Blood of the Land

Blood of the Land

The Government and Corporate War
Against the American Indian Movement

by Rex Weyler

EVEREST HOUSE Publishers

New York

LIBRARY OF CONGRESS CATALOGING IN PUBLICATION DATA:

Weyler, Rex, 1947–
  Blood of the land.

  Bibliograhy, p. 287   Includes index.
  1. American Indian Movement. 2. Indians of North
America — Government relations — 1934–   . I. Title.
E93.W54   1982   323.1′197′073   82-2349
ISBN 0-89696-134-6   AACR2

"Song for Moab, Utah" Copyright © 1982 by Winona LaDuke,
reprinted by permission of the author

TO

GRANDMOTHER ELIZABETH GOODWIN

CONTENTS

ACKNOWLEDGMENTS   11

INTRODUCTION   13

1   We Never Sold Our Church   19

2   The Trail of Broken Treaties   35

3   State of Siege   58

4   Due Process   97

5   Church and State   132

6   The Star Spangled Archipelago   166

7   The Fourth World   212

8   Yellow Thunder   251

EPILOGUE   The Two Paths   265

POSTSCRIPT   "Song for Moab, Utah"   281

BIBLIOGRAPHY   287

INDEX   291

ACKNOWLEDGMENTS

I WOULD LIKE to thank the people who helped me bring this story to print. Firstly I wish to thank all of the American Indian people who, simply by the manner of their lives, gave me that great gift of a new way to see the world. I would like to thank the many warriors and prisoners who, by their bravery, taught me dedication. I wish to thank the following: Matthew King for his wisdom and hospitality; Bill Means, Russell Means, Bob Humphries, and the people of Yellow Thunder for their friendship and generosity; Shara Griffin, Joan Price, John Trudell, Winona LaDuke, and Richard Kastl for their valuable insights and assistance; reporters Mordecai Specktor, Johanna Brand, Jerry Kammer, Michael Garrity, and Jose Barreiros whose writings and research proved helpful; David Garrick (aka Walrus Oakenbough) for kindly making available to me his extensive files, research, writing, and insights; Bob Hunter for his direction and encouragement; Bill Gannon, Maureen Zeal, Cheryl Reed, and Tusi Spong for their help in preparing the manuscript; Shivon Robinsong, Kate Wood, and Karen Lindo for critiquing the manuscript; Sandy McDonald and Peggy Taylor for their assistance with the part of this book which first appeared in *New Age* magazine; Ron Bernstein, David Lubell, and Jerry Gross for their kind and professional help; the many lawyers and legal researchers whose work has been used; and the staff and writers of *Akwesasne Notes* for so diligently documenting important events which would have otherwise been lost to history. To these generous and dedicated people I offer my most sincere appreciation. And to all others, who have helped in any way, I thank you. Royalties from this book are being donated to *Akwesasne Notes*.

INTRODUCTION

IN 1890 our forefathers surrounded and massacred 350 indigenous men, women, and children of this land and buried them in a mass grave on the Great Plains of their own Turtle Island. Eight years ago American soldiers surrounded American Indians at that same site — killing only two this time, but arresting hundreds. Today, at this hour, AMAX mines, Peabody Coal Company, Union Carbide Corporation, and EXXON Corporation dig unholy scars in the sacred ground. And tomorrow . . . ? America, when will you quit believing your treacheries are all in the past? Canada, when will you quit believing you are the free spirit after killing the free spirit of the Beothuks and offering only rye, Royal Mounted Police, and jails to the free spirit today? And when will machetes and machine guns no longer be the only greeting from generals of Chile and Guatemala and Paraguay to the people running free in the jungle? And when will corporations look for more than profits from the resources of the earth? And when will this great Western Civilization display some honor before heaven and earth?

This is the story of the most expansive geographic invasion and cultural extermination of all time: the occupation of the Americas by the Europeans. It is also the story of the resistance to that occupation, a resistance of 500 years which continues to this day, as you read these words.

At the heart of the resistance — whether it has taken the form of open warfare by the rugged Plains Indians, media confrontations by the street-wise modern American Indian Movement, or the perseverance of the peaceful Hopi — lies a common reverence for the Earth, a sacred connection to the land which for centuries has helped the American Indian people survive their battle with the invaders.

It is that same land-based spiritual tradition which gives this story some measure of hope. On the surface the story is swollen with sadness; it is a nightmare of treachery, racketeering, hypocrisy, and a corruption of the best of both cultures. Yet in these days of fuel shortages and environmental degradation it is precisely this ancient sense of reverence for the land that offers some hope for the future of humankind.

13

This, then, is not really a book *about* Indians, nor *for* Indians. The Indians do not need any more books written about or for them; this book tells of the greatest tragedy of American history for the sake of our collective future, that we might, as Chief Seattle said, "put our minds together to see what sort of future we can build for our children."

This story is set primarily in modern times, because for too long the white people of America have assumed that the crimes against the Indian people were regrettable history and nothing more. The truth is that the cultural genocide of Indian people has not let up in North and South America since the first Indian was killed by the first white settlers nearly 500 years ago. The disproportionate number of Indian people in American and Canadian jails today, compared to the general population, leads one to believe that the Indian people are innately criminal by nature or that there is something terribly wrong with the modern sense of justice. This story shows us that there is indeed something wrong.

The events described in this book will show that the American and Canadian governments, the FBI, police forces, agents, courts, attorneys, and vigilantes are guilty of: murder, assault, theft, destruction of property, arson, perjury, falsification of testimonial and material evidence, illegal surveillance, kidnapping, rape, blackmail, fraud, jury tampering, obstruction of justice, conspiracy to commit all of the above crimes, cover-up, and every imaginable sort of nastiness and depredation against the Indian people.

Why?

For the *land*. In almost every case, the Indian people were willing to *share* title of the land to which they held aboriginal right. Hundreds of treaties were signed defining Indian and white man lands; they were all broken. The Indians were forced, and still are, to resist or perish. Indian resistance has always been labeled "Indian hostility" by American courts and lawmen, whereas wholesale slaughter of Indians by settlers and modern military units has always been termed "Manifest Destiny" or "Law and Order." But white guilt serves no real purpose here; we either have a future or we do not. If we do, that future lies not in guilt, but in a spiritual reawakening and a shift from the sanctity of ownership to the sanctity of life itself, of survival.

For Indian people who may read this book I ask only tolerance for any errors of fact or failings of vision; I have tried to "tell the truth," as David Monongye, Hopi Elder, urged.

I ask white people to try to step away from your familiar world view. Stand for one moment on the wild shores of Turtle Island and witness the strange boats arriving, as the Tainos did in 1492. Join the Iroquois as they welcomed the tired and hungry trappers to their land. Observe with the Hopi as the bumbling Spanish missionaries tried to bring them "religion" by destroying Kivas and building Christian churches. Lie for a moment face down on the asphalt of an Oregon highway with young Anna Mae Aquash, a state trooper's boot in your back and the burst of gunfire all around. Imagine the thoughts of Indian activist Pedro Bissonette moments before a point-blank shotgun blast ended his life and his struggle.

The heart of the matter lies in two different philosophies of the relationship between people and land: stewardship and ownership. The schism is so deep and wide that 500 years of fighting, bickering, and legislating have failed to resolve the issue. As the Iroquois say: "The two boats are going side by side, separate. You can keep one foot in each boat for only so long. Sooner or later you must decide."

Blood of the Land

"So, you have come here to help. I hope and pray that your help will come. If you have a way to spread the truth, through the news-papers, radio, books, through meeting with powerful people, tell the truth! *Tell them what you have seen here; what you have heard us say; what you have seen here with your own eyes. In this way, if we do fall, let it be said that we tried right up to the end to hold fast to the Path of Peace as we were originally instructed to do by the Great Spirit."*

DAVID MONONGYE, HOPI
September 6, 1976

1

We Never Sold Our Church

Maybe it is early; but everything is being
prepared, waiting for the event which will
set it all off.   RICHARD KASTL, CREEK
April 2, 1981

On MARCH 16, 1981 the phone rang in my Boston magazine office; Bill Means from the American Indian Treaty Council at the UN building in New York was on the line. "On April 4 there is going to be an occupation of some land in the Black Hills," he said, but offered no further details. He said he would send some information in the mail. I asked if they expected a confrontation with the police or FBI. "We're going there peacefully to set up a camp, to build a school. There will be no weapons in the camp; no Indians will have any weapons. There will be children and elders; it will be a spiritual, educational camp. We don't know what the authorities will do; that's up to them."

Means told me I should be there if I could. I felt honored that he would bother to call me, and have faith that I would cover the story fairly. I had met Means in the course of working on several stories for *New Age* magazine. His brother Russell was perhaps the most well-known Indian rights activist in North America. For his trouble, Russell Means had been arrested countless times, indicted in thirteen court cases, framed, shot three times, stabbed in jail, and threatened by both government officials and vigilantes. Bill Means, on the other hand, had managed to stay out of the headlines, if not out of jail. He always seemed like a steadying force in the Indian movement, working diligently, but always with humor. In his capacity at the Treaty Council he met with indigenous people from around the world, government representatives, and other non-Indian supporters. People liked Bill Means; he was kind, and his amiable humor seemed to attract people to the movement.

But something in his voice and his unwillingness to give details over the phone hinted at the paranoia I had learned to accept as a part of the American Indian struggle for treaty and land rights. The Means brothers were Oglala Lakota (Sioux) from the Pine Ridge reservation in South

Dakota where some 200 unresolved murder cases hung like a cloud over Indian politics. I had seen photographs of the U.S. Army tanks and M-16-toting SWAT teams moving through Pine Ridge like Vietnam search-and-destroy missions. I had read testimony of American Indian Movement (AIM) supporters who claimed they were being shadowed by FBI agents and who later ended up dead. I was familiar with the bogus autopsies and perjured testimonies which had been used to cover up the deaths of AIM supporters while putting people like Russell Means and Oglala Sioux Civil Rights Organization chairman Richard Marshall in jail on trumped-up charges, and I had seen Leonard Peltier walk out of a Vancouver, British Columbia courthouse in 1976 raising his chained fist defiantly above his bowed head.

They were playing hard ball in South Dakota, and the stakes were high: billions of dollars worth of uranium, coal, and other resources lay undisturbed below land claimed by the Indians but desired by multinational energy companies such as Union Carbide, Kerr-McGee, Gulf Oil, and Phillips Uranium. The same scenario was being repeated in the southwestern states of Arizona and New Mexico on Hopi and Navajo land where a court order sought to relocate nine thousand Navajo people, and on virtually every other Indian reservation in North America.

The Black Hills are part of Lakota treaty land, preserved for their "undisturbed use," in the Sioux–U.S. Treaty of 1868, but later stolen from them after gold was discovered in the Hills. The U.S. Supreme Court, admitting that the United States illegally confiscated the land, awarded the Lakota people $122.5 million in compensation. But the Oglala Lakota had refused the money and insisted on the return of their treaty land. Now, it seemed, they were abandoning the courts and the halls of Congress. The forthcoming occupation of the Black Hills was to be a first step in reclaiming the land.

There was every reason to assume that U.S. authorities, particularly the FBI, would be employed to counter the move, as they had been previously employed on Indian land. Would there be another armed confrontation like the 1973 seventy-one-day siege of Wounded Knee where AIM supporters Buddy Lamont and Frank Clearwater were killed? Would the Pentagon get involved again? Would renewed media images of "militant Indians" in a "shoot-out with police" reverberate from the nightly news into the American mass mind?

The Indians were, from what Means had said, planning to present a completely peaceful front: children, elders, no guns. They were basing their claim to the land on the 1868 treaty, the 1978 Indian Freedom of

Religion Act, and an 1897 law permitting communities to occupy National Forest land to build schools and churches. A successful occupation and the establishment of a community in the Black Hills would be a powerful precedent for Indians throughout the United States and Canada, a bold new movement that the governments would surely want to suppress at once. The situation had all the earmarks of a showdown.

From the air it is easier to see that the land outlives the state, that mountain ranges and rivers are free to violate the boundaries and borders of civilizations. From a window seat of a Boston–Denver flight, on a clear day at the end of March, I surveyed the vast and varied landscape of America, the great Turtle Island which was home for 554 Indian nations prior to the arrival of the Europeans.

To the north lay the land of the Passamaquoddy and Penobscot Indians who were now claiming title to 58 percent of the state of Maine. The plane flew over the eastern shores of the Great Lakes, the land of the Haudenosaunee (Iroquois) people, the Mohawk, Seneca, and other nations all of whom are demanding the return of land illegally confiscated from them by the United States, Canada, and the State of New York.

On the western shore of Lake Michigan we passed over the land of the Anishinabe Nation where the Ojibway (Chippewa) people once lived on fish from lakes and rivers now so poisoned by acid rain, heavy metals, and radioactive contaminates that the U.S. government recommends the fish be eaten no more than once a month. Anishinabe lands have been eroded by U.S. court decisions and reduced to several small reservations in northern Minnesota. As their lands were subdivided and stolen, many Ojibway people moved south into the cities, and it was there, in the streets of Minneapolis, that the American Indian Movement began in 1968.

Over Iowa and Nebraska we entered the land of the Lakota who planted corn on the banks of the Missouri River and hunted buffalo as far west as the Bighorn Mountains in Wyoming. I could see where the Platte River emptied into the Missouri, the southeast corner of Lakota Nation as defined by the 1868 Treaty.

During the ninety-five years between the legal founding of America on July 4, 1776 and the abandoning of treaty-making with the Indians by the U.S. Congress Appropriations Act of March 3, 1871, the United States ratified 371 treaties with American Indian nations. In all cases the treaties were international instruments executed between sovereign nations. Throughout the following century and to the present day all 371 treaties have been violated, broken, ignored, or otherwise abrogated by the United States. The government of the United States of America has not kept faith with a single treaty made with Indian nations.

Though some land has been ceded by various Indian nations to the United States and Canada, most of the land in North America was stolen from the Indian people by trickery or simple bullyism. The treaties, by constitutional definition, are the "Supreme Law of the Land," on par with the Constitution itself. But the "Supreme Law" was broken as fast as it was made; might was right in the birthing of America. "Manifest Destiny," the white people said, which can be roughly translated as "God says it's okay for us to do this; God wants it this way. Look out!"

Now the Indians are reclaiming the land for which they did not relinquish title. The Iroquois, the Anishinabe, the Lakota, the Shoshonee, and Ute on the western slope of the Rockies and other Indian nations throughout the United States and Canada are demanding their treaty rights. The U.S. government finds itself in the difficult position of either denying the very basis for its existence — the Constitution — or returning the stolen land.

As we flew over the South Platte River in northeastern Colorado the Rocky Mountains rose up before us. To the southwest lay the great San Juan–Colorado River Basin, the Four Corners, Black Mesa, the "Center of the World" to the Hopi, the People of Peace. Hopi is the one Indian nation that neither fought a war nor made a treaty with the U.S. government. The Hopi prophecies foretold of the coming of the white race and their inventions. They were instructed by the Creator not to fight, to bury their weapons. They settled on the dry mesas of what is now Arizona to plant corn and wait.

The Hopi claim to be the original people of the Western Hemisphere, and their village of Old Oraibi is the oldest continuously inhabited settlement in North America. Hopi rock drawings attest to centuries of migrations throughout North, Central, and South America prior to the arrival of the Europeans. To the Hopi these stone records are their signature on the land, their title in the name of the Creator. They are the stewards of the Western Hemisphere, the Peace Keepers, the Original ones. The Iroquois in the Northeast, as well as some Eskimo and South American Indians, acknowledge Hopi ancestry.

The Hopi and their neighbors, the Navajo, have been engaged in a long battle with the U.S. government and mining companies over control of their lands. In 1974 the U.S. Congress passed Public Law 93-531, dividing Hopi–Navajo joint use land, and threatening nine thousand Navajo people with relocation. Resistance by the Navajo people has led to confrontations with police and arrests. The traditional Hopi leaders support the Navajo, but refuse to be drawn into any physical or legal confrontation. Their resistance is uncompromisingly pacific.

As we settled down through the brown smog canopy of Denver I was reminded of the ancient Hopi prophecies that a time would come when humans would fly in the air as birds, and how this would be one of the signals that the Great Purification was close at hand, the end of the "Fourth World," the world following the "flood," and the emergence into the next world. They foretold of a time when the air and rivers would be poisoned, when people forgot the way of the Creator. Their oral tradition instructs them that at that time they must cling undaunted to their humble life, planting corn, maintaining their cycle of ritual. Those who lived simply as the Creator told them, in harmony with all the natural world, would survive to live in the Fifth World. All others would perish in the Great Purification.

I stayed in Denver for several days collecting food and supplies that would be needed in the Black Hills. I had planned to arrive a few days before the scheduled occupation, to go to the Pine Ridge reservation and to find Matthew King. King (Noble Red Man) was a spokesman for the Lakota, an elder and interpreter for Fools Crow, chief of the Oglala Lakota. These men, in their roles as traditional leaders of their people, represented an unbroken lineage of chiefs dating back to the days of Sitting Bull and even further, to the time before the invasion of the white race. They held the center. The traditional people living on the reservations were at the heart of the struggle; they held title to the land. If there was to be any settlement with the government it would be decided by the traditional elders.

The night before I left Denver I met Richard Kastl who was visiting a mutual friend, and was on his way east. We had first met about a year earlier in Vancouver, B.C. where I live. We had spent several days together, during which he shared a great deal of information about the Hopi prophecies and ceremonies. Kastl is an Osage-Creek Indian from Oklahoma. He is short and powerfully built, but he carries his bearlike build with an aura of tranquility that seems to draw tension out of the air, transforming it into peacefulness. He has a gentle, knowing smile; in his presence one feels reassured.

He had been guided by his traditional medicine teachers to the land of the Hopi in 1969 where he spent the next five years learning the way of the Hopi. Then the elders endorsed him to go out into the public, to teach people about the prophecies, and to do what he could to prevent the energy companies from strip-mining the sacred Hopi lands. When I first met him in February of 1980 he was nearing the end of that public work, and by the time I met him for the second time in the spring of 1981 he was "just watching, observing, waiting for the signs."

We talked for several hours that night; I asked him about the Black Hills, what the occupation might mean. Would there be violence?

"Be observant," he told me; "watch everything carefully. The Sioux boys have never been afraid to fight; they are very brave. But if they say it is a peaceful camp, then they won't start anything.

"Back, the year before Wounded Knee — '72 — there was a protest at Mount Rushmore: elders, AIM, mostly Sioux. The cops came in and broke up the demonstration; they beat up a lot of the boys. They beat some of them up bad. It was a mess; a lot of the boys were arrested. Well, later they got together and they went into the sweatlodge [a hide-covered hut used for prayers] together to get some spiritual instruction about what to do about it. They got a message from the spirits not to seek revenge or start anything else; they were told that the people who had done those things — the beatings — would be punished by lightning. Then came the flood in Rapid City [June 9, 1972; 200 people killed, $100 million in damages] and they figured that was the revenge, the lightning.

"They were also told that there would be three major confrontations which would bring out the violence in the struggle between the Indian people and the United States. First came the takeover of the BIA [Bureau of Indian Affairs] building in Washington, D.C.; then came Wounded Knee. They were told that the spirit forces would be over the entire United States at that time. If the army troops of the United States wiped out the people, those forces would sweep the United States; if the troops pulled back, the forces would also pull back, and that would draw out the truth about the government of the United States. Well, of course at Wounded Knee the army troops did pull back. Right after that the truth began to come out about Watergate, and it seemed as if that fulfilled that particular prophecy.

"Now, could this occupation in the Black Hills be the third confrontation? I don't know, maybe not. It seems to me that maybe it is too early. The Hopi prophecy says that the last invention that the white people will be allowed to make is the platform in the sky which carries weapons and can return to earth and go back. Is that the space shuttle? I don't know. Maybe. Many of the signs that were to appear before the Purification have come to pass. Everything is being prepared, *is* prepared, waiting for the event that will set it all off. Just watch closely.

"The 'sacred' means that everything is in its proper order. Remember: the bombs and guns are really not that great a power. The natural world is the real power. The Mother holds the hammer.''

The next morning I headed north out of Denver into an icy rain blowing in over the mountains from the Northwest. Shara Griffin of Denver was driving; she had been collecting food in the city and running it to the Hopi and Navajo people in the Southwest, and to Pine Ridge reservation in South Dakota. She was going to make a stop at Pine Ridge, and then go to the Black Hills camp.

By the time we reached Cheyenne, Wyoming a heavy snow had slowed us to a crawl. The whole world was whited out, but for a few ghostly fence posts. Flakes were falling so big and fast that all tracks were covered on the road; the white curtain closed behind us as we crept along. The Mother's hammer.

This land, the eastern slope of the Rockies between the North and South arms of the Platte River was the southwestern range of the Oglala, Yankton, Hunkpapa, Two Kettle, Brule, and Santee Lakota. Here in the Platte watershed — Shell River to the Indians — the Lakota met and traded with the Cheyenne who roamed what is now Kansas, Nebraska, and Colorado. This was the "Range of the Buffalo," the heart of "Indian country," as it was known to the settlers of America.

North of Cheyenne we passed Fort Laramie on the southern bank of the North Platte, the southern boundary of Lakota Nation. Here at Fort Laramie the great Lakota war chief, Red Cloud, finally agreed to settle the long dispute with the American soldiers by signing the 1868 Treaty, defining Lakota and U.S. territory and rights.

As we turned east toward Pine Ridge reservation the snows subsided: the sun broke through, lighting the brown, flat prairie. A grand gray hawk with white belly and underwings and a bobbing, watchful head flew up before us. Short, full pine trees nestled inside the deep banks of the White River which ran north through the dry badlands, then east to the Missouri River.

These were the Great Plains; all of this land was still in dispute, claimed by the Lakota, though the U.S. government and the white people who lived on it had long ago forgotten or ignored the promises made to the Indians. I began to recognize the names of the towns from accounts of skirmishes, court cases, outbreaks of violence in little towns surrounding the Pine Ridge reservation where Indians and whites met, often at bars.

We passed through Gordon, Nebraska where in 1972 a drunk Raymond Yellow Thunder was beaten, tortured, and killed by two drunken white brothers who spent about a year in jail for their misdeed. The incident brought AIM to Pine Ridge and led eventually to the Wounded Knee takeover in 1973.

In 1975 a pregnant Jo Ann Yellow Bird was kicked by a policeman in the belly inside a bar in Gordon. She lost her baby, subsequently won a $300,000 settlement, but never received the money. On July 9, 1980 she committed suicide.

On the outskirts of Gordon stands the Hacienda Motel where in March of 1976 the FBI held Myrtle Poor Bear for three days. They intimidated her into signing affidavits (later admitted by the government to be false) claiming that Indian activists Leonard Peltier and Richard Marshall had confessed separate murders to her. The erroneous accounts led to the conviction of both men who are still in jail.

Gordon is a typical prairie town: Co-op granary; Husky gas station; livestock auction every Thursday; and a main street of coffee shop, boot shop, drugstore, and bars. Liquor is prohibited on the reservation, and the white border town bars make a killing from alcoholic Indians who have found the fog of liquor more comforting than the dry, dusty despair of reservation life.

The traditional leaders and the young AIM members have campaigned to shut down the border bars and to discourage drinking, but alcohol is still one of the major slayers of the Indians' spirit, and the main revenue for some towns in the area. These prairie towns may represent the free American spirit to the white inhabitants, but to the Indians they are like the outposts of Babylon.

At dusk we entered the Pine Ridge reservation. Along the arroyos pine trees flourished, but beyond that the land was dry and crusty, not a green hint of spring. It was dark when we entered the small town of Kyle; here I would get to talk with Matthew King. We pulled up in front of his housing-project home; two dogs lumbered up to meet us, but did not bark. This was the house of a Lakota leader, simple, no different from any of the others. The wooden and brick house was adequate, certainly not fancy; there was no yard; just the bare earth, dusty. I was reminded of something that King had told me during a previous meeting: "We don't think of leadership the same as the white man. For us there is no special privilege with leadership like all the senators and congressmen and governors of the white man's government. They are all rich, the richest people, special privilege, fancy cars and chauffeurs and big houses. For us, a warrior or a chief is always the last to eat and the first to give something away if it is needed by the people; that is the Indian way of leadership."

The screen door was smudged with the fingerprints of children. From inside came sounds of a television, chatter, and running. Here, at the heart of the struggle and all the potential sadness, life blossomed the way grass grows up through the cracks in asphalt.

Lakota Chief Matthew King, eighty-four, worked as a machinist,
farm worker, movie extra, factory foreman, and at other jobs
before returning to his Pine Ridge home to help
Chief Frank Fools Crow in the Lakota struggle for sovereignty.
King is well known in the U.S. Congress where he has lobbied
for Lakota treaty rights since 1971. (Photo by Rex Weyler)

The King family consisted of children, grandchildren, mothers, fathers, brothers, sisters, aunts, uncles, and friends. They were all graci-
ous; they gave me food and coffee and a place to sleep. Matthew King,
eighty-four, pulled out some old pictures, and told me stories. His
grandchildren and their parents went to sleep. He is a kind man with
silver hair and a contagious humor and optimism. He would break out
giggling at times as he spoke. I asked him every question I could think of;
what follows is what he told me:

A Lakota warrior smokes the sacred pipe during treaty-signing ceremony with representatives of the U.S. government at Fort Laramie, 1868. The Lakota still maintain that this treaty establishes the legal relationship between them and the U.S. government.

"The AIM boys, they have to come to us for direction; sometimes they are very eager. But it's good. This occupation in the Black Hills is good.

"We have to take our land back; the courts will never do it. That is white man's court; why would he ever give it back? When we signed the treaty [1868] we ceded certain lands — 2 billion acres — to the U.S. government, for certain provisions which he never kept. When I was a boy, 1908, 1909, some of the chiefs were still living who signed the 1868 treaty. I was old enough to understand; I always listened, and I heard what they said.

"We never gave up the Black Hills or the buffalo country, never! That is our church; we never sold our church. For us it is different from the white man. He has his Bible, but to us the hills and the sky and the water make our Bible. That is what the Creator told us, to watch the natural things; that is where we will learn how God wants us to live.

"The Black Hills is a very sacred place for us. There are seven powers of the Black Hills; there are places where we go: Bear Butte, Craven Canyon, and other places for seeking visions or sweatlodge or for the sun dance and other things. In the old days the eagles would come right down over your head when you were praying if you were really calm and if you were praying to God. Now they don't do it so much. Not too long ago, though, maybe '72 or '73, Fools Crow was praying there in a ceremony and one eagle did just come down over his head. Boy, the white people that saw that were really surprised, hee, hee. But that's the last time I saw that. There is too much disturbance now.

"Our history goes back 30,000 years; the white anthropologists don't know anything about Indian history. Our religion goes back that far. So how do they think that now we would be willing to give up our church. They're crazy.

"Our religion was given to us by the Great Spirit, and our grand-mothers and grandfathers have told us everything. Prayer is the most important thing for us. The earth gives us everything we need. White man tries to put fertilizer on the ground to make it grow better, but that is just because he is silly. He has no faith in what God has already given him. He burns up the ground, wastes it, puts poison on his food because he has forgotten.

"Our medicine comes also from the Black Hills, many plants and roots. We can cure anything; we can use a plant to make a gallstone just disintegrate. We have a medicine for everything. But many of those medicines grow in the Black Hills; that is the only place, so we have to get it back.

"So, the Black Hills are our church, our hospital, our history, and even our bank, because we knew a long time ago about all the gold and minerals in the Black Hills. But the American soldiers just came in to our bank and took out our money. How would he feel if we just walked into his house and took all his money out of his bank? Hee, hee, I remember when a white man came and saw a woman making a blanket. She was using a big piece of gold, solid gold, to run through the strings. He really was surprised; she could see how excited he was, so she gave it to him. Boy, he really went crazy. Gold always made white men crazy. The Indians used to always say that, and laugh: 'The white man is *wetko*,' crazy. He came here and saw how beautiful everything was, and he went crazy, hee, hee."

King rocked back and forth in his chair and put his fingers to his lips during his frequent flights of laughter.

"So I'm sorry to say this, but I don't think the Indian and the white man will ever get together; they have two different ways. That is why the chiefs made those treaties: you live your way, we live our way. We could see that the white people had no respect for the land; they'd just use it up and move on, always tearing everything up.

"God gave the white people a Savior and a Bible because they were so wicked and forgot the way. The Savior told them: 'My God and I are one,' but they crucified him. Where does that leave them? They are without God; I'm sorry about that, they are already condemned.

"But to us God only gave the pipe for making prayers; the natural world is our open Bible. Nature is God, God is nature. That is very simple, but the white people don't get it.

"Our grandparents told us the whole history. We were always a peaceful people. The pressure of the whites made the Indians fight. First the Pawnee came into our country, fighting for pay from the whites. We beat them. Then the Utes came, and stole all our horses. Our boys followed them south on foot, followed them all the way to Colorado. They didn't even know it. Our boys waited for the right time, then took all our horses back, plus theirs, and rode all the way back. My grandfather was in that raid. The Sioux are very good fighters if they have to be.

"Then the Cheyenne and Arapaho fled from the whites and came into Lakota country, and they joined with us.

"We were the greatest fighting force in the world; we whipped the U.S. army many times. We whipped [General George] Crook bad at Rosebud. When I was a boy I talked to Plenty Coup. He was a Crow scout for Crook in that battle. Then Custer asked him to lead the cavalry to the Sioux Cheyenne encampment. He told Custer that he would do it, but that he would not fight the Sioux again. He brought Custer to the Little Bighorn River and then he shook his hand. He told me: 'I looked in his eyes and he was already dead. I rode away.'

"Crazy Horse would ride in front of the guns; the soldiers would fire, causing a black smoke screen; then the warriors would charge. In a fair fight no one could beat us. But after they killed all the buffalo and brought in more and more soldiers and machine guns, then they stole our land.

"We never surrendered, and the chiefs today come from those chiefs, Red Cloud and Sitting Bull. Red Cloud had a son, Jack Red Cloud, who was a chief; then his son Jim Red Cloud was a chief; and then Jim's brother, Charlie Red Cloud, had a son, Oliver Red Cloud, who was made a chief. He was made a chief by me in a ceremony.

"I come from the Two-Kettle clan. Chief Fast Thunder was my grandfather. His daughter Stella Fast Thunder was my mother; she married Noble Red Man, my father. Her sister is the grandmother of the Means boys, Russ, Ted, Bill, and Dace.

"When I was born, my grandmother, Fast Thunder's wife, named me

Helper, which was also Fast Thunder's name because he helped all the people. Fast Thunder gave me the name Hard to Kill. On my father's side I got the names Kills Enemy Alone, and Big Leggings, after my other grandfather. I got the name Noble Red Man from my father. He joined the Episcopal Church, and they changed the name to King. Actually that is a mistake, a misinterpretation by the white people of the church; we don't even have such a thing as a king, but anyway, people called me that.

"I took my first sweat when I was four years old, the first time in the sweatlodge which is a sacred thing for the Lakota. It was *very* hot to me. I had my head bent down. The medicine man shot fire from his mouth, and I got scared. I tried to crawl under the side of the sweatlodge; then poof, the fire came right through my back and out my chest. I ran; everyone laughed. Later the medicine man said: 'I'm sorry to have hurt you, but now all of the sickness is out of your body. You will grow up to be an old man with a cane, and you will be a helper of your people.' Well, I don't have a cane yet, so I know I've still got some time to go.

"My grandfather did not talk very often; he said few words to me. But one time, while we sat under our horses in the shade, he said, 'The white man tells lies. I don't know what kind of human he is, but he lies. Don't ever trust him.'

"When my parents joined the Episcopal Church I also became an Episcopal. Then the Catholics came, and I joined the Catholic Church. Then the Presbyterians came, and I joined the Presbyterian Church. I even went to seminary and studied the Bible. But I don't think those people ever knew what they were talking about; they didn't even understand their own Bible. They didn't follow it. They have all those commandments, but they broke every one. The Bible said, 'By the sweat of your brow shall you earn your bread,' but they never did that; they always try to make it the easy way, stealing gold, making other people work.

"Indians learn the difference between right and wrong; then we don't need a Bible. My grandparents taught me what is right and wrong. For the Indian family, the most important thing is teaching that to the children; for us, ninety percent of life is bringing the children up right. Then there is no room for evil in this world because people know how to treat each other.

"In my life I was always a good worker; boy, I worked hard. I had a lot of jobs. After I left the seminary I took a government job in 1923 with the road department; I was a truck driver. In the '30s I was on a construction crew for the state government. They were building dams. They'd tell us to kill all the wolves and rats in a two-mile radius, and we'd do it. We also killed prairie dogs and porcupines. Boy, I'm sorry to say I ever did that; now I'm sorry I did that.

"I worked for farmers as a contractor. I'd get crews of Indians to pick potatos, top beets, pick corn. The farmers liked us. I had a lot of construction jobs, also supervising work crews. In 1944 I went to work for Martin Aircraft. I was a machine operator, hard work. When I started I worked 110 hours per week for six weeks till one day I got so tired I got dizzy, and I cut it back to 90 hours a week. There was all this excitement about the war, girls in there riveting B-29's.

"I worked for Holly Sugar Company in Sheridan, Wyoming, for American Crystal Sugar Company, and Western Sugar in Scottsbluff. I even worked on three movies, getting Indians. The movie people came and said they wanted Indians for movies, so I would get lots of Indians. And I played the trumpet in a dance band. We toured all over the country, back East. Oh boy, they loved us; they'd dance and sing. I used to write some Indian love songs and play them for people sometimes. They really liked them.

"Then in 1973, just before Wounded Knee, I came back to Kyle. I had known Fools Crow for a long time, since we were boys. I met him in 1915; we were cousins. So Fools Crow said to me: 'Matthew, now I need you. We have lots of trouble; I need your help.' We were having trouble with that Dickie Wilson [then the Chairman of the Sioux Tribal Council and opponent of the traditional chiefs] and the FBI on the reservation, and the AIM boys were starting to get mad, and the government was trying to take over more of our land. So I went with Fools Crow and Russell Means to Washington, and to the UN, and I was Fools Crow's interpreter, and I've been with him ever since. There are other headmen and chiefs: Frank Kills Enemy, American Horse, Receives the Pipe, Good Lands, and others, but Fools Crow is the head chief of the Oglala, accepted by all the Lakota people.

"We had many meetings in Washington. We told them that the so-called tribal councils were puppet governments, that they didn't represent the Indian people, the chiefs did. The goverment wanted to give the tribal council money for our land that they stole. Dickie Wilson had borrowed $400,000 from the Indian bank in Washington, D.C., and used the money to hire his goon squad and who knows what else; they were causing a lot of violence on the reservation. The government wanted to get its $400,000 back out of the settlement money, but we told them we didn't want any settlement money, we want the land back, and they could get their money back from Dickie Wilson, because the Lakota people never saw that money.

"I asked one senator how he was going to pay us for the Black Hills. He said: 'From the U.S. Treasury.' I said: 'That's not your money, that's our money; that money came from resources you stole from Indian land.' Hee, hee, boy they didn't like that. They think they can buy everything; hee, hee, oh, they're crazy. *Wetko*.

"This Senator Decker got up and said: 'This Indian shouldn't even be here. The government doesn't owe them one red cent. The government owns this country, the resources and everything.' Abourezk was the chairman [James Abourezk, D-South Dakota]; he got mad, and told Decker to sit down; he said: 'Decker, you stink!' Hee, hee. He said: 'King, do you have something to say?' I stood up, and I said: 'Mr. Decker, is that your gratitude for us letting you live in our country? You should thank the Indian; the Indians made you rich by sharing our country with you. God gave me this country; it belongs to me, not you.'

"Oh boy, sometimes those meetings were pretty funny. We were trying to get rid of that Wilson guy; that was just before Wounded Knee. Our traditional people were getting harassed by that goon squad."

By this time it was late; almost everybody in the house was asleep. The children were all in the basement in an assortment of beds. There were probably fifteen or sixteen people sleeping in the house. We were sitting at the kitchen table; I was facing toward the front wall of the house. During the course of the conversation I noticed seven holes in the front and side walls of the house, about three-quarters of the way up the wall. Each hole, about the size of a quarter, had a red circle around it. Suddenly I realized that these were bullet holes. I must have become somewhat transfixed on the holes, because King stopped talking and looked over his shoulder in the direction of my gaze.

"Oh yes, those are bullet holes," he said without hesitation, casually as if there were nothing unusual about a house having a few bullet holes in the wall. "That happened in March 1975. It was those BIA police and those goons. I yelled at them and they went away. They also set fire to Fools Crow's house while he was up at the Cheyenne River reservation. They tried every way to intimidate the people.

"That's why they put our boys in jail. Those FBIs come around here and start trouble, and the BIA police. They put Dick Marshall in jail, but he didn't kill anybody. We know who killed that Montileaux in Scenic; it wasn't Dick Marshall. Dick was a good boy; he was a leader of the Oglala Civil Rights Organization. I never knew that Leonard [Peltier] boy, but I know that he didn't kill anybody. Those FBI men that got shot came here to cause trouble, shooting at innocent people so they could get the AIM boys in jail. So they put a lot of our boys in their prisons; now they are looking out from those bars, but that is not a place for them. The government just wants to make the people afraid: if they do wrong, if they don't go along with the government, then they are going to end up in jail too.

"The white people had better examine themselves; they had better turn to God. They are causing troubles here just like all over the world, trying to run the governments of little countries with dictators, just so those companies can get resources. Well, the Indians now have friends all over the world, in the UN and in other countries. There is going to be a great catastrophe if the U.S. goverment doesn't learn to live by nature, not just by his own man-made laws.

"Fools Crow says: 'Our land is not for sale,' and we are willing to give our lives for that. The government knows that when we get our land back we will shut down the gold mines and the uranium mines, because we don't believe in those things. They use energy as an excuse to mine uranium, but they just want the uranium to make bombs. Well, we don't believe in that; we don't want to hurt somebody else. But that is why he comes here; that is why he brings guns to Indian land; that is why he calls us 'backwards.' But who is backwards? I don't hate the white people; I feel sorry for them because they think they can make a law that is above God's law. But some day they are going to be real surprised.

"Now our people are standing up. AIM did a lot of good things, showing the people to stand up for what God gave to them. You aren't free. If the government can come in and take my land any time they want, then they will come and take your land any time they want. So who is backwards?

"See that fly," he said pointing to the window; "he's trying to get out, buzzing all around. If he'd just turn around and go the other way he could fly away, and be free. But he won't do that. He'll just keep buzzing at the window.

"See that spider web there in the corner? That's where he'll end up."

The following morning, April 4, I would go to the Lakota camp in the Black Hills. To better understand the political significance of an Indian settlement on U.S. forest land, it is important to first examine both the history of the Indians' attempts to win back their treaty lands, and the origin of the American Indian Movement.

2

The Trail of Broken Treaties

I invite all of you to stay and witness the
atrocities that are about to happen
  DENNIS BANKS, OJIBWAY, AIM LEADER
  Washington, D.C., 1972

THE PRISON SYSTEM provided the environment of frustration, bore-
dom, and anger which gave birth to the American Indian Movement in
1968. Young Ojibway boys, searching for something more promising
than life on the shrinking reservations in northern Minnesota, had gravi-
tated to the city streets of Minneapolis and St. Paul. In the Indian section
of south St. Paul many of them fell onto the treadmill of alcohol, petty
crime, and prison.

Clyde Bellecourt was one of eleven children, his father a totally
disabled World War I veteran. Bellecourt had first been arrested in 1949
at the age of eleven. For his crime of truancy from a white boarding
school he was sent to the infamous Minnesota Training School for Boys
at Red Wing. From there he graduated to the St. Cloud Reformatory,
and eventually, for burglary, to the Stillwater State Penitentiary.

Inside Stillwater Bellecourt went on a hunger strike, vowing to die.
Fortunately for him and for the Indian movement a young Ojibway
spiritual leader, Edward Benton-Banai, was also in Stillwater at the
time. Benton-Banai tried throwing food into his Indian brother's cell,
but Bellecourt refused to eat. Then Benton-Banai began to teach Bellecourt about Ojibway history, and started to throw literature into the
cell. With nothing else to do, Bellecourt began to read. Before long the
two men were organizing an Indian awareness program in the prison,
teaching the spiritual history of their people and preparing Indians to
stay out of jail once they got out.

Also in Stillwater at that time was Dennis Banks from the Leech Lake
reservation, convicted of forgery and burglary, serving a three-and-a-
half-year sentence. Vernon Bellecourt, Clyde's brother — first arrested
as a teenager, and sentenced on that first offense to five years in St.
Cloud — would later recall: "They have always institutionalized our
young people, first in boarding schools where they were abused for being

35

Indians, then in prisons. We consider all the young Indians in jail to be political prisoners. That does not mean that we condone violence or crime, but those young people never have a chance. They are pushed out of an educational system that has no relevance to their needs; the courts come down heavy on them, and parole is far less likely for an Indian.''

The Bellecourts, Banks, Benton-Banai, and other Indian prisoners shared a vision of a better way of life for their people. The movement would be centered on a revitalized sense of pride in traditional Indian values in an effort to turn Indians away from alcohol, crime, and despair. A timely historical synthesis — indigenous spiritual tradition in concert with tough, street-wise fearlessness — took place inside those prison cells, and would soon reverberate across North America.

In 1968 Clyde Bellecourt, out of prison and working for Northern States Power Company, took a leave of absence from his job to work on "Indian problems" in Minneapolis and St. Paul. The first AIM chapter was started that year in Minneapolis, with the help of an older Indian woman, Pat Ballanger, who has been known since as the Mother of AIM.

Young men and women wearing red jackets, equipped with cameras, tape recorders, and two-way radios patrolled the Franklin Street bars in the Indian ghetto of Minneapolis, calling themselves the AIM Patrol. They would pick up police calls on the radio, and often beat the police to the scene to make sure that drunk Indians were not being mistreated. Bellecourt, Banks, and the others did collect evidence of rather vicious handling of Indians by police, and the result was that they became well known by both the Indians and the authorities.

This was the time of the anti-war movement and the Black Power movement, and signs of Red Power had begun to appear beside Black Power slogans across the country. But soon the Red Power graffiti changed to AIM. The movement caught on quickly. AIM was decidedly different, however, from the black movement, the anti-Vietnam War protests, or the San Francisco, Woodstock hippy generation. AIM was an indigenous, land-based spiritual movement, a call to Indian people to return to their sacred traditions and, at the same time, to stand firm against the tide of what they call European influence and dominance.

Of course, the movement was an immediate threat to the U.S. government because of the tremendous amount of Indian land that was under government control and in disputed title. A coordinated national Indian movement spelled trouble for the coordinated national land grab that was going on. Within four years of its beginnings on the streets of Minneapolis the American Indian Movement would be active in every state of the country and in Canada; the leaders would be targeted by the

FBI; senators, congressmen, and the President himself would be discussing what to do about AIM, and the U.S. military would be preparing for its first domestic counter-insurgency assault in history.

AIM was certainly not the beginning of Indian resistance to land theft and general opression, although AIM did synthesize and articulate that resistance. In 1934 the U.S. Congress passed the Indian Reorganization Act, administered by the BIA, which sought to establish "elected tribal councils" on Indian reservations. The stated purpose of this "Indian New Deal" was to bring modern democratic self-government to the Indians. The actual net effect — and probable hidden agenda all along — was to usurp traditional authority based on a lineage of chiefs or elders, and to replace that authority with governments manageable from the offices of the U.S. Department of Interior.

Traditional Indians everywhere resisted the offer to be reorganized. To sweeten the deal Congress appropriated $10 million to establish the new tribal governments. The money persuaded some Indians to go along with the plan; this faction, which has lived on to this day, became known as the progressives, or less generously as the puppet governments.

Lakota Chief Frank Fools Crow, who was a forty-four-year-old emerging traditional leader at the time, recalls: "That Act brought money to our reservation, and then corruption; it divided our people." The factionalism was fueled with more money from Washington, and soon "tribal councils" began to operate on some reservations.

The case of the Hopi tribal council offers an example of the slick maneuvering that was used to displace the traditional element on reservations. In 1936 there were approximately five thousand Hopi people living in nine villages on the mesas of the Arizona desert. The Hopi elders refused to have anything to do with the money or the "New Deal" offered by Congress. However, a few Hopi progressives were persuaded to form a council, and on October 24, 1936 they completed a constitution, approved by the Department of Interior, which they put to a vote on the reservation.

The Hopi traditionals do not even believe in voting; they make decisions based upon spiritual teachings and agreement of all the people. If they cannot come to an agreement they do not make the decision; they wait. It was precisely this style of social organization that had frustrated the efforts of the U.S. government to make land deals with the Indians. The traditional Hopi boycotted the election. As a result, only 755 votes were cast, a turnout of 15 percent. Of the votes cast, a majority favored the constitution, and the U.S. government henceforth conducted all "legal" business with the so-called tribal council. Shortly thereafter

Congress appropriated another $90 million for the "rehabilitation" of
the Hopi and Navajo.

Part of the Indian New Deal entitled them to qualify for the military
draft, serve in the armed forces, and fight America's enemies. The
Indians resisted. In 1941 six Hopi men were arrested for failing to
register for the draft, and they spent three years in jail. Fools Crow
recalls that the war years were extremely harsh, and that the Lakota
youths who did go to the war were "never the same." Many were killed
and wounded, but more came back from the army addicted to alcohol
and various hard drugs. Ira Hayes, a Pima Indian from Arizona, was one
of the marines in the famous photograph of the flag-raising on Iwo Jima.
Upon returning to the United States he was neither able to reintegrate
into his tribal life nor overcome his alcoholism. He froze to death on his
native Sacaton reservation in 1955 at the age of thirty-two.

During the decade following the war, coal, oil, and uranium were
discovered on Indian land in Arizona, South Dakota, California,
Montana, and other parts of the country. With the tribal councils firmly
entrenched, the U.S. Congress and the energy corporations began to
take the next bold steps in the great land grab. In 1946 Congress created
the Indian Claims Commission to adjudicate cases in which Indian land
had been appropriated in violation of treaty agreements. Again, the
congressional act was touted as being a better deal for the Indians but, in
fact, it was used as a means of terminating Indian title to land by paying
the puppet tribal councils cash in lieu of returning the land to the Indians.
In fact, the congressional act allowed the commission to award cash only
for stolen land; return of Indian land was not considered to be a viable
option by the commission.

In the 1950s power projects such as the Fort Randall Dam on the
Missouri River and Kinzua Dam in upstate New York required the
displacement of Indians and the flooding of their land. In such cases the
Indian Claims Commission served as a means of quieting the resistance.
The land would simply be appropriated by the government; then the
commission would work out a settlement with the tribal governments.
Three Lakota bands were paid $14.8 million in 1958 for land lost to the
Fort Randall Dam.

Operating with this system of pay-offs, Congress took the scheme one
step further: lapsing from the tradition of Orwellian euphemisms, the
U.S. government adopted the program they called "Termination." At
least they were being honest. The termination program was simple: any
tribal council that wanted to sign up only had to accept the pay-off
offered by the government; and the title to all land holdings by the
Indians would be put up for private sale, and tribal sovereignty would be

terminated. By 1958 several tribal councils including the Klamath Indians in Oregon and the Menominee in Wisconsin — both with large timber holdings — had accepted cash payments under the termination program. Over forty thousand Indian people were effected by termination during the decade of the '50s. On September 16, 1958 Congressman Lee Metcalf, a Democrat from Montana, told a meeting of the National Council of American Indians in Missoula: "The Bureau of Indian Affairs has used duress, blackmail, and pressure," to encourage tribal councils to accept termination.

But the big swindle was just gaining momentum. Later, the government would establish a fund to pay lawyers to represent the Indian claims. The result would be that lawyers appointed and paid by the government would represent tribal councils paid by the government to the commission established and controlled by the government for redress of grievances against the government. The traditional chiefs of the Haudenosaunee, Lakota, Hopi, Shoshone, Cheyenne, and other Indian nations in North America seemed powerless to counter the influence of government money on the reservations. Coal companies, oil companies, timber companies and other resource gatherers were closing in; the sanctity of money and power had eclipsed the sanctity of the land itself as a guiding principle on Indian reservations. Then a medicine man by the name of Mad Bear emerged on the scene.

Mad Bear was a Haudenosaunee (Iroquois, Six Nations) Indian from the Tuscarora reservation which straddles the New York–Canadian border. In 1958, at the age of thirty-one, he led a stand against the tide of land seizures which brought armed troops onto Indian land.

The New York Power Authority had sent a team of engineers to the home of Tuscarora Chief Clinton Rickard, seeking permission to take soil samples. The power company planned to expropriate 1,383 acres of Tuscarora land for flooding. Chief Rickard refused to allow the tests. The resistance spread quickly throughout the Haudenosaunee reservations in New York. The Seneca of Alleghany reservation and the Mohawks on Schoharie Creek both set up camps on disputed land, challenging the state to remove them.

Then, on April 16, 1958, one hundred armed state troopers and police invaded the Tuscarora lands with the intent of forcing the Indians to succumb to the engineers of New York Power Authority. They were met by the nonviolent front blocking the road, led by Mad Bear waving a sign. One hundred and fifty men, women, and children lay down, or stood, in front of the government trucks. After a few scuffles and scratched faces of police, Mad Bear and two other protestors were arrested. But the media attention and images of armed police fighting with Indian women on their own land resulted in enough public pressure to force the power company to back down. The Tuscarora Indians refused the $3 million offered by the Claims Commission and sent New York Power Authority packing.

The significance of the victory was not lost to Indians in America and Canada who glimpsed a counterforce to the power of Washington, D.C. and Ottawa. Visibility would be the important weapon against back room wheeling and dealing that were eroding Indian land. The Miccosukee Indian Nation of Florida summoned Mad Bear to help them fight the federal government, which was attempting to take land from them as a part of the Everglades Reclamation Project. In California, Nevada, and Utah the Pit River Indians led by Chief Ray Johnson refused $29.1 million of claims case money (47 cents an acre), and demanded return of the land.

The confrontations escalated a year later in the spring of 1959 when a thousand Haudenosaunee stormed the Council House on the Six Nations reserve near Brantford, Ontario, ousting the so-called tribal council and twelve Royal Canadian Mounted Police who were standing guard, Claiming sovereignty, the Haudenosaunee established a traditional government. Mad Bear exclaimed to the press: "We do not want to be absorbed into a sick society." The traditional Indians held their land for six days until, on March 12, sixty mounties retook the Council House. Television cameras caught scenes of Indians being clubbed by the charging police, and one cameraman had his camera broken by the police.

Although the "puppet regime" — as Mad Bear called it — was reinstated by the Canadian government, the Haudenosaunee people on both sides of the border stood in overwhelming support of Mad Bear and the traditional chiefs. The floodgates had broken open; Indians throughout North America had a model for resistance. The Hopi sent a letter to the President refusing to file any claims with the commission, to lease any lands to oil companies, to accept any of the "rehabilitation" money, rejecting termination, and refusing to cooperate with selective service laws of the United States. They brought a delegation to the Onondaga reservation to meet with Mad Bear and the Haudenosaunee chiefs. The two Indian nations accept common ancestry; the alliance that was renewed at that 1959 meeting predates archeological history. The Hopi had stated in their letter to the President that they "had already claimed the whole Western Hemisphere long before Columbus's great-great-grandmother was born. We will not ask a white man, who came to us recently, for a piece of land that is already ours."

*Russell Means, most outspoken of American Indian Movement leaders,
joined AIM in 1969 after meeting Dennis Banks. Shot by vigilantes,
brought to trial in thirteen separate cases, and stabbed in jail,
Means became a symbol of undaunted Indian resistance throughout the decade
of the seventies. He says that he will die fighting before he gives up
his struggle to reclaim Lakota treaty land (Photo by Lionel Delevingne)*

Thus, an infrastructure of resistance was well in place when Americans became aware of AIM in the late '60s and early '70s. In 1969 Dennis Banks met Russell Means in San Francisco. Means says that he had been an "accountant, a thief, a drunk, a computer operator, a rodeo hand, a junkie, a ballroom dance instructor, a janitor, and a farmhand" before joining AIM. He would later write in *Akwesasne Notes*: "It is the responsibility of the Indian people themselves to change realities around them when these realities are repressive and oppressive. We are simply doing those things that all Indians agree should be done, in a way that will be effective." *Akwesasne Notes* was founded in 1969 by the Mohawk nation of the Haudenosaunee. The newspaper evolved with the American Indian Movement, sending reporters throughout the Western Hemisphere to investigate stories involving indigenous people.

The AIM leaders decided to take advantage of a federal law which allowed for land once used for military purposes to revert to its previous owner when abandoned by the military. They decided that the proper symbolism would be to "retake the country from west to east," like the "wagon train in reverse." The idea matured into the Trail of Broken Treaties which would start on the West Coast and end up in Washington, D.C.

The first action would be the seizure of the abandoned federal prison on Alcatraz Island in San Francisco Bay. On November 4, 1969 fourteen Indians occupied the site. Two weeks later there were seventy-nine Indians on the island claiming Alcatraz as free Indian land. In press statements the Indians said they would pay the U.S. government $24.00 for the island, mocking the 1626 purchase of Manhattan Island by Dutch settlers. They also said that they would establish a Bureau of Caucasian Affairs to deal with any problems that whites might have in relation to the occupation. With wit and stamina, the Indians were to hold the island for nineteen months, attracting national media attention.

Bill Means recalled the time: "In 1969 I was still in the army when Russ and the others were involved in those first takeovers. I had just come back from Vietnam when my unit got a call to go up to Fort Lawton in Washington State. The Indians owned the Fort Lawton land, but the city of Seattle had swung some deal to buy it for one dollar. The army had been training us for 'riot control,' as they called it. They were going to send us up there to kick the Indians out of Fort Lawton. Well, I refused to go; I said: 'I'm not going up there to fight my own people; no way!' Nothing ever happened to me for that; I eventually got an honorable discharge, and when I got out, of course I joined AIM."

AIM began to attract bright and energetic young Indians from around the country, as well as the attention of the FBI which began targeting

AIM members as "subversives." John Trudell, a Santee Lakota from Nebraska became a spokesman for the Alcatraz takeover, and later the national chairman of AIM. FBI documents released through the Freedom of Information Act described Trudell as "intelligent and extremely eloquent when he speaks," and as a "hardliner" and an "effective agitator."

Leonard Peltier, arrested in the Fort Lawton incident, for which Bill Means had refused riot control duty, would be later described by the FBI as an "extremely dangerous" criminal although he had never been convicted of any crime. An FBI document later released from Attorney General William Saxbe's office, through a Freedom of Information Act suit by Indian Press Association editor, Richard LaCourse, would reveal the FBI's intention to "Have local police put [AIM] leaders under close scrutiny, and arrest them on every possible charge until they could no longer make bail."[1]

Peltier, Trudell, Means, Banks, Bellecourt, and other AIM leaders all spent time in jail as a result of their efforts on behalf of Indian rights. Others, less fortunate, as we shall see, fell to gunfire along the way.

Lawyer Ken Tilsen, one of the first lawyers to lend legal assistance to the American Indian Movement, recalls: "I first met Clyde [Bellecourt] and Dennis [Banks] when they were doing the street patrols in Minneapolis. I met them because they would be arrested virtually daily sometimes. They would be charged with interfering with a policeman in his duties and such things as that. The first evidence of their being targeted for arrest was simply the incredible number of times they were arrested on silly charges without being convicted. Sometimes the police would wait for them at the Bloomington [St. Paul] airport, and arrest them on old parking tickets."

In the summer of 1970, with Alcatraz Island held "in the name of all Indian people," over sixty Indian nations from across North America met in Washington State where the Nisqually, Puyallup, and Muckleshoot Indians were battling the federal government and the state of Washington over fishing rights guaranteed by treaty. From the west coast of Canada came representatives of the Nootka and Salish, from California and Nevada came the Shoshone and Pit River Indians, from the Canadian plains came representatives of the Blackfoot and Cree, from the Great Lakes came the Mohawk, Tuscarora, and Ojibway. Headmen, chiefs, clan mothers, medicine people, and others gathered in a meeting closed to whites and media. The meeting was called the North American Indian Unity Convention, and spiritual leaders such as Mad

1. *The Circle,* Boston Indian Council, March, 1979; p. 8.

Bear, Rolling Thunder of the Shoshone, and Thomas Banyacya of the Hopi spoke to the gathering urging unity and steadfastness.

Out of this gathering grew the Unity Caravan, launched in Washington State in 1970, which moved about North America supporting Indian land claims. In the state of Washington, fish and game wardens had limited fishing rights which the local Indians were guaranteed by the Medicine Creek Treaty of 1850. In August 1970 Puyallup Indians, crowded by the city of Tacoma, set up a fishing camp on nineteen acres of reservation land on the Puyallup River. At 5 A.M. on September 9 they awoke to find themselves surrounded by armed police. After a brief parley between a councilman of the tribe and the police officer in charge — during which the children were slipped from camp — the Indians stood to meet the attack. There were eight guns in the camp. Two hundred armed police moved forward, confiscating fishing nets. As the first net was touched, four warning shots were fired into the air from the camp. The police opened fire, and tear gas spread through the woods.

Miraculously, not a single person on either side was hit by gunfire that day. Sixty-four Indians were arrested and held on a total of $180,000 bail. The Indians issued a statement, saying: "Indians are being used as scapegoats to hide the real threats to the life and existence of the salmon. The white man, in the form of commercial fisheries, fish with nets at the mouth of the rivers where the salmon wait for the call of the Great Spirit which beckons them to spawn and lay their eggs miles upriver. They also fish farther out in the oceans where salmon group themselves. Sportsmen, who fish for fun and not to feed their families or to make a living, catch the salmon in great amounts each year. According to the white man's own numbers, the commercial fisheries and sportsmen catch up to 80 percent of all salmon, whereas Indian fishermen catch maybe 4 to 6 percent, if they fish at all. Industrial wastes and sewage from cities pollute the waters and burn the salmon a yellow-green color. It is not the Indian who builds dams and destroys the spawning grounds."[2]

A backlash among white fishermen turned violent. First, a boycott by fish buyers in Washington, Oregon, and Idaho closed down the market for fish caught by Indians. Then, in January 1971, two vigilantes shot Indian leader Hank Adams. While sitting in his car along the Nisqually River south of Tacoma, watching over fish nets in the river, Adams was approached by the two white men who shouted some obscenity, and fired a .22 rifle. Fortunately Adams raised up quickly at the sound of the men, and the bullet caught him in the stomach, a wound he survived.

2. *Geronimo Returns*. Zula C. Brinkerhoff; Brinkerhoff, Salt Lake City, 1973; p. 130.

Adams, an Assiniboine-Lakota from Fort Peck, Montana was the leading legal theoretician and driving force behind the fishing rights struggle. Since 1964 Adams had worked as a self-taught lawyer, writer, speaker, and organizer in "fish-ins" in Washington State. He would later recover from his gunshot wounds to become a key organizer by the time the Trail of Broken Treaties reached the streets of Washington, D.C. in 1972.

An occupation of land took place in California where the Pit River Nation had earlier refused the $29.1 million in lieu of the return of their land. After Pit River refused to accept their share of the money, other bands of the Shoshone and Paiute followed the lead by returning their checks to the Bureau of Indian Affairs. On June 6, 1970 thirty-six Indians were arrested for trespassing in Lassen National Forest. Three months later eighty club-wielding federal marshals removed seventy-five Pit River men, women, and children from the forest near Burney, California. Pomo Indians near Clear Lake, California occupied their traditional burial grounds on Rattlesnake Island, bringing a Boise-Cascade Corporation condominium development project to a screeching halt. In North Carolina, four hundred Lumbee Indians were pitted against the Ku Klux Klan. In Canada, Indian Affairs Minister Jean Cretien was advised by the Canadian Indians Claims Commission to pay an Albertan Blackfoot band $33,200 plus interest for "ammunition money accrued" since the signing of an 1877 treaty. Throughout the Americas, the indigenous people of the Western Hemisphere were making a legal, political, and spiritual stand against domination by what they considered to be colonial governments. The buck stopped. Gears jammed as lawyers scrambled after land title searches to counter the Indians' claims. Heads turned in Washington, D.C., Ottawa, and perhaps in a few board rooms in Houston, New York, and Salt Lake City.

By 1971 El Paso Natural Gas had already announced plans to build seven coal-fired electric plants on land leased from the Navajo tribal council. Peabody Coal Company had begun a coal strip-mining project on Hopi land, having negotiated a lease with John Boyden, representing the Hopi tribal council. All members of the bogus council and Boyden had received an official letter from the elders, chiefs, and villagers from the Hopi mesas protesting the leases and repudiating the legitimacy of the council. In the Black Hills, claimed by the Lakota, companies such as Union Carbide, Chevron Resources, Anaconda, and Phillips Uranium were negotiating leases for uranium exploration.

It was at this time that McGeorge Bundy, president of the Ford Foundation, announced that the foundation was kicking off a newly established Native American Rights Fund — a legal aid fund for native claims cases — with a donation of $1.2 million. Augmented by government and private support, the fund would swell to become a multi-million-dollar slush account for financing the work of tribal council lawyers such as Boyden and his former Salt Lake City firm of Wilkinson, Cragun and Barker who were then representing the Shoshone, Paiute, and Ute tribal councils, and whose senior partner, Ernest Wilkinson, had written the Indian Claims Act for his friend Utah Senator Arthur Watkins back in 1946. The Claims Commission awarded over a billion dollars to tribal councils in 1971. Boyden, for his part, had received a fee of over a million dollars from the dealings. The noose tightened around the neck of traditional Indian leadership as energy companies waited in the wings for their leases to be churned from the mill of legal maneuvering.

Back on the Trail of Broken Treaties the tide of Indian/government confrontation was moving east. In south Minneapolis Dennis Banks led a contingent of the original AIM organization over the fence of the Fort Snelling Naval Base. Startled sailors were caught flat-footed as the AIM group seized an abandoned building and established a convincing security perimeter. It was the first major action by the Minneapolis AIM chapter which had timed the move in deference to the "west-to-east" plan. The local sailors did not attempt to remove AIM, which announced plans to establish an Indian survival school on the property. The affront to the U.S. military was tolerated for only a week, but with the action AIM learned a valuable lesson: Do not negotiate with the law-making branch of the government.

AIM had entered into negotiations with senators Hubert Humphrey and Walter Mondale who were sympathetic but, as it turned out, powerless. The occupation had begun on a Sunday in April 1971; the following Friday, Mondale was scheduled to appear at Fort Snelling for a meeting with Banks. However, on that very morning, at 5:00 A.M., a heavily armed federal Special Weapons and Tactics (SWAT) unit swept the base and arrested all the Indians. When Mondale showed up there was nothing left to discuss.

In Milwaukee the AIM chapter was more successful in their August 19, 1971 occupation of an abandoned Coast Guard base. Led by Milwaukee AIM chairman, Herb Powless, the Indians immediately set up a halfway house and detoxification center for Indian alcoholics, as well as a community school for Indian children. Both state senators, the Wisconsin governor, and the mayor of Milwaukee supported the self-help site. The Indians stayed, eventually establishing a program for the elderly, job training, day care, Indian language classes, and craft workshops. Powless went on to establish Native Alcoholism groups at

Dennis Banks, co-founder of the American Indian Movement.
(Photo by Dick Bancroft)

Waupun State Prison, Fox Lake Medium Security Prison, Oregon Girls' School, Wales Boys' School, and the Milwaukee County House of Correction. By 1976, however, he would be in jail for crossing a state line with a gun in his car.

By the summer of 1972 the Traditional Indian Unity Caravan was weaving a great web of solidarity throughout North America. Between July and September the caravan traveled from New York, through the Midwest, south to Oklahoma and Texas, to Hopi-Navajo land at Black Mesa, to Pit River, Shoshone lands in Nevada and Utah, and back northeast to the Mohawk reservation in Ontario and the Caughnawaga reservation in Quebec. In October caravans from traditional camps throughout the United States were en route to Washington, D.C. where the Trail of Broken Treaties was to converge in early November.

Several shooting and beating deaths of Indians had added an edge of tension to the caravan's land-theft grievances. In February of 1972 the murder of Raymond Yellow Thunder had ignited AIM to protest in South Dakota. Yellow Thunder, drunk from a session in a Gordon bar, had been picked up by two white brothers, Melvin Hare, twenty-six, and Leslie Hare, twenty-eight. The white men drove the fifty-one-year-old Indian around in their car, beat him, abused him, tortured him, and threw him naked into an American Legion dance hall where he was further taunted. He was found dead a week later in the trunk of a car. The Hare brothers were found guilty of second-degree manslaughter, and spent about a year in jail. South Dakota Indians were outraged at the light treatment.

On July 1, nineteen-year-old Phillip Celay, a Papago Indian, was shot and killed by Deputy Sheriff David Bosman of Ajo, Arizona, who had stopped the truck in which Celay was riding, for a tail-light violation. Bosman testified that the youth had taken a gun from fellow deputy Mike Wilson at the scene, but the Indian witnesses denied the story. They said when deputies pushed the Indians against the side of the truck young Phillip pushed back. A fight ensued, Phillip ran, and Bosman shot him. Ajo Justice of the Peace M.F. Anderson ruled the death "justifiable homicide," and Bosman went free. The *Tucson Daily Citizen* called the case "kitchen justice at its worst."

Then, on September 20, as AIM leaders met in South Dakota with Lakota medicine man Leonard Crow Dog, they received news that their compatriot Richard Oakes, a Mohawk who had been a leader of the Alcatraz occupation, had been shot and killed by a white man on a country road near his home in California. A week before the killing Oakes, thirty, had broken up an argument about fishing rights between an Indian teenager and a twenty-three-year-old white youth. During that incident Michael Morgan, a thirty-four-year-old white man, had fired a shot over Oakes's head. At about 4:30 on September 20 Morgan, carrying a .9mm automatic pistol, encountered Oakes, unarmed, on the forest road northwest of Santa Rosa. Morgan claims that Oakes "jumped" at him. Nevertheless, Oakes, an AIM leader, was dead, and Morgan was cleared of manslaughter charges.

Bill Means recalls that those incidents changed the direction of AIM. "When Raymond Yellow Thunder was killed," he recalled, "his relatives first reported it to the BIA, then to the FBI, and to local police, but they got no response. Severt Young Bear [Lakota from Pine Ridge] then went to Omaha where AIM was meeting, and asked AIM to come to Pine Ridge to help clear up the case. We realized that this was a new level. We realized that AIM could not allow Indian people to be murdered, that we would have to change tactics. It was a turning point. We could not just carry signs and protest, but we would have to be willing to die to protect our people."

A 100-car caravan drove from Omaha to Gordon, Nebraska where the local law enforcement officers had been dragging their feet in the case. AIM took over the town, the mayor's office, everything. They refused to leave until the case was investigated. As a result the two Hare brothers did their year's time for manslaughter.

In this atmosphere, the Trail of Broken Treaties caravans began arriving in Washington, D.C. at dawn on November 2, 1972, with a twenty-point proposal for the remaking of the Bureau of Indian Affairs and for the establishment of a commission to review treaty violations. They had been assured in writing by Robert Robertson, of Vice-President Spiro Agnew's office, that the administration "stressed our desire that the Caravan visit result in an amicable productive discussion of all the substantive issues you plan to present." But things went sour from the start. First, the army refused to allow the Indians to perform a religious ceremony at the grave of Iwo Jima veteran Ira Hayes in Arlington Cemetery. Then the BIA, which had recently spent $50,000 funding a Washington meeting of tribal council chairmen, refused to offer any logistical support or housing. A black community organization offered the basement of a church for sleeping, but the basement was filled with rats. By noon on that first day two hundred Indian people of all ages were hanging around outside the BIA office while Russell Means, Clyde Bellecourt, and Hank Adams met with BIA officials. In the meantime someone had leaked a memorandum to the Indians which exposed the source of their difficulties.

The memo, dated October 11, 1972, was from Harrison Loesch, Assistant Secretary of the Department of the Interior for the Bureau of

Land Management to Louis Bruce, Commissioner of Indian Affairs. It read: "Subject: No direct or indirect assistance to American Indian Movement demonstration in Washington in early November. This is to give you very specific instructions that the Bureau [of Indian Affairs] is not to provide any assistance or funding, either directly or indirectly." At this point negotiations broke down; the Indians were going to get nothing from the BIA. BIA director Bruce told reporters that he was "concerned about housing for all the people," and he told the Trail of Broken Treaty negotiators, "I'm here in this concrete tepee today because I support the treaties rightfully made with you."[3] But Harrison Loesch at the Department of Interior held the power and his order for nonassistance stood: "The Commissioner [Bruce] has blown it," said Loesch by phone to BIA Navajo Area Director Tony Lincoln, "he's over there in bed with them, and we don't like it from Air Force One on down,"[4] referring to President Nixon.

By nightfall on the first day there were over four hundred Indians in the BIA offices. They had barricaded the entrances, peacefully allowed the office workers to leave, and had seized control of the building. Federal Judge John H. Pratt issued a court order, setting a midnight deadline by which the Indians were to evacuate the building. Negotiations continued past the deadline until 4:00 A.M. when the government finally offered accommodations other than the BIA offices. But by this time the entrenched Trail of Broken Treaties would settle for nothing less than a meeting with White House representatives to discuss the twenty-point proposal that was the heart of their message to the administration.

The following morning U.S. Marshal Wayne Colburn arrived at the BIA building with a contingent of armed federal officers. Colburn was there to carry out the court order for eviction, but when met at the door by painted, club-wielding protesters the marshals backed off. Dennis Banks told the press: "We are trying to bring about some meaningful change for the Indian community. If this is the only action that will bring change, then you can count on demonstrations like this 365 days a year." Russell Means said: "We didn't come here to grab hold of a building. We came here to work. The situation looks very positive because the negotiators realize our commitment here — that we are willing to die."[5]

3. *BIA*, "I'm Not Your Indian Any More," *Akwesasne Notes*, Rooseveltown, New York, 1973; p. 13.
4. Ibid.
5. Ibid.

The next few days were a stand-off. Police had surrounded the building. Between them and the Indians a circle of black, white, and Chicano supporters had linked arms, forming a human barricade. The Indians were prepared to hurl IBM typewriters and light bulbs filled with gasoline from the roof of the building should the police attack. Russell Means said, "If we go, we're going to take this building with us. There's going to be a helluva smoke signal."

Frustrated Indians sacked the offices and painted slogans on the walls. Bill Means later recalled entering the top-floor office of the BIA commissioner only to find an Indian elder standing in the middle of the room with an axe in his hand. The commissioner's mahogany desk lay on the floor in a giant V, chopped in half by the old man. "He just looked up at me and smiled," said Means. "He was grinning from ear to ear, and he said: 'I've been waiting all my life to do this.' I left him there throwing papers around the room."

The destruction of property and sacking of the offices became a rallying point for the government; their releases to the media cast the protesters as violent militants. Interior Secretary Rogers C.B. Morton broke his silence with a release, warning: "All Americans should understand that the protesters are a small splinter group of militants. They do not represent the reservation Indians of America . . . From the first announcement of their visit, we made every effort to cooperate with the advance men of the caravan. . . . It is obvious to me that the seizure and continued occupation of the building are nothing more than a form of blackmail by a small group who seek to achieve through violence objectives which are not supported by a majority of reservation Indians. . . . It is a shame that a small, willful band of malcontents should attempt to wreck the headquarters of the government's chief instrument for serving the Indian community."[6]

To prove their point, the government issued statements by several tribal council chairmen condemning the occupation. Later, however, Navajo tribal chairman Peter MacDonald accused the government of pressuring the tribal chairmen. He claimed that Robert Robertson of Spiro Agnew's office had "called all the tribal chiefs," and that the chiefs had "been pushed into making statements." Robertson denied the charge, but coming from MacDonald, a moderate with no axe to grind, it rang true. Hopi tribal council chairman Clarence Hamilton sent in a statement saying: "We had just reached a point of confidence between the BIA and the Indian. And now look. Unless we make it clear

6. Department of Interior news release; statement of Secretary Rogers C.B. Morton, November 6, 1972.

that they do not represent the masses of American Indians the good reputation of our Indian society will be destroyed.''

The Arizona Intertribal Council issued a statement from their Salt Lake City public relations firm of David W. Evans and Associates. Evans, as it turned out, was sitting at the center of a Southwestern resource development media campaign of major proportions, and was suspected of conflict of interest. Evans's firm had written speeches for Hopi chairman Hamilton defending the construction of power plants on Hopi land, and it seemed very likely that he had written Hamilton's BIA letter as well. But Evans also represented the Western Energy Supply and Transmission (WEST) Associates, a consortium of twenty-three power companies constructing coal-fired power plants on Hopi and Navajo land. Two years later, *Washington Post* writer Mark Panitch would uncover the conflict of interest, and call the relationship between the Hopi council and WEST Associates ''symbiotic,'' pointing out that ''Hamilton speeches written by Evans would be distributed through the public relations machinery of 23 major Western utilities.'' [7] Panitch also uncovered the fact that citizens writing to the U.S. Department of Interior for information about the coal development on Indian land were sent a brochure published by Peabody Coal Company. Harrison Loesch, who was, in 1972, holding a hard line against helping the Trail of Broken Treaties Indians in Washington, would, in 1976, become an executive for Peabody Coal Company.

The publicity campaign to discredit the protesters — involving David Evans; Secretary of Interior Morton; Harrison Loesch; and the office of the vice-president — did, to some extent, work. Newspapers across the country picked up on the ''violent militant'' theme suggested by Morton. The *Huntsville Times* in Alabama wrote: ''No one apparently intends to suggest that the hoodlums who occupied the BIA are typical of the greater Indian community.'' The Rochester, New York *Times-Union* called the protest ''part of the new and terrible worldwide trend toward violent action by supermilitants to obtain political objectives that can't be immediately obtained through democratic processes.''

Clyde Bellecourt countered the criticism with a statement to the press in which he said: ''The issue was not the destruction of a certain amount of property by a group of angry Indian people; the issue is, was, and forever will be the occupation of Indian land and near-destruction of a people by a nation of greedy and deceitful white men. But if you have any values higher than that of possessions of land, money, and prestige,

7. *The Second Long Walk*, Jerry Kammer, University of New Mexico Press, Albuquerque, 1980; p. 88.

I would ask you to be outraged that your government values property more than human beings.

"You will see," he said, "that for every broken window in the bureau quarters, there are a thousand broken hearts among our people which cannot be repaired."

The sacking of the BIA offices was a bold and clear statement of the traditional Indian sentiment toward the government bureaucracy that was touted as "serving the Indian community," but was, to these Indian people, the very source of the problem, the basis of land swindles, and an instrument for the planned termination of their political and cultural sovereignty. One of the senior members of the occupation was a Lakota woman by the name of Winyanwast (Good Woman) who told the *Los Angeles Times*: "I hope some good will come out of it. It was the only way, what we did. At least we were heard."

Indeed, they were. On Monday, November 6, the White House acceded to the demand for a meeting on the twenty-point proposal. Representing the Nixon administration were Interior Secretary Morton, Deputy Director of the Office of Management and Budget Frank Carlucci, and Special Assistant to the President Leonard Garment from the office of John Ehrlichman. They met with Clyde and Vernon Bellecourt, Russell Means, Eddie Benton-Banai, Dennis Banks, Hank Adams, and some of the Indian elders.

Negotiations carried over until the following day. The Indians agreed to leave the BIA building and go home; in exchange the government made five promises, three official and two under the table. First, the government agreed that there would be no prosecutions stemming from the seizure of the building. (The actual wording of the official document signed by Carlucci and Garment said only that they would "recommend" that there be no prosecutions, a loophole that Harrison Loesch would use later to urge the government to renege on this part of the deal.)

Carlucci and Garment also signed a document agreeing that "a process of decision and reform will be undertaken which will make the management and organization of the Federal Government in all matters affecting the lives of Indians more responsive to Indian needs." (The actual letter, in this case, said that they were "hopeful" the process would be undertaken.) The third written agreement by the government was to analyze and respond to the Trail of Broken Treaties twenty-point proposal within sixty days.

According to Bill Means, there were two unofficial agreements. The Indians asked for a police escort out of town, and Garment agreed to arrange it. The Indians also asked for ten cents per mile per person (equal to what the tribal council chairmen received at that time for travel expenses) to finance the return trips home. The administration, unable to cut such a deal officially without rocking the boat at the Department of Interior, executed the agreement in fine Nixon-era, Watergate style.

The total travel bill came to $66,650. The government negotiators shuffled off to the White House. An hour later, Means saw a large black limousine pull up in the rear of the BIA building. Out of the car stepped black-trenchcoated Presidential Counsel John Dean and Chief of Staff H.R. Haldeman. Dean carried a briefcase. Inside the building the two men opened the briefcase, exposing fresh, crisp hundred-dollar bills — travel expenses in cash.

The protesters distributed the money, sending some of the elders back home with first-class airplane tickets, and passing out gas money to the caravan leaders. Before leaving the building, however, the occupiers packed away twelve tons of BIA files to take back to their respective reservations to verify cases of government misconduct and conflict of interest within the BIA. A large truck was backed up to the freight ramp in the rear of the building, and entire file cabinets were loaded in. Washington columnist Jack Anderson, who later received some of the documents, called it the "biggest document heist in history," and said the papers revealed "documentary evidence of bureaucratic bungling, neglect, and outright chiselling."

"It was actually very funny," recalls Bill Means; "the police escorted the truck right out of Washington; everyone was laughing. It was a big joke, but it was also dead serious. Once the government discovered that some files were missing they became very concerned. Police radios must have been really buzzing, because caravan cars all picked up police tails, and some were pulled over and searched. Some of the papers were recovered, but some got through.

"Then they tried to get the papers back by pretending to be *New York Times* reporters," said Means. "They contacted us and said: 'The *New York Times* would really be interested in seeing the papers.' Well, they brought us to New York and put us up in the St. Moritz Hotel on Central Park South. They met with us, and told us that 'Kodak would pay for microfilm of the papers.' We didn't trust these guys, so we decided to check them out. We phoned the number that they gave us, and sure enough, someone answered 'New York Times,' and verified that the two guys worked there, so that seemed to check out. But someone was still suspicious, so we went down to the *New York Times* building; we had some friends there. Well, of course, no one had ever heard of these guys, and the number was a fraud, so we were onto them. We all went back to the St. Moritz; we stayed there for a few days, ate real well, had a nice relaxing time on their tab because we were all pretty tired from the road and all that. So we rested up in luxury there for a few days, then split.''

The pilfered BIA papers revealed shady corporate-BIA connections and eventually led to the exposure of an FBI informant who had infiltrated the Trail of Broken Treaties occupation. A memo from Vice-President Spiro Agnew to Interior Secretary Morton revealed a plan to establish an American Indian National Bank involving Spiro Agnew's old boss, banker George Olmsted and Phillips Petroleum Corporation president, W.W. Keeler.

A letter from BIA employee Peter Three Stars, an Ojibway from Wisconsin, revealed a case in which two elderly women from the Lac du Flambeau reservation east of Duluth were beaten to death on June 13, 1971. Local law enforcement personnel refused to investigate the case, and the BIA did nothing but file the letter, which read in part: ''The sheriff's office told the tribal chairman at one point to quit calling them regarding the murders . . . the local people . . . live in constant fear of being the next victims.''

The BIA papers further revealed some of the corporate liaisons between Assistant Secretary of Interior Harrison Loesch and resource developers with interests on Indian land. In relation to a timber lease on the Quinault reservation in Washington State, oil and gas leases on the Apache reservation in New Mexico, and a coal drilling lease on the Northern Cheyenne reservation in Montana, Loesch intervened to waive environmental regulations that would have slowed development. On August 18, 1972 Loesch wrote in relation to the coal leases: ''The project is being conducted on Indian land held in trust by the Secretary of the Interior for the Northern Cheyenne Indians, and is not public land. . . . Therefore, the provisions of the National Environmental Policy Act of 1969 are not applicable and no draft environmental statement has been submitted to the Council on Environmental Quality.'' This policy, issued from the desk of Loesch, future vice-president for government relations for Peabody Coal Company, created a unique, creative, and useful chameleon-like status for Indian land: on the one hand, Indian land was assumed to be ''held in trust'' by the Department of Interior; that is, *owned* by the U.S. government though occupied by the Indians with government permission. On the other hand, when convenience decreed, the lands became ''Indian land'' upon which U.S. law — in this case environmental law — did not apply. This device would prove practical to Peabody Coal a few years later when coal-fired power plants began spewing potash over the Southwest and coal strip mines began digging into the Hopi earth.

Exposure of these stories, and others, in the national media was pre-

*Mary Largo, a Navajo from Crown Point, New Mexico. The Bureau of Indian Affairs has granted mining companies uranium exploration rights on her land over her objections. (Photo by Mark Lennihan/*Gallup Independent*)*

vented because of the government's efforts to retrieve the documents as well as the arrest of Jack Anderson associate Les Whitten and Indian organizer Hank Adams. Adams, who had been chief negotiator for the Trail of Broken Treaties, had offered to help the BIA retrieve the files. He sent word throughout the Indian communities asking that the files be returned and, as a result, boxes of BIA papers were delivered to the Washington, D.C. bus depot. The FBI assigned undercover agent John Arrellano to work with Adams, and a plot was hatched to trap Adams and reporter Whitten with the documents. Arrellano knew that Adams was returning the documents to the BIA, but he also knew that he was allowing Whitten to view some of them for public news release. On January 30, 1973 Arrellano picked up several boxes of documents at the Greyhound Express office in Washington and delivered them to Adams. Whitten met Adams the following morning. The two men determined that there was no story of substance in this particular batch of papers, and loaded them into Whitten's car for the drive over to the BIA building where Adams had been returning similar boxes. Before they left the curb, however, FBI agents, acting on a tip from Arrellano, swooped down on the two men and arrested them both for illegal possession of stolen documents. They later arrested AIM publicist Anita Collins as an accomplice. When the truth of the story was revealed a federal grand jury refused to indict the three people, but Whitten was furious at his treatment. On February 8, 1973 he wrote in the *New York Times*: "The government is asserting ownership of the documents — and the contents of the documents — in a systematic effort to hide its dealings from the people. . . . My arrest signals a new step in the government's ownership of the news . . . "

The media war was on, and manipulation of information would become an important new link in the corporate, government, legal, tribal council stranglehold on Indian land and resources.

3
State of Siege

There is a prophecy in our Ojibway religion
that one day we would all stand together. I am
elated because I lived to see this happen.
        EDWARD BENTON-BANAI
        Ojibway

DESPITE THE ASSURANCE that there would be no prosecutions stemming from the BIA occupation, ample evidence surfaced indicating that by early 1973 the Nixon administration, the FBI, and local police throughout America had directed a sweeping and virulent campaign to discredit, isolate, and imprison the AIM leaders. AIM, an organization with no government strings attached, proclaiming Indian sovereignty and treaty rights, became simply too great a threat to the Indian resources pork barrel and the Indian "services" bureaucracy. "From Air Force One on down," as Harrison Loesch had remarked, militant Indians became public enemy number one.

Concerning the signed amnesty agreement, Loesch told reporters: "The Secretary [Rogers Morton] indicated that he trusted that any such *recommendation* by Carlucci and Garment would not be followed. It was only a recommendation, and I recommend otherwise," he said, adding that he and Morton had "agreed to seek full-scale prosecution,"[1] from Attorney General Richard Kleindienst.

Secretary Morton took the vendetta a step further in a special report to the Nixon administration which tacitly opened season on anyone associated with AIM. He said: "There has grown up in the wake of the black movement in this country a revolutionary Indian element. Dramatic violence is their pattern. . . . Their effort is symbolic rather than substantive. They believe that the pursuit of their cause transcends their criminal methods. Their demands are vague and change from day to day. They do not represent a constituted group with whom the government can contract or serve.

"Some of their leaders are star-struck with self-righteousness, some

1. *BIA*, "I'm Not Your Indian Any More," op. cit., p. 40.

58

are renegades, some are youthful adventurers, some have criminal records. They come forth with great gusto when there is hell to raise; otherwise, they are loosely organized, slipping from one expensive-to-the-taxpayers event to the next under a cloak of false idealism. The bloody past is the color of their banner, publicity is the course of their future. These are criminal actions, and should be dealt with accordingly."[2].

FBI documents later obtained from the office of Attorney General William Saxbe, through a Freedom of Information Act suit filed by NBC, revealed tactics used by the FBI to destroy the effectiveness of militant groups including blacks, Communists, and Indians. The memoranda directed FBI offices to "expose, disrupt, misdirect, discredit, and otherwise neutralize the groups, activities, and individual names of nationalist hate-type organizations and grouping, their leadership, spokesmen, membership and supporters. . . . Prevent the rise of a 'messiah' who can unify and electrify the nationalist movement."

During his Watergate testimony, Presidental Counsel John Dean explained that "Regular intelligence reports," from the FBI on "Indian uprisings" were sent to John Ehrlichman's aide Leonard Garment, and that the Nixon adminstration "was continually seeking intelligence information about demonstration leaders and their supporters that would either discredit them personally or indicate that the demonstration was in fact sponsored by some foreign enemy."

The BIA, under Morton and Loesch, created a Special Operations Service (SOS), a riot squad of fifty or so Indian police troops trained at the FBI National Academy at Quantico, Virginia, at the CIA training facilities in Los Fresnos, Texas, and at the BIA Indian Police Training and Research Center in Brigham City, Utah. According to *Race Relations* magazine, the FBI reports that came to Garment at the White House would then be sorted out by the Office of Indian Services, and sent to James Cooper, SOS coordinator. "His information goes to eleven BIA Area Offices," said *Race Relations,* "each having a Chief Law Enforcement Officer who maintains intelligence liaisons with local BIA agency and reservation officials."

Evidence of these administrative policies and surveillance methods began immediately to appear across the United States. Three Indian-operated schools with suspected AIM sympathies were denied promised funding from the U.S. Office of Economic Opportunity within a week after the BIA takeover in Washington. According to the *Minneapolis Star,* James Griffith, of the OEO, sent a telegram to each school advising

2. *Race Relations*, Richard LaCourse; reprint, *Akwesasne Notes*, Winter, 1975, p. 31.

them that the funding cuts were effective immediately because of "no compliance" with OEO regulations, standards, and guidelines.[3] The schools effected were the Indian School Center established by Herb Powless in Milwaukee, the Little Red School House in St. Paul, and the Survival School in Minneapolis. Attorney Larry Leventhal, acting on behalf of the schools, said that the cuts were not only vindictive, but were "illegal [because] the Economic Opportunity Act says they cannot cut off funding without reasonable notice to the recipient and an opportunity to show why such action should not be taken." Nevertheless, the deed was done.

After the Trail of Broken Treaties, Herb Powless and Leonard Peltier, who had been arrested for trespassing at the Fort Lawton occupation in Washington State in 1970, returned together to Milwaukee. On the evening of November 22, 1972 Peltier was sitting in the Texas Restaurant when two off-duty Milwaukee policemen picked a fight with him. As he left the restaurant later they jumped him, beating him so fiercely that, according to later court testimony, one of the cops broke most of the blood vessels in his hand and he could not work for several days afterward. In the struggle they found a gun on Peltier (which did not work, the firing pin being broken), and so they charged him with attempted murder. One cop received a citation for "saving" his buddy's life by foiling the "murder attempt" by dramatically thrusting his finger between the hammer and the firing pin as Peltier allegedly pulled the trigger.

After being released on bond, Peltier fled underground, but he would eventually be returned to face the murder charge. At the subsequent trial, four years later, it was determined that the entire incident had been a fraud, set up by the two policemen. Anne Guild, girlfriend of policeman Ronald Halvinka, testified that, prior to the incident at the restaurant, Halvinka had shown her a photograph of Peltier and had told her that he was going to "help the FBI get a big one."

Upon returning to his home on Pine Ridge reservation Russell Means was arrested by Del Eastman, a BIA policeman working under the direction of Sioux Tribal Council chairman Richard "Dickie" Wilson who had issued a ban on AIM members speaking publicly on the reservation or, in the case of Banks and Means, entering the reservation at all. Wilson had become a staunch supporter of the federal BIA, a vocal enemy of AIM, and a symbol of federal usurpation of traditional Indian authority. Del Eastman was a member of what came to be known as the goon squad on the Pine Ridge reservation. These were the men who put the bullet holes in Matthew King's wall, and traditional Indians were

3. *Minneapolis Star,* November 29, 1972.

accusing them of terrorizing anyone who opposed the Wilson regime.

The BIA had increased funds for "law enforcement" on reservations such as the Mohawk and Seneca in New York State, and on Pine Ridge where traditional opposition to the BIA tribal governments was strongest. Wilson later testified before a hearing on the violence, convened by South Dakota Senator James Abourezk. In answer to a question by Abourezk concerning the goon squad, he replied: "Yes, we have a police force — we call it an auxiliary force. The press named it the goon squad. We organized this force to handle the threat of people like Russell Means and other radicals who were going to have what they call a victory dance at Billy Mills Hall [on Pine Ridge reservation] after the destruction of the BIA offices in Washington. Some monies were provided, yes." When Abourezk asked if the money was provided by the BIA, Wilson replied: "By the agency, yes, to hire a small group of people to protect our buildings, bureau office, tribal offices. They were branded as the goon squad. I have no recollection of them ever beating anyone up. If I thought that was necessary I'd do it myself."[4]

Tribal council member Severt Young Bear, from the largely traditional district of Porcupine, was one of the few councilmen openly opposed to Wilson; he told a reporter at Wounded Knee: "Right from the day he took office, the 10th of April, 1972, people constantly been fighting him . . . Because of some of the under-the-table dealings . . . when he was a tribal council member before, and when he was with the Housing Authority. He was one of those guys setting up liquor on the reservation a couple of years ago . . . During the campaign he told these two guys from Rapid City that if he gets in as tribal chairman, he promised them a housing contract of $13 million, and a liquor contract . . . These two white men put a little over $10,000 into his campaign. So he was throwing money around, used wine to buy votes, and that's the kind of dealing that he done."

According to Young Bear, Wilson received $62,000 from BIA Area Director Wyman Babby and Area Supervisor Stanley Lyman shortly after the Washington, D.C. protest. Babby and Lyman have refused comment on the appropriation, and deny knowledge of funds for the goon squad. Young Bear claims this money was used by Wilson to hire "local drunks and guys that didn't have jobs." This "auxiliary force," as Wilson called it, became the local enforcer of federal Indian policy as outlined by Interior Secretary Morton. It would prove inadequate, however, and by March 1, 1973, the 82nd Airborne would be sent to Pine

4. From the film *Voices From Wounded Knee*, by Saul Landau, Institute for Policy Studies, Washington, D.C., 1974.

Ridge reservation under the direction of plain-clothed Colonel Volney
Warner in the field and, from the Pentagon, General Alexander Haig.

"We knew," said Matthew King, "because it has always been the
same. They always have two plans, a peace plan and a war plan. Our
grandfathers told us this. If they don't get what they want from the peace
plan, then they bring the soldiers. It's no different today."

In 1873, one hundred years before the presence of the 82nd Airborne
at Pine Ridge, the U.S. government committed its first sanctioned violation of the 1868 treaty with the Lakota Nation by stationing federal army
troops inside Lakota treaty lands. The military established Fort Robinson north of the Platte River and Fort Lincoln west of the Missouri, thus
ending whatever good faith may have existed during the brief five-year
span of the international agreement declaring a relationship of "peace
. . . forever." Rumors of gold in the Black Hills had lured a swarm of
America miners and prospectors into Lakota country.

The popular, latter-day version of what happened next is told by a
young blond, blue-eyed, uniformed tour guide at Fort Laramie Historical Park in 1980: "The army just couldn't keep the miners out of the
treaty land," she said, holding her palms up in the air, "and the attitude
of many Indians became so hostile that Indian agents asked for troops to
be stationed at the agencies. In 1874 General Custer led an expedition
from Fort Lincoln on the Missouri, to investigate the area, and he
confirmed the presence of gold. Later, after the famous battle known as
Custer's Last Stand, the Sioux signed another treaty turning the Black
Hills over to the United States . . ." This version of the tale has become
part of the great myopic mantra of American history.

First, it is unthinkable that the soldiers who killed ten million native
people; hunted down Cochise, Chief Joseph, Sitting Bull, and other
leaders; defeated the entire Confederate Army in the Civil War; and
whose Hotchkiss guns quelled the Metis revolt of Louis Riel on the
prairies of Canada could not control the movement of white miners in
violation of an American treaty agreement. Secondly, it is always the
Indians who become "hostile" when they defend their land against
invasion, while the American soldiers are always viewed as "peace-
keepers." Furthermore, Custer's 1874 expedition to the Black Hills was
not meant innocently to "investigate the area," but to precisely locate
the mineral wealth with the aid of prospectors; "Custer's Last Stand"
was really Custer's Last *Assault*; and the 1877 treaty was a fraud.

In 1875 the United States offered to buy the Black Hills; the Lakota
refused to sell. Then a U.S. commission asked the Lakota leaders if they
would negotiate for the Black Hills mineral rights. The Lakota said no.

The United States came back with a hard offer of $400,000 a year. The Lakota said no. On February 8, 1876 General Philip Sheridan ordered a military operation to surround the "hostiles" who were reportedly roaming the Powder and Bighorn river country in what is now southeastern Montana. The assault was to be a three-pronged military pincer operation: General George Crook came up from the south through Lakota country; General John Gibbon brought his troops from the west; and Custer and General Alfred Terry left Fort Lincoln on May 17, 1876, arriving from the east.

Crook arrived too early, encountering the Lakota at the headwaters of the Rosebud which flows north to the Yellowstone River. Crook was soundly trounced, and he limped back south. Gibbon, Terry, and Custer met at the mouth of the Rosebud, waited two days for Crook, then proceeded without him, unaware of his defeat. Custer, by all first-hand accounts, was driven by a compulsion to become famous. He pushed his leg of the pincer in an attempt to arrive at the Indian camp first, which he did, on the morning of June 25, 1876. Thus began the most honored military fizzle of American history.

Without waiting for Gibbon, Custer sent Major Marcus Reno down from their hillside, across to the western bank of the Little Bighorn, and then downstream into the Indian camp. Custer took half the troops and circled to the northeast, creating a little mini-pincer of his own. Along the river were camped the Hunkpapa-Lakota led by Sitting Bull and Gall, the Oglala led by Crazy Horse, the Minneconjous and, farther downstream, the Cheyenne. As women and children fled into the woods, Sitting Bull and Gall stopped Reno's attack cold, drove his troops into the woods and then back across the river where they dug into a hilltop. Custer was swamped by Crazy Horse, Two Moon of the Cheyenne, and Gall who returned after pinning Reno. When Terry and Gibbon arrived three days later they found only Reno and a few of his soldiers alive.

On July 22, 1876, General William T. Sherman assumed military authority over all Lakota country, ordered all Indians onto designated reservations, and sent troops after the "hostiles." The Indians were traveling with their families, including children and old people; they stood no chance against the onslaught of fresh, well-armed troops. Crazy Horse, lured to Fort Robinson with a promise of a reservation on the Powder River, was stabbed and killed by Private William Gentles at the door of the fort's jailhouse on September 5, 1877. Sitting Bull was killed by a member of the newly established Indian Police during his arrest on December 15, 1890. Disregarding a provision of the 1868 treaty which required agreement of three-quarters of the adult males of the

Lakota bands to amend it, the United States rounded up a few Lakota leaders, and extorted from them an agreement to give up all rights to the Black Hills.

The story was repeated across the plains, throughout the Rocky Mountains, and down the western slope to the Pacific Ocean. In 1885 the Major Crimes Act officially proclaimed federal U.S. jurisdiction on Indian reservations for the first time. Two years later, the Allotment Act, written by Senator Henry L. Dawes, established the policy of terminating common ownership of Indian land by alloting private parcels to individual Indians. Dawes made no attempt to obscure the purpose of the legislation which was designed to absorb traditional Indian cultures into the competitive atmosphere of the American private enterprise system. Dawes's speech to the Senate in 1885, advancing the merits of his bill, provides perhaps a glimpse at the unbridgeable philosophical chasm between the world view of the indigenous people of the Western Hemisphere and that of the European invaders. He said: "The head chief told us that there was not a family in that whole nation [Cherokee] that had not a home of its own. There was not a pauper in that nation, and the nation did not owe a dollar. . . Yet the defect of the system was apparent. They have got as far as they can go, because they own their land in common . . . there is no enterprise to make your home any better than that of your neighbor's. There is no selfishness, which is at the bottom of civilization. Until this people consent to give up their lands and divide them among their citizens so that each can own the land he cultivates, they will not make much progress."

Kit Carson had already chased down the "hostile" Navajo, burned their crops, killed their livestock, and marched them to Fort Sumner, New Mexico. Generals Nelson Miles and Oliver Howard had chased the small peaceful band of Nez Perce from their land near the Snake River, in what is now Idaho, to the Canadian border where their leader, Chief Joseph, his blanketless children scattered and lost in the snow, surrendered. The Utes were driven from their lands in Colorado, the *Denver Tribune* calling them Communist. The British North American Act of 1867 had established Canada for the British Crown, and the descendants of the Spanish and Portuguese were dividing South America.

As resources were discovered, Indian lands shrank in direct proportion. When oil was discovered in Oklahoma in 1906 the Cherokee (who had been transferred there from their original home in the Southeast), the Choctaw, Chickasaw, Creek, and Seminole Indians were moved from what had previously been considered barren, useless land. Oklahoma became a state the following year, and covered wagons raced

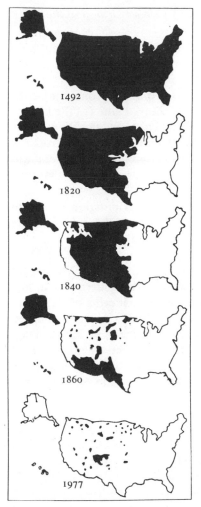

INDIAN LAND WITHIN UNITED STATES
In 1492, 541 Indian nations
— approximately 10 million people —
lived in what is now the United States.
The U.S. government ratified 371 treaties with
these Indian nations between 1776 and 1871.
Chief Red Cloud of the Lakota said:
"They made many promises to us,
but they only kept one: they promised
to take our land, and they took it."
The modern American Indian Movement
has sought to restore the Indian land base
by demanding that the United States honor
its treaty obligations with the Indian nations.

from the state line, each given a fair chance to claim a piece of former Indian land.

In the Southwest, on Black Mesa, the Hopi traditionals sternly rejected the allotment process, refusing to accept the forty- and sixty-acre plots the government assigned to them, and also refusing to send their children to the white schools that the Mormons and Mennonites had established. In 1891 the government sent troops into the Hopi villages, and arrested some of their leaders. During this period the Hopi lost 86 million acres of their land when the government sold it as "surplus" because no individual Hopi had claimed it. In 1909 coal was discovered on Black Mesa, and during the next twenty years the U.S. Geological Survey carefully mapped out the area; their efforts would eventually lead to the discovery of uranium, and would mark the Hopi mesas for multi-billion-dollar energy development projects.

In 1924 the U.S. Congress passed the Citizenship Act, conferring U.S. citizenship on all Indians born within the "territorial limits of the United States." The traditional Indians, of course, did not consider themselves to be living in the territorial limits of the United States, and did not consider citizenship in the 148-year-old nation preferable to the relationship to the land which they assumed by virtue of occupancy that predated written history.

Between the years 1860 and 1924 the Indian population of North America dropped from 340,000 to 222,000. The most shameful episode from the era was the now-famous 1890 massacre at Wounded Knee on the Lakota reservation of Pine Ridge. Lakota men, women, and children under the leadership of Chief Big Foot were surrounded by U.S cavalry troops under the command of Major Samuel Whiteside and Colonel James Forsyth. During an argument over the surrendering of an Indian gun, a shot was fired; Indians tried to flee, but Hotchkiss guns mounted on the hillside opened fire, killing 350, including the aging chief. They were buried in a mass grave at the site. The few who escaped moved through the gullies and creek beds, and hid out in what is now known as the Badlands of South Dakota. But they didn't forget, and they told their children, and their children didn't forget either.

Three separate court actions in 1904, 1906, and 1910 reduced the Rosebud reservation on the southern border of South Dakota by 75 percent. In 1911 Pine Ridge, east of Rosebud, was reduced by 25 percent. In 1970 a young lawyer, William Janklow, began a suit supposedly on behalf of the Rosebud Tribal Council to reclaim the lost land. Seven years later, as Attorney General for the state, Janklow completed the case from the other side, winning the three-and-a-half counties for the state. In 1978 he became governor of South Dakota and an avowed enemy of AIM.

By 1970, the South Dakota population was 95 percent white; 32,000 Indian people lived among 633,000 whites according to the U.S. census, but it is likely there were another 20,000 unreported Indian people. Highway 90, the main truck route between Seattle and Chicago, runs through Rapid City, just north of the Black Hills, passes north of Pine Ridge and Rosebud, through the Badlands, across the Missouri River, through the dry flat lands to Sioux Falls and then on to Chicago, Cleveland, and the eastern sea coast. The primary state revenues come from mining and tourism, both industries centered in the Black Hills where the stone faces of Presidents Washington, Lincoln, Jefferson, and Theodore Roosevelt on Mount Rushmore are America's stamp on the land.

According to a 1973 State of South Dakota Division of Human Rights report, the Indian population had a 20.1 percent unemployment rate compared to 3.2 percent for whites, and 54.8 percent of the Indian families lived below what the U.S. government has defined as the poverty level, compared with 14.8 percent of the whites. Although Indians represent 5 or, at most, 7 percent of the state population, they account for as much as 43 percent of the arrests, and up to 50 percent of the criminal convictions. The inmate population at the State Penitentiary in Sioux Falls ranges from 21 to 24 percent Indian, while the inmate population at Pennington County jail in Rapid City ranges from 50 to 55 percent Indian. The U.S Commission on Civil Right has determined that harassment, brutality, selective enforcement and manipulation of the bail system form a pattern of discriminatory abuse of Indians.

By 1973, with Janklow as Attorney General and Dickie Wilson as tribal chairman on Pine Ridge, violence against Indians escalated, and traditional Indians became the primary targets of harassment. When South Dakota Criminal Justice Commissioner Donald Holman resigned in 1977, he stated in a letter to Governor Richard Kneip that one reason was the uncontrolled practice of discrimination against Indian people. He said: "I have become increasingly aware of the fact that Native Americans who hold traditional views and are political activists are signaled out for special attention by the criminal justice system in South Dakota. Members of the American Indian Movement, in particular, are singled out for harassment. Every law enforcement agency in the state, including the highway patrol, BIA police, FBI, DCI [Division of Criminal Investigation], and seemingly all local police authorities apparently agree on one thing, that the American Indian Movement is innately evil, and that they should do everything in their power to suppress the Native peoples who adhere to the goals of that organization."

State Highway 79, running south from Rapid City to the Nebraska border, passes through a surburban country ranch-house development, past construction yards of old machinery on oiled ground, and into Custer County where a forest of billboards announces tourist sights such as Custer State Park, a "real gold rush town from the riproaring days of '76," Calvin Coolidge's Summer White House, hot springs, restaurants, and motels. Fifty miles south of Rapid City, where dry gulches cross the highway and the Black Hills rise up slowly to the west, a dirt road runs east to the little town of Buffalo Gap with rickety fences, dusty dirt

streets, post office, bank, liquor store, and bar. Here, in the streets of
Buffalo Gap, just after midnight on January 22, 1973 a thirty-year-old
white man, Darld Schmitz, stabbed and killed Wesley Bad Heart Bull, a
twenty-year-old Indian.

Schmitz was released the same day on a $5,000 bond, and charged a
week later at the Custer County Courthouse with second degree manslaughter. Wesley's mother, Sarah Bad Heart Bull, was upset because
her son's killer was not charged with murder, and was allowed to walk
free on the streets. The light treatment of whites who killed Indians
seemed like tacit approval by the state of violence against Indian people.
With the help of some traditionals on the Pine Ridge reservation, Sarah
sent word to the AIM leaders who were gathered in Scottsbluff, Nebraska at a Chicano-Indio Unity Conference. She asked that AIM come to
Custer to support her in petitioning State Attorney for Custer County,
Hobart Gates. She was asking that murder charges be leveled against
Schmitz.

AIM agreed to help, and a meeting with Dennis Banks, Russell
Means, and Hobart Gates was scheduled for February 6. On that day
over two hundred Indians and supporters converged on the town of
Custer which, by its very name and location in the sacred Black Hills,
was an affront to traditional Indians. They came from Pine Ridge reservation, Rosebud, Rapid City, and surrounding towns. The two hundred
people met at the Custer courthouse where Banks, Means, and two
other representatives went upstairs to speak with Gates. The state
attorney's office told them that as far as they were concerned justice was
being done, but that they would look into the case. The AIM people
wanted more than that; they asked for some guarantee that Schmitz
would be re-arrested and charged with murder. The discussion ended in
a stalemate.

Sheriff's deputies were standing guard at all the doors to the courthouse. Means had come down to talk with the crowd, when somebody
pushed somebody. Tempers were short on both sides, and a struggle
ensued. Sarah Bad Heart Bull was pushed down the steps of the courthouse, and the confrontation quickly escalated into a riot, police and
demonstrators participating with equal enthusiasm. According to the
police version of the story the Indians started the fight. State DCI Agent
Bernard Christenson, Sheriff Ernest Pepin, and Deputy Bill Rice were
guarding the front door. According to Christenson the police were
letting people into the building in small groups when, "All of a sudden I
was hit as I was locking the door." Christenson, with the help of other
deputies, shoved the demonstrators out the front door; he then grabbed
a gun, and ran out through the back door of the building. As he circled

around toward the bellowing riot in the street, he saw a youth carrying a burning object toward the building. He hollered: "Stop or I'll shoot!"[5] The young man fled, but soon several flaming cans were being hurled toward the courthouse. Tear gas wafted throughout the building and into the street.

According to Mildred Galligo of Rapid City: "If they'd have opened the doors for us it wouldn't have happened. All we wanted to do was be heard. They closed the doors and shoved an Indian boy down the steps. That's how it started." Upstairs in the building Dennis Banks broke a window in a gas-filled room to let air in. Down on the streets deputies dispersed and arrested demonstrators, clearing the front of the courthouse. The fire department was called.

As fire fighters extinguished the blaze at the courthouse, the Chamber of Commerce building across the street was set afire. Bottles, cans, stones, and tear-gas canisters filled the air. The Chamber of Commerce burned to the ground, an oil storage facility was partially damaged by fire, and two police cars were vandalized. Twenty-two demonstrators were arrested, including Means and Sarah Bad Heart Bull. The mother of the slain Indian would eventually serve five months of a one-to-five-year prison sentence for rioting and assaulting an officer; her son's killer served less than a day in jail.

On the day following the Custer riot Dennis Banks spoke to a meeting of citizens in Rapid City during which Rapid City Mayor Donald Barnet had promised a Racial Conciliation Commission to investigate discrimination in the city. "What does race conciliation mean?" asked Banks. "For the past thirty days I have resided in this city, and I have seen racial discrimination other places, but none like here in Rapid City. Rapid City parallels Custer in its goals and objectives to keep Indian people down. We have tried to carry signs, to bring attention to the injustices. We have carried signs from Minneapolis to Washington, and they still hurt us . . . they never listen to us, but they did listen to us February sixth in Custer. . . . These people want us to live within their system and obey their laws, but they are not ready to lay down the law against their own kind."[6] The mayor's Conciliation Commission was never established; Banks, however, was later arrested and charged with inciting to riot and destruction of property.

East of Rapid City, on Pine Ridge reservation, the traditional camp — represented by Fools Crow and other chiefs, elder women such as Ellen Moves Camp and Gladys Bissonette, the Means brothers, and

5. *Rapid City Journal*, February 7, 1973.
6. Ibid., February 8, 1973.

younger supporters such as Gladys's nephew Pedro Bissonette — had formed the Oglala Sioux Civil Rights Organization. They brought impeachment proceedings against Dickie Wilson, charging him with misuse of tribal funds, harassing opposition, and failing to protect the rights and interests of the Pine Ridge people. The erosion of the tribal land base, and the acceptance of government money for lost tribal land were at the heart of the conflict.

The Means brothers, for example, had inherited 190 acres of land, but the land, like all allotments, was held in trust by the federal government, and it was leased through the BIA to a white rancher. According to Russell Means, they no longer received lease payments after 1969 when they joined AIM.

Using the BIA tribal council system, the Department of Interior keeps an iron grip on the development and use of allotted Indian land through craftily worded grazing and mining lease contracts executed at times without the knowledge of the Indian owners. One favorite method of the BIA, devised in May of 1972, is called, in simple bureaucratese, Form 5-5525. The government form, issued from the Department of Interior, is an "Authority to Grant Grazing Privileges on Allotted Lands." It describes the land in question, and gives the superintendent of the BIA the authority to lease the land for grazing purposes. The form states: "I do hereby agree to grant any permittee (leasee) reasonable right-of-way over the above allotments, provided I shall receive reasonable compensation . . ." and adds that "the proceeds arising from the permits on the above lands shall be paid to the Superintendent of the said Indian Agency and deposited in accordance with the regulations of the Department of Interior." At the bottom there is a place for the allottee, or supposed owner, to sign.

On the surface, Form 5-5525 is a service offered by the BIA to help Indians lease their land, but it veils an insidious little plot which puts control of the Indian land in the hands of the BIA. A letter, which is sent to the landowners along with the form, states: "We believe that it is in your interest to execute the enclosed form and return it to us at an early date. If these are heirship lands and are not in use by any of the heirs, the General Grazing Regulations provide a 90-day period from date of this notice for heirs to reach an agreement with respect to the granting of grazing privileges. If an agreement cannot be reached within the 90-day period the Superintendent is authorized by law to grant a permit thereon to protect the interest of all the heirs by insuring a minimum income from their land." This paragraph may be roughly translated as saying: "If you do not sign and return this form in three months we will lease your land anyway." A range unit leased by the BIA may include land owned by ten, or twenty, or as many as a hundred different people. The forms do not allow for the owners to say "No," and after ninety days the BIA is free to lease the land as it wishes.

The standard BIA mining lease reveals what is meant by the statement that lease money is ". . . deposited in accordance with the regulations of the Department of Interior." The mining lease contract states that lease money is paid to the Superintendent *or* "to the Treasurer of said Tribe where the Tribe is organized under the act of June 18, 1934"; that is, to the tribal councils as established by the Indian Reorganization Act. By way of the 1887 Dawes Allotment Act, therefore, land is transferred from tribal to private control; then through Department of Interior lease contracts and regulations the land is leased often without the consent or even the knowledge of the "owner." Finally, the lease money — sometimes as low as twenty-five cents per acre per year — is deposited with the BIA-supervised tribal councils. On Pine Ridge in 1973 traditional supporters including the Means brothers were reporting that they were not receiving their lease money, and the suspected culprit was Dickie Wilson.

Wilson was also in favor of accepting Claims Commission money for the stolen Black Hills and, furthermore, he was in favor of a Department of Interior plan to reduce the Pine Ridge reservation by 133,000 acres, one-eighth of the reservation land. The government acquisition had been first proposed by the National Parks Service in January of 1972, just prior to the beginning of Wilson's regime. The land in question was known as the gunnery range, because it had been expropriated by the U.S. government in 1942 for use as a wartime aerial gunnery range. Rather than return the land, as promised, after the war, the government passed a statute in 1956 agreeing to compensate the Lakota people for the land. In 1968 the Department of Interior proposed that the land, situated in the northwestern corner of the reservation, be added to the Badlands National Monument; then in 1972 they brought that proposal to the Pine Ridge tribal council which rejected it. Richard Little, representing the reservation district affected by the proposal had said: "The tribe is losing a great deal of land. . . . The Park Service has no business in that area."[7]

By February 1973, Wilson had reopened negotiations with the Park Service. To the traditional Lakota people the land was like any other that they still possessed; it was simply their land, and not for sale. However, the land had a special status for the government and several energy corporations who were privy to U.S. Geological Survey information

7. Ibid., January 11, 1972.

which showed the land to be rich in uranium and oil deposits. It was in this atmosphere that impeachment proceedings were advanced against Wilson, and that the U.S. army began to move onto Pine Ridge reservation.

The impeachment hearings were scheduled for February 14, 1973 before the tribal council. Although over three hundred people showed up for the scheduled hearing, Wilson postponed the impeachment due to "road and weather conditions," and on that same day the U.S. Marshals Service, under the direction of ex-marine Wayne Colburn, moved approximately seventy highly trained counter-insurgency Special Operations Group (SOG) troops onto Pine Ridge reservation. The well-armed paramilitary SOG forces, described by Colburn as "a strike force deployed only at the request of the President or the U.S. Attorney General," set up a command post at the BIA building in the town of Pine Ridge, installing machine guns on the roof, and training the BIA police in riot formation and in various weapon and tear-gas techniques.

The FBI office in the South Dakota capital of Pierre sent agents Jim Dix and Bruce Erickson to Pine Ridge to work with Colburn's SOG unit. The town of Pine Ridge, Wilson's stronghold on the southern border of

South Dakota State Police on Pine Ridge Reservation, prior to the takeover of Wounded Knee, February 1973. (Photo courtesy of Akwesasne Notes)

the reservation, became an armed camp; Wilson, a besieged despot. The impeachment supporters drove from the council meeting hall north of town to the BIA building in Pine Ridge; there they carried signs and chanted, calling for the removal of Wilson, of BIA Superintendent for Pine Ridge Stanley Lyman, and of the U.S. marshals. The protest was led by the older women. Grandmother Gladys Bissonette recalled: "When we marched, thre were nothing but us women . . . the girls had to beat the drum and sing, because the men were afraid of being arrested, which they would have done if the men got out there." One of the women, Lou Bean, recalled that the marshals jeered at them and threatened them. She said: "Well, that's all it took . . . we told them to go ahead and come on over — we was all fired up. . . . We were willing to fight. . . . All they have to do is lay down their guns and come in, and I think us women could whip 'em."[8]

The day ended without a clash, however, and the impeachment hearing was rescheduled for February 22. In the meantime, the U.S. marshals, FBI, state police, BIA police, and Wilson's goon squad consolidated their grip on Pine Ridge and patroled the area from Rapid City through the reservation. Radio communication equipment was installed between Pine Ridge and the Hacienda Motel in Gordon, Nebraska where, according to the U.S. Marshal's Log, later released in court, a SOG Standby Unit was stationed. On February 20 the U.S. Marshals Service Director's Office in Washington, D.C. advised the Command Post that "50 additional (SOG) men will be departing for Rapid City as soon as possible." FBI Special Agent in Charge, Joseph Trimbach, arrived that day to take charge of the FBI operations. That evening Rapid City police and the FBI evicted AIM members from a meeting at the Imperial-400 Motel in Rapid City and cordoned off another suspected AIM meeting place. Seventy-five AIM members received asylum in a Rapid City church.

On the morning of February 22, the Oglala Sioux Civil Rights Organization met at the Calico Community Hall six miles north of Pine Ridge. From there a 150-car caravan drove to the Billy Mills Hall, site of the scheduled 10:00 A.M. tribal council meeting and impeachment hearing. According to the Marshal's Log for that day: "All SOG units on station: Group 1, BIA building, Group 2, located in roads building. BIA police all on station. . . . [U.S. Marshal officer Reese] Kash advises [from Billy Mills Hall] approximately 300 spectators there now and that a quorum of

8. *Voices From Wounded Knee, Akwesasne Notes*, Rooseveltown, New York, 1974, p. 23.

the Council has arrived . . . Mr. Wilson is starting to show his movie
Anarchy, U.S.A."[9]

Six hundred impeachment supporters arrived for the hearing, which
Wilson postponed until 2:00 P.M. so that he could show the John Birch
Society production *Anarchy, U.S.A.,* depicting black ghetto riots with
buildings and houses aflame. After the film, the council voted on the
impeachment request. The Civil Rights Organization had asked that
Wilson be suspended for ten to twenty days until the trial could be held.
The council voted in favor of the impeachment trial, but Wilson insisted
that the trial be held immediately, so the trial was scheduled for the
following day.

Wilson selected a judge for his trial on February 23, and according to
Gladys Bissonette: "There was a puppet if there ever was one."[10]
Dickie Wilson stood behind the selected chairman throughout the hearing, directing the course of events, frustrating attempts by opposition
council members to raise questions while allowing his supporters to
ramble on about his virtues and the threat of AIM on the reservation.
Hobart Keith, the leader of the opposition, finally rose to his feet,
announcing that the Civil Rights Organization was going to "take this to
Federal Court." Organization Vice-President Pedro Bissonette
lamented: "Every time you approach the tribe, the BIA, in the normal
way they always shut the door on us." Wilson was entrenched; the
opposition council members left the meeting in protest. The Marshal's
Log for the afternoon states simply: "Received information from BIA
police source that Dick Wilson was voted back into office, 4–0 vote."
There were twenty council members.

The traditional Oglala-Lakota people defied a Wilson ban on meetings
by congregating at the community meeting hall in Calico on February 24.
The Marshal's Log for the following day reveals the first evidence of
U.S. army involvement with the events in South Dakota. The Log
states: "Col. Simmons, Pentagon, called ref: Director [in reference to
Marshal Wayne Colburn] . . . Mr. Colburn will arrive at Rapid City
regional airport . . . on military U.S. twin engine propeller aircraft.
Have Mr. Colburn confirm his arrival at Rapid City with Col. Simmons." A Log entry at 7:47 A.M. on February 26 states: "Col. Dunn
would like the Director to call him at the Pentagon, 202-695-0441, Ext.
215." The U.S. Marshals service told Legal Aid lawyer Gary Thomas,
reporting BIA police intimidation on behalf of traditional Indians, that
the Marshal's Service was "a neutral element, and . . . we do not

9. Ibid; p. 27.
10. Ibid; p. 26.

interfere with local problems''; yet they were completely preoccupied at that time with protecting Wilson and monitoring the movement and activities of his local political opposition. What may have seemed to an onlooker to be a minor power struggle on Pine Ridge reservation had become a major concern of the Pentagon, the highest level military command post in the United States.

The elders and young traditionals continued their meeting at Calico under twenty-four-hour surveillance by the marshals. On February 26 John Terronez of the Community Relations Service of the Department of Justice attempted to intervene by arranging a meeting between the traditional leaders and U.S. Marshal officer Reese Kash. Kash, however, failed to show up at the meeting, and according to the Marshal's Log, told Bart Schmidt to ''inform Mr. Terronez that CP [Command Post] was unable to contact [me].'' Kash also concealed the military involvement from the Justice Department when he instructed Command Post personnel that ''should Mr. Terronez of the Community Relations Service request to see any of our personnel he is to be escorted to the office adjacent to Mr. Lyman's office. He is not to be admitted to the command post.'' On February 27, with the reservation swarming with armed military personnel, the traditional people called for AIM to come to the reservation in force, and they decided to make a stand by seizing the town of Wounded Knee.

Dennis Banks, who was invited by the Oglala elders to attend the Calico meeting, later described the meeting in court testimony. He said: ''I attended this meeting . . . in attendance at that meeting were Oglala Sioux chiefs, traditional headsmen, medicine men, and councilmen. Eleven out of twenty councilmen were there. I heard an Oglala Sioux woman, two women, address their chiefs and headsmen in their own language, and their interpretation to me was that . . . because the complaints that had been signed by members of the council were true . . . and because . . . the government allowed the chairman, who was under the impeachment hearing to preside over his own impeachment hearing, that they called this meeting because the president [Wilson] declared himself innocent and immediately fired the vice-president for the tribe, who had taken a stand to oppose his actions.

''The plea that they made to the American Indian Movement — two women who were truly the real warriors of Indian society, who saw their own sons dying on the reservations, who saw their own children dying — they asked the Oglala Sioux chiefs, they asked the medicine men and the headsmen, they asked them where were the spirits of so long ago that made this nation great, where was that Indian spirit that the Oglala Sioux Nation so many years ago stood up against the U.S. army.

. . . They demanded to know if there were any Indians left in the United States, Indians who were descendants of those great Indian heroes of long ago, and they asked us if we were to allow another day to go by under the dictatorship of Wilson, and they asked us where were the Indians that allowed the marshals who were surrounding us in Calico, where were the Indian warriors that allow non-Indians to come to this reservation and dictate our lives.

"They asked the American Indian Movement what was AIM going to do about it — the injustices that were happening that very minute — allowing the federal people, the federal officers, the FBI and the marshals, allowing them to turn the village of Pine Ridge into an armed camp, until people, those people who were at Calico, were afraid to go to Pine Ridge.

"It was that same BIA government that was established in 1849 under the Department of War, and . . . on February 27 it was a Department of War, and these Oglala Sioux women only asked that the spirit, that the fighting spirit, return, so that there would be no reason for Indian people to drink themselves to death, so that there'd be no reason for Indian youngsters to be slashing their wrists.

"One by one the Oglala Sioux Chiefs stood up, and their names will come before you . . . Names like Fools Crow and Crow Dog, names like Catches . . . names like Kills Enemy, Iron Cloud. . . . We'd reached a point in history where we could not tolerate that kind of abuse any longer where these women, these parents, these mothers who couldn't tolerate the mistreatment that goes on on the reservations any longer, they could not see another Indian youngster die. They could not see another Indian man meet death, whether he was in Chicago or Nebraska, or Buffalo Gap."[11]

Then one of the chiefs said: "Go ahead and do it, go to Wounded Knee. You can't get in the BIA office and the tribal office, so take your brothers from the American Indian Movement and go to Wounded Knee and make your stand there. Throw them off and don't announce that you're going to Wounded Knee. Say you're going to Porcupine for a meeting." A fifty-four-car caravan proceeded to Wounded Knee, arriving there at 7:30 P.M. They seized control of the small village, established an armed security perimeter and held eleven hostages including Clive and Agnes Gildersleeve, white owners of the Wounded Knee Trading Post from which weapons and supplies were confiscated.

Agnes Lamont was working at a reservation school dormitory when

11. *U.S. vs. Dennis Banks and Russell Means*, before Judge Fred Nichol, February 12, 1974.

the takeover occurred. She later recalled in court:[12] "The first thing you know there was a bunch of federal marshals come into the dormitory where I work. They all had these blue jump suits on, and they had guns. We put them up in the dorm. We moved our boys into the next dorm, doubled up. We were giving lunch there for the boys and I was making fried bread. One of the marshals came over and said: 'Lady, do you have a recipe for this?' [I said] 'No, I don't have no recipe, but when you eat this you be lively.'

"So he said, 'Oh, well, I better try one.'

" 'What purpose are you here, are you marshals?' I asked. 'Well, I don't know, but it's an order that we had to come.' He said they were afraid that AIM people would take over the agency. I asked 'What are they going to take over, what is there to take over? It's not like D.C. There's nothing here and it belongs to the Indians. What they're going to take is done gone. There's nothing here.'

" 'Well, that's the order we got.' So it went on and on and the marshals went to Wounded Knee. Then they came back, and I asked: 'Where did you go?'

" 'Wounded Knee.'

" 'What for?'

" 'Well, that's the orders we got so we went to Wounded Knee and thought we'll get them people out of there.'

" 'Well, I don't know, I don't think you can. They are there for some purpose. They asked for their treaty, and they want to remove this chairman. But I think he's under the U.S. government and that he's got you guys in here with guns.'

" 'Well, I really don't know,' he said."

The marshals, FBI, BIA police, and Wilson's burgeoning goon squad immediately established roadblocks on all roads leading to Wounded Knee. At 10:00 P.M. FBI Special Agent in Charge, Joseph Trimbach, arrived at the FBI roadblock on Pine Ridge Road south of the village. Shortly thereafter John Terronez from the Community Relations Service of the Justice Department, the man who had earlier attempted to diffuse the confrontation, arrived by car from the direction of Wounded Knee. Trimbach told him: "Mr. Terronez, to work with these people is one thing, but if I find that you have participated in a burglary with them I will have to arrest you."[13] Terronez handed Trimback a piece of paper on which were written the demands of the protesters: it asked that

12. *The Great Sioux Nation*, The American Indian Treaty Council Information Center, Moon Books, San Francisco, 1977, p. 47–49.
13. *Voices From Wounded Knee*, op. cit.

An FBI agent takes aim on Wounded Knee from Roadblock-1, one mile south of the Oglala Nation's Crow's Nest bunker. (*Photo courtesy of* Akwesasne Notes)

Senators William Fulbright, Edward Kennedy, and James Abourezk convene Senate committees to conduct hearings on Indian treaty rights, investigate the Department of Interior and BIA practices and procedures, and to investigate all Sioux reservations in South Dakota. The communiqué listed six people with whom the Indians would be willing to negotiate: John Ehrlichman on Nixon's staff, Interior Secretary Morton, the BIA Commissioner, and Senators Kennedy, Fulbright, and Abourezk.

In a final expression of commitment, the note — signed by Oglala Sioux Civil Rights Organization president Vern Long, Vice-president Pedro Bissonette, Secretary Eddie White Wolf, and AIM spokesman Russell Means — stated: "The only two options open to the United States of America are: 1. They wipe out the old people, women, children, and men by shooting and attacking us. 2. They negotiate our demands."

As the federal perimeter closed down tightly around the village of Wounded Knee, Russell Means slipped out a press release in which he stated: "We want full disclosure of the graft and corruption, and the fact that they are stealing our lands. Just for example, the man who runs the realty office [Tom Conroy] has been in office for twenty-three years, and is now the single largest land owner on the reservation. That is corruption . . . The BIA has perpetuated oppression and tyranny on the Indian people. The final act is the gunnery range that we let the United States use for the duration of World War II. Although the war has been over for years we have yet to get our gunnery range back on the northern edge of the reservation. . . . In order to get us out of Wounded Knee the federal government has to massacre us or meet our demands. This is it. We are making our last stand here."[14]

On February 28 the marshals acquired two armored personnel carriers (APCs, armored tanks) from the South Dakota National Guard, and began to tighten their perimeter. On that same day the U.S. Marshal's Log reported an order from Washington which said: "Do not let newspaper personnel in the Wounded Knee area . . . no TV coverage of the Wounded Knee area, authority Attorney General [Richard Kleindienst]. . . . No photos of [military] personnel." A Department of Justice information officer established an office in Rapid City to issue information to

14. *Rapid City Journal*, January 3, 1973.

U.S. Army armed personnel carrier stands watch over the besieged hamlet of Wounded Knee in 1973. When Lakota traditionalists, seeking the ouster of Dickie Wilson, took over the town, the U.S. government responded with the Sixth Army under the direction of General Alexander Haig, Colonel Volney Warner, and **Colonel Jack Potter. (Photo by Michele Vignes, courtesy of Akwesasne Notes)**

the media. The secrecy policy fit into a larger plan to disguise the fact that the federal government was violating the Constitution by employing federal military forces against civilian populations without a presidential proclamation and executive order as required by law.

On February 28 General Alexander Haig, then Vice-chief of Staff at the Pentagon, dispatched Colonel Volney Warner of the 82nd Airborne and Colonel Jack Potter of the Sixth Army to Wounded Knee. For the first time in their careers they were ordered to wear civilian clothes while on duty. At 3:00 A.M. the following morning they met with Major Vic Jackson from the California Civil Disorder Management School, FBI agent Joseph Trimbach, and Wayne Colburn of the Marshals Service at the Ellsworth Air Force Base outside Rapid City. Following their meeting they flew over Wounded Knee by helicopter; by March 3 Air Force F-4 Phantom jets were making daily surveillance passes over the besieged hamlet. Colonel Warner's daily reports to the Pentagon were

The United States Sixth Army under the direction of General Alexander Haig, Colonel Volney Warner, and Colonel Jack Potter, on location at Wounded Knee. It was the first time since the Civil War that the U.S. Army had been dispatched in a domestic operation. The Pentagon employed 17 armed personnel carriers like the one pictured here, as well as 130,000 rounds of M-16 ammunition, 41,000 rounds of M-1 ammunition, 24,000 flares, 12 M-79 grenade launchers, 600 cases of C-S gas, 100 rounds of M-40 high explosives, helicopters, Phantom jets, and personnel. (Photo courtesy of Akwesasne Notes)

passed along to Fred Buzhardt, counsel for the Secretary of Defense, to General Haig, and then to the White House. Attorney General Kleindienst issued a statement through the FBI that he wanted ''all individuals prosecuted. There is to be no amnesty or bonds set. . . . Prosecute everyone for any crimes possible.''[15]

Documents later subpoenaed from the Pentagon revealed that Colonel Potter directed the employment of 17 APCs, 130,000 rounds of M-16 ammunition, 41,000 rounds of M-1 ammunition, 24,000 flares, 12 M-79 grenade launchers, 600 cases of C-S gas, 100 rounds of M-40 high explosives, as well as helicopters, Phantom jets, and personnel. Military officers, supply sergeants, maintenance technicians, chemical officers, and medical teams remained on duty throughout the seventy-one-day siege, all working in civilian clothes. Three hundred miles to the south, at Fort Carson, Colorado the Army had billeted a fully uniformed and armed assault unit on twenty-four-hour alert.

The military equipment was dropped off, according to army records, at points several miles from Wounded Knee; it was then removed from marked military containers and transferred by civilian vehicles to the military perimeter. Department of Justice documents state that on March 2 and 13 ''representatives of the Department of Defense briefed representatives of Justice and Interior concerning certain military contingencies.'' The military contingencies were contained in a White House Option Paper prepared by Kenneth Cole of President Nixon's Domestic Council, and outlined the costs, methods, and expected number of casualties resulting from the use of ''massive force'' to evict the Indians from Wounded Knee.

The refusal of the Marshals Service to negotiate with the Indians prior to the seizure of Wounded Knee, the prompt reaction of the U.S. armed forces to a political squabble on an Indian reservation in South Dakota, the banning of the media from the scene, the undercover nature of the military operation, and the White House contingency plans indicated that the government had planned all along to force the showdown with the Indians, and to carry out what lawyer Ken Tilsen called the planned ''second massacre at Wounded Knee,'' or what Matthew King referred to as ''the war plan.'' Tilsen said: ''It has been our position that Nixon and his cronies created the Special Operations Group of the U.S. Marshals Service in January 1971 expressly to avoid the law [forbidding use of the military against civilian populations without presidential procla-

---

15. *The Nation*, New York, November 9, 1974. Further accounts of military and White House involvement at Wounded Knee may be found in the *University Review*, November, 1974; and in *Akwesasne Notes*, Early Summer, 1974.

mation]. . . . Chemical officers had completed their survey of terrain and conditions for an assault. Medical teams had surveyed the area and made plans for the injured. . . . The planned ending is quite clear.''

Dickie Wilson, in the meantime, had assembled a somewhat smaller, though equally aggressive and much more boisterous assault team of his own. On March 5, six days into the siege, he told news reporters that he had ''eight or nine hundred guns,'' and added that ''I will not be responsible for holding my people back. If necessary, I will join them with my guns.'' Mildred Galligo later told reporters: ''We parked right in front of the tribal office to see who his nine hundred were. He was going to have a big conference with his nine hundred to make plans, so we sat there and sat there. Fifteen half-drunk kids went in — those are his goons. And he's half-shot himself, so he probably kept counting them over and over until he got nine hundred. That's the size of it.''

Nevertheless, Wounded Knee, fifteen miles to the northeast of Pine Ridge, site of a mass grave for the three hundred massacred in 1890, was surrounded. Four roads lead into the village: Manderson Road from the northwest, Porcupine Road from the northeast, Denby Road from the southeast, and Bigfoot Trail from the southwest. The marshals and BIA police established roadblocks at each road, and then strung outposts between them with code names such as Cheetah, X-Ray, Dagger, Eagle, and Foxhound; a field command post called Red Arrow was established outside the federal perimeter on Denby Road. Daily the marshals and the Pentagon's finest officers closed their formation, taking hilltops, sending forays into the demilitarized zone (DMZ), and occasionally exchanging fire with the Indians. It was as real a war as had ever been fought, albeit militarily one-sided. The Indians, armed with hunting rifles, .22s, and one Russian AK-47 brought back from Vietnam by a veteran, were surrounded by the most powerful military force in the world. Their defense rested on their hope that the whole world was watching, and that the U.S. military would not expose itself to international ridicule by repeating the Indian massacres in the age of global media networks. They had little doubt that if the world turned its eye away, the Pentagon could and would disintegrate their insurgency.

Inside the village, the people went about the business of living and caring for families, as well as the military business of digging bunkers and monitoring the movements of the government troops. The hostage issue more or less dissipated when most of the hostages chose to stay with the protesters and the ones who wanted to leave were released. On March 3, eighty-two-year-old Wilbur Riegert told reporters: ''The fact is, we as a group of hostages decided to stay to save AIM and our own property. Had we not, those troops would have come down here and killed all of these people. The real hostages are the AIM people."[16]

On March 10 the government announced that it would lift the roadblocks, allowing people to peacefully leave the village; their news release said that the "militants [were] seeking publicity," and would leave if given the chance. The ploy backfired. When the siege was relaxed, a few people left, but over a hundred poured into the village, with them Frank Fools Crow and other Oglala chiefs and headmen. Drums beat through the night and the next day. Inside the village security watches were reorganized with fresh warriors, a clinic was established, a kitchen, a sweatlodge, housing was constructed, and a radio room equipped. Food, medical supplies, and ammunition were brought in, bunkers were dug and fortified, and from across the country Indian and non-Indian supporters began trekking toward Wounded Knee.

On March 11, in a ceremony led by Chief Fools Crow, the community declared itself sovereign, proclaiming the Independent Oglala Nation, and assigning a delegation to the United Nations. One hundred and eighty-two Oglala-Lakota people became citizens of the Independent Oglala Nation; in addition, 160 Indians from other tribes in the United States and Canada became dual citizens of both their home nation and Oglala Nation. Seven white supporters, members of the Vietnam Veterans Against the War, were given a naturalized citizenship status. The Independent Oglala Nation requested other Indian nations to send delegates to Wounded Knee, and they established working committees on housing, medical care, food supply, customs and immigration, internal security, information, and defense; daily spiritual ceremonies were held, as well as council meetings.

The village continued to take fire from the U.S. military outposts. According to Roger Iron Cloud, a Vietnam veteran who served in the Wounded Knee bunker security force, "We took more bullets in seventy-one days [at Wounded Knee] than I took in two years in Vietnam." By mid-March, two weeks into the siege, three people had been hit by fire from the federal marshals. Lorelei DeCora, in charge of the clinic in the village, told a reporter: "We had three guys that got shot; two were Oglala Sioux. One was shot in the leg with an M-16. The other was shot in the hand with an M-16, but the bullet went right through. And just a couple of nights ago, a Chicano medic who was here to support us, when they started to fire, he ran out with his medic's band, and he got hit in the stomach with an M-16 too. They're all okay. The medicine man took the bullets out."

16. *Voices From Wounded Knee*, op. cit.

   Vietnam veteran Stan Holder, a Wichita Indian, became the head of
security. He said: "We were born out of defense for this nation; we're
not an offensive striking force at all. . . . It's more of a brotherhood than
any army with a chain of command. . . . It's a 180-degree change from
the U.S. military. The men here don't gripe. . . . They realize that
there's a need to defend their women and children, and a need to defend
the sacred land. The American fighting forces . . . are so dehumanized
that they can't even bring the personal aspect into their wars. They just
want to wage wars on a mass scale and keep identity totally out of it. . . .
They can't see the human aspect in this fight. If they did see it they'd
realize that they should lay down their guns — that this is a fight for the
survival of the world.

U.S. Marshals' bunker on eastern perimeter of Wounded Knee.
Lawyer Ken Tilsen, who was inside the village of Wounded Knee
for two days during the siege, estimated that the
village took 20,000 rounds of fire in those two days.
(Photo courtesy of Akwesasne Notes)

"We've been receiving automatic weapons fire — M-16, it's a 7.62 NATO round; M-16, the weapon used in Vietnam by the United States Armed Forces; .30 calibers, which are either mounted or built into these armored personnel carriers. Then the 30.06, a normal hunting rifle that the white ranchers and vigilantes use — who the government says aren't there. Also, shotguns used by the BIA police, and .38s, .44 magnums, things of this nature, weapons you'd find in any sporting goods store."

The Indians were very short on ammunition and weapons, but they wanted the federal marshals to keep a respectful distance, so they used a bit of military ingenuity to give their tiny arsenal a more sophisticated appearance. One evening several of the security people stayed up late painting coffee can lids black and attaching wires to them. The following morning they meandered through the DMZ in full view of the APCs and outposts, burying the black lids in the ground. Soon there were reports in the marshal's camp that the Indians had planted mines throughout the DMZ, a fear that kept the APCs at a distance.

Following the coffee-can maneuver, the Indians were forced to create another military illusion to avoid assault. One morning in late March the Wounded Knee bunkers took heavy fire from two APCs which approached within four hundred meters of the village security perimeter. According to a radio transmission from the marshal's Red Arrow command post, they expended 3,312 rounds of .30 caliber machine-gun fire that morning. The following radio transmission from the Wounded Knee security teams indicates the imbalance of the conflict:

"Denby [bunker] to Security: Send someone out to Manderson bunker. . . . There's an APC about 400 yards straight south of 'em."

"Security to Denby: Ten-four. I just sent a guy out there. They have no radio. They can't see that APC from where they're sitting."

"Denby to Security: Right on. We'll stand by." Then one of the warriors from the bunker came into the radio room. One of the operators asked him: "Freezing, huh?"

The warrior replied: "No, I ain't freezing. Anyone around here know where I can get some .22 shells?"

"Did you check security, brother?"

"Yeah, they got one bullet."

"Check the trailer. I thought I saw a box laying around in there."

The Indians got out the black paint again. This time they painted a piece of lead pipe and draped an empty .50-caliber ammunition belt over it to make it look like a machine gun. They mounted it in view of the federal troops and fired off ten shotgun rounds in rapid succession; then they got on the radio, which they knew the government was monitoring, and began talking about where to take the .50-caliber. Again, a rumor

*An observation point inside the besieged hamlet of Wounded Knee, 1973,
where traditionalists held off state, local, and federal police,
vigilantes, Wilson's goon squad, and the U.S. military
for seventy-one days. (Photo courtesy of* Akwesasne Notes)

circulated among the marshals, this time that the Indians were armed
with a .50-caliber machine gun. Ammunition, food, and medical supplies
were smuggled in through gullies at night, past federal outposts and
roadblocks. Supporters traveled from Indian reservations on the Great
Lakes, in Canada, on the West Coast, and from the Southwest. Traditional supporters in the small towns on Pine Ridge reservation housed
and fed the travelers. Fools Crow depleted his sheep herd, using over
three hundred sheep to feed the people who camped on his land.
Matthew King opened his home to the travelers. "We had, sometimes,
thirty or forty people sleeping here," he said. "Every bit of floor was
taken up with people sleeping. And we cooked food for them. Some of
them got arrested trying to sneak into Wounded Knee with supplies, but
most got through. The Indians know this land very well. Our people
could lead them in there right past the army tanks and everything.

"Dickie Wilson doesn't know it to this day," King added, "but Fools
Crow actually saved his life during Wounded Knee. I'll tell you that
story. One night these three young Indians show up — they weren't from
here, they were Apaches — they came to Fools Crow's house. Boy, they
were tough-looking guys; they had long hair down the side of their faces,
they were all very big, and they all had guns, rifles, with them. They told

Fools Crow that they were going to kill Wilson that night. They had gotten some information from a spy in the goon squad that there was going to be a party, and Wilson was going to be there. They said they were going to go over there and kill him for all the things he had done, and that was that. Well, Fools Crow said 'No, don't do that.' He told them that it would only bring more violence, and that there had already been too many people killed. He said that violence was no good; we wanted to clear up things in a peaceful way. We didn't believe in killing people, even Wilson and his bunch. Our boys went into Wounded Knee because they had to defend our people; that's the only reason. Well, the three Apache boys listened to Fools Crow, and they said okay, they wouldn't do it. Those boys were serious, though; they would have done it. Dickie Wilson can be glad to be alive, but he doesn't even know that Fools Crow did that, saved his life.''

King also told how Fools Crow intervened to stop a planned raid on the government positions. ''Some of the boys at Wounded Knee,'' he said, ''wanted to attack the federal army. Some of them said 'Come on, we can whip those guys; we can sneak up there at night and kill them all.' Some of those boys were really mad at what the marshals had done, and they wanted to kill as many marshals and FBI as they could and they didn't care. They were not afraid to die. Well, Fools Crow stopped that, too. He told them that if they did that, the army would kill everybody in Wounded Knee, because no matter how many [marshals] were killed, they would have more. Fools Crow said 'We have to live here when this is over; we want to settle this peacefully.' So he stopped that idea. There could have been a lot more violence, but Fools Crow and some of the other chiefs kept everyone on the right path.''

On March 19 a delegation from the Haudenosaunee, Iroquois Six Nation Confederacy, arrived on Pine Ridge and entered Wounded Knee, led by Onondaga-Haudenosaunee chief Oren Lyons. Lyons read a statement that the Haudenosaunee Confederacy had sent to the White House concerning Wounded Knee: ''The solution is simple,'' he said, ''be honest, be fair, honor the commitments made by the founding fathers of your country. We are an honorable people; can you say the same? You are concerned for the destruction of property. . . . Where is your concern for the destruction of our people, for human lives? . . . What about the destruction of *our* properties . . . the thousands of acres of land, inundated by dams built on our properties, the raping of the Hopi and Navajo territories by the Peabody strip-mining operations, timber cutting, power companies, water pollution, and on and on.

''The balance of the ledger is up to you. Compare the damage of the

BIA and Wounded Knee against the terrible record, and tell us that we are wrong for wanting redress. We ask for justice, and not from the muzzle of an M-16 rifle."

A month into the siege, on March 31, the U.S. government sent a negotiating team to Wounded Knee. Kent Frizzell and Richard Hellstern, both assistants to Attorney General Richard Kleindienst, arrived by helicopter to represent the United States. A tipi was set up along Big Foot Trail to the south of Wounded Knee in the demilitarized zone. Thirteen Oglalas and their legal advisors represented the Indians; among the Indian negotiators were Gladys Bissonette, Lou Bean, Ellen Moves Camp, spiritual leader Wallace Black Elk, Russell Means, and Pedro Bissonette. Legal support included Oglala lawyer Ramon Roubideaux and the tireless, self-made treaty expert, Hank Adams.

Wallace Black Elk opened the negotiations with a prayer "to bring world peace here in the Western Hemisphere . . . to pave the way for our children." The first day was passed with greetings and good wishes. On the morning of the second day the Indians presented Frizzell with a ten-point proposal which reflected the points raised in the original twenty-point proposal that had been the purpose of the earlier march on Washington, D.C., and which the United States had since rejected in total. The first point to be discussed was the familiar demand for a Presidential Treaty Commission, in this case specifically to review the Lakota treaty of 1868. Talks immediately bogged down when Frizzell read out the 1871 Appropriation Act stating that the United States could no longer negotiate treaties with Indians. Hank Adams stopped him, saying: "We're not asking for a *new* treaty, we're talking about the treaty that the law *protects!*" referring to the provision in the 1871 law that states "No obligation of any treaty lawfully made and ratified with any such Indian nation or tribe prior to March 3, 1871, shall be hereby invalidated or impaired." Frizzell could not promise a treaty commission, so that point and other treaty points were tabled, and the discussions moved on to dealing with the current conflict on Pine Ridge reservation.

During a discussion of a demand by the Indians that the government prosecute the tribal officials and goon squad members who were harassing people, Frizzell suggested that they settle for "a sufficient number of marshals and FBI people" who would remain on the reservation to protect people from the goon squad. He added that then "there would be no Wilson men, as such, with any authority, other than the BIA police."

His suggestion was met with scorn; Ellen Moves Camp countered: "The BIA police is with him [Wilson]."

FRIZZELL SAID: "Well, of course, if the FBI and marshals are here, the BIA police would be very reluctant to take any advantage because they are subjecting themselves to a civil rights complaint."

MOVES CAMP: "They didn't do it before we came in here [to Wounded Knee]."

FRIZZELL: "Well, we didn't have any FBI and marshals on board."

MOVES CAMP: "There were U.S. marshals in here since February 14, two weeks before we came in."

FRIZZELL: "Well, of course the BIA is going to be under the close eye of the Department of Interior if an agreement is reached, and the Department of Justice and the marshals and the FBI."

MOVES CAMP: "But they've been here all this time, since two weeks before we came here, the Justice Department and all was there!"

FRIZZELL: "Well then, what would you suggest as an alternative?"

GLADYS BISSONETTE: "Throw them all in jail."

The second day's negotiations ended when the Wounded Knee people learned that the federal government had given armored personnel carriers to the BIA. Clyde Bellecourt reported that an APC had moved forward and fired on the Indian bunkers in violation of the agreed cease fire during the negotiations. Frizzell answered that it was done without authorization by a BIA roadblock. The Oglala negotiators were furious that the BIA police had been supplied with an APC. Government negotiator Richard Hellstern said that it was part of the federal Cooperative Training Program. The Indians claimed that they could not take Frizzell in good faith as long as APCs were advancing on Wounded Knee, and Frizzell promised to resolve the problem.

Negotiations continued for three more days, and by the afternoon of April 4 the Independent Oglala Nation and the United States had reached an agreement which was designed to lead to disarmament. Because Frizzell was unable to guarantee a White House-level treaty meeting prior to a stand-down of arms, the Oglalas agreed to a compromise preliminary meeting with White House staff to set in motion the treaty commission meetings; this meeting was to be followed by disarmament, investigations of tribal council and goon squad actions, and an eventual treaty meeting with the White House in May. It seemed for a moment that the confrontation could be settled before a single person had been killed by gunfire.

Richard Hellstern summed up the agreement: "We contemplate a signed agreement with everyone here. And then the next immediate step would be a preliminary meeting with the White House and Means, Chief

Bad Cob, and Crow Dog. And then the discussion will begin between
[U.S. Marshal Wayne] Colburn and your people on how we're going to
resolve the arms situation. We're on the same wavelength, aren't we?''
Russell Means replied: ''Right.''

The following morning the pipe was smoked together; Crow Dog,
Gladys Bissonette and Kent Frizzell all offered prayers that the promises be fulfilled in good faith, and the agreement was signed. But the deal
was ill-fated. After receiving a copy of the agreement calling for the
Washington meeting and the dispossession of arms to begin on Saturday, April 7, an overzealous Marshal Wayne Colburn announced that he
would lead a force of 180 marshals in a sweep of Wounded Knee on the
appointed date. The entire agreement crumbled. The Indians had agreed
that both sides would meet on the seventh, and that they would agree to a
time for the disarmament, and that both sides would simultaneously
disarm. They certainly had not agreed on a ''sweep'' of the village by
armed troops.

A frantic Frizzell pulled Marshal Colburn and AIM security head Stan
Holder into a meeting, hoping to salvage his agreement. The marshals
had a compromise plan for disarmament which called for bunkers and
roadblocks to come down simultaneously, and then for marshals to enter
Wounded Knee, set up three inspection stations, and conduct their
questioning and search. Colburn said that they wanted to ''sanitize and
neutralize'' the area, and that the marshals would be wearing their blue
uniforms and carrying only a side arm. Colburn refused to negotiate the
point further, declaring that the marshals were going into the village
armed, and he also indicated that there would be arrests, although he
promised ''No waist chains, no metal handcuffs, no leg irons. I think I'm
a helluva guy.''

The Oglala Nation negotiators disagreed. Within twenty-four hours
their disarmament agreement had turned into an armed mass arrest.
Accepting Colburn's terms amounted to a surrender. By April 8, with
Russell Means and Crow Dog in Washington, D.C., the Dickie Wilson
roadblocks went back up, the marshals continued their maneuvers, the
Indians had lost all faith in Frizzell and the village was under full siege
once again.

Meanwhile, inside the hamlet of Wounded Knee, a new society
flourished. On April 11, the first baby was born into citizenship of the
Independent Oglala Nation: Mary Moore, an Oglala, gave birth to a son.
On April 12, Anna Mae Pictou, a twenty-eight-year-old Micmac Indian
from Nova Scotia, and Nogeeshik Aquash were married in a traditional
Lakota ceremony performed by Wallace Black Elk inside the village.

Anna Mae Aquash had traveled from her Nova Scotia reservation

Representatives of the Independent Oglala Nation pose with U.S. government negotiators after the signing of the April 5th Wounded Knee agreement. Back row, from left: Florine Hollow Horn, Karen White Butterfly, Gladys Bissonnette, Clyde Bellecourt, Carter Camp, Russell Means, Hank Adams, and two unidentified U.S. government aides. Front row, from left: Ellen Moves Camp, Ramon Roubideaux, Lou Bean, Tom Bad Cob, Wallace Black Elk, Pedro Bissonnette, and government negotiators Kent Frizzell and Richard Hellstern. (Photo courtesy of Akwesasne Notes)

home to Boston, where she had worked in the Indian Center. She had then traveled to Wounded Knee to help carry food and medical supplies through the government lines. On her first supply run she had spent an entire day hiding a short distance from a government outpost awaiting night cover before she continued successfully into the village. Inside she took on work digging bunkers and eventually joined the night patrols around the village. Aquash would one day become a symbol for Indian people throughout North America as a dedicated freedom fighter, but her day was yet to come.

At 6:00 A.M., April 16, fourteen people entered the camp through the lines, carrying food and supplies. Among them were Frank and Morningstar Clearwater, Apaches, who had hitchhiked 2,200 miles from North Carolina to participate in the occupation of Wounded Knee. Frank Clearwater, forty-seven, planned to hike back out for more supplies. The following day he asked Dennis Banks if he could lie down for a nap before his return trek overland. He then went to the Catholic church on the north side of the village where he lay down and went to sleep. He never woke up. Frank Clearwater became the first casualty of the siege. As Frank slept, an APC opened fire on the Hawk Eye bunker due north of the church. Bullets were hitting the ground all around the bunker. The fire fight had started after three Cessna planes had dropped ten parachuted supply bundles into the camp. An FBI helicopter had opened fire on some people who had gone out to gather the supplies, and then the APCs moved in. Three people returning with the bundles were caught in the open, as fire from the APC hit all around them. They ran for the church where they lay down. Bullets tore through the walls of the church; someone cried out "Frank's hit!" The M-16 round shattered his skull; blood poured out into a big pool on the floor. He remained alive but unconscious for ten days before he died.

The camp was low on food, ammunition, and medical supplies. The federal perimeter had tightened, and successfully closed off some of the supply routes. Wilson's vigilantes were also roaming the hills arresting supply runners. On the evening of April 26, the rifle fire increased and confusion arose as to who was firing at whom. The marshals reported unexplained fire coming from the DMZ which was hitting both the Wounded Knee bunkers and the government APCs. The government Red Arrow command post reached Wounded Knee security by radio saying that they had honored an agreed upon cease fire, but that their Roadblock-6 was "still receiving fire." Wounded Knee security answered that they were "taking almost continuous automatic weapon fire" from a hill near Roadblock-6. Red Arrow answered: "Ten-four. A couple of our RBs [roadblocks] have reported firing and they don't know who is over in those positions. They report that it is being fired *into* Wounded Knee."

> WOUNDED KNEE: "Roger. You think you're pretty sure we got a third party out there firing on us with automatic weapons?"
> RED ARROW: "That's what it sounds like."

The vigilantes were in the hills with government-issue automatic weapons, M-16s, firing on both government and Indian positions. The government troops poured fire into Wounded Knee that night. Wounded Knee security estimated that they took 20,000 rounds from vigilantes and marshals in twelve hours. The Indians were completely pinned down; low on ammunition, they were unable to discourage the government from closing in. The marshals began using an M-79 gas grenade launcher during the early hours of the morning, in an attempt to flush the security people from their bunkers. The closest government position was Roadblock-4 on Porcupine Road, four hundred meters from Little Big Horn bunker northwest of the village center. At about 8:30 A.M. the federal troops hit Little Big Horn with gas, forcing the two occupants into the open. As he emerged from the bunker, Buddy Lamont, an Oglala, was hit with a burst of M-16 fire and lay bleeding on the ground. Because of the heavy fire the medics were unable to reach Lamont immediately. After three more hours of fire the government agreed by radio to effect a ten-minute cease fire so that medics could reach the wounded man. It was too late. By the time they had carried Buddy Lamont back to Wounded Knee village he was dead, the second casualty.

As the army closed their perimeter the FBI expanded theirs, arresting people on highways throughout America who were suspected of crossing state lines to come to the aid of the Oglalas in violation of the infamous federal Rap-Brown anti-riot laws used in the late '60s to arrest blacks and anti-war protesters. On April 28, nine Colorado State University college students were arrested by the FBI and Wyoming Highway Patrol, and held in Laramie County jail on $2,500 bonds. The FBI presented Cheyenne, Wyoming U.S. Magistrate Alan Johnson with a statement of "probable cause" for suspicion and arrest. The goverment's position was that Vernon Bellecourt had made a speech at the college the previous night, and if "what Bellecourt suggested was being pursued by the defendants . . . they would have violated federal laws."[17] None of the nine students, between the ages of 18 and 24, was able to raise bail money, and they remained in jail, accused of crossing a state line with the intention in their minds to help the Indians at Wounded Knee. The scene was repeated from Los Angeles to New York.

On Sunday, April 29, after a two-hour meeting with Dennis Banks and Leonard Crow Dog, Kent Frizzell announced that negotiations for disarmament had begun again. The format this time would be different. Banks and Stan Holder agreed to discuss the military stand-down of arms with Marshal Colburn and Richard Hellstern, while Crow Dog and Gladys Bissonette would negotiate political issues with Frizzell, FBI agent Noel Castleman, and Justice Department Civil Rights Division lawyer, Dennis Ickes. The U.S. government, however was in shambles

17. *Rapid City Journal*, April 30, 1973.

because of the Watergate scandal: Attorney General Richard Kleindienst, John Ehrlichman, and Bob Haldeman had all resigned from
Nixon's staff, and John Dean had been fired. Furthermore, the United
States was losing the battle for Saigon in Vietnam, and the imminent
defeat had thrown the War Department into a panic and Secretary of
State Henry Kissinger into a globe-trotting frenzy. U.S. government
prestige and effectiveness had disintegrated as bureaucrats in Washington tried to isolate themselves from the plague of Watergate. Interior
Secretary Morton's earlier indictment of AIM as "criminal" people who
"do not represent a constituted group with whom the government can
contract," seemed, by the spring of 1973, to be more applicable to
Nixon's fragmented presidency. Frizzell told the Indians: "Things are
happening so fast back there [in Washington], I can't tell you who they
would send [to discuss treaty violations]."[18]

The Oglala position was clear and familiar. They wanted a treaty
commission, removal of the tribal council and BIA superintendent, their
traditional government of chiefs recognized by Washington, investigations and indictments against Wilson and the goon squad, and a mutual
cease fire and disarmament. They added a request for a peaceful lifting of
roadblocks to allow Buddy Lamont's family to attend his wake and
burial in Wounded Knee.

By May 5 the two sides had reached a compromise agreement. Hank
Adams delivered a letter to Fools Crow from White House Special
Counsel Leonard Garment promising to send a White House commis-
sion in the third week of May to meet with Fools Crow and the other
chiefs, and to discuss the 1868 treaty. Dennis Ickes promised Justice
Department investigations into the dealing and action of the BIA tribal
government. Buddy Lamont's family would be allowed into Wounded
Knee for the funeral, and there would be a stand-down of arms on May 8.
The FBI insisted, however, that it would seek the arrests of anyone for
whom they possessed an outstanding warrant.

On Sunday, May 6, as federal troops let the Lamont family into
Wounded Knee, hundreds more came in unofficially between the government checkpoints. Buddy Lamont was laid in a grave next to Chief
Big Foot who fell to the army guns with his people at that very spot in
1890.

During the evening of May 7 over half the people inside Wounded
Knee, including Banks and Means, filtered out through government
lines. Federal troops entered the village at 7:00 A.M. on May 8. Justice
Department personnel disarmed those who remained in the village, and

18. *Voices From Wounded Knee*, op. cit. p. 226.

took them to Roadblock-1 for processing by the FBI and federal marshals. One hundred and fifty men, women, and children sat on the dry ground, surrounded by armed troops, as one by one they were interrogated, fingerprinted, photographed, and — in some cases — arrested. Stan Holder, who had negotiated the stand-down, was arrested and held on $32,000 bond; Oglala Sioux Civil Rights Organization vice-president and negotiator Pedro Bissonette was held on $152,000 bond. Eventually, Banks, Means, Leonard Crow Dog, and other leaders would be arrested and charged with crimes stemming from the confrontation at Wounded Knee. Between February and May 1973 the federal government arrested 562 people, Indian and non-Indian, on charges related to the occupation of Wounded Knee. According to lawyer Karen Northcott, interstate traffic and other such arrests brought the number to 1,200[19] On the other hand, Dickie Wilson and the goon squad remained untouched by the long, but discriminating arm of the law. There was not a single arrest or conviction of any tribal council or goon squad member. From a reported 150 complaints, Dennis Ickes of the Justice Department investigated 42. From those 42 complaints Ickes reported that he had "two cases that look very good against members of the goon squad," but no indictments were ever issued, no arrests made. Wilson was turned loose upon the traditional people — those who were not dead or in jail — once again.

The promised treaty commission consisted of White House Counsel Leonard Garment's assistant Bradley Patterson and four junior aides from the Department of the Interior, the Department of Justice, the BIA, and the White House. Fools Crow, speaking in Lakota translated by Matthew King, said: "Today I met one of the good representatives of the government [Patterson]. I want him to take a good look at me and my mother earth. This is my country. I want to ask him a simple question. Can we be reinstated back to the 1868 treaty? We're going to prevent all the time we could waste with that simple question. I want Mr. Patterson to say yes or no . . . ."

Patterson spent several hours fidgeting and dodging the question, repeating the familiar government reply that they could no longer *make* treaties with Indian nations and that "only Congress can change the law of 1871." He never did get around to answering Fools Crow's question. It was futile. BIA representative Leslie Gay went to great lengths to explain the Indian Reorganization Act of 1934, stating that in the eyes of the U.S. govenment the Oglalas "are under this law."

19. Ken Tilsen, "The FBI, Wounded Knee and Politics," *The Iowa Journal of Social Work,* Des Moines, Iowa, Fall, 1976, p. 20; Karen Northcott, "The FBI in Indian Communities," an unpublished account of Wounded Knee and subsequent events on Pine Ridge reservation.

Throughout the summer, there would be more beatings, stabbings, shootings, and deaths on Pine Ridge, attributed to the goon squad. The Wounded Knee trials would reveal government misdeeds including perjured testimony, fabricated evidence, and illegal surveillance. Virtually every AIM leader in the country would be either in jail, dead, or driven underground within the two years following the occupation of Wounded Knee.

4

Due Process

Language is going to ruin the whole world.
HENRY CROW DOG, BRULE LAKOTA
December, 1974, Lincoln, Nebraska

WALKING PAST the Justice Department building in Washington, D.C. where huge pillars hold up the stone inscription: "Equality under the Law," Bill Means chuckled to himself and shook his head. "*We* call it the 'Just-Us Department,' " he said. The American, Canadian, Neo-European system of justice is based on a long written history of law. (Even today the traditional Indian people view whites as "Europeans" and see modern white governments as European colonial institutions.) Every American schoolchild learns about the Magna Carta, and the Constitution and the Bill of Rights, and learns that these documents make up the body of law that guarantees justice to all. On paper, the American democratic judicial system is engineered to ensure that each individual is indeed treated equally under the law. The people elect legislators who make the laws; they elect governors and presidents who administer the laws; judges are elected or appointed by elected officials, and these judges and juries of peers impartially uphold, interpret, and protect the people's laws. Sometimes it works; sometimes it doesn't. People accept the fact that the system may not be perfect: some criminals get away with their crimes, and a few innocent people may mistakenly get convicted, but it all evens out in the end, and besides, it's as good a system as there is.

Indigenous people of the Western Hemisphere view Canadian, American, Brazilian, Chilean, and general Neo-European law with more detachment. It is a template placed over their way of life which has never quite fit their style or structure. It is a square hole for a round peg. Indian law, on the other hand, is based on what Western philosophers call "situational ethics"; a given deed is either right or wrong in a given situation based upon a tradition of spiritual belief and viewed through human eyes with whatever human wisdom is available. European law is historical, written law, whereas the law of Turtle Island, in existence when Europeans arrived, is ever-present spiritual law.

97

The Indian people saw this, and understood the significance of the difference, throughout the history of their relationship with the Europeans. The Haudenosaunee, for example, built that understanding into their first agreement with the whites, an agreement represented by a wampum belt still in the possession of their people. The belt, made of two parallel red lines on a white background, is the Haudenosaunee version of a written treaty made with Dutch settlers. According to Chief Oren Lyons: "This row is the . . . Red Man; this row is our White Brother. They are on a white background, for peace. They are equal in size, and this in between is called the river of life. And so we travel in peace and friendship down through the river of life, equal and respectful of one another's ways."[1]

Phillip Deere, a Muskogee spiritual leader from Oklahoma, says: "Understand the difference between the truth and facts . . . Facts can originate from lies, but if you get enough people to believe in it, it becomes a fact to them; it becomes a truth to them. But as Native people, we believe in truth, and not in facts. That is why we never had to sign a receipt, because we knew we were dealing with each other in an honest way. . . . We never had locks on our tipis . . . go ahead and dig all you want to search for the history of the Americas, and you will never find evidence of prisons."[2]

Hopi Kikmongwi Dan Katchongva (clan elder, spiritual leader), who died in 1974, said: 'Whiteman's laws are many, but mine is one. Whiteman's laws are all stacked up . . . but my law is only the Creator's, just one. And no man-made law must I follow, because it is everchanging, and will doom my people."[3]

And Lakota Medicine Man Wallace Black Elk, arrested after the Wounded Knee confrontation, said: "Unwritten spiritual laws — we grew up with it, so we don't need to just stipulate it and put it in a file and open that book and look whether it's there or not: 'Well, I'm guilty,' or 'I'm not guilty,' or 'Well, I'll have to see a lawyer,' and then the lawyer will take a book and start looking in the book to see if it's there."[4]

The Indian people have said it in thousands of variations throughout the last five hundred years, but the idea has yet to take root in the Neo-European mind, and certainly the position of the U.S. courts has

1. Excerpted from a speech to the Fourth Russell Tribunal, Rotterdam, Holland, November, 1980.
2. Ibid.
3. Quoted in "The Earth is Alive," by Joan Price, Colorado Plateau Project, Colorado Springs, 1979, 27 pages.
4. *Voices From Wounded Knee*, op. cit.; p. 107.

been that the whole matter is a bunch of pre-civilized, pantheistic mumbo-jumbo which has no place in a court of law.

The trials resulting from the Wounded Knee indictments would eventually involve treaty and sovereignty questions which would take lawyers, judges, and jurors back through Indian-U.S. legal history. The question eventually becomes: If the U.S. government claims jurisdiction and if the U.S. claims that the Indian nations no longer possess sovereign status, then at what point did the Indians lose their sovereignty and at what point did the United States win jurisdiction over them?

All parties agree that the Indians were sovereign nations with the right of occupancy of the land when the Europeans first arrived, and that between 1776 and 1871 the United States of America entered into 371 treaties defining the relationship between the indigenous people and the infant colonial nation. Other than that, there is little agreement; interpretation becomes nine-tenths of the law. The first U.S.-Indian treaty was ratified in 1778 describing boundaries between the United States and the Delaware Indians. By 1812 the Delaware, along with the Pequot, Narragansett, Mohican, and Pokanoket Indians had been wiped out by the settlers. When Chief Tecumseh of the Shawnee was killed in 1812, all hope was lost of a Southeastern confederated Indian resistance to the U.S. expansion.

The Haudenosaunee had played an important role during the American Revolution, holding the balance of power between the French and the English in the eastern Great Lakes region. The U.S. government borrowed extensively from their confederacy in fashioning the U.S. Constitution. In 1784 the United States entered into a treaty relationship with the Mohawk, Seneca, and other nations of the Haudenosaunee, but in that same year New York State Congressman James Bowan began negotiating with individual Mohawk Indians for land leases. In 1790 the U.S. government passed the Indian Non-Intercourse Act forbidding the state to treat with Indians, unless the agreement was approved by Congress. Nevertheless, New York State continued to expropriate Mohawk land. In 1803 the state appointed three Mohawk trustees whom they officially recognized as legal representatives of the Mohawk Nation; the state suplied the trustees with attorneys and began turning out lease contracts with the bogus Mohawk government. In this manner the state claimed title to Mohawk land in 1816, 1818, 1824, and 1825 in violation not only of Mohawk sovereignty, but of U.S. federal law.

The Cherokee agreed by treaty to confine their nation to seven million acres of the Appalachian Mountains now claimed by the states of Georgia, North Carolina, and Tennessee. In 1828 gold was discovered on their land and, in 1829, President Andrew Jackson recommended to Congress that the Cherokees be relocated "west of the Mississippi." The following year, Congress passed a law establishing Indian Territory in the West, and ordering the relocation of the Cherokee, Chickasaw, Choctaw, Creek, and Seminole Indians.

In a rare, and futile, display of honoring a U.S. agreement with Indians, the Supreme Court under Chief Justice John Marshall upheld the Cherokee bid to remain on their treaty land, and established the legal precedent that a treaty with an Indian nation must be honored. "The words 'treaty' and 'nation' are words of our own language," said Justice Marshall, "selected in our diplomatic and legislative proceedings by ourselves, and have definite and well-understood meaning. We have applied them to the other nations of the earth. They are applied to all in the same sense."[5] In 1832 Justice Marshall further upheld Cherokee sovereignty when the Supreme Court ruled in favor of a clergyman who had been jailed by the state of Georgia for interfering with the removal of Indians. Marshall said: ". . . the settled doctrine of the law of nations is that a weaker power does not surrender its independence — its right to self government — by associating with a stronger, and taking its protection. . . . Examples of this are not wanting in Europe. . . . The Cherokee Nation, then, is a distinct community, occupying its own territory, with boundaries accurately described, in which the laws of Georgia have no right to enter."

One honorable Supreme Court Justice, however, was no match for gold fever, notions of white supremacy, and the iron rule of President Jackson. Jackson sided with the state of Georgia and the white mining interests, taunting the Supreme Court with his statement that "John Marshall has rendered his decision, now let him enforce it." The government awarded the disposed Cherokee $4.5 million for the stolen land, deposited the money in the national treasury, and then charged the costs of relocating them in Oklahoma against the award money. In that now infamous Trail of Tears, thousands of Cherokee, Choctaw, Seminole, and other Indians died of starvation and exhaustion during the long trek to the barren Oklahoma plains where they would remain until oil was discovered there.

In 1814 the state of Indiana put a bounty on Indian scalps, and other eastern states followed. The United States had taken possession of the

5. *Cherokee Nation v. Georgia*, 5 Pet. 17, 8 L. Ed. 25 (1831). For a concise account of U.S. treaty relationships with Indian nations, see "Indian Sovereignty — It's Alive," by Larry Leventhal, in *The Great Sioux Nation*, American Indian Treaty Council Information Center, Moon Books, San Francisco, 1977.

909,000 square-mile Louisiana Purchase in 1803, and white settlers had begun pouring across the Mississippi River into Indian Territory. In 1827 the first American trappers ventured into the desert sanctuary of the peaceful Hopi who had already spent three hundred years ignoring the dictates of the Spanish Castillas. Mexico had just won its independence from Spain, and assumed authority over the Hopi and Navajo lands north of the Rio Grande. In that same year, on September 22, 1827, twenty-one-year-old Joseph Smith of Palmyra, New York was visited by his angel Moroni whose revelation led him to the ancient Nephite tablets, and the founding of the Church of Latter Day Saints, the Mormons. Ultimately, all of this would have serious implications in Hopi land far to the west.

By 1844 the Santa Fe Trail was busy with American trappers and traders. In 1848 the United States paid Mexico $15 million for what is now New Mexico, Arizona, Utah, southern California, and Nevada. The two countries signed the Treaty of Guadalupe Hidalgo in that year, defining the border. As far as the Hopi, Dine (Navajo), Shoshone, Ute, Paiute, and other Indian nations in the area were concerned the United States had purchased their ancestral lands from the twenty-six-year-old country of Mexico which did not own them. But in 1848 gold was discovered in California, and by 1851 sixty thousand Americans a year were passing through Hopi land on their way to the coast.

In 1854 Brigham Young, leading the Mormon Church founded by Joseph Smith, settled in the New Mexico Territory, and established the Mormon State of Deseret, "The Bee," later Utah. The Mormons took the Hopi to be Lamanites — the "wild . . . dark and loathsome" descendants of the wicked Laman, written about in their revealed scriptures. Throughout the next century the Mormons would attempt to save their supposed long-lost bretheren by abducting their children, controlling their affairs, leasing their land, and harvesting the resources of the Hopi.

The Hopi did not sign any treaty with the U.S. government or anybody else. Their claim on the land was a purely spiritual obligation to oversee and protect the land. The instructions from their Creator were to live in peace, which they did. They retired to the high, dry mesas, to consult their prophecies, watch for the signs, and wait for the Great Purification which was sure to come.

The Navajo, hunted down by General James Carlton and Kit Carson, were concentrated in an armed camp at Bosque Redondo and in 1868 signed a treaty with the United States. "Manifest Destiny" was the war cry of Carlton and other Western generals as they swept the Indians from their homelands, and routed them from their wild refuge. Law, morality, or justice had nothing to do with the American invasion and occupation of the West. Indian lands were unabashedly stolen. The only law that was honored was the prehistoric law of the biggest club or the fiercest bite. The only legal precedent set was the implied philosophy that whosoever was the toughest and meanest primate won the territory. The fact that it was called the march of civilization or that God and Christ were so often recruited to bless and witness the holocaust, added little but a taste of hypocrisy to the invasion. Between 1776 and 1876 the United States assumed ownership of over 1.5 billion acres of Indian land, leaving the Indians with less than 10 percent of their original land base; that figure would shrink to 3 percent a century later. The process was only slightly slower and no less brutal in Canada, Mexico, and South America.

The Marshall decision, recognizing Indian sovereignty and distinct Indian land, was forgotten. The 1787 Northwest Ordinance, proclaiming " . . . The utmost good faith shall always be observed toward the Indians; their lands and property shall never be taken from them without their consent," was also forgotten or ignored. Justice Marshall, in 1823, formally bowed out of the conflict and firmly established the mechanism by which federal courts would close their eyes to Indian land thefts. In the case of *Johnson & Graham's Lessee v. McIntosh* the U.S. government claimed sovereignty over Illinois and Piankeshaw Indian land. Without a legal precedent or logical reason for granting the United States position, the Supreme Court threw up its hands, turned its head, and declared the issue to be a "political question" which was the business of the executive and legislative branches of government, not the courts. Thus, with the establishment of this "political question doctrine," began a long tradition of buck-passing over the issue of stolen Indian land.[6]

In 1846 the federal courts attempted to deny that the Indian nations had ever really existed as sovereign political entities. In the case *United States v. Rogers,* a non-Indian was convicted of murder on a reservation; as an addendum to the case, Justice Taney wrote in his decision that "The native tribes who were found on this continent at the time of its discovery have never been acknowledged or treated as independent nations by European governments nor regarded as the owners of the territories they respectively occupied." Unarmed with fact or reason, Taney attempted, in this single stroke, to dispossess the entire indigenous population of the Western Hemisphere.

6. For a detailed history of U.S. law on Indian land, see R. T. Coulter, "Might Makes Right, A History of Indian Jurisdiction," *American Indian Journal*, Institute for the Development of Indian Law, Washington, D.C.; reprinted in *Akwesasne Notes*, Late Spring, 1977.

The U.S. Congress began assuming legal jurisdiction on Indian land with the 1817 General Crimes Act which gave the federal government jurisdiction over crimes committed by non-Indians on Indian land. In 1825 the Assimilative Crimes Act augmented federal jurisdiction on Indian land by proclaiming that state criminal laws, violated on Indian land, fell under the control of the federal courts. In 1885 the Major Crimes Act delineated seven (since raised to fourteen) crimes over which the federal government claimed absolute jurisdiction on Indian land. Although neither the Constitution of the United States nor any other legal precedent supported the establishment of these laws, they were not so much upheld as simply tolerated by the Supreme Court. When the Court was called upon to review the validity of the Major Crimes Act in the case of *United States v. Kagama* in 1886 — a case involving title to land acquired by the United States in the Treaty of Guadalupe Hidalgo — Supreme Court Justice Miller had nowhere to turn but to the political question doctrine. He ruled that the Court did not have the power to question whether or not the United States had legally obtained title to the land, that was up to Congress, and all the Court could do was abide by the will of the people as laid down by the laws of Congress. Underlying questions of morality, international relations, or outright land theft by the U.S. government were not considered appropriate topics of judicial investigation.

After the Dawes Allotment Act provided for the break-up of tribal land in 1887, the Office of Indian Affairs, established under the Department of War, began to set up tribal courts and judges on the reservations to protect private property and carry out the will of the federal government.

The State of New York was granted jurisdiction over Haudenosaunee reservations — jurisdiction which it had already illegally usurped — by congressional acts in 1948 and 1950 and by Public Law 280 which, in 1953, extended state jurisdiction over certain Indian lands in New York, Nevada, Arizona, South Dakota, and other specified states.

All of this was done, of course, unilaterally by the United States, certainly without the consent of the Indians living on the land, and often in violation of U.S.-Indian treaties which are defined by the Constitution as being the "supreme law of the land," on par with the Constitution itself. The unilateral abrogation of treaties and usurpation of jurisdiction over the indigenous populations were also carried out in violation of international custom and stated U.S. policy. When U.S. courts did acknowledge the indigenous political rights of the Indians those court decisions were generally disregarded.

In 1883 the U.S. Supreme Court ruled that the 1868 Sioux-U.S.

treaty constituted a "pledge to secure to these people with whom the
United States was contracting as a distinct political body, an orderly
government: the regulation by themselves of their own domestic affairs
. . . the administration of their own laws and customs" *(Ex Parte Crow
Dog,* 109U.S. 566, 1883). In 1905 the courts recognized (in the case *U.S.
v. Winans*) that the treaties ratified by the United States were "not a
grant of rights *to* the Indians, but a grant of rights from them [and] a
reservation of those not granted." In 1973 the United States Supreme
Court ruled that the State of Arizona did not have the right to tax an
Indian's reservation income, stating that "it must always be remembered that the various Indian tribes were once independent and sovereign nations, and that their claim to sovereignty long predates that of our
own Government."

Thus, the U.S. government maintained an amorphous, schizophrenic
legal relationship with the Indian nations, unable to either clearly recognize their sovereignty or carry out their annihilation, a choice which, to
the traditional Indians, was the only choice available to the United
States, the choice eventually presented to the U.S. government at
Wounded Knee in 1973. U.S. courts tried to call the Indian nations
"quasi-sovereign tribal entities" (1974), "quasi-sovereign nations"
(1956), or "dependent nations" (1965). Such judicial word salad served
not the Indians, but only the unrestrained land hunger of American
adventurers and corporations harvesting, depleting, and destroying the
wealth of the natural land base. Lawyer Larry Leventhal, an expert on
Indian treaty law, has written: "Sadly our [American] national honor
has been repeatedly blemished by our failure to live up to our word and
to extend a fragment of the human respect that first greeted visitors to
these shores. The tribal structures have, however, survived, and sovereignty, in a real, although diminished, form has continually been acknowledged by the courts. Such sovereignty must be encouraged; for it
is by the strengthening of tribal bonds and culture that not only Indian
people will be served, but our national honor as well."[7]

There is one other principle of British–American–Canadian jurispru-
dence that is worth mentioning: the principle that the law must not only
be just, but should *appear* just as well, so that the impartiality of the
courts is never questioned by the populace. The Wounded Knee trials
before American courts, and the actions of government officials revealed in those trials, would serve to undermine any such confidence.
The law would be blatantly used to arbitrarily and selectively persecute
traditional Indians and to protect the American status quo on Indian

7. "Indian Sovereignty — It's Alive," op. cit.

land. The simple statistic of over 1,200 arrests of AIM members and supporters throughout the United States and zero arrests of vigilantes and goon squad members following Wounded Knee was ample indication to the Indians and to their lawyers that the government had no intention of using the law to ensure justice. But that was only the beginning.

Criminal actions stemming from the seventy-one-day siege of Wounded Knee were conducted by the government in two separate series of trials. Dennis Banks and Russell Means were singled out in what became known as the "leadership cases." An eleven-count federal indictment charged them with larceny, burglary, assault, theft, interference with a federal officer, creation of armed roadblocks, arson, possession of destructive devices, aiding, abetting, counseling, commanding or inducing the commission of various crimes, and conspiracy. The trials, moved from South Dakota because of a ruling that the defendants could not get a fair trial there, were scheduled to begin in St. Paul, Minnesota on January 8, 1974. One hundred and twenty-seven other people were charged in the non-leadership cases, and were scheduled to appear on February 4 in Sioux Falls, South Dakota. Before the trials began, however, violence again swept Pine Ridge reservation.

On May 14, 1973, after the stand-down of arms at Wounded Knee, and just prior to the treaty meetings at Fools Crow's house, Dickie Wilson wrote a letter to tribal lawyer Bobo Dean, asking for an opinion as to how long he could legally administer tribal affairs without a meeting of the tribal council which was, at the time, split down the middle over the Wounded Knee issue. Dean's reply was that Wilson could administer tribal affairs between the four regularly scheduled meetings per year. Wilson had suspended council meetings; their last meeting had been on February 23, and when the impeachment supporters had departed from that meeting the council was without a quorum. Wilson was operating with Lloyd Eaglebull and Emma Nelson, secretary and treasurer of the council, as an executive committee. From around the reservation the reports were coming into Wounded Knee lawyers that shootings and beatings were taking place, and that the goon squad was behind the crimes.

It was a sad, dark spring on Pine Ridge, that is for sure. Von Bear Eagle reported that he had witnessed the beating of his stepbrother, allegedly by several goon squad members. Severt Young Bear's home was shot up, forcibly entered, and sacked. Chief Fools Crow's car was smashed and while he was away in Washington for promised talks with the White House, his home burned to the ground.

"Fred Two Bulls and Vincent Brewer came to my house here with a message for me and Fools Crow from Dickie Wilson," says Matthew King. "They said, 'You're safe; no one will hurt you. This is a local fight; you are not involved. You will be protected.' Then when they left they said, 'But don't trust him [Wilson].' No, well we didn't. Then those FBI boys came around here. That was the first time I ever saw that [Special Agent, David] Price fellow. We know who does these shootings. They are all in it; it is all the same. I told those guys to get out of here, and they did, they left.

"If they had shot Fools Crow there would have been a war. They knew that."

Brothers Clarence and Vernal Cross were sitting in their car by the side of the road in June when they were hit by rifle fire, according to Vernal who survived the shooting. Clarence died from gunshot wounds, and Vernal, injured but alive, was charged by the local BIA police with the shooting of his brother. Nine-year-old Mary Ann Little Bear was hit in the eye with rifle fire while riding in the car with her father. Witnesses named three Wilson hirelings: Francis Randall, John Hussman, and Woody Richards.

The BIA, the Justice Department, and the FBI were each notified of the shooting, and urged to investigate charges against the goon squad, but no investigations resulted; there were no arrests, and no convictions. Lawyer Mark Lane, speaking for the Wounded Knee Legal Offense/Defense Committee (WKLO/DC), reported that when he and photographer Carolyn Mugar went to the reservation to conduct their own investigation of the harassment cases they were "threatened at rifle point by Emil Richard, who works for tribal council chairman Dick Wilson." Lane said that he and other legal workers were confronted by both armed federal marshals and goon squad hired guns who ordered them off the reservation. Mugar reported that she was physically assaulted and shoved to the ground by goon squad members.

Throughout the summer, WKLO/DC lawyers — some of whom had traveled to South Dakota from as far away as New York and San Francisco — were kept busy preparing hundreds of defense cases, attempting to release from jail defendants whose bonds were as high as Pedro Bissonette's $150,000, investigating harassment charges, and preparing civil and criminal actions against Dickie Wilson and his goon squad. While lawyers for Bissonette — one of the Wounded Knee leaders and negotiators who had stayed within the village for the disarmament, and who had been arrested on May 8 — fought for his release on a reduced bail, Bissonette was offered a plea bargain through a court-appointed attorney. Lane, Lakota attorney Ramon Roubideaux, and

California attorney Marge Buckley had been barred from seeing their client. According to Buckley, she, Lane, and Roubideaux had traveled to the South Dakota capital of Pierre to see Bissonette. "While [Lane and Roubideaux] were talking with Pedro," she told reporters, "the sheriff came in and demanded that they leave, saying that the U.S. marshal had said nobody could see Pedro except his court-appointed attorneys."[8] Forced to leave their client, the two lawyers were then confronted in the courthouse hallway by the judge who was presiding over the government's case against Bissonette, charged with assault on a federal officer. According to Lane, the judge yelled to them: "Have you been tampering with our witnesses? . . . You take your hands off this case. It's none of your business. Pedro has good counsel. He's satisfied." Lane replied: "That's not true. Pedro wants me to be his lawyer."

The judge said: "You haven't talked to him today," to which Lane replied: "Oh, yes I have . . . Ramon and I saw him this morning and the sheriff saw us." The judge was furious, according to Buckley, who recalled: "In a bellow, the judge said, 'I gave strict orders that nobody was . . .' he paused, and added in a softer tone, realizing what he had admitted, ' to bother him.' Then he turned on his heel and stalked away. Judges have no right to prevent defendants from seeing attorneys of their choice."

While in jail Bissonette's court-appointed attorney brought to him the government's deal: if he agreed to turn state's evidence, to testify against AIM leaders on conspiracy charges stemming from Wounded Knee, he would be offered probation on his own charges. If he refused, he was looking at a ninety-year sentence. WKLO/DC lawyers told the press that Bissonette "had been pegged by U.S. officials as a weak link in the AIM command." If so, they were wrong. Bissonette refused the deal, and after winning his release on a reduced bail of $25,000, he told his lawyers the details of the government offer. Lane told the press: "Bissonette has been offered various deals to give false testimony against other leaders." The Wounded Knee legal staff made plans to call Bissonette to the stand in the upcoming Banks/Means trial to give testimony concerning the government offer as evidence supporting the defense allegation that the government had conspired to solicit phony evidence in an attempt to frame Banks and Mean.

However, on September 6 the government brought further assault charges against Bissonette, based upon the testimony of a white man who claimed that the Indian leader had threatened him in a border bar in

8. *Akwesasne Notes*, Early Winter, 1973; p. 5.

White Clay, Nebraska. Bissonette's bail was revoked, and a bench warrant was issued for his arrest. He was described in the warrant as "armed and dangerous." A few years earlier, Pedro Bissonette had been a steel worker, earning good wages, but his concern about conditions on Pine Ridge reservation had brought him home to help his people. He told a reporter at Wounded Knee: "I wanted to come home to work for my people, getting something done, and without getting pay for it. Something that would be good for every district out here, for the kids and the older generation." He had been one of the founders of the Oglala Sioux Civil Rights Organization which had sought the removal from office of Wilson and BIA Superintendent Stanley Lyman.

"Pedro would come around here," recalls Matthew King, "after he got out of jail. I told him to be careful, not to drive alone. He said, 'I am not worried.' Then they killed him; it was that Clifford." BIA policeman Joe Clifford shot Pedro Bissonette on October 17, reportedly with a twelve-gauge shotgun. He reported the time of the shooting as 9:48 P.M.; Bissonette was pronounced dead on arrival at the Pine Ridge Public Health Service hospital at 10:10 P.M. from multiple wounds in the chest. Clifford told BIA Police Chief Del Eastman that Bissonette had tried to shoot him; Eastman passed the story on to Stanley Lyman, and on the following day the BIA Superintendent told an Associated Press reporter: "Pine Ridge police began looking for Bissonette on the warrant Wednesday afternoon [the 17th]. Two officers spotted him and tried to stop him, but Bissonette fired a shot at them and they gave pursuit. Later in the evening, two officers were making a routine check of a car, and found Bissonette inside. Pedro attempted to shoot one of the officers and was shot at fairly close range."[9] Wilson issued a press statement saying "He was not killed because he was in AIM." Clifford's name was not released at that time to the press.

"Clifford was Pedro's brother-in-law, and he was working for Wilson," recalled King. "He was the brother of Pedro's wife, and so there was trouble in that family; he had a grudge against Pedro." The Associated Press, however, accepted the BIA story at face value, reporting nationally that Bissonette had been killed "while resisting arrest" by "police officers who were attempting to serve him with federal and Nebraska state warrants for his arrest."

Although Clifford claimed self-defense, WKLO/DC lawyers said: "After a preliminary investigation, we believe it is cold-blooded murder," and that Clifford was "the man that the BIA assigned to track down Pedro." Lane said that Bissonette was "the most important

9. *Rapid City Journal*, October 18, 1973.

defense witness'' scheduled for the upcoming trials, and he had been on his way to meet with Lane when he was killed. According to Lane, his examination of the body on the evening of the shooting revealed seven bullet holes in the chest ''apparently from a .38 caliber pistol in a remarkably small pattern — three by five inches — any shot of which might have killed him.'' Lane also reported a surface wound on the neck, three bullet wounds in the hand, various body bruises and tear-gas burns. Through Lane the Bissonette family demanded that the body be brought to Rapid City for an official autopsy by an independent pathologist. However, at 3:00 A.M., five hours after the body had arrived at the Pine Ridge Health Service, BIA Police Chief Del Eastman arranged for the removal of the body across the state line to Scottsbluff, Nebraska to await an autopsy by two BIA-commissioned pathologists. Eastman later told the *Rapid City Journal* that he had defied the Bissonette family instructions ''under direct orders from Bill Clayton.'' William Clayton, a Justice Department U.S. Attorney in Sioux Falls, three hundred miles east of Pine Ridge, had assured Washington, D.C. attorney Leonard Cavise — working on behalf of the Bissonette family — that the body would not be moved without the authorization of the family. Nevertheless, sometime between midnight and 3:00 A.M. Clayton, according to Eastman, ordered the hasty removal of the body across state lines and into the hands of the BIA, Department of Interior.

Clifford's report that he had shot Bissonette at 9:48 was also challenged by witnesses who reported arriving on the scene at 9:00 and seeing a ''pool of blood 45 feet from where the auto was parked.'' Matthew King said, years later: ''Pedro was very brave, everyone knew that, and he was respected. That Clifford is not around here any more; he knows he's not welcome here. He ran off to California; someone from here saw him there in a bar.'' On October 23, Bissonette was buried on Pine Ridge reservation; armed BIA police watched from a ridge above the cemetery as mourners placed flowers on the grave.

By the time Banks and Means came to trial before Judge Fred Nichol in St. Paul, Minnesota, Wilson had successfully defeated Means in an election for chairman of the Pine Ridge Tribal Council. Wilson declared his victory to be an ''historic occasion. . . . We have allowed the people to speak through the ballot box,'' he told the *Rapid City Journal*: ''Our work will continue in accordance with the established law of our land.''

Means, whose election promises included return of the 133,000-acre gunnery range and other tribal land, claimed that the election was a fraud. WKLO/DC lawyers petitioned the Department of Interior to investigate charges of election irregularities. Wilson had declared his

*Oglala Civil Rights Organization vice-president
Pedro Bissonnette was a leader of the Wounded Knee
takeover and of the move to impeach Dickie Wilson.
He was shot and killed by BIA policeman Joe Clifford
on October 27, 1973, while he was on his way to meet
with his lawyer, Mark Lane.
(Photo courtesy of* Akwesasne Notes)

victory by a margin of exactly 200 votes — 1,714 to 1,514. Although Means polled higher in the small, outlying towns such as Red Cloud, Calico, and Wounded Knee, Wilson had claimed a substantial victory in the town of Pine Ridge, enough to carry the election in his favor. Commissioner of Indian Affairs Morris Thompson, speaking for the Department of Interior, told Associated Press that "Based on our present information there does not appear to be sufficient evidence of voting fraud or irregularity to warrant federal intervention."

The U.S. Commission on Civil Rights, however, did find sufficient evidence upon which to investigate the charges; they did investigate, and they released their findings in a report which they sent to Interior Secretary Morton and Attorney General William Saxbe, who had taken over for early Watergate casualty John Mitchell. The Commission on Civil Rights was established by Congress in 1957 to "Investigate complaints alleging denial of right to vote by reason of race, color, religion, sex, or national origin, or by reason of fraudulent practices." In a letter to Morton, the five members of the commission, headed by Arthur S. Flemming, wrote: "The attached report contains findings that widespread irregularities took place before, during, and after the election."[10] The commission called Morton's attention to the Department of Interior's jurisdiction and responsibility to "assure that mechanisms of tribal government established under Federal Law are not abused."

Morton found evidence in the report that as many as "one-third of all votes cast appear to have been in some manner improper," and that "The information which was collected and analyzed shows a pattern of widespread abuses and irregularities." Examination of the voting records showed that 19.4 percent of the votes were cast by non-enrolled voters. Six hundred voters submitted improper affidavits of eligibility, and there was no procedure for disqualifying improper ballots, and "No effort was made by the Election Board to enforce the residency requirements for voting . . . [or] to check the identity of individuals presenting themselves at the polls."

The charges included eighteen counts of election fraud, each indictable under federal law, naming Dick Wilson and the BIA. The voter list was "inaccurate and out of date"; poll watchers were not present "at any time during the official count" of the votes; there was no account of "the use or distribution of all the official ballots which were printed . . . [and] ballots were permitted to be taken out of the polling places, marked, placed in the ballot boxes and counted without following any of the procedures established by the election ordinance for absentee voting." Of the three election board members, two were elected by the tribal council over which incumbent Dickie Wilson presided, and the third was appointed by Dickie Wilson in a memorandum to the council signed by Wilson and executive committee members Emma Nelson and Lloyd Eaglebull. Wilson was also cited for failing to call the council into session, as required by the election ordinance, to review the complaints of the contested election, which — according to the report — was "held in a climate of fear and tension." The report concluded: "The Bureau of Indian Affairs refused to supervise or oversee the election and afterwards refused to investigate charges of irregularities and fraud in the election." The legal opinion of the Civil Rights Commission lawyers was that "the results of the election were invalid."

The issue before Morton was whether or not to recommend to the Justice Department that charges should be placed where the report suggested they were applicable, and whether or not the election should

10. U.S. Commission on Civil Rights; Arthur S. Flemming, chairman; "Report of Investigation: Oglala Sioux Tribe General Election," October 1974.

be declared invalid, as recommended by the civil rights lawyers. Attorney General Saxbe also had a copy of the report. In the executive and judicial branches of the government, at the level of secretary of interior and attorney general, the decision was made not to prosecute or further investigate the case, and to let the election stand. According to *Baltimore Sun* columnist Theo Lippman, however, Morton was by that time "Secretary in name only."[11] His power and line to authority had been usurped by Under-Secretary John Whitaker who was reporting directly to Special White House Counsel Earl Butz. Butz, in turn, had been placed by the embattled President Richard Nixon in a newly created position as a "super Cabinet officer" in charge of the Department of Agriculture, Morton's Interior Department, and other government agencies involved with natural resources.

Russell Means gave a stirring opening statement when the leadership trials opened on February 12, 1974 before Judge Nichol. He took the opportunity to explain to the court that the issues raised in the Wounded Knee cases involved the efforts of the Lakota people to "maintain our traditional religion [and] our traditional philosophy."

He told the court: "We call ourselves 'Lakota,' which means 'allies' to us. . . . Today we are going to talk about the case of the United States of America versus Russell Means and Dennis Banks . . . really, it is the United States of America versus the Oglala people and all Indian people. We will show you that on the Pine Ridge Indian Reservation, south of that reservation sits a town called Pine Ridge Indian Village, which is the headquarters of the Bureau of Indian Affairs [and] their police, which is the headquarters of the state welfare, which is the headquarters of the puppet tribal government. We will show you that that town in no way represents the people of Wounded Knee, the people of Porcupine . . . Wanblee, or Kyle, or Red Shirt Table, or Cuny Table.

" . . . It is our philosophy that because all things come from one mother, our Mother Earth, then of course, we are all related, and we have to treat one another with the same respect and reverence that we would our own blood relatives. . . . We will introduce evidence about the United States' effort, in a concerted effort and conspiracy, to destroy our culture through concepts of cluster housing, through concepts of missionary schools, through concepts of government schools. . . . We will introduce as evidence the terror of the Bureau of Indian Affairs police on the reservation. . . . We will also offer in testimony the fact that the American Indian Movement or Oglalas who are in the American

11. *Baltimore Sun*, February 12, 1973.

AIM leaders Russell Means (left) and Dennis Banks (right)
with their lawyer, William Kunstler, during the
Wounded Knee trials, 1974. (Photo by Dick Bancroft)

Indian Movement have been systematically murdered, harassed, intimidated, put in jail since Wounded Knee. . . . The Bureau of Indian Affairs and the Department of Interior, and this will be shown in testimony, have complete control over our lives . . . we have continued to turn the other cheek too many times. We are going to ask that the United States of America in this trial, and in the future, beginning from yesterday, live up to their own laws.''

Banks told the Court: ''Wounded Knee represented the last pint, or the last blood transfusion. It was unfortunate that three Indians have died, but they died knowing — and all of us who were at Wounded Knee, and those people who called us to Wounded Knee will go to the Spirit World knowing — that the unborn generations will be given that opportunity to live the life that they choose, and not the life that somebody else dictates.''

Prosecutor Richard Hurd, a young, thirty-two-year-old U.S. Attorney from Sturgis, South Dakota, northwest of Rapid City, told the court that the government's evidence would ''show that these defendants together with their co-conspirators, in order to attract public attention to claimed grievances and demands and to extort confessions from the United States with respect to such grievances and demands, decided to seize the community of Wounded Knee, South Dakota, by force of arms.'' The young government lawyer was backed up and assisted by Department of Justice lawyer Earl Kaplan, Assistant U.S. Attorney for South Dakota David Gienapp, and his boss, William Clayton, who had earlier involved himself in the midnight interstate shuttle of the body of Pedro Bissonette.

The defense team included Mark Lane, Ken Tilsen, and Larry Leventhal from the Minneapolis-St. Paul area, Ramon Roubideaux, Doug Hall, and William Kunstler from New York who had gained a national reputation before Judge Julius Hoffman in his defense of the Chicago Seven the 1968 anti-war conspiracy cases.

Another important member of the defense team was Douglas Durham, director at that time of the national AIM office in St. Paul. Durham had first joined the Des Moines, Iowa chapter of AIM in 1972. During the Wounded Knee occupation he had traveled to South Dakota and had slipped through police lines, taking photographs for the Iowa underground paper *Pax*. Back in Des Moines, in April 1973, he and local AIM director Harvey Major had orchestrated the occupation of the First Church of the Open Bible; Durham had drawn up a list of sixteen demands, asking for church support for Indian programs. After church leaders agreed to meet with the Indians, and not to bring charges against them, the occupation ended. By June, Durham had secured a pledge of $85,000 from the United Methodist Church to be used as bail money for Dennis Banks, and another $15,000 which would go toward a joint ecumenical Indian program in the city of Des Moines. In August 1973, after an occupation of the Iowa Office of Education, Banks had traveled to Des Moines and met Durham who had been arrested with eight other demonstrators. Durham, with a propensity for visible displays of armed resistance, soon became the national chief of security for AIM.

In the St. Paul Federal Building, where the eight-and-a-half-month trial was held, the defense team met in a room assigned to them by the court. There they interviewed witnesses, planned strategy and reviewed evidence. No one was allowed in the defense room except the lawyers, the defendants, selected witnesses, and Durham, who monitored the security of the room. The case soon turned around, with the defense team launching attack after attack at the government for their negligent . . . and, eventually, criminal activities.

The first government lie was not discovered until a year after the trial, but was suspected throughout: because of apparent government knowledge of supposedly secret defense strategy, the defense began to suspect that one or more of the volunteer defense aides was an FBI informer. On March 24, 1974 lawyer Mark Lane asked witness Joseph Trimbach,

Special Agent in Charge of the FBI for Minnesota, North Dakota, and South Dakota, if the FBI had informers in connection with the Wounded Knee cases. Trimbach answered that yes, they did. However, when asked if any of these informers had infiltrated the defense camp, Trimbach said: "The answer is no."[12] Judge Nichol ordered that prosecutor Hurd check FBI informer files against a list of defense team personnel, and to report to the court any material which might indicate government infiltration of the Banks/Means defense. On March 28 Hurd met with Attorney General William Saxbe and FBI Director Clarence Kelley, and then submitted an affidavit to the court claiming that FBI files contained no material "which would arguably be considered as evidence of an invasion of the Legal Defense Camp." Both Trimbach and Hurd had lied to the court, although the truth was concealed behind FBI "top secret" status, not to be revealed until after the trial was over. The informers, for the time being, went unnamed and unknown.

Other lies, however, were discovered by the defense. On March 12, Trimbach assured Judge Nichol that there had been no illegal FBI wiretaps during the Wounded Knee occupation or investigation. On March 20 he testified on the stand that no such wiretap interceptions had taken place. But on March 29 the defense obtained from FBI agents Gerald Bertinot and Susan Rolley-Malone an affidavit signed by Trimbach which outlined conversations illegally monitored by Bertinot and Rolley-Malone. It was further discovered that prosecutor Hurd's secretary had notarized a wiretap affidavit signed by Trimbach, and Hurd, the prosecutor, was called to the stand by the defense. In answer to a defense question, the prosecutor, as witness, told the court that, yes, he had been present when Trimbach had signed the wiretap affidavit, but that he had "forgotten" about the document. Judge Nichol was disappointed in the negligence of the young prosecutor. However, as the misdeeds continued to mount the judge grew ever less tolerant. Following Trimbach's lies, and Hurd's failed memory, the court learned that the FBI had worded a teletype to its agents warning them to tailor responses to court questions so as not to provide a basis for a motion to dismiss. Nichol considered this a green light to the agents to shade the truth. The court also discovered that the prosecution and the FBI had misled the court by earlier denials that there were paid FBI informers assigned to AIM prior to the Wounded Knee siege, and that there was a general FBI Wounded Knee File. Judge Nichol said in disgust: "The

12. *U.S. v. Dennis Banks and Russell Means*, 374 F. Supp. 321, 331 (S.D. 1974), before Judge Fred J. Nichol, Chief Judge, United States District Court for the District of South Dakota; February 12 to September 16, 1974; St. Paul, Minnesota. The account of the trial is taken from the court record as compiled by defense attorney Larry B. Leventhal.

FBI in this case failed as a 'servant of the law.' The many revelations of Bureau negligence, or Bureau dilatoriness have brought this court to the brink of dismissing this case.'' However, after giving Hurd and the FBI a tongue-lashing, Nichol allowed the case to continue. The lies and the obstruction of justice, however, had only just begun.

In an earlier evidentiary hearing the court had ordered the prosecution to provide to the defense lawyers all documents in its possession which were pertinent or material to the case. Many such documents, however, were discovered by the defense after they had been concealed by Hurd. In an offer similar to the offer made to Pedro Bissonette, a sixteen-year-old youth, Alexander Richards, was given immunity from prosecution on Wounded Knee charges in exchange for testimony against Banks and Means. Under cross-examination, Richards admitted that he had lied on the stand, and documents surfaced which showed that he had been in jail during the time of events which he claimed to have witnessed at Wounded Knee. It was later revealed that Richards had signed three affidavits for the FBI prior to his release from prison, but that Hurd had turned only one of the three over to the court. The other two, contradicting the first one, had remained in Hurd's possession. Nichol reacted by disallowing Richards's entire testimony.

The government also withheld a document signed by residents of Wounded Knee requesting that government troops cease and desist from firing upon the village and the AIM members in the village. In its stead, Hurd attempted to submit to the court a bogus Oglala Sioux Tribal Council order requesting the federal presence on the reservation. When the tribal council clerk admitted under cross-examination that the document had not appeared in her files, but had been given to her just as she was leaving the reservation to testify, Hurd withdrew the document as evidence.

Hurd was also caught withholding affidavits signed by government witness Jean Fritze, financial records of the Wounded Knee Trading Post, and the arrest report of government witness Everett Little Whiteman, a BIA policeman. Photographs requested by the defense, but not provided by the prosecution, were discovered to be in Hurd's briefcase. The court was shocked by Hurd's behavior; Nichol lashed out at him once again: ''It is my feeling that the prosecutor's offering of testimony that was directly contradicted by a document [FBI affidavits signed by witness Richards] that was in his possession was inexcusable and possibly violative of American Bar Association Standards on the Prosecution Function.'' Nichol added, with generosity toward Hurd, that ''If it was not deliberate deception, it was, at least, grossly negligent conduct.'' Nichol came to the same conclusion about the FBI after a court search revealed "131 discoverable or arguably discoverable pieces of evidence which hadn't been turned over. . . . The defendants have expressed a profound mistrust toward the FBI," said Nichol. " . . . This expression of mistrust is understandable, although I can't bring myself to the conclusion that the FBI has purposely suppressed evidence. The behavior of the FBI in this case is negligent at best." He added: " . . . if our system of freedom is to be preserved . . . the FBI must be servile to our system of justice."

When the court further discovered that Hurd had withheld Senate Committee reports outlining the Pentagon's involvement in the Wounded Knee siege and that Hurd had, instead, turned over an altered version of the report, Hurd found himself backed into another corner. Although fellow prosecutor Earl Kaplan told the court that he knew there were two versions of the report, and that he assumed the defense had been given both, Hurd told the court that he was aware of only one report, the altered one. He offered the suggestion that perhaps there was a copying error. Judge Nichol said "This is about the most bizarre explanation I've heard," and addressing Hurd he asked, "Aren't you getting kind of tired of explaining your own negligence in some of these matters?" The young government prosecutor replied, "No, Judge, I'm getting used to it as a matter of fact."

The government's attempt to cover up illegal military involvement at Wounded Knee further undermined the imperious prosecutor. On June 19, Justice Department Chief of Staff Joseph Sneed testified that there existed no formal "line of authority," between his department and the Pentagon in relation to Wounded Knee. However, he said, "We did consult with the Defense Department from time to time in connection with borrowing equipment." Again Hurd kept pertinent and revealing documents from defense lawyers, and again he was admonished by Nichol as being "either deliberately or negligently dilatory" on failing to provide the information in his possession. The eventual revelations concerning unconstitutional use of the military against U.S. citizens without official presidential authorization were disclosed only after Nichol had issued a court order, releasing 120 documents from the Defense Department and a 100-page report from the Sixth Army.

Judge Nichol also ordered the White House to provide the court with Nixon tapes — revealed in the concurrent Watergate scandal investigations — concerning Wounded Knee. Former FBI director Patrick Gray and former White House Counsel John Dean both had testified that Wounded Knee was common subject matter at the White House, and that John Ehrlichman and President Nixon both received daily information about the status of the Wounded Knee siege. Nichol's court, however, was denied the Nixon tapes. Nixon sent a signed letter to the court stating that the release of the White House Wounded Knee tapes would not be in the national interest. What Nixon covered up by violating the court order remains unknown.

On August 30, the prosecution and FBI misconduct, which had reached tragic proportions, turned, for a moment, comic. While questioning FBI agent Ronald Williams concerning an alleged FBI cover-up of misconduct, attorney William Kunstler noticed that a door behind the bench was slightly ajar — a door that was usually closed. Continuing his questioning, Kunstler wandered around the courtroom, moving ever closer to the open door. As he got close enough to reach the handle, he quickly swung open the door, at which point two eavesdropping FBI agents almost fell on their faces as they stumbled embarassingly into the shocked courtroom. An incredulous Judge Nichol stopped the proceedings, and took the two agents, Dennis O'Callahan and Patrick Flynn, into his chambers for questioning. FBI agent David Price had been sequestered, awaiting his turn to testify, and Nichol wanted assurance that the two sleuths had not intended to subvert the process of objective testimony by revealing Williams's testimony to Price. The two agents assured the judge that they were only listening out of curiosity, and a shaken Judge Nichol, near the end of his patience, let them go, admonishing them for lurking around his courtroom and for carrying weapons in the courtroom in violation of court policy.

By late August, six months into the trial, the prosecution had yet to connect either Banks or Means to any of the alleged crimes. Hurd, however, produced a surprise witness, Louis Moves Camp, who testified that he had witnessed virtually every crime with which the defendants had been charged. He told the court that he had been at the Calico meeting on February 27, 1973, providing evidence of conspiracy. He told the court that he had witnessed both Banks and Means pilfering merchandise from the trading post. He said that he had seen Banks and Means handing out guns and giving orders to others, casting them as instigators of violence against the federal officers. If Moves Camp's testimony was true, the defendants could be found guilty of every charge contained in the eleven-point indictment presented by the government. The fact, however, that Moves Camp was lying was soon established by the defense; but it was the manner in which the government and FBI had secured the false testimony that finally undermined the prosecution case and pushed Judge Nichol to despair.

The witness's mother, Ellen Moves Camp, a member of the Oglala Sioux Civil Rights Organization, told the court that her son Louis had left Wounded Knee about March 12, 1973, not on May 1 as he had testified. She said he had traveled to California, had not returned, and could not have witnessed some of the events which he had described to the court. Further investigation revealed that a BIA employee had seen Moves Camp in California from March 17 through the month of June. Records from the Monterey Peninsula Cable Television Company revealed that Moves Camp had appeared on a television show there on April 23 and 26, days that he had supposedly witnessed events at Wounded Knee. Other witnesses testified that he had been on the San Jose State College campus in April. Investigation further revealed that legal aides for the prosecution had suggested that, prior to his court appearance, Moves Camp be given a polygraph (lie detector) test, but that FBI Special Agent Trimbach had ordered that the test not be given.

Awarding the government "the most favorable finding possible," Judge Nichol charged Hurd with having been "grossly negligent in failing to verify Moves Camp's testimony, and further, in failing to offer an explanation or correction of his testimony in the face of overwhelming contradictory evidence. His conduct here at least borders on violation of the American Bar Association Standards . . . "

However, further investigation by the defense exposed the government scheme to extract the false testimony and to deceive the court. The evidence convinced Judge Nichol that the government was guilty of more than borderline negligence. First, it was discovered that the FBI had paid Moves Camp $2,074.50 in expenses and fees for his testimony, and that FBI agents Ron Williams and David Price had spent several days with Moves Camp in a Wisconsin motel preparing the false testimony. Defense attorneys were suspicious when a woman approached them alleging that while in Wisconsin Moves Camp had raped her, and that the FBI and the police had covered up the incident. According to lawyer Larry Leventhal, "At the time of the alleged rape incident Louis Moves Camp was spending a few days in the presence of FBI agents Williams and Price . . . [who] by their own testimony, consumed great amounts of alcohol one evening in the presence of Moves Camp. Moves Camp thereafter left their company. The following morning a young woman attempted to press a rape complaint against Louis Moves Camp with the county attorney's office. Her complaint was initially processed, and then following contact between the FBI agents and the county attorney the complaint was sidetracked." The rape victim reported to the Wounded Knee attorneys "a very active campaign on the part of the officials to keep her from talking to anyone."

Price admitted that he had told Moves Camp not to worry about the rape charge, but he said he meant only that he would look into it. The defense, on the other hand, suspected that the FBI agents had stopped the rape investigation in exchange for Moves Camp's perjured testimony. Court records show that on August 27, 1974 defense attorney Lane, prosecutor Hurd, and Judge Nichol discussed the rape charge at the bench:

LANE: "I should like to know if Louis Moves Camp was arrested while in Wisconsin; if he was jailed for a serious charge, which may be rape; and if agents of the FBI or other representatives of the United States government arranged his release; if any of that fact situation is true." Nichol asked Hurd if he could provide the information.
HURD: "It's my understanding that he was arrested on a public intoxication charge. Now, I'm not sure of the details on that, but it was my understanding that he was arrested on a public intoxication charge. I don't believe there was ever a conviction on it; he was released. I'm not even sure he was arrested. . . . He has not been arrested on anything more than public intoxication."
LANE: "Well, I think we're entitled to this information even before we ask to call him back, Your Honor. I think we're entitled to know the date of the arrest, and what role the federal government played in having him released."
HURD: "I don't think that any of that is relevant and material; you can't impeach a witness by showing that he was arrested for public intoxication."

The defense discovered, however, that Hurd had learned of the rape charge at least a week before his denial that the charge existed. He had been told of the rape charge by the FBI Special Agent in Charge of Wisconsin, Phillip Enlow. On September 4 Hurd was again cornered, and forced to admit his lie. Attorney Lane had called Hurd to the bench again, and had asked him, "Did you have a conversation with Mr. Enlow on the 16th day of August?" Hurd answered, "Yes, I did . . . He told me that [Moves Camp] . . . had been intoxicated in Wisconsin, and that there had been a girl who was alleging that there had been intercourse, and that she had been raped."

Up to this point, Judge Nichol had shown leniency toward Hurd's behavior. But now Hurd was caught in a direct lie to the court, and Nichol was shocked that a federal U.S. attorney would so deceive a federal judge. Nichol called Hurd into his chambers and informed him that, according to Nichol, "The sordid story of what went on over in Wisconsin was going to come out." During that session in the Judge's chambers Hurd broke down and cried. "I don't know whether it was his conscience or what," Nichol said in court, recounting the incident.

Judge Nichol was moved to dismiss all charges against both Banks and

Means, In so doing, he lashed out at the FBI and the government prosecutors for their conduct and bad faith. He said, ''I blurted out, maybe unfortunately, in the early part of the trial, that the FBI had certainly deteriorated. I think that statement . . . has become justified by the manner in which the FBI has operated in this trial. . . .

''Mr. Hurd deceived the Court up here at the bench in connection with the Moves Camp incident in Wisconsin. It hurts me deeply. It's going to take me a long time to forget it . . . to that extent, I think the prosecutor in this case was guilty of misconduct; was certainly not in accord with the highest standards that we ought to expect of those officers that represent what I used to think was the majesty of the United States Government. I guess this has been a bad year for justice, a bad year for justice.''

Neither Hurd nor any of the other prosecuting attorneys was charged or indicted for offenses stemming from misconduct during the trial. Price, Williams, Trimbach, and other FBI agents also avoided prosecution for their attempts to sway the scales of justice. Furthermore, the violence on Pine Ridge had continued unabated despite the Justice Department promise to pursue prosecution of the goon squad members guilty of harassing people. Agnes Lamont and Jenny Leading Fighter reported that their car had been struck by another car driven by BIA policemen; Allison Little Fast Horse, a fifteen-year-old friend of the Bissonette family, was found dead in a ditch with a bullet in his heart; Pat Hart, another friend of Bissonette's, was shot and wounded; Philip Little Crow was beaten to death. Wallace Black Elk's brother Philip was killed when he entered his house and turned on a light switch, setting off a planted bomb. Vernal Bad Heart Bull was shot and killed in Allen, Nebraska almost exactly a year after his brother Wesley had been killed in Buffalo Gap. A rape and other beatings were also reported to Dennis Ickes, the Justice Department lawyer who had promised to seek prosecutions on the reservation, but no indictments were issued. Russell Means said: ''Not a single charge has been filed against any of the oppressors, the BIA police and goon squad; meanwhile, scores of Indians who have spoken out for liberation have been indicted and are facing many years in jail.''

The Wounded Knee arrests, high bonds, and trials served the government's purpose to ''disrupt and discredit'' the Indian movement as the FBI had earlier instructed their agents. Of the approximately 1,200 total arrests resulting from the siege or attempts to get to the scene, 185 cases were brought to court, and the government obtained 4 misdemeanor convictions and 11 felony convictions — 10 of which went to appeal courts. But AIM was forced to spend hundreds of thousands of dollars on defense, and the energy of the leadership was drained by legal battles while across the country BIA tribal councils became ever more entrenched. Hank Adams charged that the government had launched a "conspiracy" to destroy the Indian movement by tying up supporters and money with extended court cases such as the Banks/Means trial. Adams quoted a document which had surfaced during a Senate Interior Committee hearing headed by Senator Henry Jackson. The document, released as a joint Justice Department/Interior Department policy paper, stated that the Indian movement "must be stopped by criminal prosecution before they create more havoc throughout Indian America."

At the non-leadership trials in Lincoln, Nebraska, before Judge Warren Urbom in December 1974, sixty-five defendants moved for dismissal of charges based on the assertion that the United States did not have jurisdiction on Lakota treaty land. Urbom permitted thirteen days of testimony from Lakota elders, spiritual leaders, historians, and treaty lawyers. The witnesses outlined Lakota–U.S. legal history, establishing that the Lakota people had not surrendered sovereignty to the United States, and that the 1868 treaty was binding on the United States as an international agreement signed by both parties and ratified by Congress. After the lawyers established the legal history, Lakota elders recounted their oral history. Nellie Red Owl told the court, in testimony translated from Lakota by Gladys Bissonette, "I was born in 1907. I was taught by my grandparents . . . to live the traditional Oglala life for all my life. . . . We do not have these courts and these jails in our traditional life. I do not believe in these courts. . . . When the treaties were signed, the United States did not keep its promises. . . . There was an agreement that no white man was supposed to enter into Indian territory. The chiefs and headmen were supposed to govern the territory. Today the chiefs and headmen take care of us, but when they go to Washington, D.C. to negotiate with the Interior Department, they [the government] don't listen to our leaders."[13]

Reginald Bird Horse told the court: "I have been told by my grandparents, this land is not for sale. . . . My great-great-grandfather was a Hunkpapa chief who signed the 1868 treaty. . . . We are not going to change. We are Indians. We cannot live and believe like white people because we are Indians. . . . My grandfather said that they have never agreed to the Citizenship Act of 1924. It was forced upon us. Another one, the Indian Reorganization Act, was also forced. We did not agree. They did not ask the Lakotas. Another is the Allotment Act."

13. *Great Sioux Nation*, op. cit.; p. 158.

Elder Lakota Henry Crow Dog, father of Leonard Crow Dog who was on trial, spoke directly to Judge Urbom. "Your Honor, Judge," he said in English " . . . I am the law myself; I am born loyal — loyalty, and charity and salvation — on that part I don't spend one cent. I don't want nobody to spend one cent on me, to take care of me. And Christ is that way. Christ, we should save Christ. . . . We will do it in calling to serve no two masters. . . . The Great Spirit gave the white folk that Bible and the dictionary, so that they would never forget." Crow Dog urged the court to "make a law this time, this day, at this hour, at this moment, no fraction about it."

Urbom, however, ducked the issue, using the "political question" doctrine, stating that the treaty question was a legislative question and that "The defendants, then, are addressing the wrong forum for gaining relief in their sovereignty grievances." He added, however, that "It cannot be denied that official policy of the United States until at least the late nineteenth century was impelled by a resolute will to control substantial territory for its westward-moving people. Whatever obstructed the movement, including the Indians, was to be — and was — shoved aside, dominated, or destroyed. Wars, disease, treaties pocked by duplicity, and decimation of the buffalo by whites drove the Sioux to reservations. . . . It is an ugly history. White Americans may retch at the recollection of it."

Urbom's implication was that the transgressions had occurred long ago. The defendants, however, were more concerned about the transgressions that were occurring at the time, which had led to Wounded Knee, and which were continuing through the Western Hemisphere. "They say they can't give us our land back because it was so long ago that they took it, and now so many white people live there," said Matthew King, "but the Indian doesn't believe that. One hundred years is not so long for us."

In Sioux Falls, South Dakota Judge Joseph Bottum had been presiding over the trials stemming from the Custer riot the previous year. Bottum, an arch-conservative who had been defeated by George McGovern in the Senate elections of 1962, had taken a particularly tough stance against defense motions. His style had led attorney Ramon Roubideaux to remark that "He's bound and determined to show the Custer people how he's going to handle a bunch of Indians. . . . I think it's a response to a bigoted electorate." Roubideaux called the trial a "railroad" and a "legal lynching." For the first time in his twenty-four-year legal career the Indian lawyer was charged with contempt of court, fined $100, and sent to jail for one day.

When Bottum entered the courtroom on April 30, 1974 most of the spectators — including members of the League of Women Voters, four American Lutheran Church bishops, and native people — refused to stand. Bottum stalked off to his chambers, and ordered the courtroom cleared. Defendant Dave Hill turned to the bishops and asked, "What would Christ do in this situation?" The bishops went to meet with Judge Bottum in an attempt to defuse the situation, but were unsuccessful. After they returned to the courtroom, Sioux Falls police captain Earl Callahan entered, and ordered the bishops out; they refused to leave. Then, twenty-four helmeted, armed tactical squad officers entered the courtroom. Rushing past the bishops and other whites in the room, they struck at the Indians who had refused to leave. First hit was defendant Dave Hill; his head was split open from the blow of a club-wielding policeman, although, as a defendant, he had not been included in the order to leave the room. Within a few minutes the courtroom was cleared, blood was splattered across the walls, broken glass and furniture littered the floor. The South Dakota Sheriff's Association applauded Bottum for displaying "great courage in the face of potential and actual trial disruption." Governor Richard Kneip said that the Indians in the courtroom were "dedicated to destroying our constitutional system and bringing terror to the hearts of our people."[14] AIM called the confrontation a "police riot," charging that the tactical squad had made no attempt to clear the courtroom peacefully, but that they had stormed the defendants and observers with mace and clubs, and without provocation. Nevertheless, five Indian men were charged with assault as a result of the confrontation. Dave Hill was later brought back into court from the hospital on a stretcher.

On the day following the courtroom riot, AIM held a rally in front of the courthouse. Lawyer Karen Northcott recalled: "Ramon was in jail. Kunstler and Lane had come over from St. Paul, and we went to visit Ramon. On the way back, near the rally, Kunstler noticed a gun sticking out from a window of the Holiday Inn across the street. We went in to the hotel desk, but they wouldn't give us any information about the room, so we just went up to the room. When we got there the door was open and the room was empty. The phone rang, and Mark Lane answered; it was the desk. They said, 'You better get out of there, some Indians are on their way up.' It turned out that the room was rented to John Smith and paid for by the state of South Dakota."

State Attorney William Janklow was prosecuting the Custer riot cases. Janklow had previously represented the Rosebud Sioux Tribal Council. Two of his aides, John Fitzgerald and Bill Mathieson, had

14. *Akwesasne Notes*, Early Spring, 1974.

previously worked with the Wounded Knee legal team and had been intimately involved with defense strategy. During the trial Janklow had carried a pistol while traveling through Sioux Falls. He had told legal aide John Gridley III that "the way to deal with the American Indian Movement is to put a bullet in the AIM leader's head," in reference to Dennis Banks. He later confirmed this statement on television when asked by an interviewer if he had made the statement. He answered that, yes, he had; and he added "I never met anybody with a bullet in their head that bothered anybody."[15]

By October 1974, Janklow was running for South Dakota Attorney General against incumbent Kermit Sande. Janklow campaigned primarily as an enforcer of "law and order" in the face of "AIM lawlessness," gaining political points with the conservative electorate stirred and frightened by the Wounded Knee publicity. Janklow, however, had a few skeletons in his closet which Sande attempted to drag into the open. In 1955, at the age of sixteen, Janklow had been convicted of an assault on a seventeen-year-old girl in Moody County, South Dakota. Although the juvenile record was confidential, it was suspected and rumored that the charge had been rape. When Sande publicized the criminal record, Janklow countered by charging him with illegally revealing the juvenile record. He admitted to the media that he had been charged with assault, but in answer to an inquiry concerning the rape allegation he said "No, it didn't go that far, but it was preliminary to that type of thing."

Then, on October 16, Dennis Banks exposed a second rape charge against Janklow. In 1966 Janklow, working for the Office of Economic Opportunity on the Rosebud reservation, had been accused of rape by fifteen-year-old Jancita Eagle Deer, the Janklow family babysitter. The young girl alleged that Janklow had raped her at gunpoint while giving her a ride home. Medical records at the Rosebud Public Health Service hospital contained evidence of the attack and quoted her as having identified Janklow as her assailant. The rape was reported to the BIA, but with Janklow himself acting as head of the legal services program, no charges were brought against him. The FBI was also notified, but failed to bring charges against Janklow.

Banks brought the case before the Rosebud Tribal Court and Chief Justice Mario Gonzalez. AIM member Douglas Durham found the BIA officer who had investigated the charge in 1966, and he located Jancita Eagle Deer who was then twenty-six. She had dropped out of school

15. *The Life and Death of Anna Mae Aquash*, Johanna Brand, James Lorimer & Co., Toronto, 1978; p. 103.

after the rape incident, and had moved to Iowa where she had battled a drinking problem. A BIA officer identified the BIA file on the case as "file number 66." Agency Special Officer Norman Beare testified that he "located the file, had it in his possession, but was ordered by BIA Acting Area Director Harley Zephier not to deliver the same," to Gonzalez. After hearing the evidence, Gonzalez concluded that "The Court is satisfied that the rape allegations against Janklow are properly proven,"[16] adding that "Further testimony indicates that as recently as two months ago, Mr. Janklow offered Miss Eagle Deer's grandfather money after inquiring about her. . . . The depth of the suffering which Miss Eagle Deer conveyed in her testimony cannot be reproduced through words on paper. Feeling shame, she left the Rosebud reservation and returned only once until today. Her foster parents testified that her grades and interest in school fell after she was raped. She still feels frightened and inhibited by the beastly act committed against her by Mr. Janklow.

"Furthermore," added Gonzalez, "the evidence indicates that an obstruction of justice followed the rape. When a complaint was being made to the Bureau of Indian Affairs Special Officer, Janklow was there." The Tribal Court ordered "a warrant to apprehend and arrest Mr. Janklow . . . at any time that he may be found on the Rosebud reservation." The court order was signed two days before the November 2 election. Janklow claimed that the whole thing was an AIM "smear campaign" and "gutter attacks." Five months later Jancita Eagle Deer was discovered dead on a Nebraska highway near the reservation. The police report stated that the cause of death was "hit and run," although some of the wounds on her body were determined to have been caused before she was hit by the car.

After winning the election Janklow vowed to neutralize AIM in South Dakota, but the FBI would prove to be more effective at neutralizing AIM from within the organization itself. *Akwesasne Notes* reported "Tension has been high among AIM leaders because of certain knowledge that someone — fairly close to the top — was working for the government. Important information was leaking out, and police knew more about travel plans than individuals themselves knew, it seemed." Were the two Wounded Knee lawyers, who had moved over to the government's side as Janklow aides, the only two infiltrators? Who among the leadership could have been bought off by the FBI? The paranoia erupted

16. Mario Gonzalez, Chief Justice, Rosebud Sioux Tribal Court, Rosebud, South Dakota. The account is taken from Justice Gonzalez's "Judicial Opinion," from the Rosebud Tribal Court, October 31, 1974.

tragically in the late summer of 1974. Carter Camp, the newly elected AIM national chairman, had been arrested on August 25 in Mission, South Dakota on a gun charge. He was released immediately on a $100 bond. AIM leaders were accustomed to extremely high bonds, and were rarely released so quickly from custody. Camp's good fortune caused some suspicion that perhaps he had made a deal with the FBI. Was Camp an informer? Two days later an argument ensued on the Rosebud reservation; Clyde Bellecourt was shot in the stomach, and Camp was arrested for the shooting.

The incident sent a tremor through the movement as suspicion mounted and loyalties cracked. John Trudell, elected co-chairman with Camp, said that the shooting had been "conspiratorial in nature," and was the result of a larger FBI program to disrupt AIM. Bellecourt himself did a great deal to heal the organizational schism by publicly supporting Camp, and refusing to identify him as the assailant. Camp was eventually released, as there was no evidence on which to bring him to trial. Bellecourt called the shooting "the government's plot to divide and destroy the AIM organization." It was later revealed by Mission police officer Tom Rhoads that shortly after Camp was released on the original gun charge, an FBI agent had called him to order that under no conditions should the AIM leader be released. Camp regained the confidence of his compatriots, but still AIM was troubled and seriously fettered by FBI informant paranoia. Who was the leak?

In the two years since the Trail of Broken Treaties occupation of the BIA building in Washington, South Dakota had emerged as the front line of the war between the U.S. government and the traditional Indian movement. The national and international attention created by Wounded Knee, however, reverberated throughout America, Canada, and the entire Western Hemisphere where indigenous populations were battling the Neo-European nations for land rights. In Canada, the Cree and Inuit people had won a small victory in gaining a court order to delay the massive James Bay power project announced by Quebec Premier Robert Bourassa. The project called for dams on five major rivers, diversion of three rivers, and flooding millions of acres of land belonging to the Indians. Quebec Superior Court Justice Albert Malouf had written that "The Cree Indians and Inuit people have been hunting and trapping and fishing therein since time immemorial. They have a unique concept of land . . . and any interference therein compromises their very existence as a people."[17] The issue was hardly settled, however. A white backlash, government appeals, and corporate momentum swept aside

17. *Akwesasne Notes*, Early Winter, 1973; p. 22.

the court decision. The James Bay Development Corporation, the IT&T subsidiary Rayonier Corporation, and the Quebec government occupied the land, and began construction. Bourassa's government offered the Cree $100 million for the expropriated land, but the Indians refused the money. Appeals Court Chief Justice Lucien Tremblay then ruled that "the rights of the majority of Quebecers come ahead of a few thousand Indians," and allowed the project to begin. Bourassa stated in the Quebec government publication *James Bay,* "Quebec must occupy its territory; it must conquer James Bay. We have decided the time has come."

In the spring of 1974, the Mohawk Nation on the Canadian border occupied traditional land claimed by the State of New York. They established a traditional settlement which they named Ganienkeh, the original Mohawk name for the land, which means Land of the Flint Stone. Ganienkeh spokesperson Sotsisowah (John Mohawk) said, "Ganienkeh is more accurately a settlement than an occupation, a settlement on repossessed land. Since the beginning there have been any number of crises, including threats of annihilation, by the state, FBI COINTELPRO-type actions (Counter-Intelligence Program), court hearings, and shooting incidents. But . . . Ganienkeh has survived.

"The natural ways are subject to the greatest oppressions today . . . Ganienkeh is an effort to re-establish the real Mohawk culture by making available to people the means of survival."[18]

In the Western U.S. — Montana, Utah, Arizona, and New Mexico — the Nixon adminstration's "energy crisis" and "Project Independence" had brought a flurry of energy projects onto Indian land. Kent Frizzell, the Interior Department Wounded Knee negotiator, had said "America needs the Indian's coal."[19] In 1973, after the Arab oil embargo, Nixon had created the U.S. Federal Energy Administration, headed by Trilateral Commission member Dr. John Sawhill, to oversee "a major leasing program for mineral rights to Federal lands involving 10 million acres per year by 1987."[20]

Energy companies with Trilateral Commission connections had begun to swarm over federal — and Indian — land; these companies included Anaconda Copper, Atlantic Richfield, Bethlehem Steel, Climax Uranium, Exxon, Kaiser Resources, Union Carbide, Texaco, Westing-

18. Ibid., Late Autumn, 1976, p. 36.
19. Ibid., Early Winter, 1973, p. 34.
20. Michael Garitty, "The U.S. Colonial Empire Is As Close as the Nearest Reservation: the Pending Energy Wars," *Trilateralism: The Trilateral Commission and Energy Planning for World Management*, Holly Sklar, ed., South End Press, Boston, 1980.

house, Utah International, and others. In Montana, the traditional Northern Cheyenne Indians were pitted against the BIA, which had leased rights to their land to Peabody Coal Company, Kennecott Copper, Consolidated Coal (Continental Oil), American Metal Climax, and Chevron Oil. Sixty percent of the 415,000-acre reservation had been leased to energy companies through the BIA-Tribal Council system. Strip-mining projects were devastating the land. Traditional Cheyenne leaders had asked the Interior Department to cancel the leases; Secretary Morton had considered the request, but failed to do so. Richard Nixon told a governors' conference that "I'm going to have to propose some things that will drive the environmentalists up the wall. They're halfway already. How are we going to get the coal out of the ground without driving them out of their trees?"

Meanwhile, in South America Native people had been attempting to reach the ears of Europeans and Americans with the stories of atrocities brought upon them by military regimes and resource companies. In 1973 the University of Bern released a report charging the government of Paraguay with genocide for their "organized massacre of Ache Indians." The report described a typical raid: "Some specialists in killing Aches were contracted for the purpose and were paid with money from the funds of the *estancia*. . . . It was carried out with machete knives. There were between twelve and twenty killed . . . at least five small children were captured alive."[21]

Such reports, and reports of selling children into slavery were confirmed by the Roman Catholic Church in Paraguay and by Col. Patrick Montgomery, the British secretary of the Anti-Slavery Society.

Representatives of the modern Indian movements throughout the Western Hemisphere came together for the first time in the summer of 1974 on the Standing Rock Lakota reservation in South Dakota. The First International Treaty Council, which attracted ninety-seven Indian nations from Canada, the United States, and South America as well as white supporters from North America and Europe, had evolved from the organizational impetus created by the Trail of Broken Treaties and the Wounded Knee siege and trials.

John Mohawk gave an enlightening account of the history of the European invasion of the Western Hemisphere. "We hear about 'law and order' coming to the reservations," he told the gathering, "but we have to understand their theory of law. . . . A man named John Locke argued that men should not have the right to rule, but that laws should

21. *Akwesasne Notes*, Late Autumn, 1976; p. 22.

rule. He said that legislative bodies should make up the laws, not the rule of kings. Locke also said that the ones who would come to be the legislators, the lawmakers, would be the people who had vested property rights. And it is true in the United States. . . . They are not kings any more; they are corporations, and very wealthy people. That is the way of the white man today." He concluded that "It is important to be together as we are here at this convention. . . . Only a few years ago there was no one around thinking about holding the people together, no one around thinking about holding our lands. Now they are here, and I feel good about that."

A paper written by Dr. Jack Forbes of the University of California at Davis and presented to the conference read in part, "The United States, and the rest of America, both north and south, are being destroyed. The land is being ripped open and left unhealed. The rivers, lakes, and ocean shores are being polluted. . . . The destruction of the American earth and its animal and plant children is accompanied by the destruction and corruption of human beings, a corruption highlighted by the $2.5 billion pornography industry in the United States, the crisis of Watergate (with all the little Watergates both exposed and unexposed) and the continued campaign to liquidate native American tribal groups from Patagonia to Alaska."

The First International Indian Treaty Council issued a Declaration of Continuing Independence saying, "Might does not make right. Sovereign people of varying cultures have the absolute right to live in harmony with Mother Earth so long as they do not infringe upon this same right of other peoples. The denial of this right to any sovereign people, such as the Native American Indian nations, must be challenged by truth and action. World concern must focus on all colonial governments to the end that sovereign people everywhere shall live as they choose, in peace with dignity and freedom."

Thus, as the Nixon presidency crumbled, the war in Vietnam wound down to its dismal end, and America scrambled to exploit Western energy resources, the indigenous people of the Western Hemisphere formed an alliance with the intent of saving their culture, their land, and their lives in the midst of what seemed to be the death throes of a doomed, energy-intensive, industrial culture with roots in the European rational, scientific tradition. They were pitted against the full frenzy of modern American corporate industrialism: laws, courts, police, FBI, Pentagon, infiltrators, puppet regimes, goon squads, interlocking corporate dictatorships, government-corporate liaisons, media manipulation, and — it would turn out — even the organized Neo-European churches. The overwhelming odds only strengthened the movement. The Treaty

Council, frustrated by and distrustful of American courts, began to turn to the United Nations and international sentiment. Meanwhile, on the mesas of Arizona, the Hopi, who claimed to be the ancestors of all these people, were determined to maintain their humble culture in the face of encroaching energy development, and to move their message of peace out into a troubled world.

5
Church and State

*To steal in 1980 is the same as to steal in 1970,
or 1790, or 1600, or fourteen hundred and
ninety-two.*   OREN LYONS,
ONONDAGA, HAUDENOSAUNEE
Rotterdam, December 1980

EVERY SUMMER thousands of American tourists travel along Interstate Highway 40, formerly Route 66, the original Sante Fe Trail from the Midwest, through Oklahoma City to Los Angeles. The tourists visit Death Valley in California and Nevada; some blow their holiday wad under the tireless lights of Las Vegas; they visit the cowboy towns of Amarillo and Tucumcari, and they drive an hour north of Williams, Arizona to see the Grand Canyon. Billboards line the highway in the crusty desert of New Mexico and Arizona. Huge yellow signs read, "200 Miles to Indian Joe's Trading Post / Authentic Indian crafts." The yellow signs persistently remind the tourists, "150 miles"; then "100 miles, crafts, reptile garden, real garden, real Indian jewelry"; then "50 miles, don't miss it, gas, gifts, water"; "Indian Joe's, 37 miles" — "moccasins" — "bead work" — "20 miles" — "SEE: Indian craftsmen at work, exotic desert plants, reptiles" — "10 miles" — "8 miles" — "Don't miss it!" — "silver jewelry" — "sodas" — "One Mile to Indian Joe's" — "500 yards, crafts, gas, curios" — "Indian Joe's" — "THIS IS IT!!" — "STOP!"

The dusty curio shop, its gaudy turquoise watches and glass case of sleepy snakes is one of many near the New Mexico–Arizona border snuggled between the Navajo–Hopi, Zuni, Acoma, Apache, and Ute Indian reservations. "Indian Joe," of course, turns out to be a well-fed, stubble-faced white man, and the most authentic quality of the enterprise is that it sits on Indian land. The 1970 census showed 95,812 Indians in Arizona and 72,788 in New Mexico — clearly the highest concentration of Indian people in the United States. The Navajo reservation is the largest in North America, covering parts of Utah, Arizona, and New Mexico. According to the U.S. Civil Rights Commission, the

*Navajo woman herds cattle on reservation land in New Mexico.
This lifestyle is swiftly being eroded by energy-development schemes.
(Photo by Lionel Delevingne)*

per capita income there is less than $1,000 per year. The Hopi reservation is contained within the Navajo reservation, and is located in Arizona near the Four Corners.

By the time events in South Dakota had brought international attention to the American Indian land struggles, the Apache, Ute, Hopi, Navajo, Papago, Zuni, and Acoma Indians of the Southwest had already felt the pressure of mining companies moving onto their land. Kerr McGee had discovered uranium near Shiprock, New Mexico in 1949. Peabody Coal had discovered coal deposits in 1950. These two companies as well as Anaconda and Utah International had signed BIA leases and begun excavation. By 1969 Kerr McGee had abandoned their Shiprock site, leaving behind mine shafts and a uranium mill, exposing the main population center of the Navajo reservation to the site's radioactive effluents. By 1975 eighteen Navajo uranium miners had died from lung cancer.[1] Ninety-three miles south of Shiprock, Gallup, New Mexico stands on a lonely stretch of Route 66; twenty-nine miles to the east of Shiprock stands the little town of Farmington, on the San Juan River. These two towns, with mixed white and Indian populations, had

1. Fifth International Treaty Conference, "Documents from Big Mountain," report of the Dine Nation, Farmington, New Mexico, 1979.

become scenes of repeated racial violence by 1972. In Farmington, where 8 percent of the population was Indian, 84 percent of the arrests were of Indians.[2]

After participating in the 1972 occupation of the BIA building in Washington, D.C., AIM organizer Larry Casuse helped stage the occupation of the Indian Health Service Hospital in Gallup to protest racial discrimination in health-care services, and racial violence against Indian people. Then, in January 1973, Gallup mayor Emmet Frankie Garcia was nominated to the University of New Mexico Board of Regents. The local Indians protested the nomination because Garcia was considered to be a racist who profited from the alcoholism of destitute Indians. His Navajo Inn liquor store, located a few hundred feet from the Navajo reservation north of Gallup, was the most profitable liquor store in the state. As mayor of Gallup, and chairman of an alcoholism project, Garcia was considered an opportunist and a hypocrite. When Garcia's nomination came before the New Mexico Senate, Larry Casuse circulated a petition saying: "The man [Garcia] is an owner of the Navajo Inn where numerous alcoholics are born . . . does he not abuse alcohol? Does he not abuse it by selling it to intoxicated persons who often end up in jail or in a morgue from overexposure?"

The Senate, nevertheless, approved Garcia's nomination without discussing Casuse's charges. When Garcia was to be sworn in on the UNM campus in Albuquerque, Casuse attended the session, and asked to speak. He told the university regents, "These are the type of people who run our government, and these aren't *the people* — they are false people. There's no reason for me to scream or shout. There's no reason for me to bring documents. There's no reason, because you people will just turn your heads . . . you people aren't human beings."[3] Garcia was sworn in immediately after Casuse sat down.

Then, on March 1, 1973, two days after the occupation of Wounded Knee, Larry Casuse made a fatal move in his attempt to bring attention to Gallup Indian claims of direct and indirect racial violence. Casuse and his friend, twenty-year-old Bob Nakaidine, entered Mayor Garcia's office, held him hostage at gunpoint, and demanded a hearing of Indian grievances. They escorted the mayor two blocks away to the Stearn's Sporting Goods Store which was quickly surrounded by the county sheriff's officers. Gun shots were exchanged with police during which the mayor was either released or escaped; he exited the store through a

2. United States Commission on Civil Rights, "The Farmington Report," 1975; U.S. Government Printing Office, Washington, D.C.
3. Calvin Trillin, *New Yorker*, May 12, 1973.

window. The sheriff's officers poured tear gas into the store and stormed the building. A live report from a reporter with Gallup radio station KGAK described the scene following the police assault: "One of them thus far has come out . . . he has been directed by the officers to lie flat. . . . The police are now pouring into the Stearn's Sporting Goods Store. . . . They have dragged out what appears to be Larry Wayne Casuse. He is covered with blood. . . . I am approaching the body. . . . From a distance of about thirty feet, Larry Wayne Casuse appears to be dead."

Larry Casuse's tragic death did raise the profile of the Indian grievances in Gallup. A demonstration organized by Casuse had attracted 200 people in November. A demonstration organized in April, a month after his death, attracted over 2,000 people. Emmet Frankie Garcia lost the next mayoral election, resigned from the university regents, and devoted his time solely to his liquor business. Although some Indian people felt that perhaps the police had killed Casuse unnecessarily, the University of New Mexico Kiva Club, an organization of Indians, released a statement saying, "The real issue is not who shot whom, . . . but rather why Larry Casuse would so willingly sacrifice his life in order to communicate with the world his dream of unifying human beings with Mother Earth, the Universe, and Humanity."

Unfortunately, however, rather than subsiding, violence against local Indians in Gallup and Farmington increased. John Redhouse, a Navajo organizer, said, "For years, it has been almost a sport, a sort of sick, perverted tradition among Anglo youth of Farmington High School, to go into the Indian section of town and physically assault and rob elderly and sometimes intoxicated Navajo men and women. . . . There have been too few arrests. . . . The police have been ineffective and insensitive to the many complaints expressed by our people."[4]

On May 6, 1973 the bodies of Kee Jones, fifty-four, and George Dennison, forty-seven, both Navajo, were found in the hills north of Gallup. Their hands had been tied behind their backs, and their throats had been slit. In February 1974, twenty-six-year-old Navajo Gilbert Saunders was found dead near the Gallup city dump; he had been tortured to death. On Sunday, April 21 two hikers in Choke Cherry Canyon north of Farmington discovered the mutilated bodies of Navajo men John Harvey, thirty-nine, and Herman Benally, thirty-four, burned, tortured, with skulls crushed. A few days later a Farmington woman told police that she had overheard a high-school boy relaying the story of the killings as told to him by two youths who claimed to have committed the crime. A police investigation brought charges against

4. *Akwesasne Notes*, Late Spring, 1974, p. 20.

sixteen-year-old Howard Bender and fifteen-year-old Matthew Clark. During the investigation a third body — that of David Ignacio, fifty-two — was found. The youths admitted that they had killed all three men, naming a third accomplice, sixteen-year-old high-school football star, Delray Ballinger. The youths told a sordid story of the weekend ritual of picking up drunk Indians and beating them up. The game had escalated to torture and eventually to murder. The youths were tried in a closed courtroom. They received two-year sentences at the New Mexico Boys School, but were paroled a year later. A letter from Bob Gougelet in the Albuquerque newspaper *Seer's Catalogue* said, "These youths are not the only sick people in this community — they are merely representative of a white racist society in which these youths are being raised and their racist tendencies being nourished. Look through history and you will find the forefathers of these youths."

Gougelet's words proved true when, in May, the body of Willie Harrison was found in the San Juan River. A month later in June three Navajo men — Andrew Acquie, forty-seven, Arnold Cellicon, forty-four, and Alfred Yazzi, twenty-four — were found stabbed to death south of Gallup. A demonstration in Farmington on June 9, calling attention to the problem and attracting two thousand Indians, clashed with parading San Juan County Sheriff's posse deputies dressed in nineteenth-century cavalry costumes. A standard-bearer poked a Navajo youth who grabbed his flag, a fight ensued, and thirty-four Navajo people were arrested.

The violent conflicts in Gallup and Farmington, however, were merely symptomatic of a larger pressure that had been brought to bear on the Indian populations of the Southwestern United States. The massive energy developments in the area had begun to push the rural, pastoral Navajo and Hopi populations toward a labor-money economy; traditional farmers and goat ranchers were becoming construction workers or unemployment statistics as their grazing and farming land was swallowed by coal mines, uranium mines, and power plants. Furthermore, doth the traditional Hopi and Navajo leaders had been usurped by BIA-administered tribal councils. The councils, in league with the BIA, Interior Secretary and future Peabody Coal executive Harrison Loesch, Mormon lawyers, and public relations firms in Salt Lake City, had created a web of legal entanglements which came to be known as the Hopi-Navajo Land Dispute. The "dispute," or "range war" as it was sometimes called, was more accurately a legal maneuver orchestrated by government and private lawyers designed to partition common Hopi–Navajo land, relocate thousands of Indians, and open the area to coal and uranium leases. Reporter Mark Panitch wrote in the *Washing-*

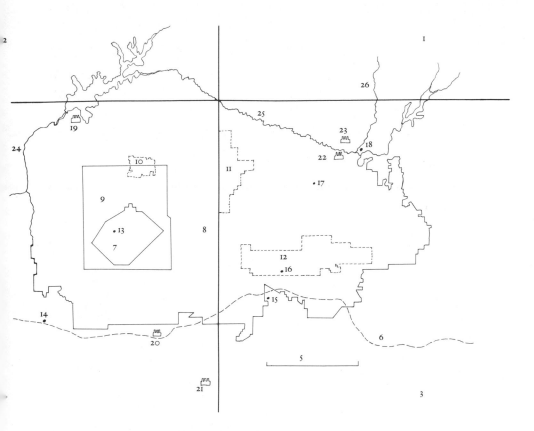

THE FOUR CORNERS (a "National Sacrifice Area," according to
the National Academy of Sciences): The Four Corners – where Colorado, Utah,
New Mexico, and Arizona meet – is known to the Hopi as the "Center of the Earth."
This ancient ancestral land of the Hopi and Dine (Navajo) people is now
the center of the most intense energy development in America. The worst
nuclear accident in American history occurred at Church Rock, New Mexico
on July 26, 1979, when a Kerr-McGee uranium tailings pond spilled over into
the Rio Puerco, contaminating drinking water between Church Rock
and the Colorado River, 200 miles to the west. 75 percent of the United States
national uraninum reserve is on Indian land under the control of the major
oil companies. Twelve oil companies own 54 percent of the uranium mines;
five oil compares own 62 percent of the uranium mills. The map shows
only a few of the more than 100 uranium mines and mills scattered throughout
the Navajo and Hopi reservations.

1. Colorado	10. Coal Strip Mine,	17. Burnham
2. Utah	Peabody Coal Co.	18. Farmington
3. New Mexico	11. Uranium lease: Exxon	19. Page power plant
4. Arizona	12. Uranium lease: United Nuclear,	20. Holbrook power plant
5. 50 miles	Tennessee Valley Authority,	21. St. John's power plant
6. Interstate Highway 40	Mobil, Conoco, Kerr-McGee	22. Four Corners power plant
7. Hopi Reservation	13. Oraibi	23. San Juan power plant
8. Navajo Reservation	14. Flagstaff	24. Colorado River
9. Joint Use Area	15. Gallup	25. San Juan River
	16. Church Rock	26. Animas River

Elvira Horseherder (right, rear), her family, and part of the neighboring Benally family stand before their home in the Navajo-Hopi Joint Use Area. Mrs. Horseherder, a Navajo, holds a letter from the BIA asking her to remove her family from the land under the relocation order that is part of Federal Public Law 93-531. 9,000 Navajo people face relocation under the law; the land is being opened for resource development. (Photo by Lionel Delevingne)

ton Post that "During 1971 and 1972 few newspapers omitted Sunday features on the 'range war' about to break out between the two tribes. . . . By calling Evans and Associates [a Salt Lake City Public Relations firm] a TV crew could arrange a roundup of trespassing Navajo stock."

By December 22, 1974 Congress had passed the Navajo and Hopi Settlement Act, Public Law (P.L.) 93-531, which supposedly settled the alleged dispute. P.L. 93-531, however, also established the Navajo/Hopi Relocation Commission, with powers to oversee the reduction of livestock and the removal of Navajo people from Hopi land and Hopi people from Navajo land. In a joint statement, the Navajo and Hopi elders officially opposed the relocation: "The traditional Hopi and Dine [Navajo] realize that the so-called dispute is used as a disguise to remove both people from the JUA [Joint Use Area], and for non-Indians to develop the land and mineral resources at Black Mesa. Peabody Coal has the right to 2 billion of Black Mesa's 22 billion tons of coal. Both the Hopi and Dine agree that their ancestors lived in harmony, sharing land and prayers for more than four hundred years. We declare our right to live in peace and harmony with our neighbors, and cooperation between us will remain unchanged.''

The dispute would eventually involve not only the Interior Department and power companies, but Senator Barry Goldwater, the Mafia, and the Mormon Church.

Hopi prophecy had predicted the arrival of the white race, actually the return of their ''lost white brother,'' Bahanna. Thus, the Hopi were not surprised when word reached them that white strangers had arrived on the eastern shore of the continent and that from the south they were approaching Oraibi via ancient Hopi migration routes. A stick which the Hopi Bear Clan had kept and marked annually for many generations had been filled with marks by the year 1520, indicating that Bahanna would soon arrive. If Bahanna was on time, the Hopi stone tablets instructed that they should meet him at the bottom of the Oraibi Mesa; if Bahanna arrived late they were to meet him at other designated spots depending on how late. In 1540 Vasquez de Coronado was raping and pillaging his way north looking for the seven lost cities of gold when he sent a party of seventeen horse soldiers, led by Pedro de Tovar, ahead to reconnoiter the area around the Hopi mesas. The Hopi prepared to meet Bahanna — twenty years later — at Tawtoma, below the village of Oraibi. They drew lines of sacred cornmeal across the earth per their instruction, and awaited the great prophesied meeting.

The Hopi were warned in their prophecy that Bahanna may have forgotten the Creator's way and they had a test ready just to make sure. When the Spanish Castillas approached the cornmeal lines the leader of the Bear Clan offered his hand, palm up, across the sacred line. If Bahanna remembered the way of the Creator he would put his hand, palm down, into the Bear Clan leader's hand, forming the *nakwach,* the symbol of peace among people. Instead, however, Pedro de Tovar dropped a gift of beads into the Hopi leader's hand, the first sign to the Hopi that Bahanna, the white brother, had forgotten the original instructions. The Hopi prophecy also foretold that if Bahanna had, in fact, lost the way, he would arrive with the ancient symbol of the four races holding the world in balance — the cross inside a circle — but that the symbol would be separated, and Bahanna would carry only the cross. The cross carried by Franciscan friar Juan de Padilla in Tovar's company fulfilled that prophecy, and the Hopi were convinced that the Castillas were not the true Bahanna, that they had strayed from the path of the Creator. They gave them the name *kachada,* white man. That was later changed to *dodagee,* dictator.

The Hopi prophecy further warned that if the white race had forgotten the path, they would bring with them many inventions. The Hopi were warned by the message in their tablets not to be enticed by the inventions, but to continue living in the manner that the Creator had given to them: planting corn and observing their spiritual ceremonies. For Tovar, finding the humble, farming Hopi on the dry mesas rather than the seven cities of gold, was a bitter disappointment, and he led his company back to Coronado. The Hopi elders knew that the invaders would be back, and they prepared for the prophesied changes.

Word of strange diseases and marauding *conquistadores* reached the Hopi mesas at this time. A smallpox epidemic had swept the Yucatan, Cortes had penetrated to the Mexican plateau, and had taken the Aztec capital of Tlaxcalan in a ninety-day siege. Far to the east the English pilgrims landed at Plymouth in 1620, and by 1637 had gone to war on the Mystic River, wiping out and scattering the Pequot. On the midwestern plains — as the story is told today — some buffalo meat hung in the forest by Lakota hunters was stolen by "something more clever than a bear." The curious Indians, hiding in the forest, caught their first glimpse of the pale-faced intruders: French trappers slipping into their food cache and making off with the best fatty meat of the buffalo. In the Lakota tradition of giving a name by first impressions, the great European civilization became forever known as *wasichu*, stealers of the fat. Between 1492 and 1776 the aboriginal population of North America was reduced by disease and warfare from 10 million to less than one million. During that same period the aboriginal population of what is now Mexico was reduced from 11 million to 1.5 million. Juan Pizarro and other Spanish raiders had begun the decimation of South American populations. The Arawak of Haiti and San Salvador — where Columbus had landed — were reduced from 8 million to zero.

Spanish missionaries penetrated Hopi land in the early seventeenth century, establishing the San Bernardino Mission in the village of Awatovi. The Hopi recorded cases of public lashings of Hopi men by Spanish missionaries who caught them practicing their "heathen" religion. Throughout the area, which is now New Mexico and Arizona, the Pueblo Indians — the Hopi, Zuni, Tewa — plotted a revolt. Ropes were knotted in the Tewa village of Taos, and carried to all the pueblos in the area, a single knot being untied each day. The last knot was untied from each of the distributed ropes on August 13, 1680, a signal to begin the revolt. Hundreds of Spanish soldiers and missionaries were killed, and churches were sacked. Today, some Hopi people maintain that the Hopi did not directly take part in the violence, in keeping with their spiritual instructions to remain peaceful; likely some did and some did not.

Nevertheless, the Spanish were temporarily driven from the area, only to be replaced by the westward-moving Americans.

At the time that the first white people had arrived in Hopi land, Dine Indians had begun to filter from the North into the area. The Dine (Navajo) had come from what the Hopi called the frozen back door of the Fourth World — this world. Stories handed down from the days of ancient Hopi migrations told of the impenetrable frozen North. The Navajo settled all around the Hopi, at times encroaching upon Hopi farmland. Paiute, Ute, Shoshone, Supais, and Havasupais people also settled around the mesas. As the whites arrived these people were confined on ever-smaller reservations. In the nineteenth century the Mormon Church laid claim to vast tracts of land in what is now Utah, and began their program to "save" their dark-skinned brethren. In 1854 Brigham Young called the Hopi a "degraded and ignorant . . . race of people,"[5] which became the rationale for confiscating their land and their children.

By 1876 a BIA field report noted that Mormons were moving onto the best Hopi farmland: "About five hundred of them [Mormons] have settled not far from the lands claimed by the Moquis [Hopi], and they are a peaceable, inoffensive tribe. . . . Their rights will be invaded with impunity, unless protected," reported BIA agent W.B. Truax. The Mormons, however, had amassed a militia of eleven hundred soldiers which had successfully defended the territory against U.S. troops in 1857; they were entrenched, and would remain so. The first recorded theft of Hopi land by Mormon settlers established a pattern of occupation and sale of title to a third party which would be repeated throughout the coming century. In 1879 BIA agent William Mateer reported that Mormon Apostle Jacob Hamlin asked and received permission from the Hopi to plant some crops and to water his stock on a section of Hopi land. When the Hopi returned in the spring to plant their own crops they were met by several other Mormons who evicted them from the land, claiming that they bought the land from Hamlin. Agent Mateer asked the Commissioner of Indian Affairs in Washington if there was not "some law by which the Indians can be protected in their rights to lands, which they have cultivated for a century or more?" The Commissioner wrote back that, no, there was not, because the Hopi had no "recognized legal rights" to the land which he called "public land." The Commissioner wrote: "As the Moqui [Hopi] occupy the public lands without any authority of law, the provisions of the statutes enacted by

5. Jon Stewart, "Cultural Genocide," *Penthouse*, June, 1981.

Congress for the protection of Indians . . . cannot be invoked to protect the Moquis, and remove and punish white settlers." The Mormons stayed, and their influence grew. They established missionary schools, enticing young Hopi children into the Mormon faith.

The Navajo, after subjugation at the hands of Kit Carson and General James Carlton, signed a treaty with the United States in 1868. The Hopi religious leaders refused to sign any such agreement but, in 1882, Congress established a 2.5 million-acre Hopi reservation surrounded by the Navajo lands. President Chester A. Arthur designated some of the land as joint use land to be shared by both Indian nations. The Hopi refused to accept any reservation or boundaries as being legitimate limits on their natural rights; the reservation boundaries had deprived the Hopi of at least 2 million acres of land. In 1884 the BIA began removing children from Hopi villages and taking them to a boarding school in Keams Canyon, twelve miles east of the mesas. In 1889 a smallpox epidemic swept the Hopi mesas, decimating the population.

At this time the U.S. government first began to use an alleged conflict between Hopi and Navajo people as a means of moving Indians off the land. In 1891 BIA agent George Parker and Indian trader Thomas Keam reported to Congress that to "protect" the Hopi from Navajo encroachment, the Hopi should be confined to 519,000 acres, one-fifth of the 1882 reservation. The Commissioner of Indian Affairs accepted the proposal, had the area mapped, and reported to the Department of Interior that the so-called conflct had been "brought to a satisfactory conclusion." The Hopi were repeatedly accused by various BIA officials of not using the land, and therefore not needing it. Between 1878 and 1907 the U.S. government expanded the Navajo land surrounding the Hopi reservation to allow for Navajo population growth. Thus, the Hopi were locked inside a double ring, first of Navajo shepherds who were in turn corralled by a burgeoning white population.

In 1906 the religious leaders of the Hopi fulfilled another of their prophecies by abandoning their spiritual center at Oraibi, and establishing the village of Hotevilla, eight miles to the north. The Hopi tablets foretold of a time when the people would be divided by outside influence; at this time the spiritual leaders were to take the ancient knowledge and move away from those who compromised the faith. BIA-sponsored private land allotment, government money, government and Mormon schools and the temptation that came with these things had indeed brought factionalism to the Hopi communities. Sun Clan spiritual leader Yukioma led the band of traditionalists to the new village. Many years later his son, Dan Katchongva, recalled that his father told him that all the knowledge of the ancient prophecies would be brought to

Hotevilla. "There is a great warning given to us as to what will happen to this land and human race if we turn away from the Life Pattern [The Great Spirit] gave us. These matters are of no small value," said Katchongva. "We must never lose faith, for if we do we will also lose our Great Spirit and we will once again destroy both Life and Land as was done before. . . . We know of many prophecies and instructions which were given to us concerning the life of the White Man, but they all hinged on the fact that when he came he would do many things for the sole purpose of getting control of this land and life for his self-glory. . . . Today we are facing the very end of this Life. It is not a small thing that is before us. . . . One of the things told to us was that the White Man will come and be very intelligent . . . bringing to us many things that he will invent. One of the inventions that our forefathers talked about was a machine or object that would move on the land with animals pulling it. Until the wagons came we didn't know what this prophecy meant. Our forefathers spoke also of a machine which would afterwards move with nothing pulling it, and when we saw the automobile we knew what they were talking about. Then the land would be cut up and there would be many roads; then there would be roads in the sky."[6]

As these prophecies came true, one-by-one, the Hopi traditional leaders clung to their faith, reading the signs, waiting for the signs which would lead to the Great Purification. As their land was unabashedly violated, those who resisted were labeled by the U.S. government as hostiles, and many were imprisoned. According to a 1977 Indian Law Resource Center report to UN Secretary General Kurt Waldheim, "Mass arrests of 'hostile' leaders were ordered and many served lengthy sentences at the U.S. prison at Alcatraz and elsewhere. To further undercut the effectiveness of traditional Hopi government, the United States gave support and aid to those Hopis, known as 'Friendlies,' who cooperated with the Bureau of Indian Affairs' policies."

The BIA jailed Yukioma after he had protested the forced enrollment of Hotevilla children in BIA schools. BIA agent Leo Crane called him a "deluded old savage, possessed by . . . witches." When Yukioma died in 1929, his son, Katchongva, became recognized as the traditional leader of Hotevilla. Katchongva braced himself for what the prophecies foretold as two "earthshaking" events, signaled by the appearance of the swastika — an ancient Hopi migration symbol — and the "rising sun," during which a "gourd of ashes" would fall from the sky, boiling the waters and spreading sickness. These events would signal a time at

6. *God's Chosen People of America*, Zula C. Brinkerhoff, Publishers Press, Salt Lake City; 1971.

which the Hopi must move their message of peace out into the world.

With the advent of World Wars I and II, the Hopi considerd these prophecies fulfilled. The religious leaders gathered in Hotevilla, in 1949, to compare the various clan prophecies and to decide on a course of action. The tablets told of a "mica" or "glass" building on the eastern shore of the continent which would be a gatherng place for all the nations of the world; they were to take their message of peace and simple living to this place, and to translate the Hopi message to the world. Katchongva, in 1949, began his spiritual life's work of communicating the Creator's Way to the world. That work would continue until his death in 1972.

In the meantime, the BIA had established the Hopi Tribal Council; Mormon lawyer Ernest Wilkinson had drafted the Indian Claims Commission legislation; Mormon Senator Arthur Watkins had taken over as head of the Claims Commission; Wilkinson's Mormon law partner, John Boyden, had become the Hopi Tribal Council lawyer; claims awards for confiscated Hopi land were being negotiated by Boyden and paid to the tribal council; the U.S. nuclear weapons industry had moved to New Mexico and Arizona; coal and uranium had been discovered on what was left of Hopi land; and Boyden was preparing lease contracts to be negotiated with mining companies. Katchongva and the traditional Hopi saw this mass assault as the potential final blow to the true Hopi people, the Original Ones, the spiritual caretakers of the Western Hemisphere. As he said, "It is not a small thing that is before us."

Katchongva wrote a letter — signed by the religious leaders of Shungopavi, Mishongnovi, and Hotevilla — to President Harry Truman on March 28, 1949 explaining the position of the Hopi elders. He outlined to Truman their opposition to accepting any Claims Commission money, the illegitimacy of the BIA tribal council government, and the traditional Hopi religion and way of life. He received no response. The following October he wrote another letter to Truman requesting an investigation of the tribal council and their lawyers, and informing the President that the Hopi people would take their grievances to the United Nations if the U.S. government refused to deal with them. Two months later the Hopi made their first visit to the United Nations. Their prophecy had told them that they would have to make three trips to the "mica" building, or the UN, before they would be received, and — sure enough — they were turned back on their first attempt. The UN assembly would not recognize them.

Legislation was pending in Congress to resolve the Hopi-Navajo land dispute, which had been initiated by Boyden and Navajo Tribal Council lawyer George Vlassis. Both tribal councils had filed conflicting claims to extremely valuable mining land. In 1956 Katchongva wrote to Senator Barry Goldwater protesting the claims and the legal case. Nevertheless, in 1958 Congress authorized the two tribal councils to enter into federal court litigation to determine the true owner of the land. The bill had been lobbied through Congress by John Boyden; the court case was under way; the Hopi and Navajo were divided, set up to be conquered by resource corporations. An editorial in the *Arizona Star* later noted that the land in question held deposits of "coal, uranium, pools of petroleum and pockets of natural gas. . . . Major oil and uranium companies had indicated that the disputed land caps one of the last great storehouses of natural resources in the United States. These companies are now awaiting the outcome of the trial . . ."[7]

Traditional Ute leaders joined the Hopi religious leaders in requesting a grand jury investigation of Boyden who had also been representing the Ute Tribal Council. The Ute Council had been paid $1.2 million for a million acres of expropriated land through the Mormon-Washington connection of Boyden, Wilkinson, and Watkins. Wilkinson had also entered a land claim for the Western Shoshone who had lost land guaranteed to them in an 1863 treaty with the United States. The Shoshone elders believed that the lawyers — Wilkinson and his Mormon partner, Robert Barker — were working to establish their treaty rights, not to sell their land to the government. Saggie Williams, a Shoshone elder, said later of the deal: "We wanted the white men to honor the treaty. I believed that the lawyers were hired to work for the Indians and to do what the Indians asked them to do. But, they didn't, they did as they pleased and told us that we didn't have any land. At that time, we didn't talk about selling our land with the lawyer because we had the treaty which settled the land, it protected our lands."[8] Although the land had been illegally occupied over many years, the law firm of Wilkinson and Barker agreed to a government proposal to fix 1872 as an official, legal date at which the Indian title had been extinguished. The lawyers, supposedly representing the Indians, were paid $2.6 million directly from the government, off the top, from money due to the Shoshone people as a result of the claim decision.

As the Shoshone, Ute, Paiute, Hopi, and other Indian nations of the Southwest lost millions of acres of land in this legal mill, the Mormons consolidated tremendous financial and real estate holdings. The Mormons, or Church of Latter Day Saints, are by far the largest profit-making religious organization in the United States. Although the finan-

---

7. *Arizona Star*, October 16, 1960.
8. Dagmar Thorpe, "The Destruction of a People," *Akwesasne Notes*, Spring, 1981; p. 6.

cial records of the Corporation of the President of the Church of Jesus Christ of Latter-Day Saints are the secret of the church, it has been estimated that their annual profits are over a billion dollars. The Church owns eleven radio stations, two television stations, a cable television franchise, 5 percent of the *Los Angeles Times,* controls a virtual media monopoly in Utah, and a complete newspaper monopoly in Salt Lake City. Aside from the church's extensive land holdings in Utah, New Mexico, Colorado, and Arizona, it owns a 700,000-acre ranch in Florida, an 80,000-acre ranch in Canada, a village in Hawaii, and interests in many businesses big and small. The Mormon Church maintains corporate board connections in Kennecott Copper, Union Pacific Railroad, Anaconda Copper, Phillips Petroleum, and Bankers Trust, among many others. In addition, church members tithe 10 percent of their personal earnings to the Church Corporation — Donny and Marie Osmond and J. Willard Marriot of hotel fame among them.

None of these holdings is, strictly speaking, illegal by U.S. law. However, when viewed in relation to the activities of the Mormon Church in the halls of Congress and in the inner workings of the Interior Department, the BIA and tribal governments, the church can be seen to wield tremendous influence over the affairs of the Indian people whom they regard as spiritually and socially inferior. On September 20, 1960 Dan Katchongva and other Hopi leaders appealed to federal Judge Frederick Hanley, Ninth Circuit Court of Appeals, San Francisco. They asked the court to overturn all legal decisions based upon the bogus Hopi-Navajo land dispute, and to recognize the authority of the traditional Hopi leaders. They further asked for an investigation into the suspect relationship between the Hopi Tribal Council, the BIA, John Boyden, the Mormon Church, Congress, President Eisenhower's administration, and energy development companies. The Hopi traditional leaders wrote to the Navajo leaders saying that they were "strongly opposed [to the] suit against you and your Navajo Tribe initiated and encouraged by the so-called Hopi Tribal Council in collaboration with their attorney, John S. Boyden of Salt Lake City, Utah, to settle a so-called Hopi-Navajo Land Dispute in a federal court."

No action was taken by Judge Hanley, and in 1962 a three-judge federal court in Prescott, Arizona ruled that the Hopi Tribal Council had exclusive rights to 624,064 acres of the 2.5 million-acre 1882 Hopi reservation, and that rights to the remaining four-fifths of the reservation land were shared jointly by the Navajo and the Hopi councils. Boyden later urged that the "Joint Use Area" (JUA) be partitioned, to establish clear legal title. As Navajo sheep farmers had long since occupied most of the JUA, Boyden urged the government to institute a "stock reduc-

*AIM organizers Larry Anderson (right), Vicky Anderson (left),
and their family at their home on Fort Defiance, Arizona.
Larry is Navajo, Vicky is Hopi; together they have fought against
the forced relocation of Navajo families, and against the destruction
of Navajo and Hopi land. (Photo by Lionel Delevingne)*

tion" program in "the best interest of both tribes."[9] But whose interest
was Boyden really looking after? He said in 1962, while lobbying for
legislation to divide the JUA, that "If partition was holding up oil
development, the oil companies would be awfully interested in getting
the legislation." Within two years, Boyden had negotiated oil leases
totalling nearly $3 million. The Mormon lawyer's fee in the deal was a
flat $1 million, paid to him by the Hopi Tribal Council in 1964.

That same year 223 Southwest utility companies — ranging from Los
Angeles, Burbank, Pasadena, and Glendale water and power authorities
on the West Coast to the four corners power companies including Utah
Power and Light Company, Public Service Company of New Mexico,
Colorado-Ute Electric Association, and El Paso Electric Company —
formed an energy consortium known as WEST, the Western Energy
Supply and Transmission Associates. The consortium drafted plans for
massive coal strip-mining and six coal-fired electricity-generating plants

9. U.S. Department of Interior, Hopi-Navajo Conference, August 6–7, 1963; quoted here
from *The Second Long Walk*, op. cit.

on Hopi and Navajo land which could supply the projected energy needs of Los Angeles, Las Vegas, and Phoenix. WEST hired the Salt Lake public relations firm of David Evans and Associates to explain the massive project to the public, and to counter the objections of environmentalists and traditional Hopi and Navajo leaders. Evans, in the Mormon stronghold of Salt Lake City, also represented the Hopi Tribal Council, writing speeches for Council Chairman Clarence Hamilton. The speeches, according to the *Washington Post,* would then be distributed "through the public relations machinery" of WEST. By 1966 Boyden had secured lease arrangements with both Peabody Coal — to strip mine 58,000 acres of Hopi land — and WEST to build the power plants, all over the strenuous objection of the traditional Hopi leaders and the simple, self-sufficient Navajo shepherds who would be displaced by the projects. The connection between the energy developers and the Hopi Tribal Council, with David Evans acting as intermediary, is revealed in a later speech written by Evans for Clarence Hamilton, in which he said, "We feel fortunate to have these power plants developed in the areas around our reservation. . . . Without the power plants we would have no market for our coal. . . ."[10] Thus, David Evans, who had initially choreographed the range war, followed through as both apologist for the energy interests and spokesman for the BIA Tribal Council and their lawyer Boyden, all from Salt Lake City. But the Mormon connection would penetrate ever further into the heart of the matter.

Katchongva and the Hopi leaders hired their own lawyer, Robert Pelcyger, and sought a federal court injunction against the lease contracts, attempting to stop payments to the tribal council and to Boyden. But the federal court ruled that since the Department of Interior recognized only the tribal council as having any legal authority, the traditionalists had no legal standing, and would have to join the suit on the side of the Hopi Council if they wished to participate. Thus, the spiritual leaders of the Hopi were told quite clearly that the only way they could enter the legal arena was on the side of their avowed opposition, the BIA Tribal Council and lawyer Boyden. Their appeal to the Department of Interior under the Lyndon Johnson administration fell to Interior Secretary Stewart Udall — member of a wealthy and powerful Mormon family. Udall disregarded the ancient authority of Katchongva and the traditionals, approving the coal and power plant leases, and remarking that the energy development would provide "new jobs, large tax benefits," not only to the Hopi and Navajo, but "for the entire Southwest."

10. *Navajo Times*, February 3, 1972.

Also in 1966, the year that Boyden sealed the lease deal with Peabody Coal, Kennecott Copper bought the huge coal company for more than $500 million. Kennecott, owned in part by the Mormon Church, operated the nation's largest open pit copper mine located outside of Salt Lake City, and produced up to 25 percent of its hundred-million-a-year profits from a copper mine in Chile. With the addition of Peabody, Kennecott became the largest producer in America of both copper and coal.

In addition to this Mormon web of political influence, the Hopi and Navajo people were further subjected to swarms of black-tied, fair-skinned Mormon missionaries teaching the revelations from Moroni, converting Indians to the faith, and placing Indian children in Mormon homes. Dr. Jane Van Deusen, a pediatrician from Tuba City, Arizona told reporter Beth Wood[11] that "In the '60s it was practically a black market adoption racket. I remember once a clerk came to me about a family who were being talked to by Mormons about their children. They gave the parents a piece of paper and said it was just to let them go to school. But the paper was an adoption form. The clerk and I told the parents what adoption was, and they said they didn't want that . . . the Mormons were absolutely furious with us because we told these people the truth."

The Latter Day Saints Placement Program removed as many as two thousand Hopi and Navajo children per year from their villages, placing them in Mormon homes throughout the United States. The Mormons felt morally justified and spiritually sanctioned to carry out the program. Their scriptures told them that the "Dark and loathsome" Indians — or "Lamanites" — had been cursed with dark skin by God because of their moral turpitude and ancient wickedness. The Mormons further believed that the children would begin to lose their dark color as they were raised by good Mormon families. "And the Gospel of Jesus Christ shall be declared among them," reads the *Book of Mormon,* "and their scale of darkness shall begin to fall from their eyes, and many generations shall not pass away among them, save they shall be white and delightsome people." Mormon Church President Spencer Kimball confirmed that the Mormons accepted that teaching literally when he stated publicly in 1960 that "The children in the home placement program in Utah are often lighter than their brothers and sisters in the hogans on the reservations." He said the Indians were living "without culture or refinement of any kind . . . then you see these boys and girls [in the placement

---

11. Beth Wood, "LDS Placement Program, To Whose Advantage," from "The Mormon Southwest," *Akwesasne Notes,* Winter, 1978; p. 16.

program] playing the flute, the piano. All these things bring about a normal culture."[12] When Senator James Abourezk introduced the Indian Child Welfare Act legislation in an attempt to establish guidelines for removal of Indian children from reservation to foster homes, the familiar Mormon law firm of Wilkinson and Barker, Mormon Congressman from Utah Gunn McKay, and the Mormon Deputy Commissioner of Indian Affairs, M.E. Seneca, lobbied for and won an amendment to the law exempting the church from the regulations. Goldie Denny, chairperson of the National Congress of American Indians' Child Welfare Committee, told reporter Beth Wood of a mass baptism which she witnessed: "They were baptizing all these Indian children one by one as they got on this bus that took them to their placement homes. Those children had no idea what was happening to them."

As Indians converted to the Mormon faith returned to the reservations they would invariably move into BIA Tribal Council positions. The most influential of these families was that of the three brothers Wayne, Abbott, and Emory Sekaquaptewa whose father had been taken from the reservation to a boarding school in 1908 and had returned eight years later, well connected to the Mormon hierarchy. Oldest brother Wayne had become a business success on the reservation, trading crafts, booking tourist excursions, winning construction contracts, and publishing a pro-BIA Tribal Council newspaper, the *Qua Toqti*. He was also the president of the local Mormon Church. His brother Abbott became the tribal council chairman in 1973, and Emory served as executive director.

Then, in early 1974, Utah Mormon Democrat Wayne Owens drafted, introduced, and facilitated through Congress Public Law 93-531, the Navajo-Hopi Settlement Act, dividing the Joint Use Area between the two tribal councils, providing for massive stock reduction, and preparing the way for the largest mass relocation of people in American history since the discovery of oil in Oklahoma, and the relocation of Cherokee, Choctaw, Chickasaw, Creek, and Seminole Indians in 1906. The Mormon Church had been instrumental in the evolution of the land division and relocation from the level of local Hopi politics to the level of the U.S. Secretary of Interior. Enormous financial dealings had hung in the balance. Peabody Coal was stripping over a quarter of a billion dollars worth of coal from Black Mesa annually.[13] WEST had constructed two coal-fired power plants and high voltage power lines to major western cities. Several top government officials who had worked

12. Ibid.
13. *Everybody's Business*, Milton Moskowitz et. al., Harper & Row, San Francisco, 1980.

on drafting and adopting the extensive legislation, transferring land title and mineral rights from the Hopi and Navajo people into the hands of these power companies, later moved into executive positions with the companies themselves. Senate Interior Committee staff director Jerry Verkler who promoted the legislation became the manager of government affairs for Texas Eastern Transmission Company, and Interior Secretary Harrison Loesch took his position with Peabody Coal.

The Hopi and the Navajo, however, were not the only Southwest Indian nations to experience government and private control of their affairs. In 1972, the *Arizona Republic* newspaper from Phoenix reported that a financial audit of the San Carlos Apache BIA Tribal Council turned up a pattern of embezzlement and general misuse of funds by tribal officials. BIA Tribal Council chairman Marvin Mull and his son were named in the scandal in which twenty-eight BIA-paid employees had pilfered at least $212,420 from tribal businesses. Harrison Loesch's assistant, Marvin Franklin of the Interior Department, leapt to the tribal chairman's defense, claiming that the audit was not an official audit, but only a "study of procedures." The Interior Department provided over $700,000 in two years to help restore the council's financial position.

Between 1949 and 1975 the financial affairs of the Cherokee Nation in Tahlequah, Oklahoma, had been under the direction of W. W. Keeler. Keeler had been appointed "principal chief" by President Truman in 1949, and reappointed to that position by Presidents Eisenhower, Kennedy, Johnson, and Nixon. He was one-sixteenth Cherokee; he was also chairman of the board and chief executive officer of Phillips Petroleum Company. Keeler maintained at Phillips a multi-million-dollar political slush fund which eventually led to an indictment against him for illegal contributions. In 1968 in the New York apartment of Richard Nixon, Keeler handed Nixon a $50,000 cash donation to the President's re-election fund. The act resulted in a 1973 conviction for which Keeler paid a $1,000 fine. Keeler and the company later pleaded guilty to concealing $2.8 million of corporate funds from the U.S. Internal Revenue Service. In tribal dealings, Keeler was no less bold in moving large amounts of money around to friends and business associates. With tribal attorney Ross Swimmer, president of Tahlequah First National Bank, Keeler formed a separate trust company headed by himself which in 1972 secured a trust indenture for all the "property, proceeds, returns, profits, and increases" of the Cherokee Nation Historical Society, for the sum of one dollar. The following year, for $10, the Keeler trust company secured a deed for a tract of land owned by the Cherokee Nation, Keeler himself signing the deed as chief. On the following day, the Cherokee Nation, again with Keeler signing, entered into a lease agreement with the trust company, agreeing to pay the company $11,099 per month to lease the land on which was located a restaurant, craft shops, and a motel. In 1975 Keeler stepped down from his post as chief, and elections were held. Cherokee James Gordon of Tulsa outpolled seven other candidates in the initial balloting, but after absentee ballots were tallied attorney-banker Swimmer was declared the winner by 278 votes. Although he received only 28 percent of the vote there was no run-off, and although six candidates filed charges of election fraud, there was no investigation by the BIA.

Attorney Edward Berger of Tucson, who was representing both the San Carlos Apache Tribal Council and the Papago Tribal Council (in southern Arizona), was fired by the Papagos in 1972 following a successful takeover of the council by a traditional faction. Berger had been negotiating mining and smelting contracts against the wishes of the traditionals. Files had been removed from his office which, according to Mike Wilson, a director of the Papago Cultural Research Center, Berger had been "reluctant to show tribal members." Berger declared that his ouster was coordinated by "People who are out to stop any development or operations on Indian land."[14] Prior to his firing he had amassed $944,080 in fees for his legal advice to the Papago Tribal Council.

The Ute Indians once ranged throughout Colorado, Utah, New Mexico, and Arizona, but in 1863 they signed a treaty with the United States ceding all Colorado east of the continental divide. Miners and soldiers, however, eventually drove them out of all their Colorado lands. Colorado Governor Frederick Pitkin said in 1879, "My idea is that, unless removed by the government, they [the Utes] must be exterminated. . . . The advantages that would accrue from the throwing open of 12 million acres of land to miners and settlers would more than compensate all expenses incurred."[15] In 1881 the Utes who survived the white assaults were marched 350 miles onto several small reservations in Utah where their affairs eventually fell into the hands of Mormon lawyers. By 1920 the original 2.5 million acres of reservation land had eroded to 360,000 acres, the balance falling to Mormon settlers. Lawyer Ernest Wilkinson negotiated claims payments to the Utes. After the establishment of a BIA Tribal Council, Ute affairs were handled by Boyden who negotiated away Ute water rights for major water diversions to Salt Lake City, and gas production leases on Ute land. The gas leases were signed

14. *Akwesasne Notes*; Late Summer, 1973; p. 13.
15. Robert Emmitt, *The Last War Trail: the Utes and the Settlement of Colorado*, University of Oklahoma Press, 1954; p. 234.

A young Navajo shepherd tends his family's flock of sheep.
In the background, the coal-fired Four Corners power plant
spews fly-ash and smoke into the air. (Photo by Mark Lennihan)

with Mountain Fuel and Gas Supply Company on the board of which sat Mormon Church president Nathan Tanner and church official Neal Maxwell. The web of Mormon lawyers including Wilkinson, Boyden, Barker, and others also negotiated cash settlements as compensation for the extinguished land rights of the Shoshone, Zuni, Gosiute, and Paiute Indian Nations. Termination legislation drafted by Mormon Senator Watkins further led to the extinction of as many as twenty Indian entities and their land rights.

By the time the American Indian Movement had established a national reputation defending Lakota land rights in South Dakota, the Indians of the Southwest were already firmly in the clutches of energy development corporations. Following the rash of racial slayings in Gallup and Farmington between 1972 and 1974, AIM members converged on the Southwest with the intent of coming to the aid of the Hopi, Navajo, and other Indians in the area. Public Law 93-531, the Hopi-Navajo Settlement Act, had put an estimated nine thousand Navajo people — old people; sheep-herding families, the traditional, land-based and least money-oriented of the Navajo — on notice that they would have to relocate. Furthermore, the government had adopted a freeze on building any structures on the divided land or improving existing roads or other facilities, private or public; stock reduction had already forced some Navajo people to leave the area.

Emma Yazzi, a Navajo elder, kept a flock of sheep near the small town of Shiprock on the reservation, east of Farmington. The Peabody coal strip mine and the huge Four Corners coal-fired power plant had encroached on her land. She could see the black plumes of smoke rising daily from the giant smokestacks. She says that the grass has slowly died away around the plant. "There is not enough grass for sheep now; and the sheep are sick. Also people get sick because of these power plants," she says. "We never had all these sicknesses before." The five units of the 2,075 megawatt power plant had begun churning out city-bound electricity and local pollution in 1969. The plant was burning ten tons of coal per minute — 5 million tons per year — spewing three hundred tons of fly-ash and other waste particulates into the air each day. The black cloud hung over ten thousand acres of the once-pristine San Juan River

Tailings (waste) from a uranium mill spill out across Navajo land near Granta, New Mexico. One government report has suggested that the area be zoned for mining only, to the exclusion of human habitation, because of the health risks due to the radioactive mine tailings. (Photo by Mark Lennihan)

Valley.[16] The deadly plume was the only visible evidence of human enterprise as seen from the Gemini-12 satellite which photographed the earth from 150 miles in space. Less visible, but equally devastating was the fact that since 1968 the coal mining operations and the power plant requirements had been extracting 2,700 gallons of water from the Black Mesa water table each minute — 60 million gallons per year — causing extreme desertification of the area, and even the sinking of some ground by as much as twelve feet.[17]

Another source of ill-health among the local people was the uranium mine tailings left behind by Kerr-McGee and Vanadium Corporation of

16. Alvin Josephy, "Murder of the Southwest," *Audubon Magazine*, September 1971.
17. *New Scientist*; July 5, 1979.

A Navajo uranium miner on the job at Mariana Lake, New Mexico. The uranium industry has brought a wage economy, environmental degradation, and cancer to the traditional farming and herding economy of the Navajo. (Photo by Mark Lennihan)

America. In a modern version of the infamous nineteenth-century smallpox blanket, the companies had provided uranium tailings as building material for Navajo homes. A 1975 Environmental Protection Agency study revealed that "concrete floors, exterior stucco, mortar for stone footings, cement floor patches . . . cement plaster"[18] had all been produced from radioactive material. Ned Yazzi, who lives near the abandoned mill tailings, told reporter Tom Barry that when he worked for Vanadium Corporation he had suffered a mining accident, and had been confined to a wheelchair. The company supplied him with tailings to build a house. "The walls, the floor, my whole house is radioactive," he says. "I wish VCA never came here." By 1975, eighteen miners had died from lung cancer, and twenty-one others had contracted various forms of cancer.

Navajo activist Larry Anderson had been elected AIM national treasurer in the summer of 1974. In the spring of 1975 he and other national AIM leaders staged an occupation of the Fairchild Camera and Instrument Company plant in Shiprock. The action was meant to draw attention to the many Navajo and Hopi local grievances, and the Fairchild plant was chosen as a target because of what local Navajo people considered to be exploitive and racist hiring practices. Young Navajo girls were hired for $85.00 a week to assemble electronic equipment. In a year the work force had slumped by 50 percent, and a recent lay-off of 140 workers caused further resentment. "There was no notice," said one worker. "They just herded the girls into the meeting room and told them goodbye. It was so sudden." The work force on the reservation is not unionized.

The AIM occupation of the plant lasted for eight days; the demonstrators asked for the rehiring of the 140 workers, but they also used the opportunity to demand a stop to strip-mining on Navajo land and a renegotiation of lease agreements held by Utah International and Arizona Public Service Company. The Navajo Tribal Council, headed by chairman Peter MacDonald, promised the protesters that the council would seek the rehiring, a civil rights investigation of employment practices, and a General Accounting Office audit of reported federal subsidy payments to Fairchild for the operation of the plant. MacDonald's offer defused the confrontation which ended peacefully, and without arrest. AIM national chairman John Trudell said that "The action was successful. Fairchild can no longer openly and quietly exploit Indian people." But the occupation became a symbol of an issue larger than 140 jobs: it signaled the arrival of AIM in the Southwest, and an escalation of resistance to energy development on Indian land.

Navajo chairman MacDonald had found himself in a difficult political position at the time. The University of Oklahoma engineering graduate had been elected to the tribal council post in 1970. Although he had taken a progressive position — supporting energy development, funding a 400-member Tribal Police Force, driving a Lincoln Continental, living in a luxury home — he had been forced by circumstances to oppose the government Hopi-Navajo Settlement Act because of the overwhelming sentiment on the reservation against the forced relocation of Navajo people. When Arizona Senator Barry Goldwater supported the legislation, MacDonald publicly denounced Goldwater, supported Democratic candidates such as George McGovern, and gained the support of the AFL-CIO union lobbyists against the legislation in return for allowing the labor organizers on to the Navajo reservation. MacDonald became a political enemy of arch-conservative Goldwater. The feud escalated to extremely hostile proportions, and Goldwater's influence dealt serious blows to the Navajo Tribal Council position in Congress.

When, in February of 1976, the U.S. General Accounting Office, the FBI, and the U.S. Attorney's office in Phoenix began an investigation of

Peter MacDonald, chairman of the Navajo Tribal Council,
has led what he calls the "modernization" of the Indian reservation,
signing lucrative coal and uranium leases on tribal land.
The traditional Indians call him "Peter MacDollars,
Shah of the Navajo." (Photo by Mark Lennihan/Gallup Independent)

Navajo Tribal Council finances, MacDonald charged that Goldwater had instigated the harassment. He claimed that "the CIA and FBI [were] being used for domestic witch hunting for political purposes. . . . The vindictiveness with which Goldwater has been attacking the tribe shows that he is not above doing anything which would do the tribe and myself in."[19] Goldwater wrote a letter to the *New York Times* denying Mac-Donald's charge, saying that "at no time did I have anything to do with it."

But Goldwater's influence was being felt, not only in the Senate, but in the internal politics of the reservation. Local BIA director on the reservation, Tony Lincoln, had attempted to put Joseph Patrick, an old National Guard service buddy and long-time friend of Goldwater's, on the BIA payroll. Personnel director for the BIA, Lee Shearin, told the *Navajo Times* that the first attempt to place Patrick failed, although Lincoln had mentioned that Patrick had a reference from Goldwater, because the applicant was not a registered civil servant. However, Lincoln eventually placed Patrick as a BIA-paid consultant for the Navajo Area School Board Association. MacDonald, caught between traditional Navajos' distrust of his lifestyle and energy development dealings on the one hand, and powerful political enemies on the other, lashed out at Goldwater and the BIA, accusing them of attempts to create "dissention within the council and to discredit the financial responsibility of my office." The federal investigation resulted in an indictment against MacDonald for submitting false travel vouchers to Tucson Gas and Electric Company, a reservation transmission line contractor. MacDonald claimed the indictment was a means of harassment, and he was acquitted by a federal judge in Phoenix.

In the spring of 1976, however, the *Arizona Republic* in Phoenix launched an investigation of their own into the sordid political affairs on the Navajo reservation. Investigative reporter Don Bolles, forty-seven, began researching the alleged relationships among Goldwater, Mac-Donald, AFL-CIO, the Mafia, the Mormon Church, coal and uranium companies, and other powers on the reservations of the Southwest. The research, however, was cut short one hot day in June of that year when Bolles was blown up by a bomb which had been planted under his car in a Phoenix hotel parking lot. Underworld figure John Adamson, thirty-six, was eventually arrested, charged, and convicted of planting the bomb that had killed Bolles. During his testimony, Adamson revealed that he had discussed the planting of the bomb with Goldwater's friend Joseph Patrick. He further testified that Patrick, in his capacity as a consultant

18. *Akwesasne Notes*; Late Autumn, 1976; p. 12.

to the Navajo school board, was, in fact, "a spy for Senator Goldwater, and reported directly to Senator Goldwater what happened on the Indian reservation, especially in regard to Peter MacDonald."[20] Adamson also revealed a plot to frame MacDonald by planting a non-exploding bomb in the car of Tony Lincoln, BIA director and Goldwater friend. Goldwater denied any connection to the bombing, and told the dead reporter's newspaper that Patrick was just a friend, not a spy. "He's no more informant," the *Arizona Republic* quoted Goldwater, "than if I might say, 'Joe, what happened on your last flight to Germany or your last flight to Saigon?' "

Hopi Kikmongwi (Spiritual leader), Dan Katchongva had died in 1972, passing on the role of traditional leadership to the other village Kikmongwis. David Monongye — known as Grandfather David — and younger interpreter Thomas Banyacya became the principal voices carrying the Hopi message out to the world. In the spring of 1976 Monongye sent an urgent appeal to all Indian People through the native journal *Akwesasne Notes*. He wrote: "Right now we Hopi are suffering the interference of industrial pressures on our people. Our poor land has always been of no real interest to the Bahanna, the Anglos. In the past ten years there has been more and more interest in our lands.

"This sudden interest comes as no surprise to those of us who still remember our ancient Prophecy. The Great Spirit told the Original People in the Beginning that this would happen. It was a grave warning. This is the Prophecy [from the Great Spirit, 'Massau'u']:

> Now you look upon me. I am a poor man. I have almost nothing. I have only my planting stick, my seed corn, and a jug of water. I live a simple life.
>
> If you wish to live like me, you must sacrifice many things. If you want me for your leader, your chief, you must prove that you can live this way of life.
>
> Now look around. See this land. It is poor land. There is not much water, and very few trees. But this is the richest land. There is a great wealth under. But hear this warning — you are not to disturb this land and take this wealth out as long as there is still war going on. If you do, these things will be used to destroy life and this will not be your salvation.

"Now there is a strip mine at our sacred Black Mesa, the Female

20. *Arizona Republic*; February 17, 1977.

Mountain. They are removing pure coal and burning it to make electricity for the big cities of the Southwest. Just recently, uranium has been discovered on our sacred lands.

"In order to gain access to this mineral, the federal government has a plan to forcibly remove all the residents from the land. These people are thousands of traditional Navajos who share this land with the Hopi.

"We know we must resist the removal of these people because, if they are not there to guard this sacred land, the miners will move in and destroy everything. They will use this uranium, which poisons everything, and cause death and misery for thousands of years. We who believe in the sacred instructions of the Great Spirit must resist and protest, for the sake of all life, both present and future."

Monongye and Banyacya carried the Hopi message to the UN on October 20, 1975 in the second prophesied attempt to contact the "World's Peoples" and as foretold, they were not recognized for the second time. Then on Sunday June 6, 1976 Banyacya fulfilled Hopi prophecy by delivering their message to the UN at the United Nations conference on World Habitat in Vancouver, British Columbia. The Hopi had arrived in late May, setting up a tipi camp in Vancouver's Jericho Park. They constructed a sacred fire circle there on the ancient spiritual grounds of Northwest Coast Indian people. The traditional name for the site was *Eealmu*, a ceremonial gathering point for the Salish, Cowichan, Haida, and other coastal Indian nations. For two weeks the Hopi conducted ceremonies and prepared for their presentation to the nations of the world. In the plenary hall of the conference Banyacya introduced four Hopi elders, blessed the meeting with sacred cornmeal brought from the Hopi mesas, and then delivered the spiritual message to the gathering. For the Hopi it was an event of great historical importance. What follows is an excerpted version of Banyacya's message:[21]

"My name is Banyacya of the Wolf, Fox, and Coyote clans, and a member of the Hopi Independent Nation. Today I brought two Hopi initiated religious leaders who were authorized by our Kikmongwis of the Shungpavy and Oraibi Pueblos, two of the oldest continually inhabited villages on Hopi land, to carry their sacred prayer feathers and message of peace, and the prophecies of warning for this day, as we were instructed by our ancestors. We have seen this destruction once before [when] mankind put more emphasis on material rather than spiritual

21. From the American Friends Service Committee reprint of the speech by Thomas Banyacya before the plenary session of the United Nations Conference on World Habitat; June 6, 1976.

things, when laws of nature were interfered with and ignored, and the world was destroyed. We do not want to see it happen again.

"The time has come to join in meaningful action. Destruction of all land and life is taking place and accelerating at a rapid pace. Our native land is continuing to be torn apart and raped of its sacredness by the corporate powers. We do have an alternative to this. Mankind has a chance to change the direction of this movement, do a roundabout turn, and move in the direction of peace, harmony, and respect for land and life. The time is right now; later will be too late. In order to do this, the Native People must return to the spiritual path as one to cure and heal our Mother Earth. It is only through the heart, prayer, and ceremony that we can bring this turbulence of evil to a halt.

"In 1948 the Hopi Kikmongwis and religious elders met for four days to compare and to remind each other of our ancient knowledge, most of which was kept in their sacred kivas. These men were around eighty, ninety, and one hundred years old, and they met in the circle, smoked their pipes, and meditated. They then delivered this knowledge for the first time in public. They talked of the present world from its creation, how we came to this land, how we spread throughout the land, how to take care of the land, and how the future will be if man again does not adhere to the spiritual balance in harmony with nature. Everything in the prophecies has been fulfilled, and I know they are speaking the truth.

"This message today is our third and perhaps final attempt to inform the world of the present status of man's existence on our Mother Earth. We come to fulfill Hopi sacred mission and ancient prophecy in order to find one, two, or three nations who should by now recognize their sacred duty to stop the destruction of the First People's land and life throughout the Western Hemisphere.

"The Hopi and all native brothers have continually struggled in their existence to maintain harmony with the Earth and with the universe. If land is abused, the sacredness of Hopi life will disappear, and all other life as well.

"It was known that the white man is an intelligent person, an inventor of many words and material things, a man who knows how to influence people because of his sweet way of talking. He would use many of these things upon us when he came. The white brother would do many things that will be good for our native brother. But when it becomes the sole purpose of getting control of this land, and he lives only for his own self-glory, then we must not listen to his sweet tongue, but watch his deeds. Those of us of the Hopi Nation who have followed the path of the Great Spirit without compromise have a message which we are committed, through our prophecy, to convey to you. The white brother, up to the present time, through his insensitivity to the way of Nature, has desecrated the face of Mother Earth. The white brother's advanced technological capacity has occurred as a result of his lack of regard for the spiritual path and for the way of all living things. The white brother's desire for material possessions and power has blinded him to the pain he has caused Mother Earth by his quest for what he calls 'natural resources.' And the path of Massau'u has become difficult to see by almost all people, even by the native First People, who have been forced into white brother's education systems and now have chosen instead to follow the path of the white brother.

"Today the sacred lands where the Hopi live are being desecrated by men who seek coal and water from our soil that they may create more power for the cities. It will destroy our Hopi and other people with smog, poison air, lack of water, and pollution of water and land. One example is sacred Hopi land in ruin all over the Four Corners area where Arizona, New Mexico, Colorado, and Utah meet in the United States. This area the Hopis call Tukunavi, and it is part of the heart of our Mother Earth and is a shrine and sacred place for the Hopi and other pueblos for many thousands of years. This desecration of our spiritual center must not be allowed to continue, for if it does, Mother Nature will react in such a way that almost all men will suffer the end of life as they know it. All we ask is that this place be respected and protected by all nations, who have sacred duty and responsibility.

"The United States and United Nations should understand that they cannot bring about peace and harmony or the good life in the world if they do not correct the wrongdoings going on within the American continent. The United Nations will never be able to reach its goals to bring about peace and harmony among all people, or make it in the future, if it does not at least support the Hopi and the other First Peoples of this land in their struggle for worldwide recognition and respect. The Hopi spiritual leaders invite world spiritual leaders to gather with them in Hopi land as soon as possible. They are waiting for you.

"To this point in time, our words have not been heeded by the nations of the world. This might be the last chance. If our words are not taken seriously, or are not heeded, only destruction will follow. We have done all the Hopi can do to notify the World's Peoples. If the people refuse to take action, the Hopi prophecy of total destruction of all mankind may be fulfilled as known to the Hopi spiritual Kikmongwis and religious headmen, who wait patiently in their sacred kivas on Shungpavy and Oraibi Hopi land with sacred stone tablets and spiritual instructions to receive all understanding beings in search for survival."

Black Mesa coal strip mine. Strip-mining is cheaper for the coal companies than shaft-mining, but in the fragile desert climate, topsoil may take hundreds of years to reestablish itself. (Photo by Lionel Delevingne)

At the time that Banyacya spoke, another Indian was in the same city of Vancouver under quite different but intimately related circumstances. Held in solitary confinement inside British Columbia's Okalla Prison, shackled twenty-four hours a day in leg irons, was thirty-two-year-old Ojibwa-Lakota Indian Leonard Peltier. Peltier, who had been arrested at the Fort Lawton occupation in Seattle in 1970, and who had been beaten up by the two Milwaukee policemen who tracked him down with FBI help following the Trail of Broken Treaties protests, claimed to be a political refugee on the FBI's Indian activist hit list. The FBI said he was a dangerous criminal, a killer. At the time of the UN Habitat Conference, British Columbia Supreme Court Justice William Shultz sat pondering whether to extradite Peltier to the United States and into the hands of the FBI, or to allow him political exile in Canada.

In the two years since the Wounded Knee trials dead bodies had continued to appear on and around the Pine Ridge reservation in South Dakota. Eventually two of those bodies turned out to be FBI agents, and suddenly the FBI and the U.S. Justice Department had a crime they felt worth investigating. The ensuing investigation, interrogation of witnesses, and trials would make the Wounded Knee trials appear tame in comparison. There would be many more dead bodies before it was all over, all of them Indians. Peltier's freedom hung in the balance of Justice

The San Juan power plant is operated by the Public Service Company of New Mexico, and is part of the vast Southwest power-generating grid. The National Academy of Sciences has declared the scarred and polluted San Juan Basin a "National Sacrifice Area." (Photo by Lionel Delevingne)

Shultz's mind. But more than that hung in the balance. Peltier claimed that he was a victim of the efforts of resource corporations to move onto Lakota land much as they had done on Navajo and Hopi land. Vancouver reporter David Garrick, writing in the *Georgia Straight*, called Peltier a "uranium refugee."

6

The Star-Spangled Archipelago

*As for us–how are we to make our way
through that rosy mist? Whom are we to ask
about it? Those who were shot aren't talking,
and neither are those who have been scattered
to the four winds.*   ALEKSANDR SOLZHENITSYN

B Y THE TIME AIM members had gathered in Farmington, New Mexico in the spring of 1975, the FBI operation, which came to be known as "Garden Plot," a domestic counterintelligence program to "neutralize" the American Indian Movement, had been somewhat successful. Informer paranoia, expensive and protracted trials, jails, and violent death had cut into the ranks of the movement. The FBI, however, concentrated their attention on the more visible men in the movement, an oversight that they would later correct. Shirley Hill Witt, an Indian woman working with the U.S. Civil Rights Commission in Denver, Colorado, wrote in a pamphlet published by Women of All Red Nations (WARN), "throughout the siege of Wounded Knee women organized, planned, provided support and material, and in effect gave continuity to the endeavor. . . . After the battle, the AIM men were arrested, neutralized, or eliminated by one means or another. The white male law enforcement officers, blinded by their own sexism, failed to recognize the power of the women, and that the heart and soul of the women would carry the movement forward."

The women offered some balance to the tough, macho image that AIM had acquired, and also brought attention to a broader range of issues in the overall Indian rights movement. The AIM women began investigating what appeared to be a massive drive to sterilize young Indian women, uncovered by Connie Uri, a Chocktaw-Cherokee doctor who had been approached by a twenty-six-year-old Indian woman looking for a "womb transplant." Discovering that the women had been sterilized at the age of twenty, Dr. Uri began investigating the records of the BIA-operated Indian Health Service Hospital in Claremore, Oklahoma. "At first I thought I had discovered a case of malpractice," she later said, but after reviewing the records she saw a larger, more frightening pattern. "I began accusing the government of genocide, and insisted on a congressional investigation. Unfortunately the study proved I was right."[1]

Dr. Uri discovered that 75 percent of the sterilizations at Claremont were non-therapeutic — that is, solely a form of population control. She discovered that Indian women were urged to sign consent forms they did not understand; they were misled into thinking the operations were reversible; and the consent forms were sometimes signed immediately after childbirth while the women were under sedation. Senator James Abourezk followed Dr. Uri's investigation by prompting a U.S. Government Accounting Office investigation which concurred that Indian Health Service sterilization programs were "generally not in compliance" with government standards requiring "informed consent," and that the sterilization programs had not "set forth as clearly as possible the fact that the procedures are irreversible."[2] Lakota Indian Barbara Moore testified later that during a caesarian child delivery "I was sterilized during the operation without my knowledge and without my agreement."[3] *Common Sense* magazine reported that the Indian Health Service was sterilizing 3,000 Indian women per year, 4 to 6 percent of the child-bearing population. Dr. R. T. Ravenholt, director of the federal government's Office of Population, later confirmed that "surgical sterilization has become increasingly important in recent years [as one of the] advanced techniques of fertility management." Further investigation by American Indian women would uncover an international sterilization program managed in part by Dr. Ravenholt's Office of Population. Ravenholt told the Population Association of America in St. Louis that the critics were "a really radical extremist group lashing out at a responsible program so that revolution will occur."

Anna Mae Aquash — the Micmac woman from Nova Scotia who had traveled to Boston and then to Wounded Knee, where she organized supply runs and stood security watches — became a central figure in the national AIM organization. The FBI would eventually bring her under close surveillance, but in 1974 and early 1975 she moved relatively freely throughout the United States and Canada organizing Indian resistance and transporting information too sensitive for the monitored phones or postal system. While she was working in the St. Paul AIM office helping with the Banks/Means trials an antagonism

---

1. *National Catholic Reporter*; May 27, 1977.
2. *Akwesasne Notes*, Early Winter, 1974; reprint from Robert McGarrah, Public Citizens' Health Research Group, Institute of Society, Ethics and the Life Sciences.
3. Ibid; Spring, 1979; translated from an interview appearing in the German magazine *POGROM*, January, 1979, Osnabruck, W. Germany.

had developed between Aquash and AIM security officer Doug Durham. Durham's treatment of women had seemed abusive to Aquash, and she began to grow suspicious of his motives. Durham had become the right-hand man to Dennis Banks, flying him to the United States from Canadian refuge in a private plane that he had secured, and controlling all financial donations coming into the St. Paul office.

In the fall of 1974 Aquash traveled to Los Angeles where AIM had opened an office and had begun to receive financial and organizational support from sympathizers in the movie and rock music industries, such as Marlon Brando and David Carradine. When Durham followed in early October Aquash became upset. She phoned the St. Paul office and pleaded that a national leader come to Los Angeles to mediate between Durham and the local leaders. She said she felt his presence was disruptive. In the first week of October Durham met with Paul Skyhorse at AIM Camp 13, in Box Canyon in Ventura County, north of Los Angeles. Skyhorse, an Ojibway from Minnesota, told Durham that he and Richard Mohawk, a Tuscarora from New York, were leaving soon for the National Indian Education Conference in Phoenix, Arizona. While at the AIM camp, Durham told several people that there were "plans to expose the racism of the sheriff's department," in Los Angeles, though he did not elaborate.

On the afternoon of October 10, after both Durham and Aquash had returned to St. Paul, Virginia de Luce, known at the AIM camp as Blue Dove, informed both Skyhorse and Mohawk of a demonstration in Los Angeles in support of Sarah Bad Heart Bull who was in jail in South Dakota following her Custer riot conviction. Blue Dove drove the two AIM leaders to the demonstration, which turned out to be not much of an event. There were very few Indians at the site, although a bevy of photographers showed up. That same evening several people who had been staying at the AIM camp departed for a reported party at TV star David Carradine's house, with Carradine's friend Lee War Lance. Marvin Red Shirt, from Pine Ridge; his girlfriend Holly Broussard, the daughter of Louis J. Broussard, a rich businessman and ex-Navy Commander from Long Beach; Marcella McNoise, with a serious felony record from Seattle; and Roland Knox, who said he was from Alaska, left for Carradine's Hollywood home in Broussard's car.

When they arrived at the house, no one was home. Knox left in Broussard's car, but the other four stayed, drinking until 10:00 P.M. Red Shirt, Broussard, and McNoise phoned for a cab. George Aird from the Red and White Cab Company arrived shortly thereafter, and began the drive back to Box Canyon. Somewhere along the way, the meter in the cab was pulled out, stopping at $6.00, and Red Shirt took over driving.

Back at the AIM camp the car was driven through the chain across the gate, and there at the camp cab driver George Aird was viciously murdered. He was stabbed seventeen times, his hair was cut off, and he was dragged around by a rope, and stuffed into a well near one of the tipis. Ventura County Police arrested Broussard and McNoise that night with bloodstains all over their clothes. The cab had been wiped down to eradicate fingerprints, but Red Shirt's fingerprints were discovered on Aird's body and on cab company papers found stuffed into an incinerator but not burned.

A week later, on October 17, Paul Skyhorse and Richard Mohawk were arrested by the FBI at the education conference in Phoenix, identified by photographs taken at the bogus Sarah Bad Heart Bull demonstration. The two AIM leaders were charged with the murder of Aird and held in the Ventura County jail without bond. The murder was reported in Los Angeles newspapers as a "ritual," and the AIM image in Southern California was seriously tarnished with imagery similar to stories of the Charlie Manson murders that had taken place in the same area and in a like manner. Doug Durham reported to the AIM leadership in St. Paul that AIM Camp 13 had seriously deteriorated, and that Skyhorse and Mohawk were probably guilty; he suggested that AIM disassociate itself from the crime. AIM took Durham's advice. Red Shirt, Broussard, and McNoise were given signed immunity agreements from prosecutors in exchange for testimony against Skyhorse and Mohawk who languished in jail without benefit of AIM legal help.

Then, on January 1, 1975, a group of Menominee Indians occupied the Alexian Brothers Novitiate, a 64-room monastery which had been virtually abandoned by the Catholic service order on a 225-acre estate near Gresham, Wisconsin. The Menominee Nation had been terminated by Congress in the 1950s, but a Menominee Restoration Committee had been established, and they were negotiating with state and federal authorities to return some of the lost land and restore the status of the tribe. The protesters claimed that the Alexian Brothers estate was Indian land. Again, both Durham and Aquash showed up at the site of the occupation, and again, Aquash suspected Durham of being a troublemaker. Durham operated a communications center from a hotel room, but before the end of the occupation — which resolved peacefully with an agreement by the Alexian Brothers to sell the Indians the abandoned monastery for $1.00 — Durham left abruptly. AIM leaders, still using the hotel room as a communications center, later discovered men with recording equipment in the room next door.

In February of 1975 AIM leaders discovered that Harry "Gi" and Jill Shafer, who had been inside Wounded Knee and had volunteered to help

with the ensuing legal work, were FBI operatives. The Shafers had
infiltrated the Students for a Democratic Society (SDS) in 1969 and later
worked in the Red Star Collective, a bogus Communist group which
served as an FBI front. Then, in March, AIM lawyers obtained FBI
papers released through court order in one of the Wounded Knee trials.
Among the papers was a report to the FBI signed by Doug Durham. On
March 7 Durham was confronted in St. Paul by AIM leaders and lawyers
with copies of the incriminating documents.

Durham, who had worked his way into a national leadership role with
AIM, told AIM lawyers and then the national media of his long history as
an undercover agent. After a stint in the Marines he joined the Des
Moines, Iowa police force. He was fired from that job in 1964, allegedly
because of his underworld connections which involved prostitution and
the fencing of stolen goods. He became a master burglar and a pilot, and
in 1971 began working as an agent for the Law Enforcement Intelligence
Unit of the National Law Enforcement Assistance Administration,
under the Department of Justice. In 1973 his assignment to Wounded
Knee required that he pose as part Indian, so he obtained brown contact
lenses to cover his gray eyes, dyed his hair black, and began passing
himself off as "one-quarter Chippewa." After Wounded Knee he
worked at displacing Des Moines AIM leader Harvey Major, and then
moved into a close relationship with national AIM leader Dennis Banks.
During the two years that Durham spied on AIM he received $1,000 per
month from the FBI, usually in cash.[4]

Perhaps fearing an AIM reprisal, Durham appeared apologetic upon
his exposure. He told AIM attorneys, "I turned 180 degrees: I also
believe that I changed the attitudes of a few FBI agents toward the
American Indian Movement. . . . After two years with AIM it's my
opinion that the American Indian Movement is a viable, legal, social
organization and if something is to be investigated they should start with
the BIA, Department of Interior, the land leases, oil rights, and possibly
really the FBI." He added, "I wish I was half the man that Dennis
[Banks] is." On March 12, Durham, accompanied by AIM leader Vernon Bellecourt, told his story to the press at a news conference in St.
Paul.

However, once out of the clutches of AIM, Durham performed another 180-degree turn. He went on a nationwide John Birch Society
speaking tour in the summer of 1975 during which he told conservative
audiences that AIM was "Communist controlled," and a "threat to
freedom." He also showed up again in Los Angeles to testify at a sanity

4. *New York Times,* March 13, 1975.

trial for Paul Skyhorse, claiming to be an Indian professor of clinical psychology from the University of Iowa, who knew all about the Indian mind. Skyhorse, previously abandoned by his Indian compatriots, had been forced into the damaging sanity trial by his court-appointed attorney, Kenneth Cleaver. Cleaver also represented Marvin Red Shirt for whom he had negotiated the immunity agreement in exchange for testimony against Skyhorse and Mohawk.

The exposure of Durham alerted AIM to re-examine the Skyhorse-Mohawk case. They soon came to the conclusion that the two AIM leaders had been framed, because of the prosecution's obvious lack of interest in bringing Red Shirt, Broussard, and McNoise — arrested on the night of the killing, covered in blood — to trial. Later court testimony revealed that not only Durham, but Blue Dove, the woman who had lured Skyhorse and Mohawk to the demonstration, was also an FBI agent. Blue Dove, a white, fifty-six-year-old ex-movie actress who had married Chicago Mafia figure Ricky Riccardo, had infiltrated AIM Camp 13 disguised as an Indian and claiming to be a Mohawk.

By the time these revelations became public, however, the damage had already been done; AIM had been seriously discredited in Southern California, a major source of financial support. While in prison Skyhorse and Mohawk complained of frequent beatings and forced drug use. The two were held in isolation cells, often in handcuffs and leg shackles. They told lawyers that they were chained to their bars, beaten and maced. They were given Thorazine and Stellazine and an experimental drug known as Millaril. After winning the right to represent themselves in court, they were held in the same cell so that they could work on their case. Skyhorse kicked his addiction to the drugs, but Mohawk had a more difficult time, suffering from the cramps and vomiting of withdrawal.

Eventually lawyers Wendy Eaton, Leonard Weinglass, Skip Glenn, Diane Orr, and Jack Schwartz took up the case, filed a $2 million civil rights suit against the prosecution for conspiring to solicit perjured testimony, and won the release of Skyhorse and Mohawk. The two AIM leaders had spent four years in jail before being found innocent after trial by jury. Red Shirt, Broussard, and McNoise were never brought to court for their roles in the murder. Juror Mildred Gable wrote later in a defense committee pamphlet that it seemed obvious that the cab driver had been killed by the three riders. "He was no match for his three joy-riding passengers," she wrote. "In the final chapter of the cab driver's life, if others were indeed involved, the evidence . . . was not there." Hank di Suvero, president of the National Lawyers Guild, commented on the case: "In a fundamental way the acquittals demonstrated that a basically unfair and repressive judicial system can be overcome when there is a confluence of popular support and resistance and thorough legal work." Jack Schwartz, a lawyer on the case, said, "The FBI urged the local Sheriff's Department to charge Skyhorse and Mohawk, and to let the three people found at the scene of the crime covered in blood go free. Two weapons — knives — were recovered, but one was supposedly lost on the way to the police station and the other one supposedly melted in the police lab. One of the knives was traceable to Holly Broussard, the white little rich girl. The case was really a media campaign — 'radical Indians,' 'ritual murder,' and all that — and it worked. But the defense strategy was that the case was a frame-up, to financially damage AIM. We proved it; it came across as a vendetta. Although the law doesn't actually recognize frame-ups; that is, the court would never officially accept the decision that the FBI framed somebody, the jury bought it; they understood."

The exposure of Durham and Blue Dove, like the revelations of FBI misdeeds during the Banks/Means trial, did little to check the FBI domestic surveillance and disruption campaigns. In South Dakota "Support Your Local Police" posters went up showing a gun-waving Indian, a big headline that read: "AIM for Communism," and announcing public speaker Eugene Rooks, "a genuine modern Indian . . . [speaking] in defense of his people and against the criminals who are trying to victimize them." The speaker on this interstate tour — sponsored by the "Support Your Local Police Committee" — was a Dickie Wilson protegé from Pine Ridge Reservation.

On February 27 three Wounded Knee lawyers — Roger Finzel from South Dakota, Martha Coplemen from New Jersey, and William Rossmore from Connecticut — flew into the Pine Ridge airport in a private plane piloted by Rossmore. They were accompanied by legal aides Eda Gordon and Kathi James. They left the plane in the airport, and spent several hours driving throughout the reservation interviewing witnesses in relation to their client Bernard Escamilla, twenty-eight, who was still facing charges stemming from the Wounded Knee occupation. When the lawyers, aides, and Escamilla returned to the plane, they found it riddled with bullets. They unloaded the plane and packed their car in preparation for the one-hour drive into Rapid City. However, before they could leave, fifteen cars sped into the parking lot, surrounded them, and goon squad gunmen leapt out, holding them at shotgun point. The five investigators and Escamilla locked themselves in their car, but the goons slashed open the convertible roof and smashed the windows.

According to a statement which the six people filed with police and the press, Dickie Wilson himself appeared at the side of the car. Referring to Finzel, one of the goons asked Wilson: "What do you want us to do with him, Dick?" Wilson's reply, as told by the lawyers and reported in the *Rapid City Journal* the next day, was: "I want you . . . to stomp 'em."

According to the lawyers' statement: "Occupants were pulled from the car and stomped, kicked, and pummeled to the ground. Others took turns kicking and stomping, while one goon slashed out at Finzel's face with a knife, cutting his hair and Eda Gordon's hand as she attempted to shield him."[5] Escamilla was the most severely beaten; he spent two days in a Rapid City hospital. Finzel, Rossmore, and Gordon were treated for multiple concussions and released.

The Associated Press version of the story quoted only Wilson and BIA administrative manager Wayne Adkinson. Wilson said: "What I can gather, mostly through rumor, is that it was a group of AIM people led by Russell Means. They shot at the airplane and also at two of our vehicles and then headed east." Adkinson's contribution to the AP syndicated story was that "since we have no data, we can't assign the blame to anyone."[6] Both U.S. Attorney William Clayton and the FBI were notified of the incident by the six victims who identified the assailants. There were no arrests.

North of the Pine Ridge on Highway 44, just across the reservation line, sits the small town of Scenic, South Dakota. Scenic consists of a general store selling auto parts and Indian jewelry to tourists, and a bar. The Longhorn Bar services local ranchers and reservation Indians. The floors are covered with a thick layer of sawdust; horns and skulls of cattle hang from the wall with trinkets and cowboy memorabilia; and the bar stools are made from milk cans and tractor seats. At the end of the bar is a small men's bathroom. There in that bathroom on the evening of March 1, 1975 Martin Montileaux was shot by a hidden assailant: he died six days later.

Montileaux had lived in Kyle, on the reservation. Some traditionals suspected him of having worked with Wilson and with the FBI. Before he died he described his assailant in a taped interview with Pennington County Deputy Sheriff Don Phillips. He told Phillips that the man who shot him was hiding in the bathroom and that he had been shot as he entered. The killer had "shaggy hair," and wore a "green coat." AIM leaders Russell Means and Richard Marshall, twenty-four, an officer in the pro-traditionalist Pine Ridge Committee for Better Tribal Government, were arrested in the early hours of March 2, and charged with

5. *Rapid City Journal*, February 28, 1975.
6. Ibid.

killing Montileaux. On March 3, the FBI issued a "Predication for Investigation of Members and Supporters of AIM."[7]

The FBI memo, issued from Washington, D.C., stated that "This investigation is based on information which indicates the subject is engaged in activities which could involve a violation of title 19, U.S. Code, Section 2383 (Rebellion or Insurrection) or 2384 (Seditious Conspiracy). . . . AIM has been actively involved in demonstrations and violent confrontations with local authorities . . . " Wounded Knee lawyers reported that at least twenty AIM leaders throughout the country were arrested within twenty-four hours, some of them supposedly in connection with the Montileaux slaying. According to the lawyers the FBI round-up was part of a "national offensive against AIM people in the wake of a civil war on the Pine Ridge reservation." In Denver, Bill Means and five others were arrested, and charged with possession of marijuana. South of Rapid City Herb Powless, executive director of the American Indian Council on Alcoholism in Milwaukee, was arrested with six other persons, and charged with illegally carrying a gun across state lines.

It was at this time that the goon squad shot up Matthew King's home, leaving the seven bullet holes in the walls. The *Rapid City Journal* said on March 4, the day after the shooting, that the BIA police "were not available for comment." However, Ted Means told the newspaper, "The attack on the Kings' home cannot be written off as another assault of one side against another on the Pine Ridge reservation. It is not a matter of AIM-Goon conflict. It is a direct attack on traditional Indian people and traditional Indian ways, and on their claims of sovereignty of the Great Sioux Nation." King said: "When that David Price came around, he said he wanted to find out who shot at my house. Ha! He knew who did it; he was probably with 'em. I told him to get off our land."

On March 21, Edith Eagle Hawk, her four-month-old daughter, and her three-year-old grandson were killed when their car was forced from Highway 44 between Scenic and Rapid City. Edith Eagle Hawk was a defense witness for Jerry Bear Shield who had been charged with shooting Wilson goon William Jack Steel. The driver of the car that struck the Eagle Hawk car, Albert Coomes, a white rancher, was also killed. Eugene Eagle Hawk, who survived the crash, said a second occupant of the car was goon squad member Mark Clifford. Police reports made no mention of the second occupant.

At approximately 1:00 A.M. on March 27 Jeanette Bissonette, sister-

7. Federal Bureau of Investigation, internal memo, March 3, 1975.

in-law of slain Oglala Sioux Civil Rights leader Pedro Bissonette, was shot and killed by sniper fire while on her way home from the wake of her friend Stacey Cottier, who had been shot a week earlier. Shootings, stabbings, beatings, and arson continued. Senator Abourezk made the comment that "Pine Ridge reservation is being run like Hitler's Germany." The town of Pine Ridge and the BIA offices there had been like an armed fortress since the Wounded Knee siege. Although FBI agents moved freely and frequently between Pine Ridge and the South Dakota FBI office in Pierre, none of the assaults reported by victims, witnesses, and lawyers led to arrests or convictions. Armed FBI agents were seen daily in Pine Ridge.

AIM leaders Leonard Peltier and Anna Mae Aquash, both of whom had traveled to the AIM convention in Farmington in the summer of 1975, returned to Pine Ridge to help the local people. Peltier set up a camp near the town of Oglala on the property of Lakota elders Harry and Celia Jumping Bull. Three other AIM men — Joseph Stuntz, Dino Butler from Oregon, and Peltier's cousin Bob Robideaux — lived at the camp with Butler's wife Nilak, several teenagers, and a few small children. The FBI had a map with the camp marked on it. Although Peltier, Aquash, and a few other AIM leaders had avoided the FBI round-up in March, they would soon be found. AIM leaders were well aware that their ranks were being systematically thinned by the FBI; documents later released by the Bureau through Freedom of Information suits would verify the fact.

The Department of Justice, created by Congress in 1870, received a budget of $50,000 in the following year for investigating and prosecuting federal crimes. In 1906 the department formed its own private Bureau of Investigation, which allied with Chicago businessman A.M. Briggs in 1917. Briggs was the founder of the anti-labor vigilante organization, the American Protective League, which had helped Justice Department investigators track down draft evaders, and had been accused of assassinating labor leader Frank Little in Montana. After World War I, in 1919, Attorney General A. Mitchell Palmer led the Justice Department in a crackdown on suspected "aliens who are members of the anarchistic classes."[8] He was assisted in his efforts by twenty-four-year-old Justice Department investigative lawyer J. Edgar Hoover. On the night of January 2, 1920, ten thousand people were arrested across the country in what became known as the notorious Palmer Raids. The questionable

8. *FBI*, Sanford J. Ungar, Atlantic-Little Brown, Boston, Mass., 1976; p. 42. For a complete history of the FBI, see this book

conduct of the agents in the fields brought accusations against the Justice Department that its investigators were out of control. Palmer replied that "alien agitators" were seeking to destroy U.S. homes and religion, and that if "some of my agents . . . were a little rough or unkind . . . I think it might well be overlooked." It was.

In the 1960s the FBI turned its attention to the civil rights movement among Southern blacks. Released FBI documents reveal that in 1961 the FBI passed information about two Freedom Rider buses to Thomas Cook, a Ku Klux Klan member in Birmingham, Alabama. In 1963 Hoover's chief aide, William Sullivan, suggested that the FBI find and support a black leader "to take [Martin Luther] King's place." King became a central target of the FBI. The FBI Counterintelligence Program, known inside the bureau as COINTELPRO, sought to "prevent the rise of a 'messiah' who could unify and electrify the militant black nationalist movement."[9]

In the 1970s the FBI turned its COINTELPRO agents onto the New Left, and when traditional Indians began protesting, the FBI turned its attention to AIM and its leaders. One FBI memo released through the Freedom of information Act recommends a "full investigation of local AIM chapters, its leaders and members," and adds that "Any full investigation involves a degree of privacy invasion and that of a person's right to free expression." After the exposure of Durham, an FBI document states: "As a result of certain disclosures regarding informants, AIM leaders have dispersed, have become extremely security conscious and literally suspect everyone."[10]

FBI documents also reveal that "friendly" media were used extensively against AIM as they had been used to discredit Martin Luther King and other black leaders. The use of the media took two forms: the manipulation of information to the general media, and the feeding of stories to the willing, cooperative media. In 1978 the National Lawyers Guild published a list of national media that had cooperated with the FBI COINTELPRO operations.[11] That list included the Hearst Newspaper chain, Associated Press (N.Y.), *New York Daily News, Chicago Tribune, Milwaukee Journal, Los Angeles Examiner, U.S. News and World Report, Arizona Daily Star,* other newspapers, and radio and television stations. An FBI memo dated March 13, 1973 outlines how a Seattle radio reporter, Clarence McDaniels, was used as an unwitting

9. FBI Memo, "Airtel to SAC, Albany," c. 1968; reprinted by National Lawyers Guild in *Counter-intelligence*, January, 1980.
10. FBI Memo, Re: "American Indian Movement, Investigative Techniques," c. 1975.
11. *Public Eye*, National Lawyers Guild, Washington, D.C., April, 1978.

informer during the Wounded Knee siege. McDaniels was sent to Wounded Knee by Seattle radio station KIXI and used by UPI because he was trusted by the Indians whereas the UPI reporter was not able to gain that trust. Little did McDaniels know, however, that KIXI was working in league with the FBI. The memo from Washington, D.C. headquarters to the Minneapolis field office reads: "McDaniels is expected to continue furnishing complete coverage of activities at Wounded Knee to KIXI by phone and tapes. He will be requested to do a special story on Seattle area participants. He is unaware that his stories are not being publicized in full or that the intelligence information and his tapes are being furnished to the FBI. KIXI officials request he not be contacted at Wounded Knee; however, if any specific information is needed by FBI, KIXI is willing to pass on the request as normal duty assignment with no reference to FBI."[12]

The military–FBI siege at Wounded Knee was later revealed as part of the Defense Department domestic counterinsurgency plan code-named Garden Plot. In 1975, Reporter Ron Ridenhour, who had exposed the My Lai massacre story, exposed Garden Plot in *New Times* magazine. The plan involved military training for state and local police units in preparation for suspected domestic insurgency uprisings. The martial law network included the FBI, Army, Navy, Air Force, Marines, Coast Guard, Federal Marshals Service, Highway Patrol, Special Weapons and Tactics (SWAT) teams, and riot police. Domestic war games were held in California, Oregon, Washington, and Arizona under the direction of the Pentagon. The plan seemed frightening to some members of Congress when the details were first exposed to public scrutiny. Claire Burener, congressman from California, called Garden Plot "subversive." Britt Snider, an investigator with Senator Frank Church's Select Committee on Intelligence, said that "If there ever was a model for a takeover, this is it." Wounded Knee was the first opportunity for the Pentagon to actually take the revolution war games into the field. According to Watergate casualty John Ehrlichman the Pentagon wanted to go "full scale." He wrote that U.S. Marshal Wayne Colburn had wanted to attack the village. "Colburn was for going in strongly," wrote Ehrlichman in a letter to Marlon Brando. "He apparently authorized the marshals to return fire, and on a given night, thousands of rounds would be fired." The paramilitary SWAT teams and marshals that made up the Garden Plot troops were trained at the Marine Corps Reconnaissance

12. FBI Memo, Headquarters to Minneapolis, teletype, March 3, 1973, Re: "Media, KIXI, Seattle, Washington."

Commando School, Camp Pendleton, California; the Military Police School at Fort Gordon, Georgia; and at the FBI National Academy in Quantico, Virginia.

In June of 1975 approximately forty FBI agents were transferred into the South Dakota area, all of them stationed in or around Pine Ridge. Among them was Jack Coler from Colorado who carried on him a map of the various known or suspected AIM houses and camps on the reservation. Also in the squad of agents was Ron Williams who had collaborated with Special Agent David Price in soliciting perjured testimony against Banks and Means from Louis Moves Camp. On June 25, 1975 young AIM supporter Jimmy Eagle visited the home of his friend Teddy Paul Pourier. Two white farm hands, Jerry Schwarting, twenty-three, and Robert Dinsmore, fourteen, arrived, and the four stayed up late, drinking. During the course of the evening an argument ensued, and one of the white youths later complained to the BIA police that Eagle had stolen his cowboy boots. On the morning of June 26, FBI agents Coler and Williams drove two cars toward Oglala; they carried high-powered rifles, several hundred rounds of ammunition, and the AIM camp map. Their official reason for being on the reservation was to serve a warrant on Jimmy Eagle for the alleged crime of stealing the white boy's boots. They drove directly to the home of Harry and Celia Jumping Bull. For a few minutes they chased a red pickup in which they may have expected to find Eagle who had been known to drive a similar vehicle. After losing the pickup they stopped a quarter mile from the Jumping Bull residence. Garden Plot was soon to have another domestic crisis to rescue.

The two agents had stopped their car in the late morning; a few hours later, by 2:30 P.M., Coler, Williams, and an Indian man, Joe Stuntz, were dead from rifle fire. Within the next twelve hours the FBI had released nationwide press statements dealing solely with the deaths of the two agents who they claimed were "executed" in an "ambush." National news media, for the most part, cooperated with the FBI version of the incident which was issued through the offices of South Dakota Governor Richard Kneip and Attorney General William Janklow. United Press International (UPI) was the first to respond with a wire bulletin in the early hours of June 27. They reported:

OGLALA, S.D. — (UPI) TWO FBI AGENTS WERE AMBUSHED AND KILLED WITH REPEATED BLASTS OF GUNFIRE THURSDAY IN AN OUTBREAK OF BLOODSHED APPEARING TO STEM FROM THE 1973 OCCUPATION OF WOUNDED KNEE.

THE OFFICE OF SOUTH DAKOTA GOV. RICHARD KNEIP SAID THE AGENTS, ON

THE OGLALA SIOUX RESERVATION TO SERVE A WARRANT, WERE SUCKED INTO AN AMBUSH, DRAGGED FROM THEIR CARS, AND SHOT UP TO 15 TO 20 TIMES WITH AUTOMATIC WEAPONS.

THE FBI CONFIRMED THE REPORT. AN AGENT SAID: ''THIS IS A REGULAR COUP DE GRAS [sic] BY THE INDIANS.''

THE AGENTS WERE TAKEN FROM THEIR CARS, STRIPPED TO THEIR WAISTS, THEN SHOT REPEATEDLY IN THEIR HEADS.

Associated Press (AP) report was similar:

OGLALA, S.D. (AP) TWO FBI AGENTS WERE DRAGGED OUT OF THEIR CARS WHEN THEY TRIED TO SERVE WARRANTS ON PEOPLE WHO WERE HOLED UP IN A HOUSE ON THE PINE RIDGE RESERVATION, GOV. RICHARD KNEIP SAID EARLY TODAY.

Neither wire service nor the FBI mentioned the dead Indian, Joe Stuntz.

Attorney General Janklow told AP, ''It looked like an execution. They were riddled with bullets.''[13] The *Rapid City Journal* quoted Kneip, Janklow, and FBI ''authorities on the scene.'' They reported that the FBI had said ''the two men were lured into an ambush . . . as many as 30 persons were waiting in the house when the agents arrived.'' Across the country headlines proclaimed that the agents had been brutally slain by Indians. The *San Diego Union* headline read TWO FBI AGENTS SLAIN AT WOUNDED KNEE. The *New York Post* declared SOUTH DAKOTA INDIANS KILL TWO FBI AGENTS. Stories told how the agents had been attacked from ''sophisticated bunkers,'' and had been ''stripped to the waist,'' before being ''executed.''

One newspaper, however, broke ranks with this official FBI story during the first twenty-four hours after the fire fight. The *Minneapolis Tribune*, familiar with AIM-FBI relations since the early days of the AIM Patrol, checked out the story with several other sources, and offered a measured headline: ''Indians, FBI, exchange fire in S.D.; three dead.'' Otherwise, the media images conjured up for mass-mind consumption were dutifully delivered from the FBI through willing state authorities, by the national media to the people. The impression that was overwhelmingly created was one of savage, violent Indians attacking innocent white people who were just trying to do their job of keeping the peace. AIM national chairman John Trudell said later, ''The FBI would

13. *Rapid City Journal*; June 27, 1975.

have us believe that their agents were out there picking flowers for their grandmothers when the wolves got them."[14]

The area was immediately cordoned by the FBI; media representatives were kept away from the Jumping Bull complex and FBI publicist Tom Coll was brought in from Washington, D.C. headquarters to provide the media with the official version of the story. That official version underwent some revision as details from the first FBI statements were exposed as being untrue. Joel Weisman, working for the *Washington Post,* was turned back from the area at gunpoint by an FBI agent. Weisman, his journalistic instincts aroused by the aggressive secrecy of the FBI, continued to investigate the case, and eventually exposed many of the FBI lies in an article in the *Columbia Journalism Review*[15] One of the first falsehoods exposed was the fact that the agents who were supposedly serving warrants on people in the Jumping Bull house, had no warrants in their possession, a fact confirmed by the U.S. Civil Rights Commission. It was also later proven that Jimmy Eagle, the subject of the phantom warrants, was not at the house, but was staying with his grandmother, Gladys Bissonette, in Pine Ridge. Coll, speaking for the FBI, was forced to revise the Bureau's position on that issue, and he announced that although the agents had no warrants in their possession, "they were trying to effect an arrest under a warrant," that had supposedly been issued.

The U.S. Commission on Civil Rights launched an investigation of the FBI reports, concluding that "Media representatives felt that the FBI was unnecessarily restrictive in the kind and amount of information it provided. It is patently clear that many of the statements that have been released regarding the incident are either false, unsubstantiated, or directly misleading." By the time FBI Director Clarence Kelley gave a press conference in Los Angeles on July 1, he had dropped the ambush theory; he admitted that Williams had removed his shirt to make a tourniquet for Coler's arm, and had not been "stripped to the waist" by the Indians; and he acknowledged that the agents had not been "shot 15 to 20 times," but had received a total of three wounds each. Later inspection by newspeople proved that there were no "sophisticated bunkers" in the area. The entire execution story was a lie.

After the shooting had begun, SWAT teams and other FBI marksmen who had been stationed around the reservation swept into the area, surrounding the AIM camp and the Jumping Bull house. Helicopters

---

14. Radio Station KGNU, Boulder, Colorado, March 19, 1980.
15. Joel D. Weisman, *Columbia Journalism Review*; excerpted in *Akwesasne Notes,* Early Autumn, 1975.

swarmed overhead. On Saturday, June 28, the *Rapid City Journal* revealed that on the day of the shootout Dickie Wilson and the tribal council completed long-standing negotiations with the Department of Interior concerning the gunnery range land. The paper said: ''The Oglala Sioux Tribal Council . . . gave approval to an agreement with the National Park Service which will allow expansion of the Badlands National Monument into scenic areas of the Pine Ridge Indian Reservation. . . . The expansion involves approximately 133,300 acres.'' Unknown to all but a select few at the time, the land in question held rich deposits of uranium and oil. Traditional Oglalas concluded that the fire fight had been instigated to provide cover for the land transfer. John Trudell said later: ''FBI agents armed with M-16's came onto the Pine Ridge reservation to serve a warrant that they didn't have on someone who wasn't there; they were accompanied by over fifty highly trained military marksmen, also with high-powered automatic weapons. These agents opened fire on a small house in which men, women, and children were asleep. Leonard [Peltier] and the others returned fire, creating cover as the people fled to safety. On that very same day, Dickie Wilson gave one-eighth of the Pine Ridge reservation to the U.S. government. Now, common sense tells us that something very unusual is going on.''[16]

According to Norman Brown, who was fifteen at the time, he and Joe Stuntz were sitting in the AIM camp waiting for breakfast when they heard shots being fired at the Jumping Bull house. He said they then ''ran up to this one hill to see what was going on, and the first thought that came into our minds was our women and children. . . . We ran back and got Dino [Butler] up there. Dino told our sisters to look for a way out, and while we were there for a while, we were all surrounded . . . you'd hear planes and stuff like that, and there were some [agents] coming from the other side of our camp . . . we saw Ivis and Angie [Long Visitor] with their kids running out with them.''[17] Brown said that Stuntz told him ''This is a time to be a good warrior,'' and sent him around to guard one side of the house while the women and children and older people ran out. While they were separated Stuntz was killed. Nilak Butler gathered some of the young people together, but there was no visible escape route. ''They told us the place was surrounded,'' said Brown, ''so we got together and started praying. We formed ourselves into a circle and as we were praying [we] saw this eagle come down, so we felt strong again.'' The party followed the eagle, taking it for a sign. As they climbed a hill behind the camp they could hear rifle fire falling all

16. KGNU, op. cit.
17. Norman Brown, affidavit, February 5, 1977.

around them. The children, women, and older people moved ahead into the trees, while Brown, Butler, Bob Robideaux, and Leonard Peltier maintained a rear guard. Brown's canteen was hit by a bullet as they climbed. By nightfall the party of about fifteen people had evaded the SWAT teams and the helicopters; miraculously slipping through the FBI dragnet, they traveled for four days and nights until they arrived at the spiritual camp of Leonard Crow Dog, one hundred miles to the east, on the Rosebud Reservation.

Pine Ridge was under siege once again. Richard Held, second to Clarence Kelley in charge of the FBI, arrived in South Dakota with new Special Agent in Charge, Norman Zigrossi, and between one hundred and two hundred paramilitary agents. This heavily armed "investigative" force included, according to the U.S. Civil Rights Commission report, FBI agents, BIA police, SWAT teams, armored personnel carriers, helicopters, fixed-wing aircraft, and tracking dogs. Commission Chairman Arthur Flemming called the ensuing investigation "a full-scale military-type invasion of the reservation . . . without due process of law . . . creating a climate of intimidation and terror."[18]

The story of thirty people who supposedly ambushed the agents had changed within a few days; Coll told reporters that they were looking for sixteen men in connection with the shootout. The suspect list reportedly contained three hundred fifty names. The Civil Rights report called the investigation a vendetta. Associated Press released a story which said: "FBI agents are seldom killed in the line of duty. When they are, it provokes feelings of outrage among other agents." The AP story quoted an FBI agent as saying, "We'll stay here as long as it takes to round up the people that did this. It may take a while, but we won't rest until we have them in custody." According to the Civil Rights report: "In the days immediately following the incident there were numerous accounts of persons being arrested without cause for questioning, and of houses being searched without warrants. One of these was the house of Wallace Little, Jr., next door to Jumping Bull's. His house and farm were surrounded by eighty to ninety armed men. He protested and asked them to stay off his property. Eliot Daum, an attorney with the WKLO/DC who had been staying in the house with the Little family, informed the agents that they had no right to search without a warrant. They restrained him and prevented him from talking further with Little while two agents searched the house."

---

18. Arthur S. Flemming, letter from the U.S. Civil Rights Commission to Attorney General Edward Levi, July 22, 1975. Also see *Wasi'chu*, Bruce Johansen and Roberto Maestas, Monthly Review Press, New York, 1979; p. 96.

At the Crow Dog camp spiritual ceremonies were taking place, as the traditional supporters pondered a way of spiriting the party of fugitives from the clutches of the FBI. Shep Gurwitz, whose brother had been serving as a lawyer for Indian cases, was at the camp. "I didn't know anything about the Indian issues when I went there," he recalled later, "but I learned fast. I just watched; I sat up on the hillside and watched the ceremonies, and praying. It was pretty intense. I saw a lot of fear, but I also saw a lot of courage; I saw young guys getting ready to be warriors. I heard Crow Dog pray and sing; I didn't know what was going on, but I knew it was serious. This one big big guy was very friendly to me, I guess we just sort of liked each other. He told me what was happening. I saw this .38 in his belt, and I thought 'There's no way!' What was that .38 going to do against those squads, those companies of troops, M-16s, helicopters. I had been in Vietnam — airborne — I'd seen all this before. I *was* one of those guys, and I knew what they could do. Those guys are top-of-the-line soldiers, highly trained. They go where they want; they can take a building down and kill everyone in it in twenty minutes — no .38 is going to stop them. I looked down at the ceremonial fires, and I knew that Crow Dog was doing the right thing. Prayers were the only thing that was going to help anybody get past those troops out there."

In the meantime, the FBI continued its sweep of Pine Ridge, visiting virtually every town and remote settlement on the 2.5-million acre reservation. Matthew King recalled a visit to Fools Crow's house by FBI agent David Price: "That Price fellow came to Fools Crow's place with another agent, I think it was that Woods [special agent William Woods]. Price asked Fools Crow a lot of questions, then he asked him, 'Do you know who killed the two agents?' Fools Crow just sat there real calm, and he said 'Yes.' Well, Price went crazy; boy, he jumped up and said 'Wait a minute, wait a minute,' and he ran out to his car, and came back in with a tape recorder and his briefcase. He got all set up, then he asked Fools Crow again: 'Do you know who killed those two agents?' and Fools Crow said 'Yes.' And Price was really excited, and he said: 'Well, then, will you tell me who it was?' and Fools Crow said: 'Yes, it was you. You killed 'em. You are the ones who brought the guns in here to our land. You are the ones who are trying to steal our land, and bringing agents around here with guns to keep the people in fear. You killed the agents, and a lot of other people too.' Well, that Price was really mad — the other one, that Woods guy, laughed — but Price was really mad. Oh boy, he stomped out of the house; you've never seen anything like it."

Two months after the fire fight, the FBI had netted only one suspect: Jimmy Eagle had turned himself in on July 9. Eventually, however, they made their way to the Crow Dog camp where they unleashed the full fury of their massive investigation. On September 3 a white man, Robert Beck, and a part-Indian, William McCloskey, came to the Crow Dog land and got into a fight with Crow Dog's nephew, Frank Running. Crow Dog had had a previous experience with strangers starting trouble on his land, so he stayed out of the conflict as several people evicted the two men from the premises. Then, at approximately 5:00 A.M., September 5, Norman Zigrossi, David Price, and fifty-four armed FBI agents entered the Crow Dog camp with a warrant for Crow Dog, accusing him of assault. The agents were looking for an indictable suspect in the June 26 shooting. Norman Brown, Dino Butler, and Anna Mae Aquash were all in the camp on the morning of the raid.

Brown later told lawyers: "I was sleeping. . . . They called out 'Hands up! This is the FBI.' One grabbed my hair; he said 'All right, [obscenity], lay down,' so I layed down, and they searched me and put an M-16 to my head. They said 'Who killed those two agents!' I told them I didn't know, so they picked me up; they pushed me with an M-16 in my back. . . . As we were standing there, these women who weren't even dressed yet, [were] crying. . . . Then they brought Leonard Crow Dog out, and he had nothing on."

Aquash later told lawyer Candy Hamilton: "They just came in and . . . raided, or busted or just pillaged . . . they were just all over the place dumping things, and just tearing things apart. . . . They came over and put a pair of handcuffs on me and took me into the house and searched me . . . [they] told me they were going to charge me with illegal possession of . . . dynamite. I could hear things crashing inside the house . . . they seemed to be having an awful lot of fun, you know, they seemed to be enjoying themselves." Aquash said that they were apparently looking for evidence, but that they destroyed religious objects such as medicine bags, pipes, feathers, and beadwork.

"While I was standing there with a group of women, waiting, I was just being brutally harassed by some of the agents. They were implying that they had been looking for me for a long time . . . they were accusing me of a number of things that I have not done . . . I just knew that I was being arrested . . . finally I hear helicopters going round up in the air; I could hear all the radio messages going back and forth and the agents were coming over and asking me questions over and over again."[19]

Brown was released, but Crow Dog, Butler, Aquash, and four others were arrested and taken to the federal building in Pierre, one hundred miles to the north. Aquash told of being taken to a third-story interroga-

19. Anna Mae Aquash, in affidavit to Lawyer Candy Hamilton; September 10, 1975.

tion room where she was questioned by David Price. "He started talking about the June 26 incident," she said. "He started referring to other things that had absolutely nothing to do with me and kept insisting that I used to live there where the incident took place, and I kept insisting that I had never lived there, and he just wouldn't believe me." Price, who had solicited the false testimony from Louis Moves Camp, was an expert FBI interrogator. The method that the FBI was using on prospective witnesses was to frighten them with serious felony charges, then offer them a deal if they would give information on other suspects. By hinting that Aquash had lived at the Jumping Bull camp, the agent was leading her along a suggested story line, one that she could follow if she so chose. Dino Butler reported later that an agent told him that day that he could "either cooperate and live, or not cooperate and die." But Butler and Aquash, experienced and fearless, refused to submit to the intimidation. Aquash told Hamilton that Price had threatened that if she did not help name some suspects she would be "dead within a year." She answered that "You can either shoot me or put me in jail. That's what you're going to do to me anyway."[20] Aquash was told later that she would be charged not with possession of dynamite, but with possession of an illegal firearm found at the Crow Dog camp. Her bail was set at $5,000. It was later reduced to $500 when the magistrate learned that she had not actually been indicted, and she was eventually released on bail. Butler and Crow Dog were held.

The FBI agents who had earlier released fifteen-year-old Norman Brown, returned to his home in an attempt to solicit testimony from him implicating others in the shooting. Agent Charles Harvey took Brown and his mother into a trailer used by the FBI as a mobile interrogation center. Brown requested that his lawyer, Jack Schwartz, be called, but Harvey refused. According to later testimony by Brown and his mother, Harvey told the youth that he would "never walk the earth again" if he refused to cooperate. Harvey told Brown that he faced two counts of first degree murder, and he told Mrs. Brown that the FBI had one of the guns that her son had supposedly used to kill the agents. Brown later testified: "My mom started crying . . . she kept telling me to talk, and I told her no. They . . . handcuffed me. I was standing there and he said 'We'll do everything in our power to see that you rot in hell.' They told my mom that she would never see me again. They kept saying 'Leonard Peltier.' They kept saying he and Dino killed the agents. They kept saying 'why are you protecting these cold-blooded killers?' " After a six-hour interrogation Brown was again released. He later compared

20. FBI summary of interrogation, *Minneapolis Tribune*, May 30, 1976.

experiences with Aquash who told him: "They are going to kill me, Norman."

Bob Robideaux was arrested on September 20, after his car had exploded on Interstate Highway 35 north of Wichita, Kansas. Arrested with Robideaux were Kamook Banks, wife of Dennis Banks, sixteen-year-old Navajo Mike Anderson, and four others. The adults were held on $75,000 bond; Anderson was interrogated for twenty-four hours without a lawyer, and in much the same manner as Brown had been.

In the meantime, Dennis Banks had fled underground after Prosecutor William Janklow had won a guilty verdict against him for his presence at the Custer riot of 1973. In that trial three defense witnesses refused to testify for fear of reprisals by the goon squad. Banks, out on bond and fearing for his life inside the South Dakota prison system, did not appear for sentencing. His bond was revoked, and a bench warrant was issued for his arrest. Likewise, Peltier and Aquash had fled underground in fear for their lives. Russell Means and Richard Marshall were facing murder charges for allegedly killing Martin Montileaux. AIM National Chairman John Trudell had been charged with assault with a deadly weapon after he had fired a pistol into the roof of a white-operated trading post in Owhyee, Nevada. The FBI certainly could have made the claim by the autumn of 1975 that their avowed campaign to "disrupt, misdirect, discredit, or otherwise neutralize," groups considered to be a threat to the U.S. "internal security" had worked in the case of AIM.

In explaining his action Trudell said: "What I did was to confront a man who was exploiting the people with high prices and racist attitudes . . . and I discharged a firearm in a public building — and that is all I have done. I do not deny it. I did it with the intention of getting at two issues. Who is going to bring these people under control, these people who flagrantly violate the law and rob our people? (and) who has jurisdiction? The tribe can't take this man to court for his practices, because there is a law protecting him from that.

"FBI agent Jack Neal told the press this was 'not a political crime,' that I was drunk at the time . . . perpetuating the racist stereotype of a drunken Indian. . . . This is an important thing, because it goes right back to the situation in Oglala, South Dakota. This goes back to the vigilante witch-hunt that the FBI, through its lies and smear tactics, justified to the American public.

"It is just my personal feeling," Trudell added, "but many [U.S. citizens] are going to have to accept some of the blame too, because it's their federal government . . . the white Americans are guilty of apathy and self-indulgence to the extent that they have allowed inhumanity to thrive."

As the FBI consolidated their version of the June 26 shoot-out — their original thirty ambushing Indians, later reduced to sixteen, had become four: Butler, Eagle, and Robideaux in custody, and Peltier at large — they continued to provide information for the prosecution of Marshall, Means, and Crow Dog. The prosecution of Crow Dog proved to be one of the more transparently invidious campaigns to undermine traditional Indian leadership. Crow Dog, from his youth, had accepted the path of the medicine society; he was regarded by his Brule-Lakota people as a healer and spiritual leader. Crow Dog's reputation, however, had spread beyond his home on the Rosebud reservation. In 1972 AIM leaders Means and Banks had visited Crow Dog to establish a spiritual direction for the Indian Rights Movement. At Wounded Knee Crow Dog had become known as a calming, clear force, diffusing anger and frustration, and helping the older medicine people maintain the spiritual direction of the action. In this capacity, Crow Dog had become an important link between the Medicine Societies and the Warrior Societies — *Pejuta* and *Akicita* in the Lakota language — of the many Indian nations that had banded together in the modern Indian land rights and treaty rights movement from Maine to California, from the Northwest territories to Chile. The warriors were called upon by circumstance to physically defend their nations; the medicine people were ordained by tradition to maintain the spiritual direction of those nations.

Crow Dog was first brought to trial in U.S. courts for his involvement in an incident on March 11, 1973 during the siege of Wounded Knee. On that day six men entered the Wounded Knee village, four of them claiming to be postal inspectors who were there to "examine the post office in the trading post." The men were detained and searched, and found to be carrying pistols and handcuffs. Two were suspected goons, and photographs later showed them toting guns on a Dickie Wilson roadblock. Crow Dog was among a group that disarmed the men and sent them away. After Wounded Knee Crow Dog was arrested and charged with assault and robbery. He was brought to trial in August of 1975 before Judge Edward McManus in Cedar Rapids, Iowa in a case prosecuted by Richard Hurd whose earlier negligence, obstruction of justice, deceit, and prejudicial prosecution had caused Judge Fred Nichol to dismiss charges against Banks and Means. Hurd found Judge McManus more cooperative, allowing the prosecutor to enter hearsay accusations against Crow Dog into the court record, and showing open disdain for the defendant and his attorneys. Crow Dog was convicted of "aiding and abetting" an assault, interfering with a federal official, and robbery, for which he received a three-year and an eight-year sentence. Because he had no previous convictions, Crow Dog was released on a five-year probation which stipulated that he was forbidden to "consort with militant Indian types." After the two-month trial, with the two jail terms hanging over his head, Crow Dog returned to the Rosebud Reservation.

A month later, in November, Crow Dog was brought before Judge Robert Merhige on new "aiding and abetting assault" charges stemming from the September 3 conflict with two tresspassers on his land two days before the FBI pre-dawn raid on his camp. On November 28, he was convicted and sentenced to five years in federal prison; his earlier probation was revoked. During that trial the home of his parents, Henry and Mary Gertrude Crow Dog, was set ablaze in a midnight arson attack. The elderly couple escaped, but the house was destroyed. In the meantime Crow Dog was swallowed by the U.S. federal prison system. He was first incarcerated in the federal prison in Sioux Falls, South Dakota, transferred to Wichita, Kansas and then to Lewisburg, Pennsylvania — all this for being present while two troublemakers were evicted from his property.

Not satisfied, the government brought a third charge against Crow Dog in January of 1976, again prosecuted by Hurd before Judge Merhige. The charges stemmed from an incident on March 25, 1975 when three white men, previously unknown to Crow Dog, visited his home. Crow Dog, his wife, Mary, and other witnesses claim that the men were drunk and aggressive. Author Richard Erdoes (*Lame Deer, Seeker of Visions*, 1972), a friend of the Crow Dog family, described the incident: "One of [the white men], Royer Pfersick, makes a crude pass at Mary . . . in full sight of everybody. Crow Dog tells him: 'This is my home, a medicine man's home. You can't do this here.' Pfersick answers, 'Who in the hell are you, telling me what to do?' He hits Crow Dog and splits his lip. A relative and a visitor take Crow Dog's part, and Pfersick is finally thrown out after a free-for-all."[21] Pfersick filed charges, and the case was taken up by Hurd. The prosecutor told the jury: "Ladies and gentlemen, we have a good system going here in this country. The government is here to protect you. I am here to protect you."[22] After presenting three witnesses who corroborated parts of Pfersick's story, Hurd told the jury that Pfersick was not "beaten because he made a pass at Crow Dog's wife. He was beaten because the Indians thought he was an informer!" The jury returned a verdict of guilty on all charges. Crow Dog was given a sentence to run concurrently with his other two. He was returned to the prison system where he was

21. *Akwesasne Notes*, Early Spring, 1976, p. 12.
22. Ibid., p. 13.

transferred to various places around the country. He first spent two weeks in the hole at Terre Haute maximum security penitentiary in Indiana; he was later transferred to Richmond, Virginia; Rapid City, South Dakota; and Leavenworth, Kansas. Inside the prison system Crow Dog became well known and well liked among the prisoners. He wrote in a letter to his wife; "They took me to Leavenworth, the grandfather of all prisons. The inmates knew about me. They took each other by the hand through the bars and began to shout: 'CROW DOG! CROW DOG!' Some white, some Indian, some black, were praying for me, praying for an Indian medicine man."

Richard Erdoes recalled that his friend Crow Dog lost forty-five pounds in the two weeks at Terre Haute, and in Richmond a medical examiner told Crow Dog that they had found a brain tumor, and that he would need an operation. Crow Dog phoned Erdoes and asked: "Richard, can they do this to me? Cut into my brain without my consent?" The National Council of Churches, the World Council of Churches, the U.S. Civil Rights Commission, and Amnesty International took up Crow Dog's case. He avoided brain surgery, but remained in prison until paroled on March 21, 1977.

"The medicine people teach by example," says Matthew King. "They are always peaceful in every way, and teach by good example. But, if that doesn't work, then the warrior — *Akicita* — comes forward. But the white people don't understand what an Indian warrior is — an Indian warrior never fights just for fun or to show how brave he is. The warrior only fights to protect the people. The warrior is always the first to help and the last to eat. When the time comes that the people have to be protected, there is no one braver than the Indian warrior; they are all ready to give their lives if that is necessary."

The warriors, however, facing a vindictive FBI, had been scattered. Banks, Aquash, and Peltier were all being sought on fugitive warrants by November of 1975 when the FBI named Robideaux, Butler, Eagle, and Peltier in a single indictment, charging them with the murder of the two dead agents. The bureau had launched a massive international search, putting Peltier at the top of their "Most Wanted" list. If they ever lost it, the FBI picked up Aquash's trail on the West Coast, and followed her to Kitsap County, Washington. According to later FBI reports released in court, two informants told the FBI that Aquash, Banks, and other fugitives would be leaving Port Madison Indian reservation in Washington. FBI agents flew over the reservation and photographed vehicles on November 8, 1975. They continued their surveillance through November 13 when a Dodge Explorer Motor Home and a white 1970 Plymouth station wagon left the reservation and entered Oregon. The

vehicle traveled southeast along Interstate Highway 80, stopping for gas
on November 14 in Baker, Oregon, about eighty miles from the Idaho
border. The FBI issued an all-points bulletin describing the occupants of
the vehicles as "armed and extremely dangerous. . . . If vehicle is
sighted, do not stop, but advise FBI, Portland, immediately for more
details." The FBI planned to follow the vehicles to their destination,
hoping to be led to more AIM people, but their plan was frustrated by
overzealous Oregon State Trooper Kenneth Griffiths. At 10:30 P.M. one
mile from the Idaho border, Griffiths decided to stop the vehicles. At
gunpoint four adults and a child exited from the two vehicles and were
forced to lie face-down on the pavement. They were Russell Redner,
twenty-nine; Kenneth Loud Hawk, twenty-one, cousin of the slain
Wesley Bad Heart Bull; Aquash; Kamook Banks, twenty, eight months
pregnant, and her two-year-old daughter.

As Griffiths waved his shotgun over their heads the motor home
moved half a mile down the road. Griffiths later testified that at least one
and perhaps two men leapt from the van and fled into the night. Griffiths
fired at the men and claimed that one shot was returned. The FBI were
soon on the scene, and they announced the following day that the two
men who allegedly excaped were Peltier and Banks. Although there was
no proof that the escapees had even existed, and certainly no evidence of
their identity, the FBI named Peltier and Banks in an indictment with
Loud Hawk, Redner, Aquash, and Kamook Banks. The six were
charged with possession and transportation of destructive devices and
firearms. On the morning following the arrests, the FBI alleged that they
had found six cases of dynamite, but in court they reported that the
dynamite had been destroyed because it had been too dangerous to
keep. Kamook Banks was returned to Kansas to face weapons charges
stemming from her September 10 arrest there; Aquash was returned in
chains to South Dakota where she was brought before Judge Mehrige
and the familiar prosecutor Hurd to face charges stemming from the
September 5 raid on Crow Dog's camp; and Loud Hawk and Redner
were detained in Oregon.

The FBI was still looking for witnesses who could or would corrobo-
rate their version of the June 26 shootout. While being transferred from
eastern Oregon to Portland, Loud Hawk was offered a deal by an FBI
agent. He told reporter Tom Bates of the *Oregon Times* that the agent
said: "If you tell me who did it [killed the agents], we could make a deal.
Transportation of firearms is a very serious charge." Loud Hawk refused to cooperate with the FBI in their search for testimony against
Peltier and the others. He and Redner were held on $50,000 bonds,
although neither of them had any previous criminal record. Redner had
been working with the United Indian Health Service in Eureka, Califor-

nia and in the Native American studies program at Humboldt State College in Oregon; he was a Vietnam veteran with an honorable discharge and seven service medals. The Oregon trials would ramble on for years, charges being dismissed in 1976, then reinstated and returned to Oregon by the Ninth Circuit Court of Appeals in San Francisco in 1979. Loud Hawk and Redner remained in jail for 110 days before being released on bond. Lawyers Michael Baily and Jack Schwartz claim that the charges were used to intimidate the AIM leaders. Linda Coelho, a volunteer who helped at the defense committee office, testified in court that an FBI agent visited her home in Portland and said to her: "I want to know how you and your family want to be buried."

In South Dakota Anna Mae Aquash was released on bond after appearing before Judge Mehrige. However, she failed to reappear in court, once again fleeing underground in fear for her life. She phoned her sisters in Nova Scotia, telling them that she was afraid the FBI was going to kill her, and that if anything happened to her, her sister Mary should take care of her two young daughters. Although weapons charges against her were dropped, Mehrige issued a bench warrant for her arrest, for failure to appear in court.

On February 24, 1976, rancher Roger Amiott found a decomposing body in a riverbed on the northwest corner of Pine Ridge reservation and called the police. He reports that BIA police arrived within twenty minutes. Also present was FBI agent David Price. The body was taken to the Pine Ridge Public Health Hospital, where BIA pathologist W. O. Brown performed an autopsy; he concluded that the woman had died from exposure. The hands were severed by Brown. Price sent them to FBI headquarters for identification, and the body was buried immediately in an unmarked grave. The death warrant read "Jane Doe." No one had been called in to attempt an identification of the body.

A week later the FBI discovered from the fingerprints that the dead woman was Anna Mae Aquash. After the FBI notified the family of the death, Aquash's sister Mary was suspicious of the exposure theory advanced by the BIA pathologist. She requested, through AIM lawyers, an independent autopsy. On March 11 the body was exhumed and examined by Dr. Garry Peterson of Minneapolis. His report: "On the posterior neck, 4 cm. above the base of the occiput and 5 cm. to the right of the midline, is a 4 mm. perforation of the skin. . . . Surrounding this is an area of reddish discoloration measuring 5 × 5 cm. Removed from the brain is a metallic pellet . . . consistent with lead."[23] Aquash did not die from exposure; she was murdered at close range with a .32 caliber

23. Dr. Garry Peterson, reprint by Women of All Red Nations, Porcupine, South Dakota, 1977.

handgun. Aquash was reburied in a traditional ceremony on March 14.

Senators Abourezk and Edward Brooke of Massachusetts contacted the Justice Department, the FBI, and Attorney General Edward Levi, urging an investigation of the FBI's behavior in the case, and of the misinformation provided by BIA pathologist Brown. The Canadian government asked the Justice Department for an "urgent investigation" of the killing of a Canadian citizen. The U.S. Civil Rights Commission concluded that "there is sufficient credibility in reports reaching this office to cast doubt on the propriety of actions by the FBI, and to raise questions about their impartiality and the focus of their concerns." The commission found that hospital personnel who first received the body "suspected death by violence because of blood on her head," and they found the failure of Dr. Brown to discover the bullet during his autopsy "incredible."

Dr. Brown told the *Washington Star* that "a little bullet isn't hard to overlook. It certainly isn't the first time a bullet was overlooked. . . . AIM is trying to stir up all the trouble they can. There's a lot of agitation by them and they're trying to wring every bit of publicity out of it that they can. It is a matter of record that Indians use every little incident that they can to create a situation. . . . They distort facts and use it to their advantage to further their cause."[24]

The FBI denied responsibility for Brown's oversight, and refused to comment on the actions of Price and other agents involved in the investigation of the case. FBI Director Clarence Kelley told Senator Brooke in a letter: "The FBI cannot account for the decisions of a medical doctor. We can only accept those decisions which we are given. . . . Dr. Brown's decision was accepted because our agents on the scene could not determine, through initial examination of the body, that any evidence of a gunshot wound . . . existed."

Like Pedro Bissonette before her, Aquash would have been a defense witness, countering the government's cases against those charged with the murder of the two FBI agents. According to defense lawyers, she would have testified that David Price had solicited false testimony from her, and that he had threatened her if she refused to cooperate. No court has ever questioned Price concerning his interest in the body of an unidentified Indian woman when hundreds of such cases had gone uninvestigated in the past. The *Washington Star* story called the killing of Anna Mae an "execution-style slaying," and said that the "curious manner in which federal authorities handled the case . . . has raised serious questions about the conduct of the FBI." FBI Special Agent in

24. *Washington Star*, May 24, 1976.

charge of the South Dakota region, Norman Zigrossi, admitted that agent Price, who had known Aquash well, had photographed her body but failed to identify it.[25]

Before her death, Aquash told lawyer Candy Hamilton that she had been very upset at the way the FBI had destroyed religious objects during the raid on Crow Dog's Camp, and at the way they had ridiculed her and other women for praying in jails and for carrying medicine bundles. "The FBI don't have any respect for these articles," said Aquash. "I think it is a very serious matter when it touches on these objects because it definitely shows that they have absolutely no respect for a religion or a belief that another nation has, and that is very discriminating, that's very racist. They don't have the ability to just allow someone to believe something that's totally different. . . . I have seen that there is something that is disturbing the agents very much. They are very frustrated or angry or there is something wrong some-where. It is not only the raid that they seem to be interested in; there were a lot of other things about Indian people in general that they are very, very concerned with. The American Indian Movement: they are very concerned with that, and I think it's not just arresting those that they went there to arrest, because they included a lot of other things: the religious items that they took, and their ridicules and remarks that were made which are totally unnecessary. I think it's a very serious thing that's coming out, it's very, very serious. I think that they most de-finitely want to destroy a nation. . . . I think that they definitely are out to destroy their own concept of freedom."

Norman Zigrossi told the *Rapid City Journal* that the FBI was con-tinuing its investigation into the death of Aquash, but no suspects were ever named. The FBI advanced the theory that perhaps AIM had killed her; an FBI spokesman told the *Rapid City Journal* that "some members of AIM might have suspected that Miss Aquash was a government informer."

Both Dennis Banks and Leonard Peltier, in the meantime, had been tracked down by the FBI. Banks was arrested in El Centro, California on January 24, 1976. He fought extradition back to South Dakota on the grounds that if returned he would be killed. After Banks won his case, allowing him to remain free in California, South Dakota Attorney Gen-eral Janklow was furious. He accused California Governor Jerry Brown of "providing a haven for our outcasts."[26]

25. *Rolling Stone*, April 7, 1977.
26. *Rapid City Journal*, April 7, 1981.

Peltier had fled to Canada where he traveled to the traditional camp of Cree Chief Robert Smallboy. In 1968 Smallboy had left the Hobbema reservation near Edmonton, Alberta, and had established a self-sufficient traditional settlement near the North Saskatchewan River in remote western Alberta. There, the FBI tracked down Peltier with the aid of an informer and the Royal Canadian Mounted Police (RCMP). He was arrested on February 6, 1976, and brought to Vancouver, B.C., where he was held in Okalla Prison under maximum security, awaiting an extradition hearing. The U.S. government was requesting that he be returned to face five charges: for the attempted murder of the cop in Milwaukee in 1972 which was later proven to be a frame-up; for the murders of the two FBI agents at Oglala; for the attempted murder of Oregon trooper Kenneth Griffiths who stopped the two AIM vehicles in Oregon; and for a burglary which took place in Oregon shortly thereafter. It was an impressive list of charges.

Peltier, on the other hand, represented by Vancouver lawyers Donald Rosenbloom and Stuart Rush, sought political asylum in Canada. His case was based upon Section 21 of the Canadian Extradition Act which stipulates that a fugitive is not liable to surrender to another country if the alleged offense is of political nature. Vancouver City Council Alderman Harry Rankin reviewed Peltier's case and then stated publicly in a defense committee newsletter that ''to deport Leonard Peltier to the United States in these circumstances is the same as deporting a political refugee to some brutal fascist country where he would face immediate death.''

On May 3, the extradition hearing opened before Justice W. A. Schultz, with Canadian Department of Justice lawyer Paul William Halprin representing the U. S. government. On May 11 the defense was shocked when Halprin presented an affidavit from a woman who claimed to be Peltier's girlfriend.[27] Myrtle Poor Bear, a woman unknown to Peltier, claimed in the affidavit that she had traveled with Peltier to the Jumping Bull camp in May 1975. (Peltier did not arrive at the camp until June, after his trip to the AIM convention in Farmington.) The Poor Bear affidavit continued: ''When Peltier arrived, he gave orders on what was to be done. He and others began planning on how to kill either FBI, U.S. government police, or BIA agents who might come into the area. Peltier was mostly in charge of the planning. . . . That day [June 26] Leonard Peltier came into the residence of Harry Jumping Bull and said 'They're coming.' I understood that to mean that police or agents of the FBI were in the immediate area.'' Poor Bear's affidavit

27. *Vancouver Sun*, May 12, 1976.

then went on to tell how she heard shooting, went outside, and found Peltier holding the two agents at gunpoint: "Peltier was facing a man I believed to be an FBI special agent. . . . This man threw a handgun to the side and said something to the effect that he was surrendering. Leonard Peltier was pointing a rifle in the direction of this man. The man was holding his arm as if wounded and was leaning against the car. There was another man who I believed to be an FBI special agent lsing down on the ground and there was blood underneath him. . . . I turned around and saw Leonard Peltier shoot the man who was standing."

In addition to this detailed "eyewitness" account, Halprin entered affidavits from BIA policeman Marvin Stoldt and FBI agent Frederick Coward who claimed to recognize Peltier as the killer, having seen him through their rifle telescopes. Halprin read a total of eighteen affidavits, two from Poor Bear and sixteen from FBI agents and BIA police, outlining the government's version of the events of June 26.

The startled defense launched an investigation but was unable to discover anything about the mysterious Myrtle Poor Bear. One person, however, knew all about Poor Bear; he had made the affidavit available to the U.S. government, which had in turn made it available to Halprin. That person was none other than FBI agent David Price.

Price first contacted Poor Bear, twenty-four, living on the Pine Ridge reservation with her five-year-old daughter, in February 1976, shortly before the body of Anna Mae Aquash was found. Throughout February and March Price and agent William Woods met with Poor Bear at her home and at least once at the Hacienda Motel in Gordon, Nebraska.[28] Their purpose in holding her there, according to her subsequent testimony, was to use her as a witness in the trials charging Richard Marshall and Russell Means with the murder of Martin Montileaux. In February Poor Bear signed three affidavits, naming Peltier as the killer of the two agents, the last two of which were presented to the Vancouver court. The first affidavit she had signed, withheld from the Vancouver court, stated that she had not actually witnessed the shooting, but that Peltier had later confessed to her.

On March 22, after a three-day stay in the Hacienda Motel with Price and Woods, Poor Bear was turned over to state authorities as a witness in the Marshall trial. (Means was tried later, which proved to be in his favor in this case.) Poor Bear was held in custody until April 2 when she testified against Marshall. As with Peltier, she claimed to have been Marshall's girlfriend, and told the court that he had confessed to her at a party that he had "followed Montileaux into the restroom of the Long-

28. FBI hotel receipts, signed by David Price, March 21 and March 29, 1976.

horn Bar in Scenic and shot him."[29] On that evidence Marshall was convicted on April 6, and sentenced to life imprisonment.

In Vancouver, the Peltier defense knew nothing of these events, although they suspected something similar. They presented a case of political harassment and government misconduct in relation to Indian activists in general and Peltier in particular. Vernon Bellecourt testified that $750,000 in bail bonds had been posted by AIM members in recent months. Sixty-nine-year-old Agnes Lamont, whose son Buddy had been killed at Wounded Knee, told the court that Pine Ridge reservation was being run by a "puppet" government, and that there had been twenty violent deaths of traditional Indians already in 1976, none investigated by the FBI. John Trudell related the story of the death of Anna Mae Aquash, and told how the FBI had drawn AIM into violence and then persecuted the leadership throughout the country. Trudell's testimony led Canadian External Affairs Minister Allen MacEachen to request the investigation of Aquash's death and the FBI's involvement.

When Peltier took the stand on Thursday, May 13, he asked the court to grant him political asylum in Canada. He said: "We were happy with the land that was originally left with us. But over the years, more and more of our land was stolen from us by the Canadian and United States governments. We were left with what white society thought was worthless land. . . . White society would now like to push us off our reservations because beneath the barren land lies valuable mineral and oil resources. This is why I am standing here today before this court in shackles. What I ask this court is: Will the Canadian system of justice and its authorities, knowing of these abuses, be used as a tool of the corrupt American state. I am asking this court and this country to grant me political asylum."[30]

Each day, outside the courtroom, Indian and white supporters of Peltier gathered, chanting, praying, handing out literature to passers-by, and cheering Peltier as he made brief appearances during his transfer from court to prison. Peltier would walk through a cordoned area, surrounded by RCMP officers, with his hands chained to his waist and leg irons hobbling his step. He would smile at his supporters, dip his head down, and confidently raise one shackled fist above his bowed head. Among his supporters, Peltier counted Homer Stevens, president of the local United Fish and Allied Workers Union; Vancouver Alderman Rankin; other politicians, labor leaders, and professionals; stu-

29. *Rapid City Journal*, April 3, 1976.
30. *Vancouver Province*, May 14, 1976.

dents, and B.C. Indian people. His presence in Vancouver served as a rallying point for local Indian grievances. By the time Judge Schultz recessed the court to ponder Peltier's fate — in June, when the Hopi delegation presented its message to the UN Conference in Vancouver — Peltier had become the most well-known political prisoner in Canada.

Concurrently, Peltier's co-indicted defendants Robideaux and Butler were being tried in Cedar Rapids, Iowa. During the proceedings, the contradictory affidavits of Myrtle Poor Bear surfaced, as did a memo from the FBI to local law enforcement agencies accusing AIM of plotting ten violent crimes including the assassination of South Dakota Governor

AIM leader Leonard Peltier in custody of Royal Canadian Mounted Police in Vancouver, British Columbia, 1976. Peltier was extradited from Canada to the United States on evidence later proven to be phony.
Convicted of two counts of first-degree murder under highly curious and unusual circumstances in Fargo, North Dakota, Peltier was sent to Marion Federal Penitentiary where a plot to murder him inside the prison system failed. His lawyers claim to be in possession of evidence that proves he was framed by the FBI. (Photo Copyright © 1976 by The Vancouver Sun*)*

Richard Kneip. What became known as the "Dog Soldier" Memo, issued in May 1976 from FBI headquarters in Washington, claimed that "AIM members who will kill for the advancement of AIM objectives have been training since the Wounded Knee incident in 1973. . . . These Dog Soldiers, approximately 2,000 in number . . . are undergoing guerrilla warfare training experiences."[31] The memo, sent to FBI offices throughout the country, accused AIM of plotting to blow up the state capital in Pierre, South Dakota; snipe at tourists; assault the state penitentiary in Sioux Falls, South Dakota; and pull off other violent guerrilla attacks. Perhaps in an effort to undermine the work of Senator Abourezk who had been seeking congressional review of FBI activities in South Dakota, the memo named his son, Charles, as being "involved with the Dog Soldiers." FBI Director Kelley, subpoenaed by the defense in Cedar Rapids, testified that there was no evidence upon which to base any of the accusations in the memo. The memo, used to stir up FBI and police sentiment against AIM, was a completely fabricated creation of the FBI.

Trudell said of the Cedar Rapids trial: "We were able to show the jury that the FBI had instigated a program to neutralize AIM. We were able to show the local media that the FBI version of the June 26 shoot-out was a lie. We developed a lot of support in Cedar Rapids. The judge wanted to hear the story, so we told him. The jury had no choice but to acquit Butler and Robideaux." The two denied shooting the agents, and testified that their actions on June 26 were solely in defense of the women and children who were fleeing the camp. They were acquitted on July 17, 1976.

In the meantime, a post-conviction hearing in the Marshall case revealed the contradictory affidavits of Myrtle Poor Bear, and the involvement of Price and Woods in obtaining them. Medical records were also presented which showed that Poor Bear had a record of 105 recent clinical and hospital admissions for "bizarre behavior," "psychosis and depression," and other physical and mental anomalies. Her father, Theodore Poor Bear, testified that she "makes up stories and other things."[32] Myrtle herself later testified that agents Price and Wood showed her photographs of the body of Anna Mae Aquash; she said they told her "if I didn't do what they said I'd be dead like Anna Mae Aquash . . . they kept reminding me I'd end up like Anna Mae."[33] She told reporter Jim Calio of *People* magazine that they threatened her and her

31. FBI Memo, "Internal Security," # 281785Z, May, 1976.
32. *Win Magazine*, December 1, 1980.
33. Myrtle Poor Bear, testimony before the Minnesota Citizens Review Commission, February, 1977; videotape by Karen Northcott.

daughter. She said, "I signed the papers without reading them; all I wanted was to go home."[34]

With the affidavits of Poor Bear proven phony, the prosecution could not use her against Butler and Robideaux, nor could she be used to convict Means who was eventually acquitted on the charge of killing Montileaux. Dick Marshall, however, remained in prison, as did Peltier, awaiting the decision of Justice Schultz. On June 18, Schultz ruled that the U.S. government had presented enough evidence to warrant Peltier's extradition. The extradition order would have to be executed by Canadian Justice Minister Ron Basford; Peltier was held in solitary confinement at Okalla prison.

On December 18, 1976 Basford signed the extradition order, and Peltier was delivered into the hands of U.S. authorities. In the meantime, charges against Jimmy Eagle had been dropped when it was proven that he had not been at the Jumping Bull complex on June 26, but had been at his grandmother's home in Pine Ridge. Prosecutor Hurd had already supplied two witnesses — prisoners Melvin White Wing and Gregory Clifford — who were willing to testify that Eagle had confessed to them in their jail cell. Eagle himself said later that he was pressed to testify against Butler, Robideaux, and Peltier, but that he refused. When charges against him were eventually dropped, Butler and Robideaux having been acquitted, Peltier became the last available suspect upon whom the FBI could pin the deaths of their agents. Peltier was held in Fargo, North Dakota, while awaiting trial. The victory in Cedar Rapids had given his defense committee confidence that they would win in Fargo. The Cedar Rapids trial had brought out evidence of FBI harassment of witnesses, tampering with evidence, brutality, perjury, infiltration of the defense, the COINTELPRO conspiracy, and the FBI "Dog Soldier" Memo against AIM leaders, the awesome military assault on Pine Ridge on the day in question, and a general FBI obstruction of justice. What had originally been described by the FBI as an ambush on June 26, 1975, had been exposed as a violent diversion from the land deal that Dickie Wilson signed with the Interior Department on that very day.

But the FBI has a way of recovering from such setbacks. The entire force of the FBI vendetta against AIM was focused on Leonard Peltier. He would be tried in Fargo, North Dakota, a truckstop crossroads in the conservative northern Midwest that had grown into a little city with a federal court. Judge Paul Benson, a Nixon friend and appointee with a reputation for being tough, sat on the bench. Judge Benson made sure that evidence would not surface before his court which might tarnish the

34. *People* Magazine, April 20, 1981.

credibility of the prosecution or the FBI: he simply disallowed any evidence that had to do with the FBI, their tactics, previous misdeeds, or crimes such as the solicitation of false testimony.

In Fargo, Peltier and his lawyers got a chance to speak with Myrtle Poor Bear. Recanting her previous "eyewitness" account of the alleged murder, Poor Bear attempted to move over to the defense side. She told Judge Benson and the lawyers that she had signed the false affidavits under the coercion of threats on her life made by FBI agents Price and Woods. Judge Benson, however, refused to allow the Poor Bear testimony to be presented to the jury, stating that "the FBI is not on trial here." Lawyer Karen Northcott said, "Defense evidence which had convinced the first jury of the innocence of Butler and Robideaux was ruled inadmissible in Peltier's trial. He was not allowed to present a case of self defense."[35] Benson sequestered the jury and placed a ban on media coverage of the substance of the case. The judge assumed complete control over the type and amount of information available to both the jury and the public.

Government prosecutors Evan Hultman and Lynn Crooks relied largely on circumstantial evidence in their attempt to connect Peltier with the deaths of the two FBI agents. They did not use the Poor Bear affidavits, knowing that the defense would be able to disprove their validity; instead they called FBI agents and informers as witnesses. The defense claims to have had evidence that the testimony of government witnesses Gregory Clifford, Marvin Bragg, Marion High Bull, and Melvin White Wing — all had signed statements claiming that Jimmy Eagle had confessed to them — was false and given under coercion; however, Benson would not allow that evidence to be presented to the jury.

Prior to the Cedar Rapids trial of Butler and Robideaux, teenager Norman Brown had told a grand jury that he had seen Peltier, Robideaux, Butler, and Eagle "down by the agents' car"; during the trial itself he recanted that story and admitted that FBI agents had threatened him with death if he refused to tell the lie. In Fargo the government presented another teenage Indian, Mike Anderson, before the jury and judge. He told the same story. Again, the defense had evidence that Anderson was lying under coercion; again Judge Benson refused to hear the evidence.

In a Watergate-like testimony an FBI stenographer claimed that she had accidentally destroyed all her notes of the radio transmissions that the two FBI agents had made before their death. She also testified that her official record of the transmissions was produced under dictation

35. Karen Northcott, "The FBI in Indian Communities," reprint by American Friends Service Committee, Minneapolis, Minnesota 1979.

from an FBI higher-up. One FBI report indicated that the record had been "typed on the 26th" but "dictated on the 30th." This same report contained a gap of four lines followed by a change of typewriters. When these discrepancies were pointed out by the defense, Judge Benson scoffed; the defense attorneys are "wasting your time," he told the jury.

One FBI agent called as a prosecution witness claimed to have identified Peltier through a seven-power rifle scope from half a mile away. The defense produced a gun expert who testified that such an identification was impossible. They offered to take the jurors out to test a seven-power scope, but Benson refused to allow the move, claiming again that it was a waste of time.

FBI agent Gary Adams had testified in Cedar Rapids that the red pickup chased by the two agents had run his roadblock at about 12:15 or 12:20; in Fargo, Adams changed his story: the red pickup disappeared. The defense assumed that the FBI had conspired to deny the existence of the vehicle and its unknown passengers to prevent the defense from raising the possibility that perhaps these unknown people had fired on the agents. By eliminating that mysterious variable, the prosecution simplified their case against Peltier which had become a process of guilt through elimination of other suspects. When the defense attempted to enter Adams's previous testimony into the court record Judge Benson prevented it; he ruled that the previous testimony was immaterial to the case. Thus, an FBI agent gave two different versions of the same story in two separate trials, and a federal judge ruled that the discrepancy was irrelevant.

In all, the government presented five weeks of testimony. Prosecutor Hultman paraded around the courtroom with a gun that he claimed had belonged to an AIM member, though not necessarily to Peltier. As he delivered his final remarks, he stated that "Sometimes circumstantial evidence is the best there is." Crooks referred to Peltier and the others who were with him on the day in question as a "brutal, cowardly, bloodthirsty bunch."

The defense had two and a half weeks of testimony planned, but Judge Benson disallowed most of it: the jury was allowed to hear two days of defense testimony. On April 18, 1977, after deliberating for ten hours, the jury of nine women and three men — all white — convicted Leonard Peltier of "aiding and abetting" in the murder of the two agents.

Prior to his sentencing, Peltier made a statement to Judge Benson. The following comments are excerpted from that statement: "Your conduct in this trial leaves no doubt that you will do the bidding of the FBI without any hesitation. . . . Each time my defense team tried to expose FBI misconduct . . . and tried to present evidence of this you claimed it

was irrelevant to this trial. . . . In the mental torture of Myrtle Poor Bear
you said her testimony would shock the conscience of the American
people if believed! But *you* decided what was to be believed and what
was not to be believed — not the jury. Your conduct shocks the conscience of what the American legal system stands for: The search for
truth by a jury of citizens. What was it that made you so afraid to let that
testimony in? Your own guilt of being part of a corrupted pre-planned
trial to get a conviction no matter how your reputation would be tarnished?

"If you were impartial, you would have had an open mind on all the
factual disputes in this case. But you were unwilling to allow even the
slightest possibility that a law enforcement officer would lie on the stand.
Then, how could you possibly be impartial enough to let my lawyers
prove how important it is to the FBI to convict a Native Indian activist in
this case? You do not have the ability to see that such a conviction is an
important part of the efforts to discredit those who are trying to alert
their Brothers and Sisters to the new threat from the white man, and the
attempt to destroy what little Indian land remains in the process of
extracting our uranium, oil, and other minerals. Again, to cover up your
part in this, you will call me a heartless, cold-blooded murderer who
deserves two life sentences consecutively.

"I honestly believe you made up your mind long ago that I was guilty
and that you were going to sentence me to the maximum sentence
permitted under the law. But this does not surprise me, because you are
a high-ranking member of the white racist American establishment
which has consistently said, 'In God We Trust,' while they went about
the business of murdering my people and attempting to destroy our
culture."[36]

The Canadian extradition agreement with the United States specifically precluded the sentencing of Peltier to death. Thus the maximum
sentence that Benson could give to Peltier was two lifetime prison terms
for the two counts of aiding and abetting first degree murder. On June 1,
1977 Benson handed down that sentence, and Peltier was taken to
Marion federal penitentiary in Illinois, the top security prison in
America.

Marion Prison replaced Alcatraz as America's darkest dungeon. The
dreaded Control Unit at Marion, a six-by-six-by-eight-foot cell, is
known inside the prison system as the "end of the line." The Control
Unit is a behavior modification laboratory using techniques designed by

36. Court Record reprint by *Akwesasne Notes*, Summer, 1977.

Dr. Edgar Schein. In Dr. Schein's own words, the Control Unit is designed for brainwashing. He said in a 1962 speech to U.S. prison wardens in Washington, D.C., "In order to produce marked changes of behavior, it is necessary to weaken, undermine, or remove the supports of the old attitudes. I would like you to think of brainwashing not in terms of politics, ethics, and morals, but in terms of the deliberate changing of human behavior by a group of men who have relatively complete control over the environment in which the captive populace lives."[37]

Official practices used in Marion Prison to break or brainwash prisoners include, according to Schein, isolation, sensory deprivation, segregation of leaders, spying, tricking men into written statements which are then shown to others, placing individuals whose willpower has been severely weakened into a living situation with others who are more advanced in their thought reform, character invalidation, humiliations, sleeplessness, rewarding subservience, and fear. Unofficial practices, according to Victor Bono, an ex-Marion inmate, include "atrocities that are on a par with Pinochet's concentration camps in Chile and with Hitler's Auschwitz." Murder is not infrequent at Marion. Between 1975 and 1979 there was an average of one murder inside the prison every four months.[38] While Peltier languished in solitary confinement, and as his lawyers sought an appeal of his case, a plot to murder him was being hatched inside the prison.

Marion prisoner Standing Deer (Robert Wilson), an Indian facing seven felony charges in Oklahoma, had developed a painful back ailment. A prison official told him that if he would cooperate with an unspecified plot he would receive medical attention. He agreed, and the next day he was transferred to the prison hospital. According to Standing Deer, on the afternoon of May 17, 1978, while in the prison hospital, he was visited by Chief Correctional Supervisor Robert "Max" Carey, and a "well-dressed stranger in a light brown suit and diagonal striped tie . . . in his late thirties, about six feet tall and 170 pounds, very erect posture, nearly blond hair, with blue eyes."[39] The stranger told Standing Deer that if he would cooperate in "neutralizing Leonard Peltier" that he would see to it that Standing Deer would be paroled from Marion.

Standing Deer asked him what he meant by "neutralizing Leonard

37. Dr. Edgar Schein, "Man Against Man: Brainwashing," a speech to social scientists and prison wardens, Washington, D.C., 1962; reprint, "Breaking Men's Minds" by the National Committee to Support the Marion Brothers, St. Louis, Missouri, 1978.
38. Michael Satchell, *Parade*, "The End of the Line," September 28, 1980.
39. Robert H. Wilson (Standing Deer) affidavit, Leavenworth County, Kansas, September 4, 1979.

Peltier," and the stranger replied that he would have to judge that for himself, but that according to Standing Deer's record he was not adverse to "going all the way." When Standing Deer asked what was meant by "going all the way," Carey interrupted, saying that he was "wasting [their] time" if he was going to "play dumb." According to Standing Deer the stranger then asked him how it felt to know that he "would never make it through the Oklahoma trial alive." Standing Deer was to be returned to Oklahoma to face state charges of shooting a police officer; he said the stranger threatened "that if I did not cooperate, he would personally see to it that I would not survive the trip to Oklahoma."

Standing Deer did not know Peltier at the time but, in fear for his life, he agreed to cooperate with the plot upon the condition that the men advanced some tangible evidence of their power to get him paroled. The stranger said: "I have the power to end your miserable life. . . . I also have the power to have all seven charges dismissed, and get you paroled out of the federal system. So, if I have the charges in Oklahoma dismissed will you cooperate?" Standing Deer agreed. The stranger outlined a plan which called for Standing Deer to gain Peltier's trust, convince Peltier to accept a prison-made zip gun, provide Peltier with wire cutters and other escape equipment, and to lure Peltier to the fence where he would be taken care of. Upon leaving, the stranger warned Standing Deer, "Don't even think of playing us for fools because, at this point, it's either Peltier's life or yours. We don't accept backing out or betrayals. You are now committed to this with your life. If you betray us you will die."

A few weeks later Standing Deer received an official letter from Oklahoma informing him that the charges against him were being dismissed. He began getting close to Peltier, who had been returned from solitary confinement to the general prison population. On July 4 Standing Deer and Peltier sat talking together in the prison recreation room. Peltier told Standing Deer about the Indian movement, the traditional elders, the demand for treaty rights. He told Standing Deer about how he had been framed, about Myrtle Poor Bear, and about the deaths on Pine Ridge reservation. Peltier's story touched Standing Deer; he began to feel a closeness to the Indian tradition that he had not experienced before. As the friendship grew, Standing Deer felt ashamed of his hidden purpose, and he told Peltier of the plot to kill him. Peltier told Standing Deer to pretend to continue to cooperate, so that the agents would not hire another assassin. This would give Peltier and Standing Deer time to hatch a counterplot.

On November 9 Standing Deer was again confronted by the stranger who took him into a prison classroom alone. There the stranger quizzed him on his progress, wanting to know what he was doing to keep his end of the agreement. Standing Deer replied that he had gained Peltier's confidence, but that Peltier had told him he was not interested in obtaining a zip gun. The stranger outlined a new aspect to the plot. According to Standing Deer: "He told me that they had come to a decision that Marion has so much security that planning a successful escape was just about impossible; therefore, unless I had firm plans to neutralize Peltier, they intended to move both me and Leonard Peltier to a less secure prison in California where an escape attempt would be hard to resist. He said I would be going to Leavenworth in December. Leonard would go to USP Lompoc about sixty days after I got to Leavenworth. I would not go to Lompoc until they had another Indian situated in Lompoc who would help me to neutralize Peltier. He said the Indian I would meet in Lompoc enjoyed their complete trust, and he would also be watching me to make sure I performed. . . . I asked why I couldn't just go to Lompoc. He replied that he wanted me on ice for a while so that Leonard Peltier would welcome me with open arms when I got to Lompoc. He said he further did not want me at Lompoc until the other Indian got himself established. I agreed to go along with him once again."

On December 9, 1978, Standing Deer was transferred to Leavenworth Prison, en route to Lompoc. In February of 1979 the Bureau of Prisons transferred Leonard Peltier — supposedly a dangerous criminal with a maximum security classification — to the minimum security facility in Lompoc, California. On March 5, the Supreme Court declined to accept the Peltier case for review. A year earlier, on April 12, 1978, the Eighth Circuit Court of Appeals in St. Louis had refused to grant an appeal, even though Judge Donald Ross grilled prosecutor Evan Hultman on the FBI treatment of Myrtle Poor Bear and stated that "what happened [to obtain the Poor Bear affidavits] gives some credence to the claim of the Indian people that the United States is willing to resort to any tactic . . . and if they are willing to do that, they must be willing to fabricate other evidence."[40]

On May 10, 1979, Charles Richards — known to traditionals and to Peltier as a former member of Dickie Wilson's goon squad on Pine Ridge reservation — entered Leavenworth Prison en route to Lompoc. Standing Deer, suspecting him of being the second assassin, sent word to Peltier. By the time Richards arrived at Lompoc two weeks later, Peltier, expecting him, had already planned his own escape with two

40. *Leonard Peltier v. United States of America*, 8th Circuit Court of Appeals, April 12, 1978.

friends whom he had met inside Lompoc: Bobby Garcia and Dallas Thundershield. Garcia urged Thundershield not to join them in the escape attempt, because he was young — twenty-one — and had only a short time left to serve. However, Thundershield was devoted to Peltier and insisted on helping to draw fire away from him during the escape. While awaiting the break, both Garcia and Thundershield stayed close to Peltier, acting as bodyguards.

On July 20, Peltier, Garcia, and Thundershield waited for dark, then went over the fence at Lompoc. Outside the fence, Dallas Thundershield was shot twice in the back by William H. Guild, a custodian in the prison power plant who had been armed and waiting. Guild handcuffed Thundershield who died there on the ground. Garcia was captured near the prison and sent back. Peltier was free — for the first time in three years. His freedom, however, was short-lived: on July 25 he was recaptured by FBI agents and state marshals, and returned to Lompoc.

Peltier's lawyers anticipated that the impending escape trial would be an opportunity to expose the plot to murder Peltier inside the prison system. However, they were to be frustrated once again, this time by Judge Lawrence Lydick, another Nixon appointee, who refused to allow testimony in his court concerning the murder plot. Twelve witnesses from Marion, including Standing Deer, were willing to testify about the plot to kill Peltier, but Judge Lydick refused to allow the evidence to be presented before the jury.

The trial, held in the U.S. District Court in Los Angeles, opened on November 14, 1979, and lasted two months. On December 12, Standing Deer was allowed to testify, but when he mentioned the plot to "neutralize" Peltier, Judge Lydick ordered the comment stricken from the record, and instructed the jury to disregard it.[41] On the following day Peltier took the stand. When he told the jury that he escaped to save his life, Lydick again ordered that the comment be taken off the record, and warned Peltier that he would be charged with contempt of court if he attempted again to raise the issue of the assassination plot before the jury. Peltier then tried to tell the jury that his conviction in Fargo, North Dakota was also due to not being allowed a defense, but Judge Lydick again stopped him and ordered the comments stricken from the record. Peltier said, "I am not going to participate in this railroad any longer," and walked off the stand in protest.

Peltier and Garcia were convicted of escape; Peltier was also convicted of being a felon in possession of a gun. He was sentenced to seven

41. Summary of testimony, "The Escape Trial," reprinted by Leonard Peltier Defense Committee, Seattle, Washington.

years on top of his two two life terms and returned to Marion Prison. Roque Duenas, a friend of Peltier's who was charged with aiding and abetting the escape from outside the prison, was tried before Judge Robert Tagasugi, who expressed a deep concern about the evidence of government misconduct. Upon sentencing Duenas to time already served, Tagasugi said that he was convinced that he was not "dealing with a common criminal, but with a man with very deep human dimensions committed to the rights of Indians." He added, "If there was even a grain of truth in the allegations of misconduct [by the FBI], the actions should be viewed as Gestapo techniques that should not be tolerated."[42]

Shortly thereafter, Peltier's lawyers were able to secure about two-thirds of his FBI file through the Freedom of Information Act; 12,000 pages were released, but, more interestingly, 6,000 pages were withheld. The reason? The FBI cited "national security." Peltier wrote from prison that "the only thing I'm guilty of is trying to help my people. For this, it is very possible I'll spend the rest of my life in prison."

On January 24, 1980 Standing Deer wrote from Leavenworth to a friend in Boston that all the prisoners who had filed affidavits with the Los Angeles court were in danger of reprisal inside the prison system for helping AIM. He noted that one such prisoner, David Owens, had been transferred recently to Leavenworth, and had been badly beaten upon his arrival. "David Owens was assaulted by Leavenworth prison guards upon his arrival from Marion on January 14, 1980. . . . David is limping badly, and from other prisoners I have learned that he looked to be in bad shape when he went to the hospital," said Standing Deer. He warned further that prisoners who helped AIM were being put into isolation cells where "anything can be done to them. . . . When Gypsy Adams 'hung himself'' in Marion he was in isolation. When Curley Fee 'hung himself'' in Marion he was in the Control Unit boxcars. . . . Something must be done about this now. The only hope to keep indigenous people alive who are Prisoners of War of the United States is to expose the machinations at every opportunity. Leonard and Bobby [Garcia] are going to Marion, the most lawless jail in the land."

Both Standing Deer and Bobby Garcia were later transferred to Terre Haute Prison in Indiana. There, in early December 1980 Garcia was removed from the general prison population and placed in an isolation cell in the prison's psychiatric ward. On December 10 he phoned his sister Priscilla Morales in Denver. "He was very nervous on the phone," she recalled. "He told us to cancel our Christmas trip to the prison. He said he was having some problems that he could not discuss

42. Ibid.

over the phone, but that he would talk to us later. The phone call was cut off by prison people, and that was the last we heard from him." On Saturday morning, December 13, officials at Terre Haute reported that Bobby Garcia had been found dead in his cell. They called the incident suicide. Garcia was supposedly found hanging by a sheet from the window of his cell. The following day, the thirteen other prisoners in the psychiatric wing were transferred to other prisons, and Standing Deer was transferred to the dreaded medical surgery wing of the federal prison in Springfield, Illinois. He wrote to his lawyers that he did not request any medical surgery, and that prior to his transfer an unidentified prison official had told him: "What you need is a good frontal lobotomy." His lawyers have continued to monitor his treatment inside the prison to protect him from persecution.

Another friend of Garcia's, prisoner Edward Lee Lawrence, swore in a petition filed in the U.S. District Court in Indiana that "On or about November 30, 1980 Bobby Gene Garcia approached this Petitioner and informed him that he'd had a verbal confrontation with his Unit Manager Robert Perdue, and Perdue had told him that he was a 'dead [obscenity]', that he 'would be dead before a month was over.' "[43] According to Lawrence, after Garcia's death, he was "discussing the murder of Bobby Gene Garcia with another inmate, Winston M. Holloway, whereupon [I] realized to [my] utter horror and great consternation that Mr. Robert Perdue was walking directly in back. . . . Mr. Perdue had overheard the comments and accusations of the Petitioner and then told me that 'Springfield is just the place to take care of sorry [obscenity] troublemakers like you.' " Lawrence had received a notice from Dr. Imre Vincze of the prison hospital that he was going to be transferred to Springfield for "testing to determine the condition of a liver disease." Six days after Garcia's death Dr. Vincze refused Lawrence's request not to be transferred. Lawrence then appealed to Terre Haute warden R.J. Lippman, but on January 7, 1981 Lippman denied Lawrence's request not to be sent to the Springfield medical wing, stating that "we decide where and when" medical attention is required. In his application for a restraining order to the District Court Lawrence said: "Petitioner swears that he is convinced he will be killed or drugged into a zombie-like state if sent to Springfield Medical Center. . . . Petitioner asserts that these are not just bare allegations without substance . . . during a verbal confrontation with a [prison] staff member, Unit Manager Robert

43. Edward Lee Lawrence, "Affidavit in Support of Application for Temporary Restraining Order," United States District Court for the Southern District of Indiana, Terre Haute, Indiana, January, 1980.

Perdue, he was told by Perdue that 'we have ways of taking care of you smart-asses; you commit suicide one day and there'll never by any questions asked.' ''

And if the questions are asked, it is quite certain that no answers will ensue from these dark corners of the law enforcement underworld. David Price denies having threatened Myrtle Poor Bear with photos of slain Anna Mae Aquash.[44] Likewise, Marion Chief Correctional Supervisor Max Carey has denied involvement in the plot to assassinate Peltier.[45] And those who would testify otherwise are all behind bars. Will the ''well-dressed stranger'' come forward? Will the FBI investigate the death of Bobby Garcia? Anna Mae Aquash? Joe Stuntz? Jeanette Bissonette? Edith Eagle Hawk? Will these names disappear one day from history? Pedro Bissonette? Raymond Yellow Thunder? AIM lawyer Candy Hamilton documented a minimum of sixty-one unsolved political murder cases on Pine Ridge in the three years following the siege of Wounded Knee, from the spring of 1973 to the spring of 1976. The murder rate there is eighteen times the national average.[46]

On the Shoshone-Paiute reservation of Duck Valley, straddling the Nevada-Idaho border, at 1:30 A.M., February 12, 1979, a fire ripped through the house of Arthur Manning and family. Manning was a member of the Duck Valley Tribal Council who was actively working for Shoshone-Paiute treaty rights. Opposition to Manning included local tribal police chief Benny Richards, a former member of the Wilson goon squad on Pine Ridge; and local BIA Director John Artichocker, also from Pine Ridge. Manning's wife, Leah, was a coordinator for social services on the reservation. Their daughter, Tina, had been working actively in a local campaign to preserve the tribe's water rights at Wildhorse Reservoir; she was opposed by the BIA, Elko County, Nevada officials, the water recreation industry, and local white ranchers. Tina's husband was John Trudell, national chairman of AIM. The Trudells had three children; Ricarda Star, five; Sunshine Karma, three; and Eli Changing Sun, one. During the Peltier trial in Fargo, North Dakota, Trudell had returned to the courtroom one day when a marshal informed him that he would not be allowed inside. An argument ensued, and Trudell was evicted. He was later arrested for the incident, charged with contempt of court, convicted before Judge Ronald Davies, and

44. *In These Times*, ''FBI manufactured AIM's Marshall's evidence'' by Karen Northcott. April 3, 1979.
45. *People* Magazine, April 20, 1981.
46. FBI Uniform Crime Reports, 1975, U.S. Government Printing Office, Washington, D.C.

sentenced to sixty days in jail. He served his time in five institutions in three states. While in Springfield Prison in Missouri, he was told by a fellow inmate that if he did not stop his Indian rights work his family would be killed. On February 11, 1979, Trudell gave a speech in front of the FBI building in Washington, D.C., condemning the FBI for their role in the persecution of Indian people. The fire at his in-law's home came twelve hours later, catching the entire family asleep. Dead were Leah Hicks-Manning, her daughter, Tina, and the three young children. Arthur Manning survived the blaze. The BIA issued a statement saying the fire was an accident. Trudell believes his family was murdered.

In September 1979 Trudell and Dino Butler sought political asylum in Canada. The Canadian government refused them, and in a subsequent statement to the Canadian public, they said: "We feel the destruction of our nations brought by racism, alcohol, bullets, poverty, poor health services, sterilization, courtroom corruption, continued takeover of our lands, attacks against our hunting and fishing rights, our water rights, our human rights. We see through the lie, and understand the U.S. government is intent on completely destroying our people's way of living. . . . The American government calls us criminals, but we are not. . . . We do not want trouble; we want the attack against the Earth and the people to stop."[47]

In California, Dennis Banks, free from South Dakota prosecution by the grace of Governor Jerry Brown, said: "What we have done, we did for the seventh generation to come, for the future. We did not do these things for ourselves, for personal gain. We work now so that the seventh generation may be born free."

Scattered as the warriors were, and as much as the FBI may have been able to claim victory in their campaign to disrupt and neutralize American Indian resistance to federal policy, AIM and the traditional Indian movement in North America had actually grown in support and effectiveness. Although most of the original leaders were either in jail, underground, in exile or dead, AIM grew as a result of worldwide publicity and public sympathy. New leaders emerged. The events of Wounded Knee, appeals from the Hopi and other traditional elders, revelations from the courtrooms, and the clarity of purpose as expressed by the Indian leaders had inspired white support from celebrities such as Marlon Brando to community organizers. By 1980 rock-music stars such as Jackson Browne and Bonnie Raitt had begun to perform benefit concerts on behalf of Leonard Peltier, Richard Marshall, and other AIM leaders in need of defense funds. To the FBI it perhaps seemed incredible and

47. *Union of B.C. Indian Chiefs' News*, September, 1979.

frustrating that all their effort had not eradicated the traditional Indian movement. In a memorandum to the White House discussing future "use of Special Agents of the FBI in a paramilitary law enforcement operation in the Indian country," FBI headquarters complained of difficulties ranging from lack of experience to political interference with their operations. The memo, signed by FBI Special Agent J. E. O'Connell, stated that during Wounded Knee, "The FBI encountered extreme problems, both in the field and at FBIHQ [Headquarters, Washington, D.C.] in adapting to a paramilitary role. The FBI was not equipped logistically to operate in a paramilitary situation in open terrain . . . "[48]

The Indian movement warriors, on the other hand, although they may have lost many battles, certainly had not surrendered the war for Indian sovereignty. On the contrary, the war had moved on to a new, more organized front: International diplomacy. It could be argued that the warriors had performed a crucial function in both holding off the government for a few precious years and by raising the Indian issues to an international level. While the battles of Wounded Knee, Black Mesa, Duck Valley, Oglala, and others raged on, the traditional Indian leadership successfully united the Indian movements from Chile to the Arctic Circle, and began a process, promised by the Hopi years earlier, of bringing their grievances before the international community.

The opposition, however, was not to be so simply outflanked: the FBI would employ CIA and international law enforcement connections to engage the Indian movement on the global front. The multinational corporations whose energy development schemes were at the root of the conflict were also no strangers to global conflict.

---

48. FBI Memo, J.E. O'Connell to M. Gebhardt, Department of Justice, April 24, 1975.

7

The Fourth World

*They arrested the trade unionists, but I did
nothing because I was not one. Then they
arrested the Jews, and again I did nothing
because I was not Jewish. At last they came
and arrested me, but by then it was too late.*

MARTIN NIEMOLLER
Concentration camp survivor

I WAS NEVER ASHAMED to be a part of the American Indian Movement
that you heard about. I was never ashamed of the incidents of Wounded
Knee and many of our protesting Indian people no matter how they are
put down, how they are pointed out. Call them militants, call them
Communists, anything you want to, but they are still my brothers and
sisters, they are still my people. We are still the evidence of the Western
Hemisphere.'' Muskogee-Creek spiritual leader Phillip Deere spoke
these words to the Fourth Russell Tribunal in Rotterdam, Holland,
November 24, 1980. He was outlining the general position of the collected indigenous people from North and South America who had
gathered before the Tribunal to bring charges of genocide against the
United States, Canada, Brazil, Chile, and other South American countries. ''I am not talking about freedom that I can place in your hands with
a paper,'' he continued. ''I am talking about something far more than
that. . . . We have the oldest government in America because our Indian
civilization was built upon the study of nature. We copied off of nature.
There we found our way of life, there we found our civilization that was
to last into thousands of years, and I do not think that life could have
begun any different for any other nation of people . . . look at your
history.

''Many of our people today are suffering. Perhaps many of our people
are standing behind the walls today in some prison; somewhere, this
very night we have some Indian persons standing behind these walls
because he was seeking freedom for his people. We have some Native
people somewhere in a grave tonight because he was seeking freedom
for his people . . . The newspapers have told you that these militant

212

Indians are terrorist groups. Before you think of how bad these people are, find out what they are fighting for, what is causing this, how come they are acting this way. . . . For many years we have had to crawl on our hands and knees and beg for this and beg for that, but in our modern times I sometimes feel proud of our younger generations though they grow up in confusion. Sometimes they make mistakes, but they have the courage to stand up. So recently you heard about the American Indian Movement. To this day I worked with them because no matter what kind of an accent they teach, they brought the attention to the world that no more are we going to crawl on our hands and knees.

"We are serious people. We didn't come here for a holiday. We did not come here to be just as the tourist people. We came here strictly for business."

By 1980 Indians were already well-versed in global politics. The Hopi had warned President Truman in 1950 that they would take their case to the UN, if the U.S. government failed to address their claims. Throughout the '60s Indian leaders from North, Central, and South America began the communicating and organizing which eventually led to the establishing of the International Indian Treaty Council office at the United Nations building in New York. In 1972 AIM founder Eddie Benton-Banai, a delegation of ten Hopi leaders including Thomas Banyacya and David Monongye, Rolling Thunder from Nevada, and other Indian leaders from Alaska to Brazil attended the UN Environment Conference in Stockholm, Sweden.

In Sweden, the Indian leaders learned much about the nature of international politics, and with whom they could align. They found, for example, that the Chinese, African, and most Third World governments were as much oriented toward energy-intensive industry as were the Americans and Canadians. The Indians pulled out of the Third World session because, according to Benton, "The groups were so internalized and so attuned to science and technology that they would not listen to the spiritualism that we were trying to project." The Indians from the Western Hemisphere found that their closest allies were such people as the Sami nomads from Lapland, the people of Brittany who claimed independence from France, the Basques who claimed independence from Spain, and other indigenous land-based people. It was here that the term "Fourth World," or global network of indigenous people, was coined. This Fourth World political, philosophical, spiritual movement brought an entirely fresh force to international political diplomacy.

"We feel solidarity with these traditional peoples everywhere," said Kanatakeniate, a spokeman for the Mohawk Nation; "these are the people who love and respect the earth, who live in harmony with their environment."[1] The Fourth World representatives saw the tired left-right political discussions as all one Neo-European debate over who reaped the spoils of industrialization while the rights of indigenous people everywhere were ignored. The Neo-Europeans continued to colonize native people around the world and destroy the environment in the name of progress. Kanatakeniate said, "Industrial civilization should recognize that, for all of its material achievements, it lacks basic spiritual values that so-called primitive lifestyles could teach. All the Indians here say they believe that neglect of such values underlies the environmental and social disorders challenging civilization today."

Furthermore, the indigenous people of the Western Hemisphere began to build political support among European countries. American and energy corporation reputations were at an all-time low in the world community due to the Vietnam War, the scandals of the Nixon presidency, and the threat of global energy war. The Indians of America found the Europeans a much more receptive audience to their charges against the U.S. government than that government itself or even the American people, who simply could not understand the concept that they did not own all the land from sea to shining sea.

By 1977 the International Indian Treaty Council (IITC) had gained Non-Governmental Organization status at the UN, and had successfully organized an International Conference on Discrimination Against Indigenous Populations in the Americas. The four-day conference, opening on September 20, 1977 in Geneva, Switzerland, was chaired by Romesh Chandra, president of the World Peace Council, and included high-ranking UN officials in the field of human rights. Russell Means, having been dragged through several trials, jailed, stabbed in the chest inside prison, and shot three times, presented the case of the Lakota people to the UN officials. He also entered documentation of CIA and multinational corporation activities in Brazil, Ecuador, Peru, Colombia, and Venezuela, accusing both U.S. and other Neo-European governments of "planned genocide" in the Western Hemisphere.

Oren Lyons spoke on behalf of the Onondaga, the Six-Nations Confederacy of the Haudenosaunee. Marie Sanchez, a tribal lawyer, represented the Northern Cheyenne; Pat Ballanger, the "mother of AIM," representing the Anishinabe people of the western Great Lakes, presented documentation of U.S. sterilization programs; and Winona LaDuke, a twenty-year-old Ojibway attending Harvard University, presented an overall analysis of the energy development schemes in operation on or planned for Indian land. Grandfather David Monongye gave a

1. *Christian Science Monitor*, June 13, 1972.

short, poignant speech: "The Indian Bureau is trying to get all of our land that belongs to us that was given to us by the Great Spirit. They want to get ahold of all our land for themselves, but do not give it up. All Indian things have been taken away from us. . . . Some of you may have eaten Crackerjacks. What does it says outside the Crackerjacks box: 'The more you eat the more you want.' He has eaten up our land already, but he wants more."[2]

Then the UN conference heard the gruesome tales from the people of South America. Antonio Millape, a Mapuche Indian from Chile, told of torture, murder, starvaton, and the terror of the military death squads under dictator Augusto Pinochet. Juan Condori Uruchi, a Mink'a Indian from Bolivia, spoke of similar atrocities against his people. After the four days of testimony, the Geneva conference issued three reports — economic, social, and legal — with accompanying resolutions. The Economic Commission, chaired by Rev. Jose Cupenda from the World Council of Churches, concluded that "the indigenous populations and nations of the Western Hemisphere are suffering from all forms of genocide, from colonialist and neo-colonialist type conditions, from racism and discrimination." They cited practices including "extermination, germ warfare, peonage, slavery, forced resettlement, . . . sterilization, forced assimilation, government bureaucratic practices, destruction of the environment, and numerous national 'development' programs." The commission charged multinational corporations with "exploitation of native peoples and resouces," adding that a "key force in this process in Latin America is the U.S. economic development and military aid,"[3] citing specifically the U.S. AID program, the World Bank, and the International Development Bank.

They called for a halt to the strip-mining of Black Mesa, a recognition of treaties between the United States and various Indian nations as legitimate international agreements, protection of native land bases from exploitation by energy corporations, and a halt to the unabashed massacre of Indian people in Chile, Bolivia, Brazil, and other South American countries.

The Social Commission charged the Neo-European governments of the Western Hemisphere with ethnocide, the systematic destruction of indigenous culture through education control, adoption, sterilization, medical experimentation, and forced assimilation.

The Legal Commission, chaired by Niall MacDermot of the Interna-

2. Transcript, International NGO Conference on Indigenous Populations in the Americas, 1977, United Nations.
3. Ibid.

tional Commission of Jurists and Chairman of the UN Special Committee on Human Rights, concluded that the testimony of the Indian nations
represented a "call for justice that cannot be ignored by the international
community." They concluded that Indian lands should be "fully
owned" by the Indian people, and that "modern international law
establishes that a nation is defined through its own sovereignty and the
principle of self-determination should express the freedom and powers
of the indigenous courts within their areas." They cited "aggression by
the military police, . . . torture, false imprisonment, . . . infiltration and
destabilization of legally constituted indigenous organization, . . . man-
ipulating legal jurisdiction, . . . failure to respect fundamental rights of
women and children, and failure to respect indigenous graveyards and
sacred places."

The conference was a major landmark for the Indian people; it was the
largest representation of Western indigenous people ever to be received
by the United Nations. Sixty Indian nations presented their cases to the
UN body, and the final resolutions of the conference ranged from UN
recognition of the Indians' sovereign land rights to the investigation of
energy companies occupying Indian land. Chairman Chandra told the
delegates who were returning to their home countries, "This I pledge: if
there is victimization, harassment, repression, terror, murder against
anyone who participated in this conference . . . then you can count on a
worldwide outcry by the non-governmental organizations who stand
beside this conference . . . we shall take all possible measures to support
and defend any participant in the conference who may face persecution
and harassment on their return."[4]

After the conference, the Indian delegates were invited by various
European countries to deliver their message among the European populations. Jimmy Durham, one of the central organizers of the International Indian Treaty Council, said: "We are moving. We have begun
something with this conference which actually began at Wounded Knee,
that cannot be stopped. Many forces are already trying to stop it, or to
confuse us. But we cannot be stopped now. Too many people know of
our struggle to allow our enemies to stop us."

An FBI memorandum from this time reveals that "in view of foreign
travel by AIM leaders and interest in AIM abroad, periodic reports from
and to foreign agencies, for information relative to [AIM] activities, as
well as an interchange of information between the FBI and the CIA, is
necessitated."[5] The CIA, in the meantime, was well versed in the affairs

4. Ibid.
5. FBI Memo, "American Indian Movement," March 3, 1975.

of the Latin American countries facing charges of genocide from their indigenous populations. The CIA had long since acknowledged its complicity in such Latin American political turmoil as the overthrow of Chile's President Salvador Allende and the installation of Pinochet. In fact, the FBI itself had intelligence specialists in Argentina, Chile, Paraguay, Uruguay, Bolivia, and virtually every other country in Latin America.[6] In Canada, the FBI worked hand-in-hand with the RCMP, as in the arrest of Peltier. The FBI maintains offices in Bern, Paris, London, Madrid, Bonn, and other European cities.

When ex-CIA agent Phillip Agee exposed the falsification of alleged Salvadorean resistance documents by the CIA in 1981 he also detailed his personal experience with CIA involvement with local police and "repressive paramilitary and military groups throughout Latin America." He told how he had "trained squadrons in the use of explosives, firearms, and techniques to disperse crowds," and he told of the CIA "Subversive Activites Control Watch List," in each country. "The people whose names appear on this list can be arrested at any time," explains Agee. "This list includes the name of the person and of all the members of his family, his children, ... In Ecuador we made use of this list to help the police carry out the necessary arrest . . . the CIA is working hand-in-hand with the paramilitary groups, in an attempt to eliminate the opposition."

When the United States was accused of complacency in the massacre of South American Indian people by the United Nations Commission on Human Rights, U.S. Envoy Richard Schifter harangued the commission as a dupe of the international Communist conspiracy: "The United Nations Human Rights Commission exists for one purpose only," he said; "that is to attack alleged rightist forces in Latin American countries. . . . The time has come to put a stop to this institution being used against U.S. interests. . . . The United States has a responsibility to help build an infrastructure and stability so that the Communists can't exploit the people there."[7]

Schifter, senior partner of a Washington, D.C. law firm, had earlier represented the Sioux Tribal Council and chairman Dickie Wilson in the Indian Claims Commission case which awarded the tribal council $122.5 million for Lakota treaty land expropriated by the United States.[8] The traditional Lakota launched a suit in federal court, refusing the award,

6. *Assassination on Embassy Row,* John Dingas and Saul Landau, Pantheon Books, New York, 1980.
7. Speech given at a meeting of the American Democrats Abroad, Geneva, Switzerland, March 4, 1981.
8. *New York Times*, May 1, 1980.

demanding the return of the land, and payment of $11 billion in damages for the plundering of the Black Hills. Concerning the settlement won by the tribal council, Lakota lawyer Mario Gonzalez said, "We weren't a party to that action."[9]

When the Fourth Russell Tribunal met in Rotterdam from November 24 to 30, 1980, they heard forty-five specific cases of alleged genocide practiced against the Indians of the Americas. The cases ranged from the incarceration of Leonard Peltier to million-acre land swindles in Canada, to brutal massacres of Indians in Latin America. Details of the horrors experienced by the representatives from Latin America added a dark and desperate urgency to the international Fourth World movement.

The Tribunal jury included Loek Hulsman, a law professor from Holland; Karl Schleseier, a West German anthropologist working in the United States; Darcy Ribetro, former Minister of Education in Brazil; Roger Jungk. an Austrian futurist author; Domitila Barrios de Chungara, the Bolivian delegate to the international women's conferences in Mexico and Copenhagen; Jose Cupenda from the World Council of Churches; Josephine Richardson, British Member of Parliament; and other lawyers, theologians, scholars, and politicians from Europe, Asia, Africa, and the Americas. When introducing the witnesses from Guatemala, the jury used the assumed names "Pedro and Juana." The two people took the stand in a hushed, tense atmosphere; their heads and faces were covered with a black cloth; only their eyes showed through. "In my country," said Pedro, "the generals rule. The army, the police force, the death squads . . . massacres, assassinations, rapes: these are now common, everyday occurrences. Our lands — what little we have left — are expropriated. If we complain, if we resist, bullets are our answer; death under torture is our answer.

"Many of you might have thought that we were strange, coming in here like this, our faces covered, like bandits. But this is our reality. . . . Since 1974 to the present there have been 70,000 political assassinations. In 1980 . . . there have been assassinations of 100 Indian leaders, 70 worker or union leaders, 63 student leaders, 41 academic leaders, 4 priests, 13 journalists, and 38 politicians."[10]

Guatemala, just south of Mexico and north of El Salvador, straddling the isthmus of Panama, was the site of the great Mayan civilization. The

9. Associated Press, Rapid City, July 18, 1980.
10. Testimony before the Fourth Russell Tribunal, Rotterdam, November 1, 1980; reprinted in *Akwesasne Notes*, Winter, 1981.

two million indigenous descendants of the Maya make up approximately 50 percent of the country's population; they live primarily in the North-western mountain provinces, where they have traditionally lived by simple corn and bean farming for at least five thousand years. The highly centralized Mayan civilization, between A.D. 1 and 850, developed a calendar more astronomically accurate than the current Western Gregorian version. Gold-seeking Spanish conquistadors decimated the populations in the sixteenth century, and for the next four hundred years the Indians lived under Spanish, British, German, and eventually American influence.

In 1901 the United Fruit Company began its banana empire in Guatemala. In 1944 the military government of dictator Ubico was overthrown by a Mayan peasant uprising, and in 1953 the popular elected president Jacobo Arbenz returned 400,000 acres of United Fruit Company farm land to the Indian and peasant families from whom it had been taken. The following year a CIA coup retook the country; planes bombed Guatemala City, mercenaries poured over the mountains from Honduras, and a new dictator, Castillo Armas, was installed.[11] United Fruit, which had supplied boats for the invasion and had launched a public relations campaign in the United States to prepare for the over-throw, got the land back, and oil companies such as Texaco and Getty began to move into the newly discovered oil fields of Peten and El Quiche provinces, home of the Mayan people. The battle raged on, and continues to this day, under the military regime of Romeo Lucas Garcia. A U.S. Army officer, Colonel Houser, and two military aides, and a U.S. ambassador were killed in the mid-sixties in Guatemala; thousands of Indians and Guatemalan peasants have been killed. Speaking of the mineral development in the northern province of Peten, Guatemalan Colonel Oliverio Casasola, an officer in the Peten Development Corporation, wrote: "No matter how much sympathy we may have for the Indian problem, they are not the human contingent that Peten needs to progress."[12]

In 1976 the Guatemalan army occupied El Quiche province; a wave of terror followed. Indians were kidnapped, tortured, assassinated, raped, and burned out of their homes and fields. Juana told the Russell Tribunal: "Sometimes, in the jungle areas, they pretend to give us lands. The Indians are given land to clear away. Then, when the work is done, the army is moved in. The people must move on. Some resist. Then the

11. *Everybody's Business*, Milton Moskowitz, ed., Harper & Row, New York, 1980; p. 79.
12. *Grandezas y Miserias del Peten*, Oliverio Casasola, Government of Peten, Paraguay, 1969.

night raids: a village is occupied. The men are shot or kidnapped; the
women abused, sometimes by fifteen to twenty soldiers on one
woman.''

In the fall of 1979 seven Mayan leaders who had been sought by the
army for questioning disappeared. They were found dead. According to
Juana, the army dressed the Indian leaders in green fatigues, shot them,
and issued a statement that the men were guerrillas. The Indians sent a
delegation to Guatemala City to complain officially. After being ignored
by the government, the delegation spoke with Ish Campari of the Partido
Unido Revolucionario, a popular reform organization. Campari had
offered his help, but in late January 1980, a few days after the visit from
the Mayans, he was assassinated. On January 31, the Indians, in fear for
their lives, and hoping to attract international attention to their predica-
ment, occupied the Spanish Embassy in Guatemala City. They were
joined in sympathy by several students and ex-government workers.
The army of President Lucas surrounded the building, and ordered the
Spanish staff out; the ambassador and several Spanish workers stayed,
in support of the Indians. The army then firebombed the building, killing
twenty-one of the twenty-two Indians, seven embassy staff members,
two ex-government officials, four students, and five other supporters.
The body of the one surviving Indian was found the next day in front of
the University of San Carlos, a bullet hole in his forehead, and a note
pinned to his shirt warning the Spanish ambassador that he risked a
similar fate if he continued to side with the local Indian people.

The Mayan Indians who are being forced from their land have but few
choices: they may apply for jobs as oil company executives; they may
pick bananas for Del Monte (which bought out United Fruit in 1972) for
$2.80 per day if there are any openings; they may starve; or they may
resist. Those who choose resistance face torture and death. ''You must
excuse us, our painful words,'' said Pedro as he finished his testimony
before the Tribunal,''but from the north to the south, from the east to the
west, all over our country, this is our reality.'' Sadly, the story told by
the Mayan witnesses was not an isolated case.

The Tribunal heard from the Purace Indians of southern Colombia
who provided evidence that their land in the province of Cauca had been
seized by the Colombian government for the mining of sulphur, agribusiness cash crops, and the creation of a tourist park. In Colombia,
occupying the northeast corner of South America, the Indian population
has been virtually exterminated: approximately 179,000 Indians live in
the wild headwaters of the great Amazon River basin, dominated by
over 23 million Spanish-speaking Colombians. The Russell Tribunal

found the Colombian goverment guilty of violating international and their own national laws in the expropriation of Purace land, and they found the multinational mining company Ceanese and its subsidiary Industrias Purace guilty of violating trade union, pollution, and safety agreements which they had signed in their occupation and exploitation of Purace land. The Tribunal collected evidence of forty-five Indian resistance leaders murdered since 1971 in the Purace area alone. These crimes, however, were only indicative of a much larger government-industry program to "deindianize" Colombia.[13]

The New York Times reported in 1973 that the small band of Guahibo Indians living in remote southeastern Colombia near the border of Brazil were "being hunted and killed by the Colombian army and white settlers who believe that there is oil beneath the tribe's land."[14] *The New York Times* report quoted a white landowner as saying: "There will not be any peace in this region until the Indians are gone."

In 1967 two white ranchers, Anselmo Aquirre and Marcelino Jim-minez, and a local politician, Luis Enrique Morin, lured a band of Cuibas Indians, living along the Capanaparo River in northeastern Colombia near the Venezuelan border, to a "Christmas feast," which turned into a macabre massacre. Nineteen Indians had gathered at the LaRubiera ranch house on December 27; as the promised feast was served, the men and several accomplices leapt from hiding places with guns, machetes, hatchets, and clubs. They slaughtered sixteen of the nineteen Indians, including an infant and five small children. The three who escaped reported the incident, and a trial ensued in the town of Villavicencio.

Morin and the others freely admitted the massacre, but told the court that killing Indian people was a common practice, and that they "didn't know it was wrong to kill Indians." When the judge asked one of the participants, Eudoro Gonzalez, why he committed the act, Gonzalez replied: "I've heard that Don Tomas Jara ordered Indians killed. That's why I killed those Indians because I knew that the government would not reprimand us."[15] Under a Colombian law which recognizes "invincible ignorance," the killers were ruled innocent on the grounds that they did not know that their deed was wrong. A 1973 *New York Times* story reporting the incident stated that "Cuiba-killing on the llanos

13. "Report of the Fourth Russell Tribunal on the Rights of the Indians of the Americas," Russell Peace Foundation, Nottingham, United Kingdom, November, 1980; p. 25.
14. *Sunday Times*, 1973; London; *New York Times* News Service, 1973.
15. *El Tiemp*, Castro Ceycedo; translated by Nan Lopez in *Akwesasne Notes*, Summer, 1972, p. 26.

[Colombian prairies] continues,"[16] citing the fact that Colombian Navy riverboats cruise the rivers, machine-gunning Indians on the bank.

The systematic extermination of indigenous populations in Colombia has paralleled, predictably, the development plans of energy corporations and other corporate interests in the area. In 1960, a Texaco-Gulf oil consortium began exploration in southern Colombia; by 1968 they operated forty-seven productive wells and a 193-mile pipeline from the region to an oil terminal on the Pacific Coast. In 1970 the World Bank began a loan program to Colombia for development of the remote Amazon region. In March of 1979 the Colombian government under Julio Cesar Turbay signed a $500 million contract with the National Uranium Company of Spain for the exploration of uranium in the southeastern province of Vaupes where the Guahibo Indians had been continuously hunted and slaughtered. In the southern province of Cauca, home of the Purace Indians who testified at the Russell Tribunal, 51,000 acres of the Indians' subsistence bean crop was reduced to 7,200 acres in the 1960s. During that same time, the multibillion-dollar international farm feed company, Ralston Purina, had gained control of some 200,000 acres in the province for the production of chicken feed.[17]

Most of the vast, virgin Amazon basin, however, is contained within the borders of Brazil; uranium, oil, gold, tin, bauxite, timber, and other resource bonanzas have brought to Brazilian Indians an influx of corporate resource harvesters, government development projects, and extermination. Three million Indians once occupied the rich Brazilian jungles; today approximately 100,000 remain, 3 percent of the original population. A massive mineral exploration project, funded in part by an $11.2 million grant from the Canadian International Development Agency and a loan from the World Bank, has opened the last Amazon frontiers to corporate interests, and forced the indigenous populations into a final, desperate stand.

Companies involved in the resource bonanza and land grab in the Amazon Basin include Georgia Pacific and MacMillan Bloedel in timber; Swift-Armour in agribusiness and cattle raising; Reynolds Metals, Royal Dutch Shell, W. R. Grace Co., Alcan, Rio Tino Zinc, Inco, Gulf and Western, Falconbridge, Cominco, and others in the mining of bauxite, zinc, copper, nickel, tin, titanium, and coal; Anglo-American Corporation in gold; Gulf, Texaco, and Mobile oil companies; Litton Industries, Westinghouse, Komatsu, Fiat, General Motors, Caterpillar, Easton

16. *New York Times* News Service, January 6, 1973.
17. *Hungry for Profits*, Robert J. Ledogar; International Documentation, New York, 1975.

Corporation, and others in exploration and construction services; and U.S. Steel and Bethlehem Steel in iron ore and manganese. The native populations living in the Amazon Basin have been systematically exterminated. Between 1950 and 1968 the Cacass Novas tribe was reduced from 30,000 people to 400.[18] In 1974 a group of Brazilian anthropologists at the 41st International Congress of Americanists in Mexico City accused United States Steel Company of distributing influenza-contaminated blankets to Paracana tribesmen in the iron ore fields near the mouth of the Amazon River. Although proof of the plot was circumstantial, the company did distribute blankets, and the tribe was decimated by an epidemic of influenza.

The most isolated of the Amazon indigenous nations had been the Yanomami Indians until gold, diamonds, and uranium were discovered in their land in 1974. The Yanomami had already been pushed north by early Spanish settlement and the rubber industry, and had established their home in the Branco River valley, a remote Amazon tributary in the northernmost Brazilian province of Roraima. After the discovery of uranium in the area, the Brazilian government immediately began construction of the Northern Perimeter Highway, cutting through 225 kilometers of Yanomami land. Fourteen of the southern villages were soon decimated by highway workers, vigilante raids, and disease. Population in the villages was reduced from 400 to 79 by 1975.[19] In 1975 Fernando Ramos Pereira, governor of Roraima Province, told the press that the area "is not able to afford the luxury of conserving a half-a-dozen Indian tribes who are holding back development."[20] A 1972 report from Reuter news service detailed the existence of hunting parties in the Amazon jungles which "murdered and raided the peaceful Indian tribes." According to the report from Cuiaba, Brazil, an army official, two priests, and an agricultural engineer testified before a Brazilian court that on one documented occasion white hunters shot a baby in a young woman's arms, then hung the woman from a tree and hacked her to death with a machete. "On other occasions," reported Reuter, "planes bombarded the Indian villages with dynamite or dropped poisoned food into villages."

The Russell Tribunal found the Brazilian government and the World Bank guilty of the "systematic dispossession" of Indian people of their

18. *Brazilian Information Bulletin*, American Friends of Brazil, Berkeley, California, 1973.
19. Anthropology Resource Center, "The Yanomami Indian Park," Boston, 1981.
20. From the North American Congress on Latin America, quoted from *Akwesasne Notes*, Late Summer, 1975, p. 27.

Testimony before the Fourth Russell Tribunal, December 1980, in Rotterdam, Netherlands, brings tears to the eyes of delegate Dyhani Fisher Ywahoo, Cherokee-Cayawba from Vermont. (Photo by Dick Bancroft)

land. They found that through the Brazilian Agency for Indian Affairs (FUNAI, the Brazilian BIA) the government "consistently and illegally encourages settlement on land occupied by Indians." *U.S. News & World Report,* outlining development opportunities in Brazil, noted that obstacles included "soil deficiences, tropical diseases, insects, and hostile Indian tribes."[21]

Deeper into the Neo-European structure of South America lies land-locked Paraguay, ruled by the most openly repressive military regime on the continent. Paraguay was a favorite asylum for World War II Nazi war criminals such as Auschwitz's Herr Dr. Josef Mengele, who, to this day, basks in the neo-Nazi climate of General Alfredo Stroessner's government.

Paraguay is unique among countries of the Western Hemisphere: because of isolation, way-station use, and a relatively small Spanish population, the native language of Guarani was adopted in part by the ruling Spanish minority, and is still in use as an official language of the country, though Spanish, the other official language, is now taught in the

21. *Akwesasne Notes*, Spring, 1972; p. 29.

schools. Nevertheless, since declaring its independence from Spain in 1811, the country has been run by a lineage of absolute military dictators. General Higinio Morinigo supported the Axis powers during World War II. Stroessner assumed power in 1954, and has maintained an unabashedly repressive profile. The country still serves as a way-station and sanctuary for the neo-Nazi global underworld. Ousted Nicaraguan dictator Anastasio Somoza fled there in 1979, and in 1976 the Chilean assassins who blew up former Chilean ambassador Orlando Letelier in the streets of Washington, D.C. used the U.S. Embassy in Paraguay to obtain U.S. visas.[22].

In this climate, the local Ache Indians are the most ruthlessly oppressed of all the Indians in South America. Hunting parties employing helicopters, dogs, guns, machetes, and enslaved Indian guides have been widely reported. Nazi-style concentration camps and an open slave trade have been documented to the present day. Dr. Mark Munzel, a German anthropologist, documented first-hand reports of one such camp called the Colony, established in 1968, and operated by the notorious General Manuel de Jesus Periera.[23] According to Munzel, Periera sent hunting parties out after Aches; most of the Ache men were killed; those who would submit were used as free labor in the forest industry, and many died of starvation in the camps. Children were sold in open slave markets; women and young girls were forced into sexual slavery. Munzel accused Periera of maintaining several young Ache girls at his home for such purposes. Chilean entomologist, Luis Pena, working for the Peabody Museum of Yale University, offered a first-hand report in 1971 of the slave trade in San Juan Nepomuceno, one hundred miles southeast of the Paraguayan capital of Asuncion.[24] He reported that an Ache child could be purchased there at prices ranging from $18 to $72. Paraguayan anthropologist Miguel Chase-Sardi organized a humanitarian group in 1974 in Asuncion with the Catholic Church; they reported that as common practice Ache Indians "are hunted; they are pursued like animals. The parents are killed and the children sold."[25] Chase-Sardi was arrested and tortured, Pena was banned from the country, and Munzel was deported. The international outcry included reports from the University of Bern, the British Anti-Slavery Society, the Roman Catholic Church, and the World Council of Churches.

22. *Assassination on Embassy Row*, op. cit.
23. *The Ache Indians: Genocide in Paraguay*, Dr. Mark Munzel, International Work Group for Indigenous Affairs, Copenhagen, 1973.
24. *The Nation*, September 24, 1973.
25. *Akwesasne Notes*, Late Autumn, 1976, p. 23.

When American Dr. Richard Arens, author of *Genocide in Paraguay*, was invited by the Paraguayan government to tour an Indian reservation, he went, curious to know what he would be shown. Oddly, the camps to which he was escorted were as gruesome as reports had indicated. He was later interviewed by a General Samaniego who offered him a bribe to be a "reasonable man."[26] Arens reported: "When I said, 'Mr. Minister, I thought I had come to discuss with you the fate of the forest Indians,' he pressed a buzzer and in goose-stepped — and it was literally the Nazi-type goose-step — six uniformed characters who escorted me into another room. . . . I was told such things as 'anybody who puts out a book like this [*Genocide in Paraguay*] is obviously interested in subverting the only stable anti-Communist government in South America. It follows that he is a Communist. There's only one thing that ought to be done with him.' One doesn't feel very comfortable under such circumstances." Arens was relieved to be deported alive.

In spite of its well-documented repression, Paraguay has been a consistent recipient of U.S. economic and military aid. In 1974 Senator Abourezk said on the Senate floor that "Genocidal activities [are] still rampant in Paraguay . . . a government which is bent on the mass extermination of a part of its people does not deserve our aid." But the U.S. State Department continued to view Paraguay in a favorable light. Both the International League for the Rights of Man and former U.S. Human Rights Commissioner to the UN, Morris G. Abram, have accused the U.S. State Department of attempting to cover up the atrocities of the Stroessner regime in Paraguay. Abram wrote a letter to Senator James Buckley of New York claiming that Assistant Secretary of State Robert McCloskey had personally withheld information damaging to the Stroessner regime. As late as 1978, the U.S. State Department maintained in their Human Rights Report that extermination of Indians was non-existent, and that the government had made great strides in improving the lot of the Aches. In their report they ignored the volumes of evidence to the contrary, and quoted a Professor Robert C. Smith of the University of Kansas to support their case. The report led Richard Arens, who had been recently expelled from Paraguay, to investigate. He phoned Professor Smith, who told him that the State Department had manipulated his report by quoing out of context that in one area of Paraguay "the manhunt against the Aches appeared to have stopped because they have killed almost all of the Aches in that area and there is no one left to hunt."[27]

26. Ibid., Autumn, 1979, p. 6.
27. Ibid., p. 13.

The U.S. interest in propping up the reputation of the Stroessner government is different than in other South American countries. Although some oil and uranium, timber, and other resources in the country have commercial value, Paraguay's place in the web of global politics has more to do with the stability of its entrenched anti-Communist government. To seriously consider the human rights of the Ache Indians, the U.S. government would have to stir the hornets' nest in the global haven of neo-Nazi militarism.

The longest successful indigenous resistance to Neo-European occupation in Latin America was staged by the Mapuche Indians of what is now southern Chile. The Mapuche confiscated the Spanish invaders' horses and weapons in guerrilla raids along the rugged Andes Mountains, and held off the Conquistadors until 1884 when the newly formed independent nation of Chile amassed enough military strength to overrun and occupy their lands. Paralleling events in North America, the Chilean government established reservations, and then began to erode them and break them up through individual allotment. In the 1920s American mining interests began to move into Chile, and onto former Indian land. Anaconda Copper, owned at the time by the Rockefeller family and Standard Oil Trust, bought the Guggenheim family's Chile Copper Company for $70 million.[28] At that same time the Guggenheims' Kennecott Copper Company operated the world's largest underground mine in Chile. As the Mapuche were forced to become farm and mining wage laborers, the U.S. resource giants built enormous empires on Chilean profits. Kennecott took 7 million tons of copper out of Chile over the next fifty years. By 1969 Anaconda was selling half a billion dollars' worth of Chilean copper annually, claiming three-fourths of its corporate profits from that enterprise. All went well for the mining companies, and downhill for the Mapuches, until the democratic government of Chile elected Salvador Allende as president in 1970. In a move virtually unheard of in Neo-European politics, Allende began returning stolen land to the Mapuche people. Citing the fact that 600,000 Mapuche and Chilean peasant children were mentally retarded because they had lacked protein in their formative years, Allende instituted a daily half-litre-per-child milk distribution plan among the poor, and began a program of establishing family farms among the Indians and poor white populations. On July 11, 1971, Allende nationalized the Chilean copper industry, noting that foreign resource investors had taken from Chile earnings of $10 billion in sixty years. He told Saul Landau of the Washington-based Institute for Policy Studies that "the

28. *Everybody's Business*, op. cit.

total value of all the capital accumulated in Chile over the last four hundred years has left its frontiers."[29] On Mapuche land, farming cooperatives were formed, a Mapuche radio station was established, and medical clinics were established. But in Washington, D.C. Henry Kissinger, Richard Nixon, the CIA, ITT, Anaconda, Kennecott, and the Export-Import Bank had other plans for Chile.

As early as May 1970, ITT board member and former CIA Director John McCone had pledged $1 million for a joint ITT-CIA program to defeat Allende.[30] When that plan failed, Kissinger, Nixon, and current CIA Director Richard Helms initiated a plot to undermine Allende. On September 15, 1970, a few days after the Chilean election, Kissinger, Nixon, Helms, Attorney General John Mitchell, and Pepsi-Cola president Donald Kendall met with Don Agustin Edwards, publisher of Chile's ultra-conservative *El Mercurio* newspaper. Notes scribbled that day by CIA Director Helms, later surfacing in a Senate investigation, reveal the essence of the plot: "One in ten chance perhaps, but save Chile!/worth spending/not concerned risks involved/no involvement of embassy/$10,000,000 available, more if necessary/full-time job — best men we have/game plan/make the economy scream/48 hours for plan of action."[31] The Export-Import Bank cut off loans to Chile; millions of dollars flowed into *El Mercurio*, and other anti-Allende newpapers; the CIA infiltrated unions and engineered devastating strikes; economic aid was cut off from Chile; military aid increased; Kissinger warned the American people of a "Communist government" in Chile which presented "massive problems . . . for democratic forces and for pro-United States forces in Latin America and indeed to the whole Western Hemisphere"; friendly Chilean generals were bankrolled; and — on September 11, 1973 — Allende was assassinated in a military coup led by General Augusto Pinochet, who suspended the Chilean constitution and took over the country.

Bodies of the Mapuche leaders began to appear floating down the Allepen River south of Sanitago, from farmlands, through the village of Pitrufquen, to the Pacific Ocean. The only government-sponsored Indian land reform movement in the Western Hemisphere was over. Felix Hunentelaf, a Mapuche leader who had worked at the new radio station and had been elected to the Chilean Congress, was arrested and executed. Pinochet reinstituted the allotment program, selling off Indian land under the new Mapuche Land Law No. 3568. In December 1980,

29. *Assassination on Embassy Row*, op. cit., p. 45.
30. *Everybody's Business*, op. cit., p. 828.
31. *Assassination on Embassy Row*, op. cit., p. 39.

the international edition of *El Mercurio* proudly announced on page one that under the new law 2,168 individual property titles had been issued in the province of Cautin. The Mapuche people who were not killed after the coup were left landless and, once again, in poverty.

In 1977 Mapuche leader Antonio Millape told the UN: "Go to any Mapuche home today, and you will find that the dog outside will not bark, because it is too weak. If you go inside you will find one or more children lying sick, dying of starvation. There may be children outside, and they will tell you their parents are not home. Do not believe them. If you go inside you will find them, too, dying of starvation and extreme malnutrition. That is the form of extermination today under Pinochet."[32] Bank loans and American corporations returned to Chile. In 1979 the U.S. Justice Department dropped perjury charges against ITT's senior vice-president Edward Gerrity who had lied about ITT's role in the overthrow of Allende.[33] Federal lawyers, in the interest of national security, determined that the prosecution of Gerrity would reveal too much sensitive information concerning the cooperative dealings of the CIA, American corporations, and Latin American military regimes.

The stories of other Latin American Indian populations are similar, with local variations. Argentina, like Paraguay, has been ruled by the military, and has systematically exterminated most of the indigenous population; 200,000 survive in a population of 23 million. Uruguay has virtually eliminated all Indians inside its borders. In Bolivia, on the other hand, the Quechua-Aymara Andean Indians account for 75 percent of the population, and maintain a strong independence movement which has been viciously opposed by the military regime of President Huygo Banzer. In Peru, Quechua-Aymara Indians make up about half of the 11 million population; their land has been continually eroded by forest, oil, and mining industries. Development pressures in Ecuador, Venezuela, Guyana, and Surinam have, likewise, driven the indigenous populations from their traditional lands. The same is true in Central America, from Panama to Mexico.

Although left-leaning governments such as Allende's Democratic Socialists and the Sandinista Front of the recent Nicaraguan revolution have proven to be sympathetic to the Indians' claims, the Fourth World indigenous peoples' movements of Latin America and North America have made a particular effort to communicate to the world community that they do not represent just another facet of Third World left-vs.-right

32. Transcript, International NGO Conference, op. cit.
33. *Everybody's Business*, op. cit., p. 829.

ideology. One reason is that even the most socially enlightened leftist governments have failed to recognize the Indians' cultural and political sovereignty, which lies at the heart of the Fourth World movement. A Nicaraguan Indian woman interviewed by *Akwesasne Notes*, after the revolution there, said: "I don't mean to sound negative about the people in the Sandinista Front, about anyone who struggled in Nicaragua. It is just that the Indian experience within the left political parties has been . . . that they are inevitably maneuvered so as to become ineffective for their home communities. This victory — the expulsion of Somoza — is only a partial victory because within the directory [ruling junta] even now there are to be found some of the biggest industrialists, some of the politicos who were very sweet on Somoza while he was in strength."[34]

The Bolivian Indian sovereignty organization, Movimiento Indio Tupac Katari (MITKA), representing the Indian majority in Bolivia, has written that both the left and the right are "imported from Europe," and are fighting for what rightly belongs to the Indians. "They all unite and fight against the Indians when the latter claim their rights," says MITKA. "The whole range of leftist groups have not got the liberation of the Indian people in their platform either."[35]

The famous Peruvian peasant leader Hugo Blanco was half Quechua Indian. When he turned his support toward Quechua land rights, the Communist Party of Peru dropped him. The rightist government already had a price on his head, so he became a hunted, isolated reformist, roaming the hills with three hundred Quechua guerrillas. In his fascinating book, *Land or Death*,[36] Blanco recounts that while at university "I saw . . . that becoming a professional meant becoming part of the fabric of a system, that my knowledge would be only to the tiniest degree useful to my people, and to a great degree useful to the enemy's apparatus. I understand that although my country needed technicians, it needed fighters more." Blanco scoffed at the liberals who gave food to the Indians during a famine: "I don't ask that they distribute that charity to us; I ask that they return to us what is ours, so that there will be no famines."

This sentiment among Latin American Indians was generally shared throughout the American Indian Treaty Council which had often been termed leftist. AIM, likewise, had been labeled Communist by William Janklow, the John Birch Society, and others. In a brilliant speech to the Black Hills Survival Gathering in South Dakota in July of 1980, Russell

34. *Akwesasne Notes*, Autumn, 1979, p. 10.
35. MITKA reprint, International Working Group for Indigenous Affairs, Frederikshoms Kanal, Copenhagen, 1978.
36. *Land or Death*, Hugo Blanco, Path Finder Press, New York, 1972.

Means delivered what has already become a classic statement of Fourth World philosophy. Accurately tracing modern Neo-European beliefs to their sixteenth-century Cartesian roots, he went on to explain the difference between the European world view and that of the Indian nations: "Hegel and Marx were heirs to the thinking of Newton, Descartes, Locke, and Smith. Hegel finished the process of secularizing theology. . . . Then Marx put Hegel's philosophy into terms of 'materialism.' That is, Marx despiritualized Hegel's work altogether. This is now seen as the future revolutionary potential of Europe . . . but American Indians see it simply as still more of that same old European conflict between *being* and *gaining*. Being is a spiritual proposition; gaining is a material act. . . . Philosophers have despiritualized reality, so there is no satisfaction [for them] to be gained in simply observing the wonder of a mountain or a lake or a people *in being*.

"You can't judge the real nature of a European revolutionary doctrine on the basis of the changes it proposes to make within the European power structure and society. You can only judge it by the effects it will have on non-European peoples. This is because every revolution in Europe's history has served to reinforce Europe's tendencies and abilities to export destruction to other peoples, other cultures, and the environment itself. I defy anyone to point out an example where this isn't true . . .

"Look beneath the surface of revolutionary Marxism and what do you find? A commitment to reversing the industrial system which created the need of white society for uranium? No . . . a commitment to our rights, as peoples, to maintaining our values and traditions? No . . . Revolutionary Marxism is committed to even further perpetuation and perfection of the very industrial process which is destroying us all. . . . Marx himself called us 'precapitalist' and 'primitive.'

"I see that the territory of the USSR used to contain a number of tribal peoples, and that they have been crushed to make way for the factories. . . . I see China explode nuclear bombs, developing uranium reactors . . . it's the same old song . . .

"There is another way. There is the traditional Lakota way and the ways of the other American Indian peoples. It is the way that knows that humans do not have the right to degrade Mother Earth, that there are forces beyond anything the European mind has conceived, that humans must be in harmony with all relations or the relations will eventually eliminate this disharmony. . . . All European traditions, Marxism included, have conspired to defy the natural order of all things. . . . Things come full circle. Back to where they started. That's revolution . . . It is the role of American Indian peoples, the role of all natural beings to survive. A part of our survival is to resist. We resist, not to overthrow government or to take political power, but because it is natural to resist extermination, to survive . . . I don't care if it's only a handful of red people living high in the Andes, indigenous people will survive, and harmony will be re-established. That's revolution.''

Thus, through the Geneva convention, the Russell Tribunal and other international forums, the indigenous people of the Western Hemisphere had made a clear and consistent statement: they were sovereign nations — colonized, brutalized, driven to take, at times, desperate recourse, but determined to survive. The Russell Tribunal indicted virtually every country in the Western Hemisphere, from Chile to Canada, for practicing genocide and ethnocide against the native populations. They charged these countries with breaking the United Nations Charter (1945), the Universal Declaration of Human Rights (1948), the International Covenant of Economic, Social and Cultural Rights (1966), the Covenant on Civil and Political Rights (1966), the Convention on the Prevention and Punishment of Genocide (1948), the International Convention on the Elimination of All Forms of Racial Discrimination (1965), UN General Assembly Resolution on Permanent Sovereignty over Natural Resources (1962), the Declaration on the Granting of Independence to Colonial Countries and Peoples (1960), the American Convention on Human Rights (1969), the Helsinki Final Act (1975), and the Convention concerning the Protection and Integration of Indigenous and Other Tribal and Semi-Tribal Populations in independent Countries (1957).

Canada, the United States, Guatemala, Panama, Colombia, Peru, and Brazil were also charged with breaking their own internal laws in their persecution of Indian people. The Tribunal, however, like the United Nations itself, has no more power than the power of information and world opinion. The International Indian Treaty Council was well aware of the fact, and harbored no illusions that the United States or Guatemala or Paraguay would recoil in shame at the exposure of their misdeeds. The real value of the international forums had been twofold: internally, the Indian nations had created a united front that spanned the Western Hemisphere, and externally they had raised their issue of sovereignty to the international level in which whatever repression did continue against them would have to take place in the full light of world scrutiny. General Periera, William Janklow, and David Price suddenly became known as notorious bit players in an international tragedy; no longer would Indian leaders in South Dakota or Paraguay die anonymously, nor would they languish forgotten in prisons; the play had been moved to center stage. Oren Lyons of the Haudenosaunee told the Tribunal: "There are millions of people looking in this direction. . . . It is a great responsibility to all the delegates who are here, and I must commend the Russell Tribunal for the courage to take this issue — because we are challenging the major powers of this world.''

Back in North America, the struggle for Indian land rights and treaty rights had broadened, deepened, and intensified. In Canada, a furor had erupted among the legal profession, the Justice Ministry, and the Native people following the revelation that Leonard Peltier had been extradited illegally using the bogus accounts from Myrtle Poor Bear's affidavits. When lawyer Paul Halprin, who had prosecuted the extradition case for the U.S. government, was implicated in the misconduct, he sued the *Vancouver Sun* and accusing lawyer Peter Grant in an attempt to clear his name. His suit backfired when he was forced in court to admit that he had taken the FBI-supplied affidavits at face value, but that legal procedure placed upon him a duty to verify the information. He said he was "shocked"[37] when he received the third affidavit which contradicted the other two, eliminating Poor Bear as an "eyewitness." He said that he would have expected all the material in the case to be provided, and agreed that the word "misconduct" was not too harsh to describe the holding back of relevant material. Lawyers, labor leaders, Indian leaders, and Members of Parliament demanded the return of Peltier, but to no avail. The Canadian government under Pierre Trudeau failed to challenge the U.S. officially, and the U.S. government ignored the outcry.

Likewise, the Canadian government let their "urgent investigation" of the murder of Anna Mae Aquash wane into oblivion. When External Affairs Minister Allen MacEachen was questioned on June 29, 1976 in the House of Commons on the progress of his investigation, he produced an FBI press release issued by Clarence Kelley. When questioned on the progress of the investigation once again in October, the new External Affairs Minister, Donald Jamieson, produced an updated FBI press release which stated that "175 agents" had been used to investigate the killing, but that they were not able to crack the case. A year later the matter had long since disappeared from the agenda of the House of Commons.

Canada's complicity in the FBI's disruption of AIM, unwitting or invidious, was not at all out of character. In spite of Canada's global reputation as a benign, liberal, freedom-loving country — sort of a big North American Switzerland — the federal government in Ottawa wields extraordinary power. Trudeau's government possessed the

37. *Vancouver Sun*, April 26, 1979.

power to declare marshal law under its War Measure Act, and had done so at 4:00 A.M., October 16, 1970. Following the abduction of British Trades Commissioner Richard Cross and Quebec Minister of Labour and Immigration Pierre Laporte by the separatist *Front de Liberation du Quebec* (F.L.Q.), Trudeau's government closed counterculture newspapers across the country and arrested F.L.Q. sympathizers on the streets.

Canada, the second largest country in the world with a tiny population of 20 million, is a member of the Commonwealth of Great Britain. Its provinces form a confederation which has been a shaky alliance at best of times, as angry Newfoundland fishing communities, the separatist *Parti Quebecois,* and oil-rich Albertans have threatened to pull out. Ottawa's fragile grip on centralist control began with the British North American Act of 1867, in which the Crown granted its colony the right to form a parliament and run its own affairs, albeit under the watchful eye and for the greater glory of the empire.

British imperial policy had considered the Indian nations as either allies or enemies in their maneuvering to establish their colony in North America. The enemies fell prey to the British military; the allies to the British legal system. Although the Indians signed treaties with Britain, and then with Canada, those treaties were freely and unilaterally abrogated by the Canadian Parliament, and the courts have consistently upheld that acts of Parliament take precedence over the treaties. Canadian lawyer Kenneth Lysyk has written that "Federal legislative competence with respect to Indians is unfettered by treaties — either Indian treaties or international treaties."[38] As in the United States, treaties with Indians served only a transitory function for Neo-European expansionism.

Canada always followed America's lead in its dealings with the Indians, establishing reservations, breaking up the reservations into individual allotments, and installing tribal governments, always one or two years after the U.S. Congress set the format. In a flair for originality betraying the true intent in both countries, the Canadian Parliament followed the establishment of the BIA in the United States with their own ministerial portfolio of Indian Affairs and Northern Development. The entire Northwest Territories, the size of the western United States, are governed as a subdivision of this department.

The vast Northwest Territories actually stretch east to Baffin Island,

---

38. "The Unique Constitutional Position of the Canadian Indian," *Canadian Bar Review*, December, 1976.

two hundred miles from Greenland; west to the Mackenzie River which runs north into the Beaufort Sea; and north from the 60th parallel, across the Arctic Circle to the frozen islands of the Arctic Ocean. It is the home of the Inuit, Cree, and the Athabascan Dine people, ancient relatives of the southern Dine or Navajo.

In the 1920s the Canadian government sent Federal Commissioner Henry Conroy and Oblate Bishop Gabriel Breynat to the Mackenzie River valley to negotiate a treaty with the inhabitants; the result of their mission was Treaty Eleven, upon which they collected a few Indian signatures from people who may or may not have known that they traded their entire homeland for $25 per chief, $5 per family head, a few new axes, handsaws, and grindstones. In 1947 the Geological Survey of Canada discovered vast petroleum reserves in the area, and the familiar corporate land grab followed. In 1968 Imperial Oil, which had established a corporate outpost on the British Columbia coast as early as 1880, announced the discovery of oil and gas reserves in Prudhoe Bay, off the northern coast of Alaska. Thus began a major conflict with the Inuit, Cree, and Dine people.

Exxon Corporation, the owner of Imperial Oil, announced a proposal for a pipeline to carry the resource riches of the North through Mackenzie River valley to the American markets. Both the World Wildlife Federation and the Canadian Wildlife Confederation opposed the massive construction project on environmental grounds, and the Indians opposed it on the grounds that they owned the land. In 1973 Judge William Morrow ordered a freeze on all land sales and development in the area until the issue could be settled. In 1977 the Canadian government appointed Justice Thomas Berger to conduct an inquiry. The Berger Inquiry warned that the project would destroy vast tracts of land, endanger the grizzly bear, Dall sheep, and other animals of the North; and disrupt or destroy the Native cultures in the area. Berger then handed the matter back to the Parliament stating that, "Canada should have, and indeed must have, the right to overrule the wishes of the Native people. That's the Parliament's prerogative . . . but I want them to understand the price they'll pay."

An uproar in Canada over the destruction of the North for America's energy consumption provided a reprieve for the Indians. The Council of Yukon Indians, representing 6,000 native people, claimed land and mineral rights to 207,000 square miles of territory, virtually the entire Yukon. The Committee for Original Peoples' Entitlement, representing 2,500 Inuvialuit people of the Western Arctic, claimed 169,000 square miles. In 1978 they signed an agreement in principle for $45 million, ownership of 37,000 square miles, and full sub-surface rights to 5,000 square miles. Leaked documents[39] later revealed that the federal government had second thoughts about following through with a final agreement. The Inuit Tapirisat, representing 17,000 people, have claimed 750,000 square miles, and declared themselves the sovereign nation of Nunavut. In 1979 Justice Patrick Mahoney ruled that the Baker Lake Inuit do indeed have aboriginal rights, defeating a federal government argument that the 1670 Hudson's Bay Charter had extinguished those rights. However, uranium was discovered in northern Canada and, with the stakes raised, the rules of the game were amended. Justice Mahoney allowed uranium exploration and mine development to proceed, saying that aboriginal rights were not necessarily property rights.

In 1971 Quebec Premier Robert Bourassa announced the massive hydroelectric project on the eastern shore of James Bay, the southern finger of Hudson Bay. The proposed project was to take twelve years to complete; cost $6 billion; involve ITT, American banks, and American power companies; and, when finished, would be the largest such electricity generating station in the world. It would also flood out 9,000 Cree and Inuit Indians who happened to be living in the Opinaca and Kanaaupscow River valleys. On Thursday, November 5, 1973 Justice Albert Malouf of the Quebec Supreme Court issued a 170-page injunction, halting work on the project until the land rights could be cleared up. The injunction was later overturned by the Quebec government, which offered to pay the 6,000 Cree $45 million over ten years.[40] A spokesperson for the Indians pointed out that that equalled $750 per person per year, and that a store-bought chicken cost $7.50 in the area, "so the government is offering us two chickens a week each, for ten years, in exchange for our land and self-sufficient life. Then what?" A protracted court case left the Cree with a 2,000-square-mile reservation and the Inuit with some hunting and fishing rights only; the original Cree-Inuit homeland around James Bay had covered 400,000 square miles. They were left with ½ of 1 percent of that land. The James Bay Development Corporation patrolled its realm with a private police force; visitors to the area had to acquire special passes from the corporation.

Understandably, Canadian Indian people began to move their battle from Canadian courtrooms into the streets. Furthermore, North American Indian movements, unlike the Neo-European governments, were not defined by the 49th parallel and other borders. The Anishinabe Ojibway of Ontario, and the Anishinabe Ojibway of Minnesota, for

39. *McLean's*, February 23, 1981, Toronto, Ontario.
40. *Akwesasne Notes*, Early Winter, 1974, p. 12.

example, are one and the same. In 1959 the Department of Indian Affairs sold a twelve-acre parcel of land, held in trust for the Ojibway by the federal government, to the city of Kenora, Ontario. On July 22, 1974, while the Wounded Knee trials were going on three hundred miles to the south in St. Paul, the Ojibway Warrior Society occupied the land. They demanded that their lands be administered by them, rather than by Indian Affairs. Crown attorney Ted Burton said three weeks later that if the armed Indians did not leave the land, they would be evicted "by whatever means the police think are desirable."[41] When AIM leader Vernon Bellecourt, an Ojibway from just across the border, visited the site, Ottawa took the opportunity to tell the public that the takeover was due to outside agitators. Nevertheless, Kenora Mayor Jim Dairdson said that Kenora had purchased the land in good faith, and that if there was a land title dispute he was willing to negotiate with the Ojibway people. Dairdson managed to diffuse the confrontation somewhat by his stance and the whole affair was ended without a violent clash, but the land was not recognized by either government as belonging to the Ojibway people.

Much more devastating to the Ojibway people of Ontario, however, was the death by mercury of the two rivers which had traditionally provided them with food. Mercury discharged from the Dryden Chemical Company plant upriver had accumulated in the English and Wabigoon rivers. By 1974, cats on the White Dog and Grassy Narrows reserves had begun to lose coordination and die spasmodic deaths. The sign was familiar to Dr. Jun Ui from Japan, who had experienced the mercury tragedy of Minamata Bay, following which Japanese courts found Chisso Chemical Company directly responsible for crippling the nervous systems of 798 villagers. In Japan, cats had begun to die first; 120 villagers subsequently died from the disease.[42] The government of Canada had responded to the crisis by putting "Fish for Fun" signs along the river to discourage tourists from eating the poisoned fish. Dr. Ui warned the Canadian government on a trip to Canada in 1975: "If you don't start action you will have a more serious result than we had . . . the Dryden area is worse than it is in Japan."[43] The Ontario Health Minister maintained that the government had warned the Indians "not to eat the fish," and some of the Ojibway on the reservation confirmed that they had received the letters. While the government scientists milled about their labs searching for conclusive proof, and Ottawa played down the

41. *Georgia Straight*, January 9, 1975; Vancouver, B.C.
42. *Minamata*, W. Eugene Smith and Aileen M. Smith, Alskog-Sensorium Books/Holt, Rinehart and Winston, New York, 1975.
43. *Akwesasne Notes*; Summer, 1975, p. 16.

affair with deference to tourism, the Indians of the Restigouch Reserve on the St. Lawrence River began shipping salmon to White Dog and Grassy Narrows reserves. Dryden, in response to a study by Environment Canada Thunder Bay office director Ian Ramsay, promised to install filtering equipment as soon as they could scrape together the money.

A thousand miles to the west, in the interior of British Columbia, Chief Ken Basil of the Bonaparte Indian Band, supported by the local American Indian Movement, established a roadblock on B.C. Highway 12 where it passed through the Bonaparte reservation between the towns of Lillooet and Cache Creek. To dramatize the poor housing conditions on the several small reservations in the area, water diversion by the provincial government, and other grievances, the Indians collected a $5.00 toll from motorists. The confrontation tactic brought the issues to the fore, forcing the province and Indian Affairs into negotiations. Such affronts to the Crown, as well as events in the United States, had stirred the RCMP to mobilize against "Red Power militancy" across Canada. In 1975 the *Montreal Gazette* uncovered a report from the RCMP to Solicitor-General Warren Allmand warning that "certain Indian militants" were collecting arms, and that "if their demands are not met rapidly, it is conceivable that the Indian militants will try to reach their objectives through violence."[44]

During the Wounded Knee incident in 1973, the FBI had sent a telex[45] to the RCMP, alerting them to watch for AIM members crossing the border. The RCMP had responded with their own counterinsurgency military exercises and stepped-up surveillance of Indian groups. After the arrest of Leonard Peltier in Alberta in 1976, western Canadian Indian leaders complained of increased harassment from the RCMP. Urban Calling Last, director of the Calgary Urban Treaty Alliance, told the press that an unidentified undercover RCMP officer had approached him for information about AIM leaders, and in return "my organization would not have to worry about funds anymore," Calling Last said.[46] "I told him to go to hell." He said that another officer returned in the middle of the night with a bottle of whiskey and tried to get him drunk and pry information from him. RCMP Inspector Roy Byrne, head of security for Alberta, admitted to the press that an officer did visit Urban Calling Last, did share a bottle of whiskey with him, and did try to get information, but that it was "just a social visit."

44. *Montreal Gazette*; quoted from *Akwesasne Notes*, Autumn 1975, p. 41.
45. *The Life and Death of Anna Mae Aquash*, Johanna Brand, James Lorimer & Co., Toronto, 1978; p. 154.
46. Gillian Lindgren, *Calgary Herald*, February 19, 1976.

Alberta AIM leaders Nelson Small Legs and Roy Littlechief complained of constant surveillance by the RCMP. Littlechief said that he had been picked up several times by the RCMP on old traffic tickets, and questioned. Then, on February 20, 1976, three weeks after Peltier had been arrested, Ken Basil, who had led the B.C. Indian people in their picket of the Cache Creek highway, was arrested by the RCMP on a fourteen-month-old charge of creating a disturbance, stemming from the blockade.[47] The arrest signaled a general round-up of AIM members in western Canada. Two Oglalas from South Dakota, in Vancouver to help with the Peltier defense, reported that their hotel room door was kicked in by RCMP at 12:30 one night. Edgar Bear Runner and Louie Bad Wound said they were ordered to stay in bed while the two officers ransacked their room.[48] Bear Runner said: "What may have precipitated the whole thing was that an FBI agent that we've seen on the reservation [Pine Ridge] was milling around the courthouse all day yesterday. He must have set this up on us."

In 1977 Ed Bernstick from the Cree nation of Canada told the UN conference in Geneva that "When the people took over the Bureau of Indian Affairs offices in Washington [1972] there was a contract paper that was discovered there between the Department of Indian Affairs in Canada and the BIA in the United States. This White Paper policy was introduced by the Canadian government. At the same time there was a new economic development program set up called the Mid-Canada Corridor. This is the Northern Development Plan, designed to take all economic basis away from Indian people. It involves the Department of Northern Saskatchewan and Northlands in Alberta, the Department of Northern Manitoba where there is a huge hydrodevelopment project going on, and the development programs in Northern Ontario, Quebec, British Columbia, and the Northwest Territories."

Part of that Canadian resource development plan included the mining of uranium in northern Saskatchewan, in the land of the Athabasca Dine people. In 1953 Eldorado Nuclear had established Uranium City on land north of Lake Athabasca, claimed by the Dine. There, they began mining from Canada's largest known uranium field. The Canadian government took the position that the land was Crown land, and Eldorado Nuclear began exporting uranium to the world market, piling up the toxic mill tailings (residue left after the ore is extracted) on the land, and dumping the deadly waste sludge into the lake system of the area. From 1959 through 1974 Eldorado Nuclear participated in a uranium cartel with the British Rio Tinto Zinc, France, South Africa, and Australia,

47. *Vancouver Sun*, February 21, 1976.
48. *Georgia Straight*, op. cit., May, 1976.

driving the price of uranium up to $40 per pound from about $9 per pound in the early 1960s. Pressure from the United States broke up the cartel in 1975, but Eldorado Nuclear was then entrenched in Dine land.

John Graham, a Dine who helped organize the Group for Survival, an anti-uranium organization in Saskatoon, told Mordecai Specktor of the *University of Minnesota Daily*: "They have a program in the prisons; to get good time or to get paroled, inmates can go into a program to work in the uranium mines. It's the same thing with the welfare system: you have to apply to work in the mines before you're eligible for welfare. It's slave labor. It's genocide."[49] Graham and others began working with the International Indian Treaty Council in an attempt to bring their claims before the UN, citing the documented lung cancer deaths of their Dine relatives, the Navajo uranium miners of New Mexico.

In the pattern that now ran from Chile to the Arctic Circle, the resource boom invariably brought corporate squatters to Indian land, and the struggle that ensued invariably pitted a self-sufficient, labor-intensive collective community against hit-and-run, capital-intensive corporate development which could turn a quick dollar or a quick million to capitalize its next venture.

For hundreds of years the Nishga Indians lived in small fishing villages on the remote northwest coast of what is now British Columbia. A 1916 Royal Commission on Indian Affairs — which had conducted a whirlwind three-day tour of British Columbia to establish Indian reservations — had confined the Nishga to several tiny parcels of land along the Portland Canal, a hundred-mile-long, branching fiord that serves as the border between the southern tip of the Alaskan panhandle and the province of British Columbia. In 1968 Kennecott Copper began mining molybdenum at Alice Arm, a branch of the fiord. They abandoned the site in 1972. In 1974 AMAX mining corporation, through its subsidiary Climax Molybdenum Corporation of B.C. Ltd., hired consultant J. L. Littlepage to write a report on the impact upon the local environment and upon the Nishga people should AMAX dump mine tailings into the inlet. Littlepage determined that neither the ocean life nor the Nishga people would be seriously affected.[50] The process had worked before for AMAX. In Colorado in 1967 the company had formed a task force called an Experiment in Ecology to soften the hearts and minds of local residents before opening a $500 million molybdenum mine forty miles west of Denver.

AMAX had its beginning as a mining company in Hanover, Germany

49. Mordecai Specktor, *University of Minnesota Daily*, October 9, 1980.
50. David Garrick, *Mine Talk*: July/August, 1981.

in 1700. The company established branches in Frankfurt, London, and then in New York in 1880. In 1920 the U.S. government seized the German interests of the company and sold them to American investors, establishing the American Metal Corporation. That company merged with Climax Molybdenum on December 23, 1957 to form American Metal Climax, which they adroitly shortened to AMAX in 1974, the year they began their environmental study at Alice Arm. On the basis of the Littlepage data, the province of B.C. and the government of Canada offered AMAX special exemptions from existing environmental regulations protecting such waterways. On January 12, 1979 the B.C. government issued a pollution control permit allowing AMAX to discharge up to 400,000 mg/liter of suspended solids into the waters of Alice Arm.[51] The B.C. Pollution Control Board standard recommendation is 25 to 75 mg/liter. The federal standard is 50 mg/liter, but the federal cabinet amended the Fisheries Act to clear the way for AMAX. The company's discharge limit was thus established at 8,000 times the normal recommendation. AMAX operates similarly in Africa, Australia, Arizona, Colorado, Missouri, Japan, New Caledonia, New Brunswick, Botswana, and Zambia. In 1972 stockholding heirs of Climax Molybdenum founder Max Schott sued AMAX for operating "illegally and immorally" in southern Africa.

The Nishga were among the Northwest Coast Indian nations — including the Haida, Nootka, Kwagluth, and others — who traditionally gathered each year at the summer Potlach, a giant give-away feast during which the various nations would show their faith in the community by giving away their accumulated wealth: skins, dried fish, copper shields, medallions, and other material possessions. The ceremony — banned by the Canadian government from 1919 to 1940 — established the people's dedication to and faith in the interdependent community. In 1979, when AMAX announced its plans, the Nishga were quietly living as they always had, from the bountiful fishing waters of the coastal inlets.

The Nishga rallied to stop the mine as AMAX ran full-page ads across the province proclaiming that "Saving your environment is our business!" David Garrick of the Canadian Society for Pollution and Environmental Control says that the mine tailings will kill the inlet, and thus destroy the life of the Nishga. "The waste tailings contain mercury, cadmium, lead, arsenic, zinc, and trace amounts of other dangerous metals. In addition, the ore contains Radium-226, uranium, and thorium in unknown quantities. These radioactive heavy metals are not only toxic, but water soluble. Radium decays into deadly radon gas." In May

51. Ibid.

of 1981 the first mine wastes were spotted at Alice Arm near the AMAX tailings pipe outfall, fifty meters below the surface of the water. The AMAX mine, if the company can hold off environmentalist and Nishga efforts to stop it, will discharge about 12,000 tons of tailings per day — totalling 100 million tons over the twenty-six-year expected life of the mine — into the inlet. Watching from the wings are two other mining companies — Borax Metals Corporation and Rio Tinto Zinc — both of whom have similar plans to mine molybdenum in the area. The mine would produce molybdenum, used to harden steel alloys, for twenty-six years. AMAX, which reported profits of $365 million and sales of $2.9 billion in 1979, would then move on to new ventures.

From these coastal inlets, to the mercury-laden rivers in Ontario and the lifeless lakes of acid-rain-drenched Quebec, Indian nations within the borders of Canada had experienced the destruction of their way of life, and had risen to confront the government with land claims that would protect their means of survival. The Russell Tribunal found Canada guilty of violating the Universal Declaration of Human Rights, the American Convention on Human Rights, and the International Convention on Racial Discrimination in their dealings with those Indian nations. In 1977 Art Solomon from the American Indian Movement chapter in Toronto, Ontario, told the UN Conference in Geneva: "If I trusted only in what men and women can do, then I would be afraid for what comes after, but I've seen the power, the Sacred power of the Creator working among us. . . . We are brothers and sisters wherever we come from on the earth. . . . All those who are using their power against us, to oppress us, to kill our people, to steal our land, to steal our humanity, they're following the way of the great negative power. They cannot win. If we turn to the Creator . . . we cannot lose."

By 1980 the traditional Indian movement in the United States, though consistently a land-based spiritual movement at heart, had evolved strategically at the level of practical political activity. The national chairmanship of AIM had been disbanded in 1978, as the position had served little function other than to target the person who held it. AIM offices throughout Canada and the United States continued to function as local entities; the decentralization not only conformed to Indian social organization, but presented a network less easily infiltrated, since there was no longer a central leadership upon which the FBI could focus their attention. John Trudell, who had previously held the national chairmanship, had worked to forge an alliance with the burgeoning environmental and no-nukes movements among the young white community. He had toured with musician Jackson Browne in a series of benefit concerts which had raised money for the many defense funds, and had served to raise the white organizers' awareness of Indian issues.

In July of 1980 Trudell spoke during a Browne performance at the Black Hills Survival Gathering, organized by a coalition of South Dakota environmentalists, Indians, and sympathetic farmers. Trudell told the crowd: "We must go beyond the arrogance of human rights. We must understand *natural* rights, because all the natural world has a right to existence. . . . One of the things I hope that you all learn while you are here is the energy and power that the elements are: that of the sun and the wind and the rain. This is the only real power. . . . There is no such thing as military power; there is only military terrorism. There is no such thing as economic power; there is only economic exploitation. That is all it is. We are an extension of the earth; we are not separate from it. . . . The earth is spirit, and we are an extension of that spirit. We are spirit. We are power.

"I look around in the white community, and I see people who are not oppressed, but they say they feel powerless. Then I look around in the Indian community, and I see people who are totally oppressed, but it is important for you to understand that they do not feel powerless." That power, the strength of the Indian movement now spanning the entire Western Hemisphere, emerged as the one unifying element among the U.S. environmental movements. Whites concerned about the survival of the environment could suddenly see that the Indians had been giving environmental speeches for four hundred years. Suddenly, when, to the more pessimistic ecologists, prospects for a fruitful future seemed most dark, the Indian movement lit the way with a convincing and healthy relationship to the land.

In 1980 Leonard Peltier's case was taken up by California Congressman Don Edwards, movie star Robert Redford, and literally thousands of non-Indian supporters. When Peltier appealed to exiting President Jimmy Carter for a commutation of sentence, letters poured into the White House from every state in the union. The letters came from lawyers, entertainers, environmental groups, and religious organizations, and even from schoolchildren. "I am 13 years of age, and although that may decrease your respect for my opinion, please listen to what I have to say," wrote Tauna Lockhart of Rapid City, South Dakota to the President. "I know from documents I have knowledge of that the FBI seems to have set up Leonard. . . . Please, I ask of you to pardon Peltier, because Peltier is innocent, and only you can help Peltier and be just by pardoning him. Thank you."

Sixteen congressmen signed a letter urging the President to review the case, but the effort failed to penetrate the Oval Office. In March 1981, however, a California appeals court ruled that Peltier had not received a fair trial before federal Judge Lydick when he was convicted of escape from prison. The Ninth Circuit Appeals Court ruled that Peltier had been denied the right to base a defense on duress because of the assassination threat. The court also ruled that he had been denied the right to cross-examine the government witnesses who had been presented against him. The reversal meant that if the government did not consent to a new trial, then the charges against Peltier for escape would have to be dropped. If they did consent to a new trial, Peltier would then be able to present evidence of the plot to murder him, implicating prison officials. The government chose to let the matter drop rather than re-open the potentially embarrassing case.

Congressman Don Edwards's House Subcommittee on Civil and Constitutional Rights questioned the FBI on their activities regarding Peltier during FBI oversight hearings, but as a committee staff lawyer said: "It doesn't matter what we find out, really, because the FBI has all the votes they need in Congress to stop any serious investigation. The FBI has most congressmen totally intimidated; the FBI has the votes, we don't. And it doesn't really matter what the law is or what regulations we establish, the FBI does what it wants." In the meantime, Peltier, a humble man who claims to hold no special status in the Indian movement, had become an international figure. In April 1981 *People* magazine quoted a friend who called him a "symbol for the Indian struggle." His lawyers claim to be in possession of evidence that proves he was systematically framed by the FBI, but there is not a court in the land that wants to hear it. Likewise, Richard Marshall, also convicted on fabricated evidence, languishes in jail while courts dodge his case.

On the Pine Ridge reservation itself, Dickie Wilson had lost his grip on power in a tribal election monitored by the Federal Mediation and Conciliation Service, on January 27, 1976. Prior to his defeat, Atlanta attorney Reber Bouldt told a reporter: "I think the FBI and the BIA consider the excesses of the Wilson regime to be more than they can deal with. Wilson is like Thieu in Vietnam — the United States many times talked about dumping Thieu, as he was carrying things too far and embarrassing the U.S. government. Dick Wilson is doing the same. He's totally, openly, and unabashedly corrupt."[52] Wilson, however, had served his purpose, overseeing the transfer of 133,000 acres of uranium-rich reservation land to the federal government. He was ousted by Al Trimble who had been earlier forced from a BIA superintendent job by Wilson. The Oglala-Lakota had refused claims money awarded them by

52. *Akwesasne Notes*; Summer, 1975, p. 9.

the government, and tribal attorney Mario Gonzalez had launched a suit against the government demanding return of the Black Hills and $11 billion for damages and stolen resources.

East of the Great Lakes, the Mohawk people of Akwesasne live on 22,000 acres of their original eighteen-million-acre homeland along the St. Lawrence Seaway. They are Haudenosaunee, members of the Six Nations Confederacy with the Onondaga, Cayuga, Seneca, Oneida, and Tuscarora. Ten law enforcement agencies claim at least partial jurisdiction over their 22,000-acre reservation land: the Canadian and U.S. federal governments, New York State police, Quebec and Ontario Provincial police, Canadian and U.S. border police, local police on both sides of the border, and the BIA tribal police known as the Akwesasne Police. In 1980 their continuing dispute with these agencies erupted when a Mohawk chief was arrested for seizing the logging equipment of several men who were felling trees on his land.

The traditional Haudenosaunee system is based upon their Great Law of Peace which guarantees equal decision-making power to all people of the community. The women hold the nation's title, and the clan mothers select the chiefs. Chief Oren Lyons says: "It offends us to be questioned: 'Are women equal?' Our prophecies told of a time when man would be pitted against woman."[53] He says that a failure of Neo-European governments is that they are controlled by "only men; they do not respond to the voice of the mothers, so naturally there is conflict."

The first white man that the Haudenosaunee saw was the Frenchman Jacques Cartier in 1537. In 1754 they met with the colonial revolutionaries, struck an alliance of peace, and loaned many of the concepts of their confederation system to the new American government. By 1776 they had over two hundred treaties with other Indian nations and European governments. In 1784 they signed their first treaty with the United States, and in that same year New York State Congressman and land speculator James Bowan began a process of negotiating land leases from individual Mohawks, persuading them with cash. The Haudenosaunee objected, and in 1790 the federal government passed the Indian Non-Intercourse Act which prohibited states from negotiating land deals with Indian nations in violation of U.S. treaty agreements. New York State continued, however, and these land deals were negotiated with tribal trustees whom the state had appointed in 1803, all of this being technically illegal. In 1892 the state legislated a mandatory elected form of government to supposedly rule the Haudenosaunee people. When the Mohawks voted to reject the trustees — in 1935, 1948, and again in

53. Testimony before the Fourth Russell Tribunal, op. cit.

1951 — the state militia was sent in to enforce the trustee government. In 1972 the federal government, through the BIA, began to fund the Akwesasne police. In the meantime, both Canada and the United States had declared them citizens of their respective countries, and thus claimed police jurisdiction over the Mohawk people.

On May 22, 1979 Chief Loran Thompson found a federal work crew cutting down trees on his land, supposedly under agreement from the trustees. Thompson seized the equipment, and ordered the men from his land. Later the same day New York State police and the Akwesasne police arrested Chief Thompson — allegedly beating him severely — and charged him with grand larceny. On May 27 several hundred traditional people marched on the Akwesasne police headquarters, evicted the police, and announced that the police had been illegal, and were no longer recognized as having any jurisdiction on the reservation.

When the state police issued indictments for twenty-three Mohawk leaders, two hundred traditional people established an armed encampment on Raquette Point, where the Raquette River empties into the St. Lawrence. The reservation was invaded by state police, and the Akwesasne police force was beefed up with a $204,987 CETA grant. The state police made a few forays into the area, but Raquette Point was held by the Mohawk people through the winter and spring. In the summer of 1980 a new force was added to the equation: a white vigilante group began sending armed teams into the woods around the encampment.

On June 13, Akwesasne police, state police and vigilantes surrounded Raquette Point and established a tight perimeter. A delegation of Haudenosaunee led by Onandaga Chief Oren Lyons met in Albany with Raymond Harding, an assistant to Governor Hugh L. Carey. A tense conversation ensued:[54]

> HARDING: "Everything has gone to hell. It's nose to nose; it looks like war." (Harding had offered a deal that would involve bussing the occupiers past police lines to the state court where they would be indicted. Lyons had said "No.")
> HARDING: "They [the vigilantes] say that if *we* don't go in, they are going in."
> LYONS: "So, are you going to be the assaulting force?"
> HARDING: "Well, what should we do?"
> LYONS: "Let the vigilantes go in."
> HARDING: "What will happen?"
> LYONS: "Oh, there'll be a big fight; I don't think they'll make it."

54. Ibid., as recounted by Chief Oren Lyons.

HARDING: "We're trying to avoid that."

LYONS: "Well, if you go in, there will be the same big fight, and I don't think you're going to make it either." They continued to discuss the situation and Harding eventually asked Lyons if there was anything else that he knew. "Oh, yes, there is one other thing," said Lyons. "There is another perimeter other than yours."

HARDING: "Oh? Where's that?"

LYONS: "Behind you."

Lyons informed Harding that the entire Haudenosaunee alliance of six nations had been alerted, and that if a single bullet was fired by the police, the Haudenosaunee people would come to the aid of the Mohawk. "If you kill one Mohawk," said Lyons, "the rest of their relatives will help their people. Once you fire that bullet, you will never be able to bring it back. From that point we may have a very serious fight."

In the meantime, Onondaga Chief Vincent Johnson had initiated a phone-tree system which had telegrams flooding into Governor Carey's office and into the White House, demanding that the New York State police and the vigilantes back off. Then Chief Johnson phoned Allied Chemical Company and informed them that if the state police went into Raquette Point, their pipelines, passing through the reservation land, would be cut, and that they should get in touch with Governor Carey and President Carter. Then he called the Niagara Mohawk Electric Service Company and informed them that their high tension wires would be cut, and that they should call the governor and the President. Then Chief Johnson phoned the Tennessee Gas Company and informed them that their gas lines would be cut; he then phoned the county sheriff's office and the state police to update them on the new stakes.

Within ten minutes the Gas Company called back saying that they had talked with Governor Carey and that he had assured them the police would not go in. Shortly thereafter the police phoned Chief Johnson and assured him that the police were not going in, and requested that they not carry out any of the actions they had threatened. Chief Johnson told the police that if they did not attack the camp, and if no vigilantes attacked the camp, everything would be fine. He then phoned the local hospitals and — so they would not be caught by surprise — warned them to prepare for a possible loss of power, due to the high tension wires coming down. The Tuscarora Haudenosaunee said that they would cut the Niagara Falls power lines, and the Caughnawaga Mohawks near Montreal agreed to close the seaway through their land.

Governor Carey's office was sufficiently impressed with the potential

*Mohawk children join the picket line protesting the presence of state
and BIA police on traditional Mohawk land during the siege of
Raquette Point in June 1979. (Photo courtesy of Akwesasne Notes)*

for crisis, and they ordered the police not to enter Raquette Point, and to
keep the vigilantes away. (Two months later, in mid-August, a truce was
negotiated between the traditional Mohawks, the tribal trustees, and the
state police pending a resolution between the trustees and the traditionals.) The state police took the position that they were a peace-
keeping force, and that the argument was between the two Mohawk
camps: traditionals against trustees. But the traditional Mohawks saw
the federal government, the state government, and the BIA-funded
tribal police as one unified system of oppression. Most of the national
media picked up the Indian vs. Indian theme: under a photograph of
sixteen armed, riot-equipped state police, the *New York Times* headline
referred to "Armed Mohawk Factions";[55] the *Christian Science
Monitor* cited "Feuding Mohawk groups."[56] The traditionals see such
reporting as the media's willing participation in the Neo-European ploy
to divide and conquer the Indian people and to usurp their traditional
lineage of leadership. According to John Mohawk, a leader of the

55. *New York Times*, June 16, 1980.
56. *Christian Science Monitor*, June 24, 1980.

Raquette Point encampment: "The budget for BIA police is over \$3 million per year in the United States. They are on every reservation in the United States. They train the Indian to become the police, the occupation force, to police our territories."[57]

At a fund-raising tour throughout New York State, a speaker from the Mohawk Nation said: "We don't need instructions on how to govern ourselves. Two-thirds of the United States Constitution comes from the Great Law of Peace. We don't need to be told about equality and democracy."[58] As on Pine Ridge, with the Lakota, as with the Hopi, the Navajo, the Shoshone, Papago, Cheyenne, Crow, Ojibway, and some two hundred other existing Indian nations in the United States, the heart of the matter is quite simple: sovereignty. The dilemma for the U.S. government is how to face that question of sovereignty. The Indian people demand that the United States either acknowledge and respect their claim to sovereignty as established in their treaty relations — and, in that case leave them alone to run their own affairs — or, if the U.S. government takes the position that the Indian nations are not sovereign nations, the Indian people are asking the U.S. government to explain when and how that status was terminated, and what status the treaties hold.

As John Trudell has said: "If the treaties are just so much paper, then so is the Constitution." Russell Means said at the 1980 Survival Gathering in South Dakota: "This is the last chance for the white man. We have always maintained that there is enough to share, but the white man has never seen that, never accepted that; America wants to own everything. Now they are coming to the Black Hills for the uranium, but they will have to kill us first. I've been shot three times and stabbed once, and I'll die fighting right here on this land."[59]

Matthew King says that the Lakota people have taken their case to the local farmers, and that many of them have responded with support: "We've told them," says King, "that they will be a lot better off under the jurisdiction of Lakota Nation. For one thing, we don't have taxes! Ha! that really gets 'em. We've told them that we do not want to just kick them all off our land, but that we just want what was promised to us; let us run our own affairs. The white people can stay if they want to learn to live like the Indian people. In our way, everybody shares; there is enough for everybody. That way no one has to try to store up more than the neighbor; no one has to try to steal or cheat anybody. The white people can destroy their land, but not ours, no way."

57. Testimony before the Fourth Russell Tribunal, op. cit.
58. Sea Cliff, Long Island; June 9, 1980; recorded by Julie Shpiesel.
59. From the film *Sacrifice Area*, by Otto Shuurman, 1981.

Rancher Marvin Kammerer is convinced that the Lakota people are legally and morally right; he offered his land as a site for the Survival Gathering which attracted about eight thousand people. He told the crowd: "It's the law [the 1868 Treaty]; we can't do anything *but* accept the treaty. We have to practice what we preach."[60]

Winona LaDuke, an Ojibway working with the Navajo relocatees and Women of All Red Nations (WARN), has written: "Last century the federal government found oil in Oklahoma Indian Territory. Within a few decades Oklahoma Indians had lost land, oil, and lives so that the United States could grow strong. That was the last time we had an 'energy crisis.' The oil companies which sprouted during the last energy crisis have expanded to become the largest corporations in the world. This time, the oil companies are interested in all energy sources: coal, oil, uranium, etc., and are busy trying to restage the Oklahoma tragedy. If they succeed, Indians will lose land, resources, and lives again, and this time it's all we have left. . . . Three percent of our lands is what we have left, and in order to remain as Indians we have to fight to keep that. I want to have grandchildren born and raised on Indian land."[61]

The native alliance of the Western Hemisphere is as ancient as any known civilization, and yet it has also been newly forged as a modern force in global politics. So long ignored by Neo-European and world politicians, it has endured five hundred years of colonization and genocide to emerge not only as an agent of survival for the Indian people, but perhaps as a much needed model for survival of our planet scarred by war and environmental degradation. The modern Indian movement, represented by AIM, WARN, the International Indian Treaty Council, and traditionalist movements throughout the hemisphere, was born in response to that call for a struggle of survival. So, what does the future hold? The Indian nations certainly are not a "vanishing race" as photographer Edward Curtis stated at the beginning of this century. The issues are not going to go away, and the Indian people are not going to compromise their position. Something has to give.

60. Ibid.
61. "Resources of Red Nations," Winona LaDuke, WARN, Porcupine, South Dakota, 1980.

8

Yellow Thunder

*It is a myth of European warfare that one
man's victory requires another's defeat.*
GEORGE MANUEL, 1974
Neskonlith, Shuswap

I AWOKE BEFORE the sunrise on the morning of April 4, 1981, after my late-night talk with Matthew King as recounted in Chapter One. I thought about the young, blond tour guide at Fort Laramie with her palms in the air, her shoulders shrugged, and her lips contorted as she told how the U.S. Army just couldn't keep white prospectors out of Indian treaty land; she seemed to be the personification of the American legal system: law that had been designed to obscure, not to clarify.

King, however, had clarified the issues in a way that the courts never could, or at least never would. "Those are the white man's courts," he had said. "Why would they ever give us our land back? They took it; they want to keep it for themselves." That had seemed true enough. How would America look on the map with Lakota Nation drawn in with its treaty borders? A great red heart on the great plains? Surely no court in the land would go for that, nor any senator, nor most American citizens. Another country *inside* America? Unthinkable.

Yet, to King, to the Lakota people, as well as to the Hopi, the Haudenosaunee, Cree, Inuit, or Yanomami it was quite thinkable. Was there any solution other than bloodshed, murder, and genocide? Later that day, the Lakota people were to occupy a valley in the Black Hills. They were no longer relying on U.S courts to return their land; they were going to establish a traditional, self-sufficient community in the sacred Black Hills. The sun rose red-orange through the front door of the Kings' home. The temperature had dropped below zero during the night, freezing the prairie ground. But the sky was clear, and soon the meadowlarks were twittering.

Over breakfast King said, "I'll be up there in a few days. They said they're going to have a big meeting there tomorrow, but that's Indian time; they'll take a while to get set up; it'll be a few days. The Indians like

"THE UNITED STATES NOW SOLEMNLY AGREES...":
EXCERPTS FROM THE 1868 TREATY

ARTICLE 1: *"From this day forward all war between the parties to the agreement shall forever cease."*

ARTICLE 2: *"The United States agrees that the following district . . . commencing on the east bank of the Missouri River where the forty-sixth parallel of north latitude crosses the same, thence along low-water mark down said east bank to a point opposite where the northern line of the State of Nebraska strikes the river, thence west across said river, and along the northern line of Nebraska to the one hundred and fourth degree of longitude west from Greenwich, thence north on said meridian to a point where the forty-sixth parallel of north latitude intercepts the same, thence due east along said parallel to the place of beginning . . . is set apart for the absolute and undisturbed use and occupation of the Indians . . . and the United States now solemnly agrees that no persons except those herein designated . . . shall ever be permitted to pass over, settle upon, or reside in the territory."*

ARTICLE 16: *"The United States hereby agrees and stipulates that the country north of the North Platte River and east of the summits of the Big Horn Mountains shall be held and considered to be unceded Indian territory, and also stipulates that no white person or persons shall be permitted to settle upon or occupy any portion of the same."*

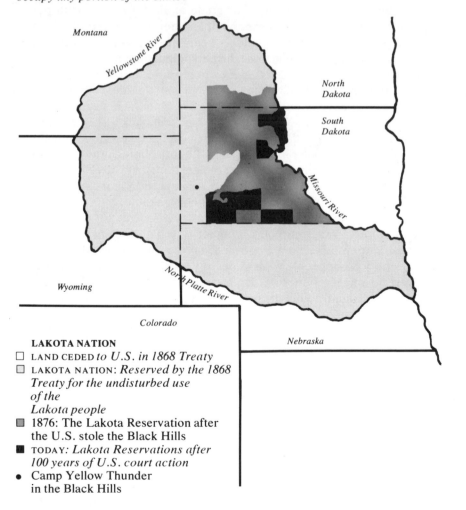

LAKOTA NATION

☐ LAND CEDED *to U.S. in 1868 Treaty*

☐ LAKOTA NATION: *Reserved by the 1868 Treaty for the undisturbed use of the Lakota people*

▨ 1876: The Lakota Reservation after the U.S. stole the Black Hills

■ TODAY: *Lakota Reservations after 100 years of U.S. court action*

● Camp Yellow Thunder in the Black Hills

to do things slow, so we only have to do it once, so things are just right."
Later, Frank Kills Enemy, eighty-seven, came by to talk with King.
They spoke for some time in Lakota, then Frank Kills Enemy said
something to me. King translated: "After Big Foot was killed [1890,
Wounded Knee Massacre] some warriors were in the hills hunting. They
said they couldn't decide what to do because it was foggy, everything
was foggy, not clear. It's still foggy, smoky, can't decide; not right now.
But it will come clear."

A caravan of some twenty cars which had gathered that morning in
Porcupine, between Kyle and Wounded Knee, by mid-morning was
headed northeast along Highway 44 between the reservation and Rapid
City, carrying several sets of tipi poles, mountain survival gear, food,
materials for a traditional sweatlodge, pipes, and other sacred objects.
With red flags waving, the cars passed through Rapid City, turning
southwest toward the Black Hills. Twelve miles into the hills the caravan turned from the main road, continuing for four miles along a
seldom-used forest service road to a place called Victoria Creek Canyon. A sheer rock bluff rose to the north and west, shielding the site from
the prevailing winds; the surface of a spring-fed lake was broken by the
ripples of feeding trout.

As the Indians and the few non-Indian supporters climbed from their
cars to gaze at the pine-covered hills, a huge, white cloud blew over the
stone cliffs, darkening the otherwise clear sky. The winds whipped up
suddenly, dusting the entire camp in a light snow, and then the cloud
disappeared as quickly as it had come. "A good sign," someone said, "a
purification." Within an hour the first tipi was standing, children were
running through the hills, and a meal was being prepared at the central
campfire. A hawk flew overhead, surveyed the encampment, and disappeared.

"The whites say possession is nine-tenths of the law," said Bill
Means. In addition to the 1868 treaty rights, the Lakota were claiming
the land under the 1978 Indian Freedom of Religion Act, and an 1897
federal law allowing schools and churches to be built on U.S. forest land.
When James Mathers, forest supervisor of the Black Hills National
Forest, heard of the occupation, he told the *Rapid City Journal* that "we
have the legal muscle and the law enforcement muscle to evict them very
quickly." On Monday morning, April 6, Mathers met with local sheriff
Mel Larson, representatives of the FBI, and Assistant U.S. Attorney
Jeff Viken to plan an official response.

However, by the time of that meeting, the FBI had already responded
by sending a contingent of agents to prowl the hills around the community site, dressed in camouflage fatigues and armed with automatic
weapons. On Sunday, the second day of the occupation, FBI agent Rob

Miller drove up to the security checkpoint at the gateway of the camp; his Mini-14 automatic rifle and his newly issued fatigues lay in the seat beside him. He told Bill Means: "I'm one-eighth Indian; I just came here to see what was going on." Means told him that FBI agents weren't allowed in the camp, that guns were not allowed in the camp, and that he should leave. Although he was sent away, Miller was spotted later on the ridge above the camp with his weapon and a pair of field glasses.

The following day more agents were spotted creeping around the camp. On Monday afternoon a camp security patrol came across two camouflaged agents attempting to sneak up to the ledge above the camp. The agents carried Mini-14 automatic rifles with 120-round "banana clip" cartridges. When questioned by the young Indian men, the agents said they were turkey hunting. They were told that no guns were allowed in or around the camp because of the children, and they were asked to leave. But agents came daily, stalking through the woods, occasionally firing their weapons at who knows what. Camp security kept a twenty-four-hour watch, and twice during the first week discovered FBI agents slipping to the perimeter of the camp.

Building tipis at Camp Yellow Thunder, teaching traditional survival skills to a new generation of American Indians. (Photo by Rex Weyler)

Matthew King filed a claim with the Pennington County Title Department on Monday morning, April 6, defining an 800-acre site around the camp, and stating that "the Lakota Nation wishes to hold worship services in our church, and to build an alternative natural school for the young people of the Indian Nation." More tipis went up at the site; sweatlodge ceremonies were held each morning, and a meal was cooked at the central campfire each evening. Earl, the camp cook, kept a pot of coffee on through the night for the security watches. The young security crew that was stationed on the ridge above the camp each night — who came to be known as the Ridge Rats — straggled into camp each morning at dawn, ate breakfast, and then went to sleep as the other camp residents busied themselves with another day's activities.

Ridge Rat Randy Thomas, a Santee Lakota from Nebraska, wrote to the Lakota newspaper *Oyate Wicaho*: "When I first came to the camp I was worried as to whether we would be able to stay or not. After we got there, I found an inner peace within myself and with a lot of prayers with the Sacred Pipe, I knew the camp would survive. . . . All my life I've never really known what peace and happiness was. Now in the camp I feel at home. There aren't the tensions like in the city or on the reservation. . . . We are all brothers and sisters and we all respect one another's thoughts and ideas. This is the only time that I've ever been with the Movement, and thanks to the Movement and a lot of supporters I've finally found out what life was like. Words can't really describe the peace a person feels at camp. You would have to be there to know how it really feels." In the meantime, the FBI snipers had set up a rifle range in a clearing about a quarter-mile from the camp, and the crack of their rifle fire could be heard daily.

Each morning, during the sweatlodge ceremony, the men of the camp would sing the AIM song which had been sung first in 1972, after the beating-torture murder of Raymond Yellow Thunder had brought AIM to South Dakota. The song had originally been dedicated to Raymond Yellow Thunder, and had since been sung in his memory. On the morning of April 11, the people of the camp decided to name the camp after the slain Lakota Indian, and from that day forward the camp was known as Camp Yellow Thunder.

On that same morning people began arriving from Lakota and Cheyenne reservations throughout the area, as well as from Colorado, Montana, Wyoming, and Nebraska. Chief Fools Crow came with Matthew King, Frank Kills Enemy, and James Holy Eagle, representing the Oglalas; Leonard Crow Dog came from Rosebud reservation; representatives came from the Yankton, Standing Rock, and Cheyenne River reservations. Lakota elder James Holy Eagle, a grandson of Sitting Bull,

Chief Frank Fools Crow of the Oglala Lakota was born in Porcupine on the Pine Ridge reservation in 1892, two years after the brutal massacre at Wounded Knee. In 1917 he received Chief Iron Cloud's pipe, and in 1925 he was made a chief of his people. (Photo courtesy of Akwesasne Notes*)*

told the gathering: "I will fight for my land, and I'm not talking about with a gun, but with my voice. We must all speak up. The 1868 treaty was a nation-to-nation deal. We won't go to the white man's court any more; we will go to the world court. Our land is not for sale." He quoted Sitting Bull, saying: "If anyone tries to take this land, I will fight."

Greg Zephier from Yankton reservation said: "This land is our school, our church, our Bible — it gives us everything we need. This spot — Camp Yellow Thunder — is the only thing I see that can bring the people together; not the courts, the government, the tribal council, the BIA, but only this community and others like it."

Melvin Garreau, a former Cheyenne River Sioux tribal chairman, agreed: "I resigned from the tribal government because I saw which direction it was headed." He told the gathering: "The BIA governments are puppet governments of the United States."

Pearl Yellow Feather from Fort Peck, Montana wept as she recalled how few real Indians were left. "All my people have forgotten the true way," she said, "they have lost their spiritual traditions." She urged the people at the camp to "be strong," and to maintain their ways.

Leonard Crow Dog spoke in both English and Lakota; he said: "Is this really happening before my eyes? . . . For me Wounded Knee never went away — that spirit still lives; it lives here in this camp."

Following the meeting, a large pot of mutton stew was served to the two hundred people at the gathering; white rancher Marvin Kammerer had donated the sheep for the feast. All seemed well and at peace. A full week had gone by, and the FBI and federal marshals had not made an attempt to evict the people. Except for the FBI turkey hunters and snipers at the target range, there was no disruption of the community of about fifty permanent residents.

The federal guns were held off in part by the 800-acre claim filed with the Forest Service by Matthew King, citing the 1868 treaty as well as federal Forest Service law. The bureaucracy would have to first process the claim before they sent in an armed eviction squad. As the summer days grew long and warm the camp installed a solar hot water heater and shower, a solar oven and food dryer, planted a garden, and brought in goats and chickens. Then, on May 29, Camp Yellow Thunder filed a Special Use Application with the Department of Agriculture which called for the construction of schools, ceremonial buildings, and homes and the "utilization of solar and wind and energy-efficient underground buildings."

Craig Whittekiend, District Ranger for the Forest Service, Department of Agriculture, answered the application with a long list of questions, such as "What type of entity is the 'Lakota Nation'?" [Whittekiend always enclosed the term *Lakota Nation* in quotes.] Starting from square one, Bill Means wrote a return letter answering all the questions, describing the 1868 treaty and Lakota history. Whittekiend had asked: "Which, if any, of the members of Camp Yellow Thunder or the 'Lakota Nation' group are recognized as medicine men? What specific powers do each of the medicine men claim to have?"

Means answered: "The question is completely incoherent and hasn't any meaning or basis in legal and/or political, cultural relationships between members of the Lakota Nation and the United States. However in an attempt to act in good faith, we must explain there is no such thing as medicine men in any Indian nation in the entire Western Hemisphere. Anthropologists at the Smithsonian Institution will tell you the very same thing. Therefore, because medicine men are nonexistent among the Red people of the Western Hemisphere, they don't have any power.''

WHITTEKIEND ASKED: ''Does either Camp Yellow Thunder or the 'Lakota Nation' claim that the tract, or any part of such tract described in the special use permit application, has been used traditionally for any traditional ceremonies or rites?''

MEANS: ''Camp Yellow Thunder and the Lakota Nation have been using the Black Hills traditionally since the beginning of time until we came under the auspices of the U.S. military in 1877 and were illegally forced to leave the Black Hills.''

WHITTEKIEND: ''Please describe or state for each site or holy place the specific use to be made of the area.''

MEANS: ''To treat with the utmost respect and reverence, to live in humility, with prayer, and to walk in the sacred manner upon our Grandmother the Mother Earth, and to teach our children and our unborn to live with their relatives rather than conquering, raping, and murdering.''

Lakota author Vine Deloria, Jr. (*Custer Died For Your Sins, God is Red*, and others) wrote to the Forest Service on behalf of the application, saying: ''Indian people everywhere see in this effort the first and best means of returning social and community institutions to the hands of the traditional Indian people. For that reason this project is one of the most progressive proposals to be received by the federal government in the last century of Indian relationships.''

At a public hearing on July 8, it was revealed by a local resident who held a timber contract for the area around Yellow Thunder, that there were plans to log the area. The plan, as told to the citizens at the hearing, called for building new forest roads and widening existing roads to carry out the logging enterprise. The road construction would require gravel, and it was told that the gravel pit would most conveniently be dug right on the site of Camp Yellow Thunder. Then, on August 24, James Mathers, Forest Supervisor for the Black Hills National Forest, sent a certified letter to Bill Means informing him that the Yellow Thunder special use application was denied. ''I have based my decision upon an evaluation of several alternatives,'' wrote Mathers, ''and have determined that your proposed community development is not in the public interest.''

Bill Means, Lakota from Pine Ridge Reservation, is the chairman of the International Indian Treaty Council, and one of the original occupants of Camp Yellow Thunder in the Black Hills. (Photo by Lionel Delevingne)

Mather's letter cited disruption of "multiple use activities" and an "environmental assessment" as reasons for the denial; he informed Camp Yellow Thunder that they were ordered to vacate the land within two weeks, by September 8. He threatened forced eviction, imprisonment, and fines. The Lakota people, however, resolved to stay. Russell Means said: "I'll die in these hills," rather than leave. Camp Yellow Thunder prepared for a forced eviction attempt. "We will defend ourselves," said Russell Means.

Letters from across the country came into the Forest Service offices in Washington, D.C. urging the government to negotiate a peaceful settlement with the camp. Thirty-eight members of the House of Representatives signed a letter in support of the camp; the Urban Affairs Commission of the Catholic Archdiocese of St. Paul/Minneapolis, Minnesota issued a statement of support; The American Friends Service Committee, Greenpeace, Mobilization for Survival, and other groups sent letters of support. Nick Meinhardt of the American Friends Service Committee had been offering legal and organizational help to the camp since April. He told the *Rocky Mountain News* in Denver: "In this country we have respect for the law and the Constitution. We feel those things give us freedom and protect us — but when we look back and see all these broken treaties, it has to psychologically affect us. . . . Sometimes people think that treaty history is only Indian history, but half of that is ours. It's like saying that any problem over two hundred years old is no longer a problem. People in this country fear their history because they know something bad happened back there." The Rocky Mountain Greenpeace office issued a statement saying: "Greenpeace supports the Lakota people in their claim to the Black Hills . . . on the basis of treaty rights and environmental concerns. . . . The [Yellow Thunder] proposal establishes alternatives to the non-renewable energy system, and provides systems for implementation. It is critical that the people of this nation support those seeking ecological solutions to difficult problems. The counter proposal of the United States Forest Service is to log the area, expand roads, and build gravel pits at the exact site of Yellow Thunder encampment. This will have a destructive impact on the environment of the area. . . . We encourage the United States government to solve this issue in a dignified and responsible manner, and return to the Lakota people the land that is theirs by law."

On September 7, the American Friends Service Committee and Greenpeace established two camps just outside the perimeter of the Yellow Thunder camp as a statement of support for the Lakota, and as a nonviolent resistance to the anticipated armed eviction. Camp Yellow Thunder maintained twenty-four-hour radio contact with the Black Hills

Alliance office in Rapid City, and announced that they would defend their community by any means necessary. Roving security watches patroled the Yellow Thunder perimeter in anticipation of an invasion.

On September 8, the children were moved from the main camp. The day passed without incident. As darkness fell, the roving patrols continued their watches; campfires were kept low or extinguished altogether. During the middle of the night the Ridge Rats' truck backfired on a trip up the hill to their post, and the entire camp was frozen in readiness until the patrol radioed back that it had been their truck, and not rifle fire, which had disturbed the silent night. At dawn, not a single federal agent was to be found in the bush; the government had obviously decided to take another tack. The bird chorus began peacefully as it had for thousands of years.

By noon on September 9, the camp was notified by radio that government lawyer Jeff Viken had sent the matter to federal court, seeking a permanent injunction against the camp. "I assume the status quo will prevail until a judge hears the case," Viken told the *Rapid City Journal.* "The defendants will remain at the camp, but I want to make it clear that there has been no agreement with the federal government." All campfire permits were revoked, and the camp was informed that their continued occupation of the site was considered illegal by the government.

This effort by the government to remove fifty Lakota people from a community on their treaty land on the grounds of multiple use and environmental considerations is, in a larger context, absurd. The Black Hills is one of those areas of America which have been designated by the National Academy of Sciences as a National Sacrifice Area, and thus slated by government and energy corporations for resource exploitation. There are over five thousand uranium leases held in the Black Hills region by such companies as Tennessee Valley Authority, Union Carbide, Chevron Resources, Anaconda (ARCO), the British-Canadian Rio Algom, Wyoming Mineral (Westinghouse), Kerr-McGee, and others. Union Carbide holds a lease in Craven Canyon, site of sacred Lakota rock writings. Only the companies know the extent and the value of the uranium holdings, but they are estimated to be in the hundreds of billions of dollars, covering hundreds of thousands of acres of the Black Hills.

Union Carbide public relations officer for South Dakota, Dudley Blanca, said in a phone interview concerning his company's uranium holdings in the Black Hills: "Our expectations are modest. We think we know pretty well how much there is, but that is classified information — I mean, that's competitive information. I can't tell you exactly how much the uranium is worth." Bill Harris at the South Dakota State Surface Mining Licensing Office stated: "The companies won't even tell us how

Fence around uranium mine site on Lakota Indian treaty land, South Dakota. (Photo by Lionel Delevingne)

much uranium they think they have. . . . Of course they won't tell us exactly what they've learned, but the first thing they do is take a water sample: if the water sample shows a relatively high level of radioactivity, then they know that the uranium is there somewhere, and they explore to find it. I know that the water samples from Pine Ridge showed a considerable amount of uranium, one of the highest. They know it's there. It's one of the prime spots.''

Records at the Licensing Office indicate that twenty-one companies share the five thousand-plus active, pending, or inactive claim sites in the area. Each productive site may yield from one million to a hundred million pounds of ''yellowcake,'' the 1 to 2 percent of the uranium ore that is extracted and sold. The current price of uranium is $30.00 per pound on the world market. The many variables and the information withheld by the companies makes an exact calculation impossible, but it is safe to say that several hundred billion dollars worth of uranium lie under Lakota treaty land. Lowest estimates are in the range of fifty to eighty billion dollars.

In addition to the uranium, there are rich deposits of coal, oil, and other minerals in the Black Hills. The Homestake Gold Mine in the

Black Hills, in operation since the U.S. Army invaded the region and removed the Lakota people, has produced more than a thousand tons of pure gold, worth over $14 billion today. For all of this the U.S. Supreme Court has awarded the Lakota people $122.5 million; taking all the lowest estimates, this amounts to less than one-tenth of one percent of the value of the mineral resources in the Black Hills, not to mention the land itself, and not to mention the rest of the 150-million-acre treaty claim in addition to the Black Hills. To expect the Lakota people to willingly forfeit their land for that amount of money is absurd, particularly in view of the fact that they have stated for over a hundred years that they are not willing to give up the land for *any* amount of money.

"They think we're stupid," Matthew King said, laughing. "How would you feel if someone came and stole your house, and kicked you out, and then came back and said: 'Oh, okay, I'm sorry, here, I'll give you $fty cents for your house!'? Boy, they must think the Indian is pretty stupid."

Camp Yellow Thunder is asking to be left alone on 800 acres of a 150-million-ace land claim, and yet the government expends considerable legal and law-enforcement effort and expense to evict them. This government, which cannot accept the presence of a self-sufficient community of fifty Indian people on the land that they have occupied for thousands of years, bankrolls uranium exploration in the Black Hills at the expense of the U.S. taxpayer. Through the Department of Energy National Uranium Resource Evaluation program the U.S. federal government pays Union Carbide and other companies millions of dollars in subsidies to scour the hills for uranium. Union Carbide's total Department of Energy subsidy is worth $2.3 billion per year, 25 percent of its annual gross sales. Thus, billions of dollars flow into the coffers of multinational resource companies to fuel the search for ever more fuel, to fuel an ever-more-wasteful society, while an attempt at benign self-sufficiency is squashed at even further expense to the taxpayers.

According to Dennis Holt, public relations spokesperson from Union Carbide's headquarters in New York: "The [Lakota] land claim has no effect on us; that's old history. The Supreme Court ruled that the United States should pay the Indians for the land, so that's what we go by. It's a moot issue."

According to Russell Means: "This is the final act; the final indignity: they want to sacrifice our homeland for a few more years of energy, a few more dollars. We are the most colonized people in the world, right down to the poisoned water on the Pine Ridge reservation; they've even poisoned the Indian soul. We live in the belly of the monster. But rather than submit to this final act of genocide, we will fight. Our struggle began with the land, and it will end, if it does end, right here on the land."

AIM founder Clyde Bellecourt said to the 1980 Black Hills gathering: "Multinational corporations don't care what color you are, they're going to step on you, they're going to slap you in the face just like they did to the Indians. So you are going to be the next Indians, my brothers, non-Indians who have come here to support us. You will be the next Indians."

EPILOGUE

The Two Paths

*What is life? It is the flash of a firefly in the
night. It is the breath of a buffalo in the
wintertime. It is the little shadow which runs
across the grass and loses itself in the sunset.*
CROWFOOT, 1890

THE PROPHET of the Seventh Fire of the Ojibway Nation told of a
"New People" that would come forward at a certain time to rediscover
the old ways of the people after a period during which children would
have turned against their parents and grandparents. Edward Benton-
Banai says: "There are Indian people today who believe that the New
People are with us today in the form of our youngest generation . . .
seeking out the few elders who have not forgotten the old ways."[1].

The Cree Nation of Canada has a similar prophecy that just when the
hour is darkest, when the air and the water have been poisoned by
greedy people, there will come a reawakening of the Indian spirit, which
will serve to unite all the races of the world. These people will come
together to protect the earth from destruction.

Phillip Deere tells of a Muskogee prophecy which says that after the
invasion of the white race, that particular civilization will eventually
come to an end. A sign of that end will be the return of the animals to the
land. The recent return of the beaver and deer to Muskogee land in
Oklahoma is seen as the beginning of the fulfillment of that prophecy.
The Muskogee prophecy says that at that time there will be a spiritual
rebirth among their people, and a renewed pride in their culture. Deere
told reporter Mordecai Specktor: "Even today some [Indian people]
cannot recognize the American Indian Movement as the ones responsible for bringing pride to the Indian people, but they were responsible for
that. . . . From the time when their culture was taken away from them
. . . [Indian people] became sad people . . . [then] our young Indian boys
began to wear their hair long, they began to braid their hair. They began

1. *The Mishomis Book*, Edward Benton-Banai, Indian Country Press, St. Paul, Minnesota, 1979.

265

to put on their feathers and showed up, identified themselves according to the prophecies. They brought back identity, they brought back pride with their people. This is the spiritual rebirth, the beginning of a spiritual rebirth of our Indian people."[2]

The Muskogee also have a prophecy that strange people would show up on their land; they would appear overnight, and the Indians would not know where they came from or where they were going. This would be a sign of the coming of the spiritual rebirth. Then, in the mid-sixties, hippies wearing long hair and raggedy clothes appeared hitchhiking through Muskogee land. "We didn't know where they came from," Deere told Specktor, "but here they were, strange people that came overnight. . . . The hippie days are gone now because they came here only as a sign to us; and so the spiritual rebirth began."

The Muskogee prophecy mentions that at the time of the strange people and the spiritual rebirth, a man in a red coat will appear. This reference to the man in the red coat clearly links the Muskogee prophecy to the vast Hopi prophecy which tells of previous worlds and future worlds, and offers some insight into the fate of this one. The Hopi prophecy also speaks of a short-haired generation which would follow the clever ways of the Bahanna (white race), followed by a long-haired generation which would signal the spiritual rebirth. The Hopi prophecy adds an interesting detail to the telling of the strange people. In the Hopi version, the new people were to have a name that sounds like Hopi, thus, when the hippies began showing up on the Hopi mesas in the 1960s, the Kikmongwis interpreted that as a fulfillment of that part of their prophecy.[3].

The Hopi prophecy also speaks of a "man coming from the East wearing a red hat or cape." This person, in the Hopi prophecy, will be the "Purifier," who will arive at the time when the Bahanna has begun

2. From an interview with *University of Minnesota Daily* reporter Mordecai Specktor, June 8, 1981.
3. The Hopi Prophecy is an oral transmission passed to successive generations, different parts of which have been maintained by the individual clans, the symbols of which have been retained on stone tablets and other stone carvings. The entire prophecy was pieced together for the first time in modern history when the clan Kikmongwis gathered in 1948. There is no official written version, and the entire prophecy takes many days to tell. Sources used in this telling include: Dan Katchongva, Sun Clan, "From the Beginning of Life to the Day of Purification," translated by Danaqyumptewa, Wer-mi Jo-vow-ma, Spiritual Unity publication, *Land and Life*, Los Angeles, 1972; Richard Kastl in conversation and public talks; *Techqua Ikachi*, traditional newspaper of the Hopi Nation; "The Essence of Hopi Prophecy," by Thomas V. Tarbet, Jr., *Land and Life*, Los Angeles California; Thomas Banyacya, Wolf, Fox, and Coyote Clans, public talks; *Book of the Hopi*, Frank Waters, Viking Press, New York, 1963.

to dig into the heart of their sacred land, and when the Bahanna's last invention — the "house in the sky" — is sent from earth into space. The Hopi offer no hint as to who this person might be. The obvious parallels between the Hopi prophecies and those of the Muskogee, the Cree, Ojibway, as well as the Haudenosaunee and many other American Indian nations, suggests more than just the cultural intercourse which might be assumed by a Neo-European anthropologist; it provides for us an understanding of the modern Indian movements of the Western Hemisphere, because it points to the unified heart and spirit of those movements, providing some glimpse into where those movements came from, and where they are headed.

The Hopi tell that at the time of these signs, there will be two paths: the path of the Bahanna with their inventions; and the path of the Hopi, the People of Peace. When the Purifier comes, only the people of peace will survive. Throughout this book we have looked back at some relevant periods of history in an attempt to shine some light upon the conflicts between the American Indian Movement and the Neo-European governments. Our excursions into history have taken us as far back as the fifteenth and sixteenth century when the white race first met the red race. Now, the future seems to be inexorably linked to events and teachings that predate the European incursion into the Western Hemisphere. When the Indian spiritual leaders talk about a rebirth, they are talking about returning to roots which predate written history. When Phillip Deere talks of the difference between truth and facts, he is talking about the difference between material knowledge and spiritual knowledge, between knowledge that you can hold in your hand, and the knowledge that you can hold in your heart. Be grateful that this violent and often sad story has led us here; if we go back beyond the realm of facts for a moment, we may discover some truth.

"There is a great answer that is going to come from the Hopi,"[4] said Tuscarora Haudenosaunee leader Mad Bear in 1969, "because this is the place where even my people come from, where all Indian people come from. A long time ago it is told that Tha-ronda-na-waga, who was the Holder of the Heavens, as it's interpreted in our way, guided my people across the mountains to the East, across the great river, the Mississippi, across the plains to the place where it appeared that the Great Spirit had placed his hand upon the ground [the Great Lakes]. Many went North, South, and to the West. My people went out there to a place in New York where the Finger Lakes are. That's where the Haudenosaunee, the People of the Longhouse, got their message. This is the message I'm

4. From a talk given to the Hopi people, Hoteville village, October 11, 1969.

bringing not only to the Indian people, but to the people of the world. So, it is important that we look back to the prophecies, back to the instructions, that we remove any hate and ill feelings that we might have for our brothers and sisters, remove it and be at peace again, so that our minds could be clear and we could see the great path."

Anthropologists and archaeologists ("grave robbers," the Indians call them) tell us that there were about 100 million people in the Western Hemisphere in 1492, most of them in South and Central America.[5] Between 1430 and 1530 a steady population of 6 million Incas lived primarily on the western slope of the Andes Mountains from Southern Colombia to central Chile. Anthropologists date the major settlement of the great North American plains and Mississippi River Valley between 700 and 1500 A.D. although there is evidence of communities there much earlier. In 1168 the ancestors of the Aztecs migrated from the southern isthmus into the Valley of Mexico.

What anthropologists call the Anasazi culture, including the Hopi, Zuni Pueblo, Laguna Pueblo, Acoma, Mesa Verde Indians, and others, migrated into the Black Mesa area from at least 31 B.C. until the establishment of Oraibi by the Hopi in about 1150 A.D. The date 31 B.C. derives from a dated monument of the Olmec culture in Veracruz. Feathers from tropical birds and seashells have been found in the pueblos of the Southwest. The people of Chaco Canyon in New Mexico used highly skilled mortarless masonry to construct Pueblo Bonito, covering three acres, standing five stories high, with thirty-two sacred Kivas or round ceremonial rooms, and a total of eight hundred rooms, all of which housed as many as twelve hundred people.

Sometime around 1,000 A.D. the Vikings landed in what is now Newfoundland, penetrated North America to the Great Lakes, and may or may not have encountered Native people. People had been living around the lakes by 100 A.D.; these were the ancestors of Mad Bear and the Haudenosaunee. At about 100 B.C., walrus-hunting Aleuts settled what is now the Aleutian Islands of Alaska. The regions of Louisiana, Florida, Ohio, and Wisconsin were settled between 500 and 200 B.C.

The calendar of the Mayan culture dates back to a beginning in 3113 B.C. The Mayan city of Tikal was at its peak in the Yucatan in 550 A.D., and the Mayan temples were abandoned about three hundred years

5. Estimates, of course, vary among Western archaeologists; the figure of 100 million has been advanced by Dr. William R. Jacobs, University of California at Santa Barbara. See his book, *Dispossessing the American Indian*, Scribner's, New York, 1972.

later. The city of Teotihuancan (now the site of Mexico City) was established in 200 B.C. and burned a thousand years later.

At the time that people were beginning to farm in Egypt and the Middle East, 7000 B.C., basket-making Indians were living in Oregon. Indians migrated along and across the Mississippi in 9000 B.C., hunted with flint tools in the Minnesota region in 10000 B.C., hunted mammoths in the Southwestern U.S. regions in 12000 B.C., and made obsidian tools in Tlapacoya, Mexico in 19000 B.C. Carbon-14 dating techniques place Indian cultures in the Valley of Mexico in 22000 B.C., at the height of the last Ice Age. Western guesses of the earliest settlements in the Western Hemisphere have slowly moved back into time, and now range from 25000 to 37000 B.C. — some anthropologists now even say 100000 B.C. Before that, it's all a dark mystery.

Western anthropologists assume that the Indians must have arrived in North America via the frozen Bering Land Bridge, but that is only a theory. And even if it could be conclusively proven that there was ancient traffic across the Bering Strait, that would not preclude another arrival by other means. Matthew King says: "They'd better go up there and check the direction of those footprints." Neither does the theory explain why the populations would then move so far south before establishing major centers of civilization, nor why the migration patterns tend to move from the centers in Guatemala and Mexico north into Black Mesa and other regions of North America. The Neo-European scholars are also confused as to why certain major sites were suddenly abandoned, such as the cliff pueblo at Mesa Verde, or the Mayan centers in Guatemala which were abandoned in the ninth century A.D. Drought has been suspected in some cases as a likely cause. In relation to the Mayan case, scholar William H. McNeill guesses that "in absence of any signs of violence at the deserted sites," the civilization scattered as Mayan priests were replaced in function by a "simpler, popular religion that allowed individual farmers to assure the fertility of their maize fields by appropriate private ceremonies."[6]

According to the Hopi's own version, handed down orally and by stone tablet, McNeill is right and yet, at the same time, wrong: the spiritual movement of corn growers was not an offshoot of the Mayan civilization; the Mayan civilization was an offshoot of the corn growers.

6. *The Rise of the West*, William H. McNeill, University of Chicago Press, 1963; p. 529. This book provides a lucid example of the typical Western historian's inability to grasp the subtleties, richness, and ultimate value of the indigenous civilizations of the Western Hemisphere. McNeill says: "The loss to human culture involved in the Spanish extirpation of Amerindian civilizations does not . . . seem very great."

To the Hopi, the Mayans represent a corruption, a following of the wrong path which flowered and died like many others. The Hopi have grown corn and carried their instructions and prophecies from the time beyond the flood, past many civilizations. The mysterious migrations were governed by spiritual reasons rather than by material pressures, leaving but subtle clues for latter-day anthropologists.

The Hopi call the Creator *Taiowa*. *Taiowa* created *Sotuknang* who manifested the land, air, and water, and then *Kokyangwuti*, Spider Woman, who made all living things including two twins who sit at the poles of the earth maintaining the balance. The four races of humans — yellow, red, white, and black — were made in mating pairs, and given that First World, *Tokpela*, in which to live. They were given corn to sustain their physical bodies, and speech to honor the Creator. The people, as most ancient stories concur, became corrupted by their powers and pleasures. Those who had remained simple and true to their instructions from the Creator hid below the ground as *Sotuknang* erased the First World with fire.

The faithful emerged into the Second World, *Tokpa*, to try again. In the Second World some of the people learned to barter for goods; the Creator's plan decayed again, as possessions became important to people, and the faithful corn growers were overrun by a greedy merchant-class civilization. *Sotuknang* asked Spider Women to do something, so she brought the twins back from their posts, the earth went off balance, and the Second World was ended by a pole shift. Interestingly, modern science agrees that there have been pole shifts during the long history of the earth.[7] Evidence includes traces of deer in the Antarctic, tropical fossil remains in Alaska, flash-frozen mammoths with undigested grass in their bellies in the Siberian ice, fresh-frozen fruit trees under the Arctic tundra, and the well-known tilts, wabbles, and polarity changes of the earth throughout its estimated 4.5-billion-year history. However, we are concerned here not so much with proving the Hopi case as with understanding it.

Emerging again from below the ground, the faithful entered the Third World, *Kuskurza*. The people in the Third World became very clever; they built great cities, and many inventions, including a flying shield. The cities eventually went to war with each other, employing their flying machines in aerial attacks. In the cities, the people corrupted sex, and used power to manipulate others and to gain riches or status. *Sotuknang* and Spider Woman destroyed this Third World in the Great Flood; the story of the Flood is told by virtually every culture in the world including

7. *Pole Shift*, John White, Doubleday, New York, 1980.

the Greeks, Egyptians, Chinese, Judeo-Christians, and American Indians.

The Hopi tell that the simple people, who faithfully grew their corn and honored the Creator, survived the flood by sailing from the doomed land of the Third World in the hollow stems of large plants. As the corrupted cities were lost below the waters of the sea, the ancestors of the Hopi sailed until they found land. They stopped at many small islands — stepping stones — but were instructed to continue. They were told that the bountiful islands would make life too easy, leading to corruption again. They were instructed that they were on a journey to a place where life would be difficult, where a scarcity of water would make corn growing difficult, and where they would have to rely on their faith and ceremony to keep life in balance.

The Hopi eventually migrated by sea to the land of the Fourth World, *Tuwagachi*, "World Complete," where they would find their home. They landed on the shores of what they now believe to be the isthmus between North and South America, in the place now known as Guatemala. When they emerged onto this land they were met by the Creator, the Great Spirit, in the form of *Massau'u*, a humble farmer. They asked Massau'u if they could live on that land. He told them: "All I have is my planting stick and my corn. If you are willing to live as I do . . . you may live here with me."[8]

Massau'u told them, however, that the tropical lands were still too bountiful, that they must follow a migration pattern which would lead them to the heart of the earth, where they would find barren land suited for a rich spiritual life. Massau'u laid out many different colors and sizes of corn, and asked each leader to select one. The people who waited, and who chose last, took the smallest corn. These people, Massau'u called Hopi, the People of Peace. Massau'u gave the Hopi stone tablets which carried their spiritual instructions and which served as their symbol of "Power and Authority over all Land and Life to guard, protect, and hold in trust for me until I shall return to you in a later day, for I am the First and I am the Last."[9]

After Massau'u left them, one of the leaders had two sons who took over the responsibilities of leadership when he died. The older brother was fair-skinned and the younger was dark-skinned, fulfilling a prophecy of the tablets. According to instructions, the set of tablets was broken, each brother taking half. The white brother was instructed to go to the

8. "From the Beginning of Life to the Day of Purification," Dan Katchongva, Sun Clan, translated by Danaqyumptewa, Wer-mi Jo-vow-ma, Spiritual Unity publication, *Land and Life,* Los Angeles, California, 1972.
9. Thomas Banyacya in a letter to M. Muller-Fricken, Frankfurt, Germany, 1961.

East, where he would learn to write, learn inventions and other skills which would be used to carry out his mission of helping the younger brother bring about Purification Day. The brothers were told that a great white star would appear in the sky at a future time. When that star appeared it would be a signal that the white brother had reached his destination in the East; also at that time the dark-skinned brother and his clans would have completed their long migrations, and would be at the heart of the earth, their spiritual home. They should then stop, plant their corn, and wait for the return of the white brother who would come from the East.

The Hopi then began their great migrations, some going in each of the four directions, traversing the Western Hemisphere to the tip of South America, to the Atlantic and Pacific coasts, and to the frozen back door of the North American Arctic. Some stayed in the rich, comfortable lands of Central America where the Mayans in Guatemala, the Aztecs in the Valley of Mexico, the Olmecs in Veracruz, and the Incas of Peru developed great cities of civilization. The Mayans share with the Hopi the stories of the flood, the ocean crossing, and the previous worlds. Other cultures which share the conception of three, in some cases four, previously destroyed worlds include Hindu, Tibetan Buddhism, Persian Zoroastrianism, Chinese, Polynesian, and Icelandic. The Greek historians Heraclitus and Hesiod concur.[10]

For many thousands of years the Hopi clans moved about the Western Hemisphere, the Badger Clan leading the people to the North, the Eagle Clan leading the people to the East, the Parrot Clan leading the people to the South, and the Bear Clan leading the people to the West. The record of these migrations are the clan signatures, drawings on stone which appear throughout the hemisphere. Clan drawings consistent with those in Oraibi appear in Mesa Verde, Colorado; Chichen Itza, a Mayan city in the Yucatan; Springerville, Arizona; Senora, Mexico; Ohio; New York; Texas; Ontario; Quebec; Guatemala; and in the Andes Mountains of Ecuador. These signatures trace the outlines of the Hopi migrations which took the ancestors of the Haudenosaunee to the Great Lakes region, the Parrot Clan to the southern Pasa at the tip of South America, and the Spider Clan and the Flute Clan to the frozen North. Some members of each clan stayed at the many sites along the way, some forgot the instructions, some remembered, some continued the migration to the spiritual home. The Bear Clan was the first to reach Black

---

10. For a more detailed account of cultures which describe "previous worlds," see *Mexico Mystique*, Frank Waters, 1975.

Mesa; when they saw the great white star, they stopped, and there they established Oraibi.[11]

In Oraibi the Hopi planted their corn in the dry ground, and continued their cycle of ritual to show their eternal dedication to the Creator. As members of the other clans arrived, those who had still remembered the instructions given by Massau'u were allowed to settle in or around Oraibi. The Hopi waited for the return of the white brother who would be carrying the other half of the tablets, and would also possess the migration symbol: the cross inside the circle. The founders of Oraibi also carved in stone a petroglyph which depicts the Creator's instructions and prophecies. The petroglyph shows the true Hopi who had cast away a bow and arrow symbolizing the People of Peace. Extending up from that figure is the Hopi life plan which splits into two paths. The upper path shows the arrival of the white race, and a bridge, a connection, between that path and the lower path, the path of the Hopi, the path of peace.

At this point, the Hopi tell of many prophecies which, as we have seen, they consider fulfilled by events of the last five hundred years: the cross-bearing missionaries, the horse-drawn wagons, the horseless wagons, roads, sweet food, sweet tongues, cobwebs in the sky, the house of glass where the nations of the world would gather, and the gourd of ashes which would fall from the sky and boil the water. The Hopi life path as drawn on the petroglyph is intersected by two circles which represent two earth-shaking events which would occur in the days of the later inventions. These events, signaled by the appearance of the swastika and the rising sun, interpreted as World Wars I and II, are followed by a second bridge between the two paths. (To the Hopi, the Iron Cross is the female version of the swastika.) At this point, the Hopi were to deliver their message to the world, which they did by way of Thomas Banyacya's presentation to the UN and other public expressions of the prophecies. The seventeen clans met for four days in 1948 to compare their tablets and piece together the parts they had carried and passed on for thousands of generations.

After this second bridge, the paths do not meet again. This is the time when each person must decide which path to take. According to the Hopi, we are at that time right now. There are four figures on the top path representing the people who took the path of the inventors, the path of those who relied upon human cleverness, but who forgot the way of the Creator. The last person on this path is past the last bridge; that figure appears to lose its head and become deformed. The top path becomes

11. *Book of the Hopi*, Frank Waters, Viking Press, New York, 1963.

crooked, aimless, and eventually ends. The prophecy tells that the last invention of the Bahanna will be the house in the sky; after that the Bahanna's path is finished in this world.

A lone figure on the bottom path is depicted with a staff, standing among growing corn. This, of course, symbolized the people who chose to follow the path of humility and spirituality; the path is straight, and leads on. But a half-circle drawn on the petroglyph, which does not yet intersect the Hopi life path, symbolizes potential disaster. If the Hopi are not strong enough, or if they are unable to get their message to the world, or if the destructive inventions are not checked, a third earth-shaking event threatens even the People of Peace. The prophecy tells the Hopi that if nations are still fighting wars, they are not to let the inventors dig into the sacred ground at the heart of the earth. If they do, the prophecy says, they will use the wealth for destructive purposes, the world will be put off balance again, and there will be a catastrophe.

If the world avoids the catastrophe, the True White Brother will return wearing red. That will bring the Day of Purification. According to Dan Katchongva: "The Purifier, commanded by the Red Symbol, with the help of the Sun and the Meha [the Four directions, or Swastika symbol] will weed out the wicked who have disturbed the way of life of the Hopi, the true way of life on Earth . . . the ills of the Earth will be cured. Mother Earth will bloom again and all people will unite into peace and harmony for a long time to come.

"But if this does not materialize, the Hopi traditional identity will vanish due to pressure from Bahanna. Through the white man's influence, his religions, and the disappearance of our sacred land, the Hopi will be doomed. This is the Universal Plan, speaking through the Great Spirit since the dawn of time.

"With this in mind, I as a Hopi do not make wars against any country. . . . I am not sending my children across the ocean to fight. If they want to that's up to them, but they will no longer be Hopi if they do.

"Since I am Sun Clan, and the sun is the father of all living things, I love my children. If they realize what I am talking about they must help me save this world.

"The Hopi have been placed on this side of the Earth to take care of the land through their ceremonial duties, just as other races of people have been placed elsewhere around the Earth to take care of her in their own ways. Together we hold the world in balance, revolving properly. If the Hopi Nation vanishes, the motion of the Earth will become eccentric, the water will swallow the land, and the people will perish. Only a brother and a sister may be left to start a new life."[12]

12. "From the Beginning of Life to the Day of Purification," op. cit.

The Oraibi petroglyph depicting the Hopi prophecy. The figure on the lower left represents the Hopi, the people of peace, who have cast away the bow. The cross inside the circle is the symbol of the four sacred directions and the four races of people holding the world in balance; the Hopi were instructed to look for this symbol when the Bahanna — the white brother — returned. If the Bahanna returned with the cross without the circle, as was the case with the Spanish missionaries, the Hopi were to take that as a sign that the Bahanna had forgotten the Creator's instructions for living a simple and peaceful life. The top part of the petroglyph depicts the two paths with two bridges between them. The upper path is the path of those who forgot the Creator's instructions, those who relied on inventions and cleverness rather than on spiritual faith. The lower path represents the path of the Hopi, the path of peace. The two circles between the two bridges connecting the paths represent two earth-shaking events which the Hopi interpret as World Wars I and II. After the second bridge, the two paths do not meet again. For those who have chosen the Bahanna's path of inventions, the way becomes crooked and aimless and ends in destruction. The bottom path shows a third event — the half-circle — which represents potential disaster if the Hopi allow the Bahanna to dig into their sacred land and remove the riches; the Hopi interpret this as the U.S. government's search for uranium on their land. The figure on the bottom path is shown with a staff, standing among growing corn; this figure represents the true Hopi who has followed the path of peace, simple living, and faithful observance of ritual and prayer. The Hopi warn that now the earth is near disaster if the people of the world do not turn away from greediness and war, toward a spiritual, peaceful life.

Who could deny that a third earth-shaking event hangs over us in these days when Russia and the United States combine to spend over $300 billion a year to prepare for the next — and in that case, last — war? The Hopi could certainly make a case that the fate of the world hangs in the balance. They say that if enough people turn back to the simple chores of living, and honor the spirit of the living things, then disaster can be avoided. The Hopi can see now that their land is surrounded, as Peabody Coal and Tenneco and Mobil and Exxon and Kennecott and Climax Uranium move in to dig into the heart of the earth. They've watched the sky turn dark with fly-ash. They've witnessed the ground literally sinking below their feet as the Black Mesa aquifers are drained for power projects. They've heard the National Academy of Sciences declaration that their land is a "national sacrifice area."[13] And they understand that they are the nation that is going to be asked to make the sacrifice so that the Department of Defense can stockpile plutonium and oil, so that Las Vegas can keep a billion light bulbs flashing right up to the grand, sad finale.

The clear and ancient commitment of the Hopi to the natural ways has continually provided support and direction for the modern Indian movements of the Americas, and now defines the only real future. Throughout the Indian movements, the leaders are calling for a return to the family, to the land, to the spiritual life, to the ways that were handed down from the generations before the Europeans arrived. Edward Benton-Banai, who helped spark the American Indian Movement when he tossed Indian spiritual literature into Clyde Bellecourt's cell in Stillwater Prison, established, in 1972, the Red School House as an alternative to Neo-European education. "The road to knowledge is eternal," says Benton-Banai. "We must establish an alternative education system to equip our children, the future leaders, with the tools of survival. The tools of survival are those provided by a good, sound, relevant education. That education must not be offered at the price of one's identity, religion, music, heritage, or pride; indeed, it must be built upon these things, utilizing them as a cultural core emanating from all dimensions of instruction."[14]

At the Red School House, in St. Paul, Minnesota, everything is done in a circle. Classes are conducted in a circle, the students are taught that knowledge "does not come in steps 1, 2, 3, . . . but that knowledge comes from the Circle of Learning which is sharing, mutual respect, and

13. "Rehabilitation Potential of Western Coal Lands," National Academy of Sciences, Washington, D.C., 1974.
14. Edward Benton-Banai, opening statement, "The History of the Little Red School House," slide presentation, Indian Country Press, St. Paul, Minnesota, 1977.

a merging of spiritual learning, survival skills, and intellect.'' The school teaches that cooperation, not competition, makes the nation and the family and the individual strong. In June 1975, the Red School House graduated its first six students, two of them twenty-two years old. By June of 1977 the school enrolled one hundred twenty students, thirty-three interns at Hamline University, and thirty adults in the adult education program. A year later the school had raised enough money to purchase its building. Students learn native health and pharmacology; U.S. and native law; local, cultural, and world history; survival skills such as farming and community crafts; as well as English, native language, mathematics, and science. They have a weekly women's hour, and a men's hour.

Benton-Banai has also written a series of books, which serve both children and adults as a history of his people, the Ojibway people. The books and the school are a part of the rebirth that Phillip Deere speaks of. A sign at the Red School House greets the students at the entrance: ''Don't feel you're a stranger here. This is your land. This is my land. This is Indian Country. My ancestors lived here; the Great Mystery put them here, just like he did the oak trees and the water. Feel welcome. Let your spirit be free.''

In Oklahoma, Phillip Deere and the Muskogee Nation operate an annual Youth and Elder Conference to which they bring people from all over the hemisphere to teach and learn Indian culture and ways. At the conference, everything is done in a traditional way, with the elders leading the instruction. Deere says, ''We mention a lot of things to our young people: What it is to respect our own children; what it is to respect our grandfathers; because we believe in the sacred circle, we believe in that circle which represents the cycle of life.

''In our homes is where it begins; at our tables is where it begins. In ancient times we had room for grandpa; we had a place for our grand-children in our houses; we had a complete family circle at one time, but the system took it away from us by placing our children in nurseries, so we could go out and slave for the system, working every day, man and woman.''[15]

So, the Indian people are turning away from the culture which placed their children in boarding schools, their old people in nursing homes, and their bravest and strongest in jails or in graves. They are turning back to the center, to the family, the community. Sotsisowah, John Mohawk, a leader of the Haudenosaunee occupation at Raquette Point in 1979, also helped organize Ganienkeh, a self-sufficient Mohawk community in the

15. From interview with Mordecai Spector, op. cit.

Adirondack Mountains. He wrote in *Akwesasne Notes*: "When we talked about the decline of our culture, the old people pointed to the evidence of the decline of our families. . . . The future," he says, "is the family. . . . Modern industrial society does not require stable families any more than people require dogs to have stable families. In fact, the society is based on the need for children to learn highly specialized skills, and to leave the home to practice those skills wherever the jobs may be. That is why the society is so mobile.

"The traditional people urge the re-establishment of natural ways of life as a way of strengthening and promoting family unity." A statement of purpose from the Ganienkeh community says: "Ganienkeh is an effort to re-establish the real Mohawk culture by making available to people the means of survival. The movement has essentially two objectives: to secure enough land to once again make possible the practice of the Mohawk material culture by a community of people, and to maintain enough autonomy to enable people to continue the Mohawk social culture without interference."

In September 1978, Indian women from everywhere in the United States gathered in Rapid City, South Dakota, to discuss "the destruction of the family, sterilization, abuse, theft of Indian children through white-controlled adoption procedures, and the erosion of the reservation land base." Among them was Pat Ballanger, another of the original founders of the American Indian Movement. Women of All Red Nations (WARN) was founded at this meeting; national committees were established in the fields of education, sterilization, women's health, midwifery, political prisoners, law, and national and international organizing.

Madonna Gilbert, Lakota from South Dakota, said that the intention of the organization was "not . . . to separate Indian men from Indian women. . . . So far," she said, "we haven't had to deal with that issue because we do not believe in separating, and we haven't done it in the past. So, right now, it isn't an issue. We don't have a separate heading for the youth — we consider them young adults on the way, and we need their help. We do not need special contingencies for the elderly. We do not want to separate our people. Time is too short. The family is what is important, and our men know this, and the women know it, and so there isn't an issue."[16]

Lorelei Means wrote later that "In many native cultures, women hold positions of power as women, and in some, women are unquestionably both spiritual and political leaders of the communities. . . . Women not only hold up half the sky, they are also the carriers of the future. . . . The

16. *Akwesasne Notes*; Winter, 1978, p. 15.

Four generations of Navajo family: Elder Ashikie Bitsie (left)
with her daughter, granddaughter, and great-grandchildren outside
their reservation home. These traditional families are being asked
by the BIA and the Federal government to leave the land which is rich
in coal and uranium reserves. Like other Navajo families, they are
resisting the forced relocation. (Photo by Lionel Delevingne)

organization of a national women's organization, coming ten years after the formation of the American Indian Movement, should be viewed as another major step in the maturation of the struggle."[17]

Matthew King says: "In the Indian way, everything is for the children. They learn respect because we show respect for them; we let them be free, but at the same time, there is always someone there to teach them how to act, the right way to treat people. When we get our land back, the first thing we will do is make places for spiritual things and for the children, places where the children can learn the right way to live, to be generous, to be respectful, and to love all the living things. We believe in the Great Hoop: the Great Circle of Life; everything comes back to where it started. We believe this. That is the Indian way."

Patty Wind, a thirteen-year-old student at the Red School House, wrote this poem:[18]

I want to be free
Fly with you my brother
I want the experiences to live like you live
To be free, not for the white man to shoot at
like they did to our ancestors and brothers
    and sisters
Carry me off
Go now, my brother, fly
into what's still yours
Hurry my brother
before they discover what's yours
and claim that, too.

17. Ibid.
18. *Time of the Indian*, Indian Country Press, St. Paul, Minnesota, 1977.

Song for Moab, Utah

In the beginning, the Earth Mother was alone
Longing for company
She invited friends

The Ant people
carefully worked their way through her hair
Softly touching her skin
They loved her with each gift
each moment

The ant people too
were in want of company,
metakwease *— relations*
The people were invited to the surface
the skin of the earth.

Quiet people,
they asked the Earth Mother for water
Never taking, only gathering
They prayed for food
Never taking, only gathering
They prayed for life
Never taking, only gathering
They cared for Eachother.

The Earth
the ants
the people
And the Creation grew.

Their marks on the earth
dissipated over the generations of
wind, rain, and power.
Their baskets and sacred pottery
remained
A legacy for remembering.

This was the beginning of our eternity
only the beginning
They were the Anasazi, the old ones
The ancestors.

The Dine came to live on this sacred place
here in this place
here in this place
Living carefully, they gathered,
they prayed.

The Spaniards only sought
the riches of the land
Not to possess it for eternity
Only to possess the riches
These they took
and they left
left their cross
burned into the Earth
burned into the skins
of the
Dine, Keresan, Tewa.

They left their fathers and brothers
to continue collecting
the Booty of the land.

The Spaniards were soon sent home
twice
Once by the red
and then by the white.
The Mericanos won,
they said
and they were called
"the Mericanos."

Song for Moab, Utah

In the new alchemy
the Mericanos found uses for
the black golds — coals and oils.

The people told to starve or move
to work
or starve
became the oil workers.

Standard Oil
killed their food — livestock, sheep and
green relatives — metakwease
killed their coworkers at
Ludlow
very close to them
and brought them wage work.

It was called the capitalist system
but this system was
for some
and not
for others.

In the 1940s *a new sort of*
capitalism
came to the Dine
came to the Land.

They were sent to Moab, Utah
an internment center
a "Jap Camp"
a relocation center
for Japanese
non-patriotic Japanese Americans
that is.

On the reservation
in old Bureau of Indian Affairs buildings
the Japanese people were
confined
in isolation
isolation centers.
And together they
lived in
those isolation centers
like a special flower —
yellow surrounded by red
all
carefully monitored by
those federales.

And all the while
those Indians (as they were called)
were sent over
to fight those
wars
against those people
thousands of
those Indians
fighting
those Japs
over there.

Then in what they called
the Final Ceremony
the Black Magicians
came together
in their new religion they
brought atoms out of
those sacred rocks
prayer rocks of the
Dine, Keresan, and Tewa people.
Those sacred rocks
who they said
boiled up the slaughter
of those Japs
those people
who lived elsewhere
but who also
lived here.

And it was still Moab, Utah
when those Mericanos
with all that power —
who had allowed those
gentle farmers and ranchers
the Mormons
to settle like
their special story said —
did that to them.

The Mericano Defense Department
dropped their bombs
made of that sacred Earth
on those people
near Moab.

And the Earth screamed
and the wind screamed
and the people of the
creation
lived with those radiation poisons
and screamed
in the night.

Moab,
that place with all those
uranium mines, uranium mills
That nuclear fallout
those voices in the wind
the voices of the Japanese
interred forever
embalmed in those mesas
the voices of the wageworkers of
the new alchemy
making their fast money
in the night.

The old people
and the shadows of
the Anasazi
who will not go away
who will remain
who cry in the night
those sacred songs
in the night.

Only the ants remain
to tell all the stories
they stay
never changing their paths
never changing their houses
never changing their lives
never changing their prayers.

And the Earth never moved
offended, pained
She was still in need of
company and prayers.

WINONA LADUKE
April 1981
for Lawson Inada

BIBLIOGRAPHY

THE FOLLOWING bibliography is intended to assist those who would wish to investigate the subject further. It seems appropriate, however, to mention that there are two very distinct sources of the history of the Western Hemisphere: Indian history and Neo-European history. Whereas history in the European tradition is written, American Indian history is, for the most part, an oral history. The author used both sources, and wishes here to acknowledge the vast oral tradition which is essential if one is to piece together a balanced view of North American history.

Included in this bibliography are books and reports by Indians and non-Indians which the author used in the preparation of the text. Not included are the newspaper and magazine articles used, many of which are referred to in the notes. A major source throughout the text are the periodic issues of *Akwesasne Notes* from Autumn, 1969 through Autumn, 1981, published by the Mohawk Nation, Rooseveltown, New York.

Akwesasne Notes, ed. *B.I.A. I'm Not Your Indian Any More.* Akwesasne Notes, Rooseveltown, New York. 1973.

Akwesasne Notes, ed. *Voices From Wounded Knee.* Akwesasne Notes, Rooseveltown, New York, 1974.

Anthropology Resource Center, ed. *The Yanomami Indian Park, A Call for Action.* Anthropology Resouce Center, Boston, Massachusetts, 1981.

Benton-Banai, Edward. *The Mishomis Book.* Indian Country Press, St. Paul, Minnesota, 1979.

Blanco, Hugo. *Land or Death.* Path Finder Press, New York, 1972.

Black Hills Alliance, ed. *The Keystone to Survival, The Multinational Corporations and the Struggle for Control of Land.* Black Hills Alliance, Rapid City, South Dakota, 1981.

Blue Cloud, Peter. *Back Then Tomorrow.* Blackberry Press, Brunswick, Maine, 1978.

Brand, Johanna. *The Life and Death of Anna Mae Aquash,* James Lorimer & Company, Toronto, Ontario, 1978.

Brinkerhoff, Zula C. *God's Chosen People of America,* Publishers Press, Salt Lake City, Utah, 1971.

———. *The Spirit of Geronimo Returns.* Brinkerhoff, Salt Lake City, Utah, 1973.

Brown, Dee. *Bury My Heart at Wounded Knee*. Holt, Rinehart & Winston, New York, 1971.

————. *Showdown at Little Big Horn*. G.P. Putnam's Sons, New York, 1964.

Buitrago, Ann Mari, and Leon Andrew Immerman. *Are You Now Or Have You Ever Been in the FBI Files?* Grove Press, New York, 1981.

Caso, Alfonso, *The Aztecs, People of the Sun*. University of Oklahoma Press, Norman, Oklahoma, 1958.

Cheney, Roberta Carkeek. *The Big Missouri Winter Count*. Naturegraph Publishers, Happy Camp, California, 1979.

Cloutier, David, trans., ed. *Spirit Spirit, Shaman Songs*. Copper Beech Press, Brown University, Providence, Rhode Island, 1980.

Clymer, Theodore, ed. *Four Corners of the Sky*. Atlantic Monthly Press, Little, Brown and Co., Boston, 1975.

Coulter, R. T. "Might Makes Right, A History of Indian Jurisdiction," *American Indian Journal*. Institute for the Development of Indian Law, Washington, D.C. 1977.

Dawson, R. MacGregor. *The Government of Canada*. University of Toronto Press, Toronto, Ontario, 1947; Fifth Edition, 1970.

Deloria, Vine Jr. *Custer Died for Your Sins*. Avon Books, New York, 1970.

————. *We Talk, You Listen*. Dell Publishing Co., New York, 1970.

Dinges, John and Saul Landau. *Assassination on Embassy Row*, Pantheon Books, New York. 1980.

Edmonson, Munro S., ed. and trans. *The Book of Counsel: The Popol Vuh of the Quiche Maya of Guatemala*. Middle American Research Institute, Tulane University, New Orleans, 1971.

Emmitt, Robert. *The Last War Trail: The Utes and the Settlement of Colorado*. University of Oklahoma Press, Norman, Oklahoma, 1954.

Flemming, Arthur S., chairman. "Report of Investigaton: Oglala Sioux Tribe General Election," U.S. Government Printing Office, Washington, D.C., 1974.

Garitty, Michael. "The U.S. Colonial Empire is as Close as the Nearest Reservation: The Pending Energy Wars;" from *Trilateralism: The Trilateral Commission and Energy Planning for World Management,* Holly Sklar, ed. South End Press, Boston, 1980.

Grey Owl. *The Men of the Last Frontier*. Macmillan Co., Toronto, Ontario, 1931; current edition, 1972.

Hieb, David L. *Fort Laramie*. National Park Service, Washington, D.C., 1954; reprint, 1961.

Hoebel, E. Adamson. *The Cheyennes, Indians of the Great Plains*. Holt, Rinehart & Winston, New York, 1960.

Indian Country Press, ed. *Time of the Indian*. Indian Country Press, St. Paul, Minnesota, 1977.

Jacobs, William R. *Dispossessing the American Indian*. Scribner's, New York, 1972

Johansen, Bruce and Roberto Maestas. *Wasi'chu, The Continuing Indian Wars*. Monthly Review Press, New York, 1979.

Josephy, Alvin M. Jr., ed. *Red Power, American Indians Fight For Freedom.* McGraw-Hill, New York, 1971.

Kammer, Jerry. *The Second Long Walk, The Navajo-Hopi Land Dispute.* University of New Mexico Press, Albuquerque, New Mexico, 1980.

Katchongva, Dan; trans by Danaqyumptewa. *From the Beginning of Life To the Day of Purification, Teachings, History & Prophecies of the Hopi People.* Committee for Traditional Indian Land and Life, Los Angeles, California, 1972; revised edition ed. by Thomas V. Tarbet, Jr., 1977.

Kroeber, A. L. and E. W. Gifford, *Karok Myths.* University of California Press, Berkeley, California, 1980.

Kwartler, Richard, ed. *Behind Bars, Prisons in America.* Vintage Books, Random House, New York, 1974.

LaDuke, Winona. *The Council of Energy Resource Tribes: An Outsider's View In.* Women of All Red Nations, Rapid City, South Dakota, 1980.

Lame Deer, John Fire and Richard Erdoes. *Lame Deer, Seeker of Visions.* Simon and Schuster, New York, 1972.

Ledogar, Robert J. *Hungry for Profits.* International Documentation, New York, 1975.

Leon-Portilla, Miguel, ed. *Native Mesoarmerican Spirituality, Ancient Myths, Discourses, Stories, Doctrines, Hymns, Poems, From the Aztec, Yucatec, Quiche-Maya and other Sacred Traditions.* Paulist Press, New York, 1980.

————. *The Broken Spears: Aztec Account of the Conquest of Mexico.* Beacon Press, Boston, 1961, 1966.

Lopez, Barry Holstun. *Giving Birth To Thunder, Sleeping With His Daughter, Coyote Builds North America.* Sheed Andrews and McMeel, Kansas City, Missouri, 1977.

Lowman, Bill. *220 Million Custers.* Anacortes Printing & Publishing, Anacortes, Washington, 1978.

McNaught, Kenneth. *The Pelican History of Canada.* Penguin Books, Harmondsworth, Middlesex, England, 1969, 1981.

McLuhan, T. C., compiled. *Touch The Earth, A Self-Portrait of Indian Existence.* Simon and Schuster, 1971.

McNeill, W. H. *The Rise of the West, A History of the Human Community.* New American Library, New York, 1965.

McNeley, James Kale. *Holy Wind in Navajo Philosophy.* University of Arizona Press, Tucson, Arizona, 1981.

Mails, Thomas E. *Fools Crow.* Doubleday, New York, 1978.

Minnesota Citizens' Review Commission, ed. "Report on the FBI." Minnesota Citizens' Review Commission, Minneapolis, Minnesota, 1978.

Moskowitz, Milton, Michael Katz, and Robert Levering, ed. *Everybody's Business, The Irreverent Guide to Corporate America.* Harper & Row, San Francisco, 1980.

Munzel, Dr. Mark. *The Ache Indians: Genocide in Paraguay.* International Work Group for Indigenous Affairs, Copenhagen, 1973.

National Committee To Support the Marion Brothers, ed. *Breaking Men's Minds: Behavior Control and Human Experimentation at the Federal Prison in Marion, Illinois*. National Committee to Support the Marion Brothers, St. Louis, Missouri, 1978.

Neihardt, John G. *Black Elk Speaks*. University of Nebraska Press, Lincoln, Nebraska, 1932, 1979.

Ortiz, Roxanne Dunbar, ed. *The Great Sioux Nation, Sitting in Judgement on America*. American Indian Treaty Council Information Center/Moon Books, San Franscisco, 1977.

Perry, John Weir. *Lord of the Four Quarters*. Collier Books, Macmillian, 1966, 1970.

Price, Joan. *The Earth is Alive: The Southwest as a Holy Land, Native American Tradition and the New Physics*. Colorado Plateau Project, Colorado Springs, 1979.

Rosen, Kenneth, ed. *Voices of the Rainbow, Contemporary Poetry by American Indians*. Seaver Books/Viking Press, New York, 1975, 1980.

Russell Tribunal, ed. "The Rights of the Indians of the Americas," The Fourth Russell Tribunal, Rotterdam, Netherlands, 1980.

Sandoz, Mari. *Crazy Horse*. University of Nebraska Press, Lincoln, Nebraska, 1942, 1961.

Scudder, Thayer, et. al. "Expected Impacts of Compulsory Relocation on Navajos, With Special Emphasis on Relocation from the Former Joint Use Area Required by Public Law 93-531." Institute for Development Anthropology, Binghamton, New York, 1979.

Sejourne, Laurette, *Burning Water, Thought and Religion In Ancient Mexico*. Thames and Hudson, London, 1957.

Smith, W. Eugene and Aileen M. Smith. *Minamata*. Alskog-Sensorium Book/ Holt, Rinehart and Winston, New York, 1975.

Taylor, Flint, ed. *Counter-Intelligence, A Documentary Look at America's Secret Police*. National Lawyers Guild, Chicago, Illinois, 1980

Tilsen, Kenneth. "The FBI, Wounded Knee and Politics," from *The Iowa Journal of Social Work,* Des Moines, Iowa, 1976.

Unger, Sanford J. *FBI*. Little, Brown and Company, Boston, 1976.

Water, Frank. *Book of the Hopi*. Viking Press, New York, 1963, 1972.

———. *Mexico Mystique*. Viking Press, New York, 1975.

White, John. *Poleshift, Predictions and Prophecies of the Ultimate Disaster*. Doubleday, New York, 1980.

Williams, Paul, ed. *The International Bill of Human Rights*. Entwhistle Books, Glen Ellen, California, 1981.

INDEX

Note: Figures in italics indicate illustrations

Abourezk, Charles, FBI and, 198
Abourezk, James, 33, 61, 78, 150, 167, 175, 192, 226
Abram, Morris G., 226
Aches, 129, 225–7
Acquie, Andrew, killing of, 136
Adams, Gary, at Peltier trial, 201
Adams, Gypsy, hanging of, 207
Adams, Hank, 44-5, 49, 53, 57, 88, *91,* 94, 122
Adamson, John, and Bolles murder, 158-9
Adkinson, Wayne, 173
Agee, Phillip, and CIA, 217
Agnew, Spiro, 49, 51-2, 55
Aird, George, murder of, 168-9, 171-2
Akwesasne Notes, 42, 126, 159, 230, 278
Alcatraz Island, Indian seizure at, 42-3
Alexian Brothers Novitiate, 169
Allende, Salvador, 217, 227-9
Allmand, Warren, 238
Allotment Act, 64, 71, 103, 122
AMAX, 13, 240-2
Amazon Basin, 222-3
American Indian Movement (AIM), 13, 20, 24-6, 28, 32-4, 36-7, 42, 49-50, 60, 68, 75, 82-3, 94, 107, 121-2, 127, 153, 156, 169-71, 238-9, 250; beginning of, 21, 34-6; spread in membership of, 36, 42; Indian resistance predating, 37-40; harassment and arrests, 43, 67, 96, 105, 112-13, 174; campaign against, 58-60; and treaty obligations, 65; Janklow and, 66, 125-6; Wilson and supporters and, 74; women at Calico meeting and, 75-6; and Wounded Knee, 76-7; and Custer trial, 124; and leaks, 126-7; and Fairchild occupation, 156; in Farmington, 166; in Los Angeles, 168; Camp 13 of, 168-9, 171; accused of Escamilla attack, 173, media and, 176; at

Pine Ridge, 178; Dr. Brown and, 192; bonds posted by members of, 196; and Kneip, 198; and prisoners who helped, 207; growth in support of, 210; Deere and, 212-13; labeled Communist, 230; decentralization of, 242; and Victoria Creek camp, 255; and Indian pride, 265; and Neo-European governments, 267; and FBI, *see under* FBI
American Indian Treaty Council, 19, 230
Amiott, Roger, finding of body by, 191
Anaconda Copper, 45, 128, 146, 227-8, 261
Anarchy, U.S.A., 74
Anderson, Jack, 54, 57
Anderson, Larry, 156
Anderson, Larry, Vicky, and family, *147*
Anderson, M. F., and Celay killing, 48
Anderson, Mike, 186, 200
Anishinabe, 21-2, 214, 236-7
Apache, 55, 133
Appropriation Act, and treaties, 88
Aquash, Anna Mae, 15, 90-91, 175, 184-6, 189-91; and FBI, 167, 175, 189-93, 196, 233; and Durham, 168-9; at Alexian occupation, 169; to Hamilton, 184-5, 193; and Price, 185, 192-3; goes underground, 186, 191; and sister Mary, 191; murder, autopsy and, 191-3, 196, 209; Canada and, 192, 233; and Myrtle Poor Bear, 198, 209
Aquash, Nogeeshik, marriage of, 90
Aquirre, Anselme, 221
Arbenz, Jacobo, and United Fruit, 219
Arens, Dr. Richard, 226
Arizona, 20, 22, 38, 132, 144
Arizona Daily Star, 145, 176
Arizona Intertribal Council, 52
Arizona Republic, 151, 158-9
Armas, Castello, and Guatemala, 219
Arrellano, John, and BIA files, 57
Arthur, Chester A., 142
Artichocker, John, and Manning, 209

291

Assimilative Crimes Act, 103
Associated Press, 108, 110, 173, 176,
    179, 182
Athabascan Dine, 235, 239-40
Aztecs, 268, 272

Babby, Wyman, and Wilson, 61
Bad Cob, Chief Tom, 89-90, *91*
Bad Heart Bull, Sarah, 68-9, 168-9
Bad Heart Bull, Vernal, murder of, 121
Bad Heart Bull, Wesley, 68, 121
Bad Wound, Louie, and RCMP, 239
Bahanna, 139, 159, 266-7, 274
Baily, Michael, and Oregon trials, 191
Ballanger, Pat, 36, 214, 278
Ballinger, Delray, killings by, 136
Baltimore Sun, and Morton authority, 112
Banks, Dennis, 35-6, 42, 46, *47,* 50, 53, 60,
    68-9, 92-4, 105, *113,* 114, 178, 186-7, 193;
    arrest and jailing of, 43, 69, 95; and
    Calico meeting, 75-6; trials of, 107, 109,
    112-15, 115n, 116-22, 167, 172, 186-7, *see
    also* Wounded Knee, trials of; and
    Durham, 114, 168, 170; and Janklow,
    125, 193; FBI and, 189-90, 193; statement
    by, 210
Banks, Kamook, 186, 190
Banyacya, Thomas, 44, 159, 213; at UN,
    160-1, 163, 273
Banzer, Huygo, and Indians, 229
Barker, Robert, 145, 153
Barnet, Donald, 69
Barry, Tom, Ned Yazzi to, 156
Basford, Ron, and Peltier, 199
Basil, Chief Ken, 238-9
Bates, Tom, Loud Hawk to, 190
Bean, Lou, 73, *91*
Bear Eagle, Von, and goon squad, 105
Bear Runner, Edgar, and RCMP, 239
Bear Shield, Jerry, 174
Beare, Norman, and BIA rape file, 126
Beck, Robert, at Crow Dog camp, 184
Bellecourt, Clyde, 35-6, 43, 49, 52-3, 89, *91,*
    127, 264, 276
Bellecourt, Vernon, 35-6, 53, 93, 170,
    196, 237
Benally family, *138*
Benally, Herman, assassination of, 135
Bender, Howard, killings by, 136

Benson, Paul, and Peltier trial, 199-202
Benton-Banai, Edward, 35-6, 53, 58, 213,
    265, 276-7
Berger, Edward, 152
Berger, Justice Thomas, inquiry of, 235
Bernstick, Ed, and contract paper, 239
Bertinot, Gerald, and Wounded Knee, 115
Bible, 28, 30-1, 123
Big Foot, Chief, 66, 94, 253
Bird Horse, Reginald, testimony of, 122
Bissonette, Gladys, 69, 73-4, 88-90, *91,* 93,
    122, 180
Bissonette, Jeanette, 174-5, 209
Bissonette, Pedro, 15, 70, 74, 78, 88, *91,* 95,
    110, 192, 209; government offer to, 106-7,
    116; murder and autopsy of, 108-9
Bitsie, Ashikie, and family, *279*
Black Elk, Philip, murder of, 121
Black Elk, Wallace, 88, 90, *91,* 98
Black Hills, 23, 28-9, 67, 217-18, 245;
    planned occupation of, 19-21, 23-4, 28,
    251, *see also* Victoria Creek Canyon *and*
    Camp Yellow Thunder; and uranium
    exploration, 45, 249, 261-3; U.S. and,
    62-4, 71
Black Hills Survival Gathering, 243, 250;
    Means and, 230-1, 249
Black Mesa, 65-6, 138, 150, 155, 159, *163,*
    268, 272-3
Blackfoot, 43, 45
Blanca, Dudley, and uranium holdings, 261
Blanco, Hugo, and Quechua, 230
Blue Dove, 168, 171-2
Bolivia, 215, 229
Bolles, Don, 158
Bonaparte Indian Band, 238
Bono, Victor, and Marion Prison, 203
Bosman, David, shooting of Celay by, 48
Bottum, Joseph, and Custer trials, 123-4
Bouldt, Reber, and Wilson excesses, 244
Bourassa, Robert, 127-8, 236
Bowan, James, and land leases, 99, 245
Boyden, John, 45-7, 144-9, 152
Bragg, Marvin, and Jimmy Eagle, 200
Brando, Marlon, 168, 177, 210
Brazil, 97, 212, 215, 222-4, 232
Brewer, Vincent, and King, 106
Breynat, Bishop Gabriel, and treaty, 235
Briggs, A. M., 175
British Columbia, 238, 240-1

British North American Act, 64, 234
Brooke, Edward, and Aquash death, 192
Broussard, Holly, 168-9, 171-2
Brown, Gov. Jerry, and Banks, 193, 210
Brown, Norman, 181-2, 184-5, 200
Brown, W. O., autopsy by, 191-2
Browne, Jackson, concerts of, 210, 242-3
Bruce, Louis, and Unity Caravan, 50
Byrne, Roy, and Calling Last, 238
Buckley, James, Abram to, 226
Buckley, Marge, and Bissonette, 107
Bureau of Indian Affairs (BIA), 33, 37, 39,
    45, 49-50, 55, 59-60, 67, 70, 74, 76, 78-9,
    89, 94-5, 106, 108-9, 111-13, 150, 152,
    158, 175, 210, 244, 257; takeover of
    building of, 24, 50-5, 58-9, 61, 127, 134,
    239; files of, 54-5, 57; leasing of Indian
    land by, 70-1, 129, 133; and Janklow
    rape, 125-6; and Hopi, 136, 142-3, 146;
    Monongye on, 215; and Canadian Indians
    Affairs Dep't, 234, 239; Tribal Councils
    of, *see under names of nations; see also*
    police
Burener, Claire, and Gardon Plot, 177
Burton, Ted, and Ojibway occupation, 237
Butler, Dino, 175, 181-2, 184-5, 187, 189,
    197, 200, 210
Butler, Nilak, 175, 181
Butz, Earl, 112
Buzhardt, Fred, and Wounded Knee, 81

Calico, meeting in, 73-6, 118
California, 38, 40, 45, 101
Calió, Jim, Poor Bear to, 198-9
Callahan, Earl, and Custer trial, 124
Calling Last, Urban, and RCMP, 238
Camp, Carter, *91*, 127
Camp Yellow Thunder, *252, 254,* 255-7,
    258, 260-61, 263
Campari, Ish, 220
Canada, 13, 14, 22, 36, 40, 64, 127, 129,
    210, 233-5, 237, 241; and Indian land, 21,
    102, 196, 218; system of justice in, 97,
    104; and James Bay, 127-8, 236; and
    Aquash, 192, 196, 233; extradition
    agreement of, 202; treatment of Indians
    by, 212, 234-42; Tribunal charges against,
    232, 247; and uranium, 239-40; and
    Mohawks, 245 6; *see also* RCMP

Carey, Hugh, and Raquette Point, 246-8
Carey, Robert "Max," 203-4, 209
Carlton, James, and Navajo, 101, 142
Carlucci, Frank, 53, 58
Carradine, David, 168
Carson, Kit, and Navajo, 64, 101, 142
Carter, Jimmy, 243, 247
Carter, Jacques, Haudenosaunee and, 245
Casasola, Colonel Oliverio, 219
Castleman, Noel, and Wounded Knee, 93
Casuse, Larry, 134-5
Catches, Chief, at Calico, 76
Cavise, Leonard, 109
Ceanese, Fourth Tribunal and, 221
Celay, Phillip, murder of, 48
Cellicon, Arnold, killing of, 136
Central Intelligence Agency (CIA), 59, 158,
    214, 216-17, 219, 228-9
Chandra, Romesh, 214, 216
Chase-Sardi, Miguel, 225
Cherokee, 64, 99-100, 100n, 150-2
Chevron Oil, 129
Chevron Resources, and uranium, 45, 261
Cheyenne, 25, 30, 39, 63; Northern, 55,
    129, 214
Chicago Tribune, and FBI, 176
Chickasaw, relocation of, 64, 100, 150
children, Indian, 142-3, 149-50
Chile, 13, 97, 149, 212, 215, 227-29
Chisso Chemical Co., and poisoning, 237
Choctaw, 64, 100, 150
Christenson, Bernard, 68
Christian Science Monitor, 248
Christmas feast, 221
Chungara, Domitila Barrios, 218
Church of Latter Day Saints, *see* Mormons
Citizenship Act, 66, 122
Clark, Matthew, killings by, 136
Clayton, William, 109, 114, 173
Clearwater, Frank, 20, 91-2
Clearwater, Morningstar, 91-2
Cleaver, Kenneth, 17
Clifford, Gregory, 199, 200
Clifford, Joe, shooting by, 108-9
Clifford, Mark, and car crash, 174
coal, 52, 55, 136, 149, 158, 250; on Indian
    land, 20, 38, 65-6, 128, 133, 144, 160, 262;
    see also strip mining
Coast Guard, occupation of base of, 46
Coelho, Linda, and FBI, 191

COINTELPRO, 128, 176, 199
Colburn, Wayne, 50, 72, 74; and Wounded
  Knee, 80, 90, 93, 177
Cole, Kenneth, 81
Coler, Jack, 178, 180
Coll, Tom, 180, 182
Collins, Anita, arrest of, 57
Colombia, 220-2, 232
Columbia Journalism Review, 180
Commission on Civil Rights, 67, 110, 132-3,
  180, 182, 189, 192; and tribal council
  election, 110-11, 111n
Commissioner of Indian Affairs, 141-2
Committee for Original Peoples'
  Entitlement, claims of, 235-6
Common Sense, and sterilization, 167
Conroy, Henry, and Indian treaty, 235
Conroy, Tom, and Pine Ridge land, 78-79
Cook, Thomas, FBI information to, 176
Coomes, Albert, and Eagle Hawk, 174
Cooper, James, reports to, 59
Coplemen, Martha, attack on, 172-3
Coronado, Vasquez de, 139
Cottier, Stacey, shooting of, 175
Council on Environmental Quality, 55
Coward, Frederick, affidavit of, 195
Crane, Leo, and Yukioma, 143
Crazy Horse, Chief, 30, 63
Cree, 43, 127-8, 235-6, 251, 265, 267
Creek, 64, 100, 150
Cretien, Jean, 45
Crook, General George, 30, 63
Crooks, Lynn, and Peltier trial, 200-1
Cross, Clarence, killing of, 106
Cross, Richard, abduction of, 234
Cross, Vernal, shooting of, 106
Crow Dog, Henry, 97, 123, 188
Crow Dog, Leonard, 48, 76, 90, 93, 187-8,
  255, 257; arrest, prosecution, and trials
  of, 95, 123, 184, 187-8; camp of, 182-4,
  193; and prison system, 188-9
Crow Dog, Mary, 188-9
Crow Dog, Mary Gertrude, 188
Cuibas Indians, 221-2
Cupenda, Jose, 215, 218
Curtis, Edward, and Indian nations, 250
Custer County, 67-9, 123-5, 186
Custer Died for Your Sins, 258
Custer, George Armstrong, 30, 62-3

Dairdson, Jim, 237
Daum, Eliot, and Little house, 182
Davies, Ronald, Trudell before, 209
Dawes, Henry L., 64, 71, 103
Dean, Bobo, Wilson letter to, 105
Dean, John, 54, 59, 94, 117
Decker, Senator, and Indian claims, 33
DeCora, Lorelei, 83
Deere, Phillip, 98, 212-13, 265-7, 277
Defense Department, 81, 117
Deloria, Vine, Jr., 258
deLuce, Virginia, *see* Blue Dove
Dennison, George, assassination of, 135
Denny, Goldie, and baptism, 150
Denver Tribune, and Utes, 64
Dep't of Indian Affairs, Canada, 234, 237-9
Dine, 101, 138, 141
Dinsmore, Robert, 178
Dix, Jim, to Pine Ridge, 72
"Dog Soldier" Memo, 198-9
Dryden Chemical Co., and mercury, 237-8
Duenas, Roque, and Peltier, 207
Dunn, Col., and Pine Ridge, 74
Durham, Douglas, 114, 125, 168-72, 176
Durham, Jimmy, 216

Eagle, Jimmy, 178, 180, 183, 187, 189,
  199, 200
Eagle Deer, Jancita, 125-6
Eagle Hawk, Edith, killing of, 174, 209
Eagle Hawk, Eugene, and car crash, 174
Eaglebull, Lloyd, 105, 111
Eastman, Del, 60, 108-9
Eaton, Wendy, 171
Economic Opportunity Act, 60
education, Indians and, 276-7
Edward, Don, and Peltier case, 243-4
Edwards, Don Agustin, 228
Ehrlichman, John, 53, 59, 78, 94, 117; letter
  of, to Brando, 177
Eisenhower, Dwight D., 146, 151
El Mercurio, 228
El Paso Natural Gas, plans of, 45
El Quiche, Guatemala, 219
energy, 66, 128-31, 136, *137,* 146, 148, 153,
  156, 214, 222, 235, 250
Enlow, Phillip, and rape charge, 120
Environmental Protection Agency, 156

Erdoes, Richard, 188-9
Erickson, Bruce, to Pine Ridge, 72
Escamilla, Bernard, attack on, 172-3
Evans, David W., 52, 138, 148
Ex Parte Crow Dog, 104
EXXON Corp., 13, 128, 235, 276

Fairchild Camera and Instrument Co., 156
Farmington, N.M., 133-6, 153, 166
Fast Thunder, Chief, and wife, 30-1
Fast Thunder, Stella, 30
Federal Bureau of Investigation (FBI), 14,
    26, 32-3, 49, 55, 57, 59, 93, 125-8, 147-8,
    169-71, 173, 175-7, 180, 207, 209, 211,
    244; and Black Hills, 19, 20, 253-5, 257;
    and AIM, 20, 33, 42-3, 58, 67, 73, 115-21,
    126-7, 166, 170, 172, 174-6, 179-80, 186,
    193, 196-9, 216, 233, 242; and Peltier, 33,
    43, 164, 175, 185, 189-90, 193-5, 199-201,
    207, 244; and Trudell, 43, 210; and Pine
    Ridge, 73, 106, 174-5, 178-84, 196, 199;
    and Wounded Knee, 77, 87-9, 92-5; and
    Banks/Means trial, 114-21, 172; and Louis
    Moves Camp, 119-20; and shooting of
    agents, 164, 178-87, 189-90, 192, 198-201;
    and Aquash, 167, 175, 189-93, 196, 233;
    and Skyhorse/Mohawk, 169, 172; Durham
    and, 170-1, 176; use of media by, 176-80;
    at Crow Dog camp, 184-5; and
    prospective witnesses, 185, 192; and
    fugitive warrants and indictments, 189-90;
    and Brown, 192, 200; and RCMP, 194,
    217, 238-9; "Dog Soldier" Memo of,
    198-9; and radio transmissions, 200-1; in
    Latin America and Europe, 216-17; *see
    also* Garden Plot
Federal Energy Administration, 128
Fee, Curley, hanging of, 207
Finzel, Roger, attack on, 172-3
Fifth World, Hopi and, 23
First Church of the Open Bible, 114
First International Treaty Council, 129-31
First World, 270, 272
fishing rights, 43-5, 48-9
Fitzgerald, John, 124-5
Flemming, Arthur S., 111, 111n, 182
Flood, story of, 270-1
Flynn, Patrick, eavesdropping by, 118

Fools Crow, Frank, 23, 29, 32-4, 37-8, 69,
    76, 83, 86-7, 94-5, 105-6, 183, 255, *256*
Forbes, Jack, at Treaty Council, 130
Ford Foundation, legal aid fund of, 45-6
Forsyth, James, and Wounded Knee, 66
Fort Laramie, 25, 62, 251
Fort Lawton, occupation of, 42-3, 60
Fort Lincoln, 62-3
Fort Robinson, 62-3
Fort Snelling, occupation of, 46
Four Corners, *137;* power plant of, *153*
Fourth Russell Tribunal, 212-13, 218-21,
    223, *224, 232-3, 242
Fourth World, 23, 213-14, 218, 229-31, 271-2
Franklin, Marvin, defense of Mull by, 151
Fritze, Jean, and Wounded Knee trial, 116
Frizzell, Kent, 88-91, *91,* 93-4, 128
Front de Liberation du Quebec, 234
Fulbright, William, and Oglala Sioux, 78

Gable, Mildred, and Aird case, 171
Gall, Chief, and Custer and Reno, 63
Galligo, Mildred, 69, 82
Gallup, N. M., 133-6, 153
Ganienkeh, 128, 277, 278
Garcia, Bobby, 206-9
Garcia, Emmet Frankie, 134-5
Garden Plot, 166, 177
Garment, Leonard, 53, 58-9, 94
Garreau, Melvin, 257
Garrick, David, 165, 241
Gates, Hobart, AIM meeting with, 68
General Crimes Act, 103
Geneva, conference in, 214-16, 239, 242
genocide, 141n, 212, 214-15, 217-18, 226,
    232, 240, 250, 263
Genocide in Paraguay, 226
Gentles, William, and Crazy Horse, 63
Georgia Straight, Garrick in, 165
Gerrity, Edward, and perjury charge, 229
Gibbon, General John, 63
Gienapp, David, 114
Gilbert, Madonna, 278
Gildersleeve, Clive and Agnes, 76
Glenn, Skip, 171
God is Red, 258
gold, 34, 100-1, 222-3; Black Hills and, 20,
    29, 62, 263

Goldwater, Barry, 139, 145, 157-9
Gonzalez, Endoro, 221
Gonzalez, Mario, 125-6, 126n, 218, 245
goon squad, 32-3, 60-1, 73, 77, 87-9, 92,
    94-5, 106, 174, 186-7; arrests, beatings,
    and shooting by, 92, 96, 121; nonarrests
    of, 95, 105-6, 121
Gordon, Eda, attack on, 172-3
Gordon, James, election of, 152
Gordon, Nebraska, 25-6, 73
Gougelet, Bob, and white racism, 136
Graham, John, and uranium miners, 240
Grant, Peter, Halprin suit against, 233
Gray, Patrick, and Wounded Knee, 117
Great Plains, occurrences at, 13, 25
Great Purification, Hopi and, 23-4, 101,
    143, 266-7, 272, 275
Greenpeace, and Camp Yellow Thunder,
    260
Gridley, John III, Janklow to, 125
Griffin, Shara, 25
Griffith, James, 59-60
Griffiths, Kenneth, 190, 194
Guahibo Indians, treatment of, 221-2
Guatemala, 13, 218-20, 232
Guggenheims, copper companies of, 227
Guild, Anne, and Peltier, 60
Guild, William H., 206
Gulf Oil Co., 20, 222
Gurwitz, Shep, at Crow Dog camp, 183

Haig, General Alexander, 62, 80-1, *80*
Haldeman, H. R., 54, 94
Hall, Doug, and Wounded Knee trials, 114
Halprin, Paul William, 194-5, 233
Halvinka, Ronald, and Peltier, 60
Hamilton, Candy, 184-5, 193, 209
Hamilton, Clarence, 51-2, 148
Hamlin, Jacob, and Hopi Land, 141
Hanley, Frederick, and Katchongva, 146
Harding, Raymond, and Lyons, 246-7
Hare, Melvin and Leslie, 48-9
Harris, Bill, and uranium, 261-2
Harrison, Willie, killing of, 136
Hart, Pat, shooting of, 121
Harvey, Charles, and Brown, 185
Harvey, John, assassination of, 135
Haudenosaunee, 21, 39, 40, 87, 98-9, 103,
    245-7, 249, 251, 267-8

Hayes, Ira, 38, 49
Hearst Newspapers, and FBI, 176
Hegel, G.W.F., Means and, 231
Held, Richard, to Pine Ridge, 182
Hellstern, Richard, 88-9, *91, 93*
Helms, Richard, 228
High Bull, Marion, and Jimmy Eagle, 200
Hill, Dave, and Custer trial, 124
history, Indian, 29-30, 35, 267-73, 275; *see
    also* Hopi *and* prophecies
Holder, Stan, 84-5, 90, 93, 95
Hollow Horn, Florine, *91*
Holloway, Winston M., Lawrence and, 208
Holman, Donald, 67
Holt, Dennis, and Lakota land claim, 263
Holy Eagle, James, 255-6
Homestake Gold Mine, 262-3
Hoover, J. Edgar, 175-6
Hopi, 22, 25, 37-40, 55, 66, 101, 133, 136,
    140-4, 146, 148, 150, 153, 156, 251, 270-6;
    resistance by and imprisonment of, 13,
    22-3, 131, 140, 143; and Spanish
    missionaries, 15, 140-1; and relocation,
    20, 138; as original people, 22, 40, 131,
    144, 159; prophecies of, 22-4, 101, 139-40,
    142-4, 159-61, 162, 266, 266n, 267-8,
    270-1, 273, 274; and Oraibi, 22, 139, 142,
    162, 268, 272-3; and tribal council, 45,
    136, 144-6, 148; power plants on land of,
    52, 147-8, 150-1; rejections by traditionals
    of, and loss of land by, 65, 141-2, 145;
    Mormons and, 101, 136, 141-2, 144-9;
    uranium mines and mills on reservation
    of, *137;* and Bahanna, 139, 266-7, 274; to
    UN conferences, 160-1, 162, 197, 213;
    and Mayans, 269-70, 272; and petroglyph,
    273, 274, *275*
Hopi-Navajo Land Dispute, 22, 136, 138-9,
    142-7
Hopi-Navajo Settlement Act, 138, 150-1,
    153, 157
Hopi Tribal Council, 37, 45, 52, 144-8, 150
Horseherder, Elvira and family, *138*
Hotevilla, Hopi and, 142-4
Houser, Colonel, 219
Howard, General Oliver, 64
Hultman, Evan, 200-1, 205
Humphrey, Hubert, and Fort Snelling, 46
Hunentelaf, Felix, 228
Hunkpapa Lakota, 25, 63

Huntsville Times, 52
Hurd, Richard, 113-21, 187-8, 190, 199
Hussman, John, 106

Ickes, Dennis, 93-5, 121
Ignacio, David, assassination of, 136
Imperial Oil, 235
Inada, Lawson, song for, 281-6
Incas, 268, 272
Independent Oglala Nation, 83, 89, 90
Indian Claims Act, 46
Indian Claims Commission, 38, 40, 46, 71,
  144, 217
Indian Child Welfare Act, 150
Indian Freedom of Religion Act, 20-1, 253
Indian Health Service Hospital, 134, 166-7
Indian Non-Intercourse Act, 99, 245
Indian Reorganization Act, 37, 71, 95;
  Lakotas and, 122
Indian School Center, 60
Indians, 14, 26, 30, 35-6, 64, 66-9, 97, 100,
  130, 202, 210-11, 213, 215, 222, 226, 231,
  243, 250, 276-7, 280; and resistance and
  confrontation, 13, 14, 19, 20, 22-4, 30, 33,
  36-40, 42-5, 46, 50-1, 62-3, 72, 114, 134-6,
  140, 156, 167, 169, 219-20, 227, 232,
  236-8, 242, 246-7, 251, 253-7, 259-61, *see
  also* Wounded Knee *and* Hopi; and cash
  for land, 20, 32, 38-40, 45, 62-3, 70-1,
  100, 128, 144-5, 152-3, 217-18, 236, 244-5,
  263; and sovereignty, 99-100, 102, 104,
  122-3, 174, 211, 216, 230, 232, 236, 249;
  Canada and, 233-42; spiritual rebirth of,
  265-7; earliest settlements of in North
  America, and migration patterns of,
  268-72; history of, *see* history; *see also
  names of nations, individuals, etc.*
Industrias Purace, 221
Interior Dep't, 37, 52, 55, 70-1, 78, 89, 95,
  113, 122, 139, 148, 151, 181, 199; and
  tribal council election in, 109-11
International Conference on Discrimination
  Against Indigenous Populations in the
  Americas, 214-16
International Indian Treaty Council, 213-14,
  232, 240, 250
Int'l League for the Rights of Man, 226
Inuit, 127, 235-6, 251
Iowa Office of Education, 114

Iron Cloud, Chief, at Calico, 76
Iron Cloud, Roger, and bullets, 83
Iroquois, 14, 15, 21-2
ITT, 228-9, 236

Jackson, Andrew, and Cherokee, 100
Jackson, Henry, 122
Jackson, Major Vic, 80
Jacobs, Dr. William R., 268n
James Bay project, 127-8, 236
James, Kathi, attack on, 172-3
Jamieson, Donald, and Aquash, 233
Janklow, William, 66-7, 124-6, 178-9, 186,
  193, 230, 232
Jara, Don Tomas, and Indians, 221
Jimminez, Marcelino, 221
John Birch Society, 74, 170, 230
Johnson, Alan, FBI to, 93
Johnson, Chief Vincent, 247
Johnson & Graham's Lessee v. McIntosh,
  102
Johnson, Lyndon B., and Keeler, 151
Johnson, Ray, and Pit River Indians, 40
Joint Use Area, 138, 142, 146-7, 150;
  Horseherder and Benally family in, *138*
Jones, Kee, assassination of, 135
Joseph, Chief, 62, 64
Jumping Bull, Harry and Celia, 175, 178,
  180-1; Camp, Peltier and, 194
Justice Dep't, 79-81, 89, 94-5, 97, 106, 122,
  175-6, 192, 229

Kammerer, Marvin, 250, 257
Kanatakeniate, and Fourth World, 213-14
Kaplan, Earl, 114, 117
Kash, Reese, 73-5
Kastl, Richard, 19, 23-4
Katchongva, Dan, 98, 142-6, 148, 159, 274
Keam, Thomas, and Hopi, 142
Keeler, W. W., 55, 151-2
Keith, Hobart, and Wilson, 74
Kelley, Clarence, 115, 180, 182, 192,
  198, 233
Kendall, Donald, 228
Kennecott, 129, 146, 149, 227-8, 240, 276
Kennedy, Edward, and Oglala Sioux, 78
Kennedy, John F., and Keeler, 151
Kenora, Ontario, Ojibway in, 237

Kerr McGee, 20, 133, 155, 261
Kikmongivis, and Hopi prophecy, 266, 266n
Kills Enemy, Frank, 32, 76, 253, 255
Kimball, Spencer, and children, 149
King, Martin Luther, 176
King, Matthew, 23, *27,* 31-3, 95, 106, 108-9,
  123, 189, 249-51, 253, 255, 257, 263, 269,
  280; and Fools Crow, 23, 32, 86-7; home
  and family of, 26-7, 30-1, 33, 86, 174;
  author's conversation with, 27-34, 251;
  and bullet holes, 33, 60, 174; re peace
  plan and war plan, 62, 81; and Price, 106,
  174, 183
Kissinger, Henry, 94, 228
Kleindienst, Richard, 58, 79, 81, 88, 94
Kneip, Richard, 67, 124, 178-9, 198
Knox, Roland, and Carradine party, 168
Kunstler, William, *113,* 114, 118, 124

LaCourse, Richard, 43
LaDuke, Winona, 214, 250, 281-6
LaRubiera ranch house, massacre at, 221
Lakota, 23, 25, 31, 38-9, 62-4, 66, 122, 140,
  153, 214, 249-50, *252,* 262-3; and treaty
  rights, 20-2, 62, 251; warrior of, 28; and
  Black Hills, 62-4, 71, 217-18, 251, 253-7,
  259-61, 263; suit of, and refusal of money,
  217-18, 263; *see also* Oglala-Lakota
Lamont, Agnes, 76-7, 121, 196
Lamont, Buddy, 20, 93-4, 196
land, Indian, 13, 14, 34, 55, 62, 64-6, 70-1,
  99, 127, 141-2, 153, 159, 219-20, 227-8;
  philosophy about, 15, 29, 64, 66; claims
  to, 19-22, 25, 28, 39, 42, 44-5, 66, 123,
  145, 169, 187, 220, 229-30, 235-6, 242,
  250-1, 253-7, 259-61, 263; confiscation of,
  20-2, 32-4, 36, 38-40, 70-1, 78-9, 100,
  102-3, 123, 142, 145, 196, 215, 217, 227,
  235, 244, 251; resources on, 20, 33, 38,
  64, 72, 145, 196, 202, 222-3, 235, 250,
  261-2, *see also names of minerals*; ceding
  of, to U.S., 22, 28, 62, 152, *see also*
  treaties; energy leases and projects on,
  55, 99, 128, 214; in 1492, *65;* and 1868
  Treaty, *252;* cash for, *see under* Indians
Land or Death, 230
Landau, Saul, Allende and, 227-8
Lane, Mark, 106-9, 114-15, 120, 124
Laporte, Pierre, abduction of, 234
Largo, Mary, *56*

Larson, Mel, 253
Latin America, 217-18, 257, 229-30; *see also
  countries of*
Lawrence, Edward Lee, 208-9
Leading Fighter, Jenny, 121
Letelier, Orlando, 225
Leventhal, Larry, 60, 100n, 114, 115n, 119
Levi, Edward, and Aquash death, 192
Lincoln, Tony, 50, 158-9
Lippman, R. J., Lawrence appeal to, 208
Lippman, Theo, and Morton authority, 112
Little Bear, Mary Ann, shooting of, 106
Little Bighorn, battle at, 63
Little Crow, Philip, murder of, 121
Little Fast Horse, Allison, 121
Little, Frank, assassination of, 175
Little Red School House, 60
Little, Richard, 71
Little, Wallace, Jr., 182
Littlechief, Roy, and RCMP, 239
Littlepage, J. L., and tailings, 240-1
Locke, John, 129-30, 231
Lockhart, Tauna, and Peltier, 243
Loesch, Harrison, 49-50, 52-3, 55, 58-9,
  136, 151
Long, Vern, signing of demands by, 78
Long Visitor, Ivis and Angie, 181
Los Angeles Examiner, and FBI, 176
Los Angeles Times, 53, 146
Loud Hawk, Kenneth, 190-1
Lumbee Indians and Ku Klux Klan, 45
Luce, Virginia de, *see* Blue Dove
Lucas, Garcia Romeo, 219-20
Lydick, Judge Lawrence, 206, 244
Lyman, Stanley, 61, 73, 75, 108
Lyons, Oren, 87-8, 98, 132, 214, 232-3,
  245-7
Lysyk, Kenneth, and treaties, 234

McCloskey, Robert, and Paraguay, 226
McCloskey, William, 184
McCone, John, and Allende, 228
McDaniels, Clarence, as informer, 176-7
MacDermot, Niall, 215-16
MacDonald, Peter, 51, 156-9, *157*
MacEachen, Allen, and Aquash, 196, 233
McKay, Gunn, 150
McManus, Judge Edward, and Crow Dog,
  187
McNeill, William H., 269, 269n

McNoise, Marcella, 168-9, 171-2
Mad Bear, 39-40, 43-4, 267-8
Mahoney, Justice Patrick, and Inuit, 236
Major Crimes Act, 64, 103
Major, Harvey, 114, 170
Malouf, Albert, and James Bay, 127, 236
Manning, Arthur, fire at home of, 209-10
Manning, Leah Hicks, 209
Mapuche Indians, 227-9
Marion Prison, description of, 202-3
Marriott, J. Willard, and tithing, 146
Marshall, Justice John, 100, 102
Marshall, Richard, 20, 26, 33, 173-4, 186-7, 195-6, 198-9, 210, 244
Massau'u, and Hopi, 271, 273
Mateer, William, and Indian land, 141
Mathers, James, 253, 258, 260
Mathieson, Bill, and Custer trial, 124-5
Maxwell, Neal, 153
Mayans, 218-20, 268-70, 272
Means, Bill, 19, 20, 30, 42-3, 49, 51, 53-5, 69-71, 97, 174, 253-4, 257, 258, *259*
Means, Dace, grandmother of, 30
Means, Lorelei, and women, 278, 280
Means, Russell, 30, 32, *41,* 42, 49-51, 53, 60-1, 68-71, 78, 88-90, *91,* 94, 109-10, *113,* 121, 173-4, 178, 187, 195, 199, 214; arrests of, 19-20, 43, 60, 69, 95, 105; trial of, 107, 109, 112-15, 115n, 116-22, 167, 172, 187; and Montileaux murder, 173-4, 186-7; statement of, on Fourth World philosophy, 230-2; and Black Hills, 249, 260, 263
Means, Ted, 30, 174
media, 20, 40, 42, 50-2, 55, 57, 78-9, 81-3, 170, 176-81, 198, 200, 248; *see also names of periodicals*
Medicine Creek Treaty, 44
Medicine Societies, 187, 189
Meinhardt, Nick, 260
Mengele, Dr. Josef, and Paraguay, 224
Merhige, Judge Robert, 188, 190-1
Metcalf, Lee, 39
Mexico, 101-2, 140
Miles, General Nelson, 64
Millape, Antonio, to UN, 215, 229
Miller, Rob, and Black Hills, 253-4
Miller, Justice Samuel F., 103
Milwaukee Journal, and FBI, 176
Minamata Day, mercury tragedy of, 237
Minneapolis, 21, 35-6, 47

Minneapolis Star, 59
Minneapolis Tribune, 179
Minneconjous, 63
Mitchell, John, 110, 228
Moab, Utah, song for, 281-6
Mohawk, 43, 61, 99, 245-6, *248,* 248-9; and Ganienkeh settlement, 128, 277, 278; *see also* Haudenosaunee
Mohawk, John, 128-30, 249, 277, 278
Mohawk, Richard, 168-9, 171-2
molybdenum, mining of, 240-2
Mondale, Walter, 47
Monongye, David, 14, 159-60, 213-15
Montgomery, Col. Patrick, 129
Montileaux, Martin, shooting of, 33, 173-4, 186, 195-6, 199
Montreal Gazette, and RCMP report, 238
Moore, Barbara, and sterilization, 167
Moore, Mary, birth of baby of, 90
Moqui, Mormons and, 141-2
Morales, Priscilla, 207-8
Morgan, Michael, and Oakes killing, 49
Morin, Luis Enrique, 221
Morinigo, General Higinio, 225
Mormons, 101, 136, 139, 141-2, 145-6, 149-50, 152, 158; Hopi and, 65, 101, 146, 148-50
Morrow, Judge William, 235
Morton, Rogers C. B., 51-3, 55, 58-9, 61, 78, 94, 110-12, 129
Mount Rushmore, 24, 67
Moves Camp, Ellen, 69, 88-9, *91,* 118-19
Moves Camp, Louis, 118-21, 178, 185
Movimiento Indio Tupac Katari, 230
Mugar, Carolyn, 106
Mull, Marvin, and misuse of funds, 157
multinationals, 20, 211, 214-15, 263-4; *see also names of*
Munzel, Dr. Mark, and the Colony, 225
Muskogee, 265-7, 277

Nakaidine, Bob, and Garcia, 134
National Academy of Sciences, 261, 276
National Environmental Policy Act, 55
National Parks Service, 71, 181
Native Alcoholism groups, 47-8
Native American Rights Fund, 45-6
Navajo, 22, 25, 38, 64, 101, 106, 132-3, *133,* 135-6, 141, 146, 148-9, 153, *153,* 156, 158; and relocation, 20, 22, 136, 138, *138,*

153-4, 157, 160, *279;* power plants on land of, 52, 133, 147-8, 150-1, 154-5; uranium mines and mills on reservation of, *137; see also* Hopi-Navajo
Navajo Times, Shearin and, 158
Navajo Tribal Council, 45, 145-6, 150, 156-8
Neal, Jack, and Trudell, 186
Nelson, Emma, 105, 111
Neo-Europeans, 97-8, 127, 130, 214-15, 227, 231, 234, 236, 245, 248-50, 267, 269, 276
New Mexico, 20, 132, 144
New Times, and Garden Plot, 177
New York Daily News, and FBI, 176
New York Post, and death of agents, 179
New York State, and Indian land, 21, 99, 103, 128, 245-7
New York Times, 54, 57, 158, 221-2, 248
Newton, Isaac, Means and, 231
Nez Perce, 64
Nicaragua, 229-30
Nichol, Judge Fred, 109, 112, 115, 115n, 116-21, 187
Nishga, 240-2
Nixon, Richard M., 50, 53, 58-9, 81-2, 94, 112, 117-18, 128-30, 151, 228
Noble Red Man, 30-1; *see also* King
North America, 14, 39-40, 66, 140, 229-30
North American Indian Unity Convention, 43
North Carolina, 45, 100
Northcott, Karen, 95, 124, 200
Northern Development Plan, 239
Northwest Ordinance, ignoring of, 102
Northwest Territories, 234-5

Oakes, Richard, killing of, 48-9
O'Callahan, Dennis, 118
O'Connell, J. E., and FBI, 211
Office of Economic Opportunity, 59-60
Office of Indian Affairs, 103
Oglala, 19, 25, 63, 83, 181; refusal of money by, 20, 33, 244-5; demand of, at Wounded Knee, 88-90, 94
Oglala Sioux, 75-6; Civil Rights Organization, 20, 70, 73-4, 77-9, 108; Tribal Council, 116, 181
oil, 55, 128, 147, 149-50, 219, 250; on Indian land, 38, 64, 72, 100, 181, 202, 219, 221-2, 235, 250, 262

Ojibway, 21, 35, 43, 237, 277; prophecy of, 58, 265, 267
Oklahoma, discovery of oil in, 64, 100, 150, 250
Olmec, 268, 272
Olmsted, George, and bank, 55
Onondaga, 40, 214
Oraibi, Hopi and, 22, 139, 142, 163, 268, 272-3; petroglyph at, 273, 274
Oregon, 44, 190-1, 194
Orr, Diane, 171
Osmond, Donny and Marie, 146
Owens, David, beating of, 207
Owens, Wayne, 150
Oyate Wicaho, Thomas to, 255

Padilla, Juan de, and cross, 139
Paiute, 45, 47, 101, 141, 145, 153
Palmer, A. Mitchell, raids of, 175-6
Panitch, Mark, 52, 136, 138
Papago, 133; Tribal Council, 152
Paracana tribesmen, 223
Paraguay, 13, 129, 224-6, 232
Parker, George, and Hopi, 142
Partido Unido Revolucionario, 220
Patrick, Joseph, 158-9
Patterson, Bradley, 95
Pax, Durham and photos for, 114
Peabody Coal Co., 3, 45, 52, 55, 129, 133, 138, 148-50, 154, 276
Pedro and Juana, 218-20
Pelcyger, Robert, 148
Peltier, Leonard, 20, 26, 33, 43, 60, 175, 186-7, 199-207, 209-10, 218, 243-4; beating of, and murder charge against, 60, 164-5; and shooting at Jumping Bull house, 181-2, 185, 194-5; Poor Bear and, 194-5, 200, 202; and Canada and extradition, 194-7, 199, 233, 238-9; in custody of RCMP, *197;* and FBI, *see under* FBI
Pena, Luis, 225
Pennington County Jail, 67
Pentagon, 20, 75, 80-2, 117; armed personnel carrier of, *80*
People, 198-9, 244
Pepin, Ernest, at Custer courthouse, 68
Pequot, 99, 140
Perdue, Robert, 208-9

Pereira, Fernando Ramos, 223
Pereira, Manuel de Jesus, 225, 232
Peterson, Dr. Garry, 191-2
Pfersick, Royer, and Crow Dog, 188
Phillips, Don, and Montileaux, 173
Phillips Petroleum Co., 146, 151
Phillips Uranium, 20, 45
Pictou, Anna Mae, marriage of, 91
Pine Ridge, 19-20, 25, 61, 66, 69-73, 75-6, 175, 182, 196, 209, 262; U.S. military and police in, 20, 62, 72-3, 75, 182; gunnery range on, 71, 79, 109, 160, 181; Tribal Council, 71, 105, 109-11; South Dakota State Police at, 72; FBI and, 72, 164, 174-5, 178-87, 189-90, 192, 196, 198-201; violence at, 96, 105-6, 121, 196; goon squad on, *see* goon squad; and Wounded Knee, *see* Wounded Knee
Pinochet, Augusto, 215, 217, 228-9
Pit River Indians, 40, 43, 45
Pitkin, Gov. Frederick, and Utes, 152
Pizarro, Juan, 140
Plenty Coup, and Custer, 30
police, 14, 19, 24, 26, 39-40, 44, 49, 51, 54, 60, 73, 124, 245-8; AIM and, 36, 58, 67, 126; Indian, 59, 63; South Dakota State, at Pine Ridge, 72; BIA, 72-4, 77, 82, 85, 88-9, 106, 108-9, 121, 174, 178, 191, 195, 248-9
Pomo Indians, occupation by, 45
Poor Bear, Myrtle, 26, 194-5, 197-200, 202, 205, 209, 233
Poor Bear, Theodore, 198
population, Indian, 66-7, 132, 140, 167, 220, 222-3, 229; in 1492, *65,* 268, 268n
Port Madison reservation, FBI and, 189
Potlach, Northwest Coast Indians and, 241
Potter, Colonel Jack, *80,* 80-1
Pourier, Teddy Paul, 178
Powless, Herb, 47-8, 60, 174
Pratt, Judge John H., 50
Presidential Treaty Commission, 88, 94-5
Price, David, 106, 118-19, 121, 174, 178, 183-5, 191-3, 195, 198, 200, 209, 232
prison system, 35-6, 188-9, 202-3, 206-7
Pueblo Indians, planned revolt by, 140
Purace Indians, 220-2

Quechua-Aymara, 229-30

Qua Toqti, 150
Quinault reservation, 55

Race Relations, 59
Racial Conciliation Commission, 69
Raitt, Bonnie, benefit concerts of, 210
Ralston Purina, and Cauca province, 222
Ramsay, Ian, and mercury poisoning, 238
Randall, Francis, 106
Rankin, Harry, and Peltier, 194, 196
Rap-Brown anti-riot laws, 93
Rapid City, 24, 69, 73, 279
Rapid City Journal, 109, 173-4, 179, 182, 193, 253, 261
Raquette Point, 246-9
Ravenholt, Dr. R. T., 167
Red Cloud, Chief, 25, 30, 65
Red Owl, Nellie, and Lakota history, 122
Red Shirt, Marvin, 168-9, 171-2
Redford, Robert, and Peltier, 243
Redhouse, John, and Farmington, 135
Redner, Russell, 190-1
relocation, 20, 22, 100, 136, 138, *138,* 150, 152-4, 157, 160, *279*
religion, 29-31, 193
Reno, Major Marcus, attack by, 63
reservations, U.S., and state jurisdiction on, 64, 70-1, 102-3, 122
Reuters, and raids on Indians, 223
Rhoads, Tom, and Camp, 127
Riccardo, Ricky, 171
Rice, Bill, at Custer courthouse, 68
Richard, Emil, harassment by, 106
Richards, Alexander, 116
Richards, Benny, and Manning, 209
Richards, Charles, and Peltier plot, 205
Richards, Woody, 106
Richardson, Josephine, 218
Rickard, Clinton, 39
Ridenhour, Ron, and Garden Plot, 177
Riegert, Wilbur, re hostages, 82-3
Riel, Louis, U.S. Army and, 62
Rio Tinto Zinc, 222, 239, 242
Robertson, Robert, 49, 51
Robideaux, Bob, 175, 182, 186-7, 189; trial of, and acquittal, 197-200
Rochester *Times-Union,* 52
Rocky Mountain News, Meinhardt to, 260
Rolling Thunder, 44, 213

Rolley-Malone, Susan, 115
Rooks, Eugene, against AIM, 172
Rosebud reservation, 30, 63, 66, 182; Tribal
    Council, 66, 124-6
Rosenbloom, Donald, and Peltier, 194
Ross, Judge Donald, 205
Rossmore, William, attack on, 172-3
Roubideaux, Ramon, 88, *91,* 106-7, 114,
    123-4
Royal Canadian Mounted Police (RCMP),
    13, 40, 194, 217, 238-9; and Peltier, 194,
    196, *197*
Running, Frank, at Crow Dog camp, 184
Rush, Stuart, and Peltier, 194

Samaniego, General, and Dr. Arens, 226
San Carlos Apache Tribal Council, 151-2
San Diego Union, 179
San Juan, power plant at, *164*
Sanchez, Marie, at UN conference, 214
Sande, Kermit, Janklow *vs.,* 125
Saunders, Gilbert, assassination of, 135
Sawhill, John, 128
Saxbe, William, 43, 59, 110, 112, 115
Schein, Dr. Edgar, and Marion, 203
Schifter, Richard, 217
Schultz, Justice W. A., 194, 197, 199
Schwarting, Jerry, 178
Schwartz, Jack, 171-2, 185, 191
Schmidt, Bart, Kash instructions to, 75
Schmitz, Darld, 68-9
Seattle, Chief, and the future, 14
Second World, 270, 272
Seer's Catalogue, Gougelet in, 136
Sekaquaptewa, Wayne, Abbott, and
    Emory, as Mormon converts, 150
Seminole, 64, 100, 150
Seneca, 21, 39, 61, 99
Seneca, M. E., 150
Shafer, Harry and Jill, 169-70
Shearin, Lee, and Patrick, 158
Sheridan, General Philip, 63
Sherman, General William, 63
Shoshone, 22, 39, 43, 45, 101, 141, 145, 153,
    209; Tribal Council, 47
Shultz, William, and Peltier, 164-5
Simmons, Col., and Pine Ridge, 74
Sitting Bull, Chief, 23, 30, 62-3, 255-6
Sioux, 19, 20, 24, 28-30, 72, 78; Treaty of
    1868, 20-1, 25, 28, *28,* 62-3, 88, 94-5,
    103-4, 122, 250, *252,* 253, 256-7; Tribal

    Council, 32, 217-18
Sioux Falls State Penitentiary, 67
Skyhorse, Paul, 168-72
Small Legs, Nelson, and RCMP, 239
Smallboy, Robert, Peltier and, 194
Smith, Adam, Means and, 231
Smith, John, and Holiday Inn, 124
Smith, Joseph, 101
Smith, Robert C., and Paraguay, 226
Sneed, Joseph, 117
Snider, Britt, and Garden Plot, 177
Solomon, Art, to UN conference, 242
Somoza, Anastasio, 225, 230
Sotsisowah, *see* Mohawk, John
South America, 22, 64, 102, 140, 268;
    Indians of, and atrocities, 14, 129, 212,
    215, 217
South Dakota, 20, 38, 48, 66-8, 78, 124,
    127, 153; Sheriff's Association, 124; *see
    also places in*
Southwest, 133, 136, 145, 147-8, 153,
    156, 158
Spain, 15, 140-1, 220, 227
Special Operations Group, *see* U.S.
    Marshals Service
Specktor, Mordecai, 240, 265-6
SWAT (Special Weapons and Tactics), 20,
    46, 177, 180, 182
Standing Deer, and Peltier plot, 203-8
Steel, William Jack, shooting of, 174
sterilization, 166-7, 214
Stevens, Homer, Peltier supporter, 196
Stillwater State Penitentiary, 35
Stoldt, Marvin, and Peltier, 195
strip mining, 55, 129, 148, 150, 154-6,
    159-60, *163; see also* coal
Stroessner, General Alfredo, 224, 226-7
Stuntz, Joseph, 175, 178-9, 181, 209
Sullivan, William, 176
Supreme Court, 20, 100, 102-4, 205, 263
Survival School, and funding cut, 60
Suvero, Hank di, 171-2
sweatlodge, 24, 28, 31, 83, 255
Sweden, UN conference in, 213-14
Swimmer, Ross, 151-2

Tagasugi, Judge Robert, 207
tailings, uranium, *154,* 155-6, 239-42
Taney, Justice, and Indians, 102
Tanner, Nathan, 153
Tecumseh, Chief, death of, 99

"Termination," 38-9, 169
Terronez, John, 75, 77
Terry, General Alfred, 63
Texaco, 128, 219, 222
Third World, 213, 270-2
Thomas, Gary, and Marshals Service, 74
Thomas, Randy, 255
Thompson, Chief Loran, 246
Thompson, Morris, 110
Three Stars, Peter, and BIA files, 55
Thundershield, Dallas, 206
Tilsen, Ken, 43, 81-2, 114
Tovar, Pedro de, and Hopi, 139-40
Trail of Broken Treaties, 42, 45, 47-50,
  52-5, 57-8, 127, 129; proposal of, 49-50,
  53, 88; *see also* Unity Caravan
Trail of Tears, 100
treaties, 43, 45, 88, 95, 101, 103, 123, 142,
  234-5, 245, 260; between U.S. and
  Indians, 14, 21, *65,* 99, 100, 100n, 152,
  234, 249; violation of, 22, 62-4, 103, 145
Treaty Eleven, 235
Treaty of 1868, *see under* Sioux
Treaty of Guadalupe Hidalgo, 101, 103
treaty rights, 19, 22, 34, 78, 187, 190, 209
Tremblay, Lucien, and James Bay, 128
tribal councils, 32, 37-40, 46, 51, 61, 71,
  88-9, 94-5, 112, 122, 129, 136, 148; cash
  awards to, 37-9, 47, 144-5; *see also names
  of individual councils*
Trimbach, Joseph, 73, 77, 80, 119; and
  Wounded Knee, 114-15, 121
Trimble, Al, succeeds Wilson, 244
Truax, W. B., and Mormon land grab, 141
Trudeau, Pierre, 233-4
Trudell, John, 43, 127, 156, 179-81, 186,
  196, 198, 209-10, 242-3, 249
Trudell, Tina Manning, 209
Truman, Harry, 144, 151, 213
Tucson Daily Citizen, and Celay, 48
Turbay, Julio Cesar, and uranium, 222
Turtle Island, 13, 14, 21, 97
Tuscarora, 39-40, 43
Two Bulls, Fred, King and, 106
Two Kettle Lakota, 25, 30
Two Moon, Chief, and Custer, 63

Udall, Stewart, and leases, 148
Ui, Dr. Jun, and mercury poisoning, 237
Union Carbide Corp., 3, 20, 45, 128, 261,
  263

United Nations (UN), 32, 34, 83, 131,
  160-62; Hopi and, 144, 160-62, 197, 213;
  conferences of, 160, 197, 213-16, 239,
  242; Commission on Human Rights, 217
United Press International (UPI), 177-9
United States, 14, 21, 34, 36, 51, 62-3, 65,
  71, 79, 89, 93-4, 101, 121-2, 129, 214, 217,
  226-9, 232-3, 263, 276; and Wounded
  Knee, 79-81, 88, 127; system of justice in,
  97-9, 104; departments of, *see under name
  of department*
U.S. Army, 24, 29-30, 37, 49, 62-3, 66, 74-5,
  94, 117, 251, 262
U.S. Forest Service, 257, 259-60
U.S. Geological Survey, 66, 71-2
United States v. Kagama, 103
U.S. Marshals Service, 72-6, 81-3, 106-7,
  257; Log of, 73-5, 79; at Wounded Knee,
  77, 79, 85-93, 95, 177-8; bunker of, *84*
U.S. News and World Report, 176, 224
United States v. Rogers, 102
U.S. Steel Co., and blankets, 223
United States v. Winans, 104
Unity Caravan, 44, 48-9
uranium, 34, 136, 155, 158, 239-40, 249-50;
  on Indian land, 20, 38, 45, 66, 72, 133,
  144, 160, 181, 202, 222-3, 236, 239, 261-3;
  mines and mills, *137*; Navajo miner of,
  155; fenced mine site of, *262*; *see also*
  tailings
Urbom, Warren, 122-3
Uri, Connie, and sterilization, 166-7
Uruchi, Juan Condori, 215
Uruguay, and Indians, 229
Ute, 22, 30, 64, 101, 133, 141, 145, 152;
  Tribal Council, 47, 145, 152

Vancouver Sun, Halprin suit against, 233
Van Deusen, Dr. Jane, and adoption, 149
Verkler, Jerry, 151
Victoria Creek Canyon, 253-5
Viken, Jeff, 253, 261
Vincze, Dr. Imre, and Lawrence, 208
Vlassis, George, 145

Waldheim, Kurt, report to, 143
War Lance, Lee, and Carradine party, 168
Warner, Colonel Volney, 62, 80, *80*
Warrior Societies, 187, 189, 210-11, 237
Washington Post, 52, 136, 138, 148, 180

Washington Star, 192
Watergate, 24, 94, 117, 130
Watkins, Arthur, 46, 144-5, 153
Weinglass, Leonard, 171
Weisman, Joel, 183
Western Energy Supply and Transmission
    (WEST) Associated, 52, 147-8, 150
Westinghouse, 128-9, 261
White Butterfly, Karen, *91*
White House, 81, 87-9, 95, 117-18
White Wing, Melvin, and Eagle, 199, 200
White Wolf, Eddie, 78
Whitaker, John, power of, 112
Whiteman, Everett Little, report of, 116
Whiteside, Major Samuel, 66
Whittekiend, Craig, 257, 259
Whitten, Les, arrest of, 57
Wilkinson, Cragun, 46, 150
Wilkinson, Ernest, 46, 144-5, 152
Williams, Ronald, 118-19, 121, 178, 180
Williams, Saggie, and 1868 treaty, 145
Wilson, Dickie, 32-3, 60-1, 71-4, 76, 82,
    87-8, 90, 94-5, 106, 108, 172-3, 181, 187,
    199, 217-18, 244; and tribal council, 67,
    74, 105, 109-11; and impeachment, 70,
    72-5, 105; *see also* goon squad
Wilson, Mike, 48, 152
Wilson, Robert, *see* Standing Deer
Wind, Patty, poem of, 280
Winyanwast (Good Woman), 53
Witt, Shirley Hill, 166
WKLO/DC lawyers of, 107-9, 172-3, 182
Women of All Red Nations (WARN), 166,
    250, 279
Wood, Beth, 149-50
Wood, William, 183, 195, 198, 200
Wounded Knee, 75-8, 82-3, 85-6, 88-94,
106, 117-18, 127, 129, 157, 164, 166, 170,
176-7, 187, 211-12, 238, 257; battle, siege,
and massacre at, 20, 24-5, 66, 75-9, 81-8,
90-2, 117, 187; Trading Post, 76, 116; and
roadblocks, 77, 82-3, 89, 91-5, 187; FBI
agent on roadblock at, *78*; military
equipment, personnel, and contingencies
for, *79,* 79-82, 85-6, 92, 117; U.S.
Marshals' bunker at, *84*; observation
point at, *86*; negotiators of agreement of,
91; arrests at and following, 91, 94-6, 105,
121; *see also* Wounded Knee trials
Wounded Knee trials, 96, 99, 104-5, 109,
114-16, 118, 170; leadership, 105, 112-21;
non-leadership, 105, 122-3; *see also*
WKLO/DC

Yanomami, 223, 251
Yazzi, Alfred, killing of, 136
Yazzi, Emma, power plant on land of, 154
Yazzi, Ned, and uranium tailings, 156
Yellow Bird, Jo Ann, mistreatment of, 26
Yellow Feather, Pearl, 257
Yellow Thunder, Raymond, 25, 48-9, 209,
255
Young Bear, Severt, 49, 61, 105
Young, Brigham, 101, 141
Youth and Elder Conference, 277
Yukioma, 142
Ywahoo, Dyhani Fisher, *224*

Zephier, Greg, 256
Zephier, Harley, 126
Zigrossi, Norman, 182, 184, 193
Zuni, 133, 140, 153